How Successful Organizations Implement Change

Integrating Organizational Change Management and Project Management to Deliver Strategic Value

Compiled and Edited by
Emad E. Aziz, PRINCE2P, CSSGB, PMP, PgMP, PfMP
Wanda Curlee, PhD, PMI-RMP, PMP, PgMP, PfMP

Library of Congress Cataloging-in-Publication Data has been applied for.

ISBN: 978-1-62825-386-3

Published by: Project Management Institute, Inc.
14 Campus Boulevard
Newtown Square, Pennsylvania 19073-3299 USA
Phone: +610-356-4600
Fax: +610-356-4647
Email: customercare@pmi.org
Internet: PMI.org

To inquire about discounts for resale or educational purposes, please contact the PMI Book Service Center.

PMI Book Service Center
P.O. Box 932683, Atlanta, GA 31193-2683 USA
Phone: 1-866-276-4764 (within the U.S. or Canada) or
+1-770-280-4129 (globally)
Fax: +1-770-280-4113
Email: info@bookorders.pmi.org

Dedication

On behalf of the board of BRISK Business Inc. and myself, I would like to express our utmost appreciation to the world-renowned, seasoned, and knowledgeable change leaders and practitioners who have generously taken the time to share their battle-tested best practices, lessons learned, and tips and tricks for making this work a possibility.

Without your valuable contributions, we could have never been able to achieve our dream: to contribute to the efforts of those who work tirelessly around the globe to make the world a better place and improve the lives of millions of people by transforming one organization at a time.

We are also very grateful to the Project Management Institute (PMI) for giving us the honor and pleasure of publishing this work, and for their continued support of, and contribution to, the profession of portfolio, program, and project management.

Sincerely,

Emad E. Aziz, PRINCE2P, CSSGB, PMP, PgMP, PfMP
President and Chief Executive Officer
BRISK Business Inc.
www.brisk-business.com

The authors and editors of this book would like to thank and dedicate this work to*:

Barbara Walsh
Dave Jones
Donn Greenberg
Eloise Sikma
Elsa Abajy
Ezzat Aziz Abdelsayed
Garry Marsh
Gary Heerkens
Harold Kerzner
Janet Snyder
Jerry Brightman
John and Phoebe Gordon
Jon Warntjes
Katie Porter
Kay Wais
Linda Kim Gordon
Madison Porcelain
Malak Aziz
Michael Porcelain
Mounir Nassif
Mostafa Hashish
Nadia Nassif
Nazly Aziz
Noah Porcelain
Nora Bahgat
PJ Porter
Shady Fayed
Stephen Townsend
Stewart Lockie
William Snyder

We would also like to thank and dedicate this book to our families for their love and support, and the many executives and portfolio, program, and project managers we have worked with, learned with, and shared stories with, especially those in our extended PMI family. You have all provided us with the motivation to find ways to give back to the worldwide project management community.

May those who would rather seek solutions than complain about problems make the best out of this book.

*Listing is in alphabetical order by first name

Table of Contents

About the Contributors

Emad E. Aziz, Prince2P, CSSGB, PMP, PgMP, PfMP

With experience in managing programs and projects worth over US$10 billion in the sectors of oil and gas, business, IT, construction, banking, politics, government, healthcare, and economic development, Emad has accumulated a rich pool of knowledge and experience that he utilizes to enable organizations to transform their strategic directives into tangible results and realize anticipated benefits. Emad specializes in the management of complex programs and rescuing troubled projects, as well as the setup, alignment, and operations of portfolio, program, and project management offices (PMOs).

Emad is the founder of BRISK Business Inc., (BBI) (www.brisk-business. com) is a New York City-based international service provider specializing in strategy execution, business transformation, organizational change management, and portfolio, program, and project management. BBI helps clients realize strategic benefits through one or more of its service delivery mechanisms: consultancy, training, capacity building, and/or managing and delivering programs and projects on their behalf.

BBI is a Registered Education Provider (R.E.P.), and 1 of 133 members worldwide of the Registered Consultant Program (RCP) with the Project Management Institute (PMI). BBI's team members hold certifications in good standing with PMI, and are recognized for their contributions to the profession through participation in the creation and update of PMI's standards, frameworks, and practice guides, receipt of PMI awards, authorship of various published white papers and books contributing to thought leadership, as well as having served in multiple leadership roles with PMI.

Emad is a member of the core team developing the Third Edition of the *Project Manager Competency Development Framework*, and a subject matter expert contributor to the *Standard for Organizational Project Management (OPM)*, *The Standard for Program Management* – Fourth Edition, and *The Standard for Portfolio Management* – Fourth Edition for the Project Management Institute. He is also the last manager of the PMI Information Technology and Telecommunications Community of Practice (IT & Telecom CoP), the founder and first chair of the PMI Egypt Chapter, and a board member of the Agency for the Development and Empowerment of Women (ADEW). In 2013, Emad was an evaluator of submissions for the PMI Professional Awards for Individual Recognition, and a steering committee member and chair of the consultancy, training, and development committee of the Egyptian Junior Business Association (EJB). In 2015, Emad was a member of the advisory panel to the White

House Business Council on International Trade, and in 2016, a member of the Industry Advisory Council to the American Public University System (APUS).

Emad actively participates in outreach and best practices-sharing activities, through the publishing of books, white papers, features, and articles in various publications, including *PM Network®*, as well as speaking engagements, including but not limited to Rutgers University Business School, PACE University, and PMI® Global Congresses in North America and EMEA since 2012. He is also the founder of the Projects to the Point (P2P) Conference and Exhibition (www.p2pevents.net).

In 2008, Emad facilitated a cooperation between PMI and the Government of Egypt, the first ever agreement between PMI and a government.

Simona Bonghez, PhD, PMP

With a solid theoretical background and practical experience in management (including expertise in change management, process management, organizational design, strategic management, and business planning), Simona has carried out several development programs in these areas, supplemented with consulting and training services, both in Romania and worldwide.

Simona is an author and international speaker who runs her own training and consulting company, Colors in Projects, specializing in project management services. She is collaborating as a principal consultant with BRISK Business Inc., and maintains her connection with the National University of Political Studies and Public Administration, a renowned university in Romania.

Simona has been a volunteer for Project Management Institute since 2004, starting as president of the PMI Romania Chapter, and later serving at the global level as a member in the Leadership Institute Advisory Group and Chapter Member Advisory Group. She is now enjoying collaboration within the Ethics Member Advisory Group.

Even though professional experience is a defining aspect in her activities, Simona thinks that she would not have come this far without a good sense of humor. She believes that games and metaphors are powerful tools for having interactive and enjoyable workshops, presentations, and training sessions, thus enforcing the learning process.

Alfonso Bucero, MSc, PMI-RMP, PMP, PMI Fellow

Alfonso Bucero is the founder and managing partner of BUCERO PM Consulting. He managed IIL Spain for almost two years, and was a senior project manager at Hewlett-Packard Spain (Madrid Office) for 13 years.

Alfonso has a computer science engineering degree from Universidad Politécnica (Madrid) and is now completing a PhD in project management at the University of Zaragoza in Spain. He has 27 years of practical experience, with 22 of these years devoted to project management worldwide. He has managed and consulted on projects in different countries throughout Europe.

Since 1994, he has been a frequent speaker at international project management congresses and symposiums. Alfonso has delivered project management training and consulting services in Spain, Mexico, the United Kingdom, Belgium, Germany, France, Denmark, Costa Rica, Brazil, the United States, and Singapore. As a project management advocate, he defends the idea that passion, persistence, and patience are keys to project success.

Alfonso authored the books *Dirección de Proyectos: Una Nueva Vision* (2003) and *Today Is a Good Day—Attitudes for Achieving Project Success* (2010); contributed a chapter in the book *Creating the Project Office*, edited by Graham, Dinsmore, and Englund (2003); and coauthored the book *Project Sponsorship* (2006) with Englund. Alfonso has contributed articles to many magazines at the national and international levels.

Yves Cavarec, MBA, PMP

Yves Cavarec connects leaders to help them become more innovative, agile, and people centric. He provides professional services with a mission to develop collective performance and team success and believes that organizations are places where all stakeholders can thrive at the same time through cooperation.

Yves spent 20 years in organizational transformation through project, program, portfolio, and change management. He worked mainly for large organizations, including Societe Generale, ABN Amro, La Banque Postale, Europcar, Ubisoft, Veolia Water, Vallourec, and SNCF.

As a professional speaker, Yves has addressed audiences in Europe and North America, whose members included executives, professionals, managers, and consultants. He is bilingual and speaks French and English.

Yves has a master's degree in economics and an executive MBA from the prestigious business school ESCP Europe in Paris. He holds a Project Management Professional (PMP)® certification. He is a CQ Certified Change Leader®.

Yves's history with PMI since 2004 has been, and continues to be, a rich and rewarding leadership, sharing, and learning experience.

Wanda Curlee, PhD, PMI-RMP, PMP, PgMP, PfMP

Dr. Wanda Curlee is the general manager of PM POWERED®. Her career spans several industries, including IT, government, insurance, telecommunications, and consulting. She is active on PMI's certification and standards teams and served on the core teams for *Requirements Management: A Practice Guide* and *The Standard for Program Management* – Fourth Edition. In addition, Wanda was part of the item-writing team for the Portfolio Management Professional (PfMP)® certification.

Dr. Curlee has published three books: *Complexity Theory and Project Management* (coauthored with R. L. Gordon, 2010), *Successful Program Management: Complexity Theory, Communication, and Leadership* (coauthored with R. L. Gordon, 2013), and *The Virtual Project Management Office: Best Practices, Proven Methods* (coauthored with R. L. Gordon, 2011). She has earned four PMI certifications: the PMI Risk Management Professional (PMI-RMP)®, Project Management Professional (PMP)®, Program Management Professional (PgMP)®, and Portfolio Management Professional (PfMP)® certifications. She is proud to be the mother of three children who have served or currently serve in the U.S. military. She met her husband, Steve, while both were serving in the U.S. Navy.

Jack Ferraro, CSM, PMI-ACP, PMP

Jack Ferraro has more than 20 years of business management consulting experience with a focus on executing strategic projects and increasing organizational project management effectiveness. He has extensive knowledge of the current PMI standards for project, program, and portfolio management.

Jack strives to be a trusted advisor to organizations seeking to optimize limited resources to effectively manage the growing list of organizational strategic priorities. He has experience in the pharmaceutical, manufacturing, higher education, nonprofit, and financial industries, and is a seasoned project management practitioner experienced in team development while leading complex enterprise technology, vendor management, change management, and business process improvement projects.

Jack is the author of two books on project management: *The Strategic Project Leader: Mastering Service-Based Project Leadership* and *Project Management for Non-Project Managers*. Jack is passionate about using project management to effect positive organizational change. He enjoys consulting, training, and mentoring project stakeholders and teams seeking to spearhead organizational change and he has designed a project leadership program based on *The Strategic Project Leader* to help project managers build their leadership and communication skills.

Robert Lee Gordon, DM

Robert Lee Gordon is currently the program director for the Reverse Logistics Management department at American Public University. Robert has more than 25 years of professional experience in supply chain management and human resources. Robert earned his doctorate in management and organizational leadership and his master's degree in business administration from the University of Phoenix, and a bachelor's degree in history from UCLA.

Robert has been teaching for over 14 years and regularly teaches courses in reverse logistics, transportation, project management, and human resources.

Robert has more than 40 published articles pertaining to reverse logistics, supply chain management, project management, human resources, education, and complexity. Robert has also four published books on the topics of reverse logistics management, complexity and project management, virtual project management organizations, and successful program management. He maintains a blog about logistics and reverse logistics hosted by DC Velocity at http://blogs.dcvelocity.com/reverse_logistics/.

Dave Gunner, MSc, PMP, PfMP

Dave Gunner has more than 25 years of extensive experience in project, program, and portfolio management. He currently works for one of the world's largest multinational information technology corporations. His experience extends from managing the United Kingdom and Ireland's Java capability to setting up and managing the Project and Program Management Academy. He has worked closely with PMI for a number of years, including participation as chair of PMI's *Navigating Complexity: A Practice Guide,* as a member of PMI's consensus body, and on the PMP Role Delineation Study steering committee.

Dave was the vice chair on the creation of the third edition of PMI's *Project Manager Competency Development Framework* and is currently the vice-chair on PMI's new OPM Standard committee. He also regularly presents at various PMI events. Dave has held the Project Management Professional (PMP)® certification since 2003 and is one of the few to attain the Portfolio Management Professional (PfMP)® certification. He also holds an executive MSc in project and program management from Cranfield University.

Ginger Levin, DPA, PMP, PgMP, OPM3 Certified Professional

Dr. Ginger Levin has worked in the project management field for over 50 years specializing in consulting and training in portfolio and program management, organizational project management, change management, and knowledge transfer. Dr. Levin had a career in the U.S. government and with a consulting firm in Washington, D.C., which focused on project management, information systems, and organizational development.

Since 1996, Dr. Levin has worked on her own in the project management field and is an active PMI volunteer. In 2014, she won PMI's Eric Jenett Project Management Award of Excellence for her contributions to the field. She presents regularly at PMI and other organizations throughout the world.

She is also an adjunct professor in project management for the University of Wisconsin–Platteville's MSPM program and for SKEMA in Lille, France, in its doctoral program in project management. Six of her students have won PMI's Student Paper of the Year Award.

Dr. Levin is the author, editor, or coauthor of 21 books, and has a book series with CRC Press. She received her doctoral degree from George Washington University and won the outstanding dissertation award for her research on large organizations.

James Marion, PhD, PMP

Jim Marion has more than 22 years of experience in managing programs and projects in excess of US$100 million in the wireless telecommunications sector. He is a member of the subteam that is developing the *Project Management Competency Development Framework* – Third Edition.

Jim has experience in process improvement and developed process flow and layouts for a new startup customization operation where he clarified responsibilities, structures, and processes for operations in the United States, Japan, China, and Europe.

Jim's experience in change management helped change the culture in one company from a high-turnover environment with a high rate of project failure to one with a string of high visibility project successes and minimal staff turnover.

Jim received a PhD from Capella University, an MBA/MSc from the Edinburgh Business School of Heriot–Watt University, and an MS in engineering from the University of Wisconsin–Platteville.

Barbara Porter, MSc, MBA, CSM, PMP

Barbara Porter has more than 15 years of experience in internet retail, primarily in the consumer goods and gifting spaces. She has been the chief technology officer of FragranceNet.com since 2010, where she has led many large-scale change initiatives that have transformed and streamlined the operations of the organization. Prior to joining FragranceNet.com, she worked for 1800flowers.com for 10 years in various IT management roles before transitioning to the operations side of the organization as the director of enterprise initiatives, where she was chartered with identifying and sponsoring projects for operational improvements throughout the organization that would reduce costs and/or increase customer satisfaction.

Barbara graduated summa cum laude from the New York Institute of Technology with a bachelor's degree in computer science and a minor in electrical engineering and graduated summa cum laude from the University of Massachusetts–Amherst with an MBA. She is a Project Management Professional (PMP)® certification holder, Certified ScrumMaster (CSM), Scaled Agile SAFe Agilist (SA), and is Six Sigma Black Belt trained. She is an adjunct business school professor, a sought-after conference speaker, and a recognized thought leader in the areas of technology management, operational improvement, and change management.

Frank P. Saladis, PMP, PMI Fellow

Frank Saladis is a consultant, instructor, motivational speaker, and author within the discipline of professional project management. He is the owner/ founder of Blue Marble Enterprizes, Inc. and Project Imaginers. Frank is an accomplished leader and is the author of 12 published books, including *Positive Leadership in Project Management*, and he coauthored the book *Value Driven Project Management* with Harold Kerzner, PhD. He is a past editor of the internationally circulated *All PM* newsletter and the author of more than 160 articles and papers related to the field of project management. He has presented at numerous project management seminars and has been providing training to aspiring project managers for more than 20 years.

Mr. Saladis holds the Project Management Professional (PMP)® certification and has been a featured presenter at PMI® Global Congresses and many other project management events. Mr. Saladis is a graduate of the PMI® Leadership Institute Master Class and has held several positions within PMI, including president of the PMI New York City Chapter and president of the Assembly of Chapter Presidents. Mr. Saladis is the originator of International Project Management Day and was recognized as PMI Person of the Year in 2006. Mr. Saladis was awarded the prestigious title of PMI Fellow in October 2013 and received the PMI Distinguished Contribution Award in October 2015.

Bryan R. Shelby, BA, CSM, PMP, PgMP, PfMP

Bryan Shelby is director of the IT project management office for KPMG North America, charged with establishing and maintaining consistent standards and practices for all IT projects across the firm. Prior to taking this position at KPMG in early 2017, he had been vice president at The Blackstone Group, working with the operations groups in their Hedge Fund Solutions business line where he managed a number of business process and system development re-engineering programs and technology efforts. Before joining Blackstone in 2010, Bryan founded and operated Contek Systems, a consulting business providing portfolio/program/project management and life cycle methodology expertise to large corporations in the telecommunications, publishing, pharmaceutical, and financial industries.

Prior to founding his consulting firm in 1993, he was vice president and group project manager at Bankers Trust, where he was responsible for all applications supporting the master trust/master custody business. Bryan received a bachelor's degree in mathematics from Harvard University, is a past member of the American Society of Pension Actuaries, and earned the Project Management Professional (PMP)®, Program Management Professional (PgMP)®, and Portfolio Management Professional (PfMP)® certifications from Project Management Institute as well as the Certified ScrumMaster (CSM) credential from the Scrum Alliance. For PMI, he contributed to the Program Management Professional (PgMP) and Portfolio Management Professional (PfMP)® exams, has participated in the project to revise PMI's *Project Management Competency Development Framework*, served on the PMI Lexicon Committee, and has been an active member of both the PMI New Jersey Chapter and PMI New York City Chapter.

Gary J. Sikma, MBA, MSM, CSM, SAFe 4.0 (SA), PMI-ACP, PMP

Gary J. Sikma is a transformational change leader who has provided vision to the strategic planning process and who ties complexity of information technology to business needs. He has more than 30 years of leadership experience in government, for-profit, and not-for-profit organizations in healthcare, insurance, manufacturing, customer service, and intelligence. He has developed and turned around enterprise project management offices (PMOs) for multiple organizations.

He has been an active member of PMI since 2003, when he was instrumental in starting the PMI Sioux Empire, South Dakota Chapter and earned his Project Management Professional (PMP)® certification. He has been a leader for PMI publications and an author, serving as a significant contributor or core team member to a number of PMI publications. He is currently the vice chair for *The Standard for Portfolio Management* – Fourth Edition.

Bob Tarne, CSM, PMI-ACP, PMP

Bob is an engagement manager with IBM Systems Group, where he specializes in leading business process improvement initiatives following lean/agile project management techniques. Prior to joining IBM, he was a managing consultant with PM Solutions, where he was responsible for improving clients' project management practices. He also worked as a project manager for 7 Sprint and Owens-Illinois. Bob's career began in the U.S. Navy, where he served for seven years as a cryptologist. Bob is an IBM Certified Executive Project Manager; he holds a PMI Agile Certified Practitioner (PMI-ACP)® certification, a Project Management Professional (PMP)® certification, and is a Certified ScrumMaster (CSM). Bob holds a bachelor's degree in electrical engineering from the University of Illinois and an MS in business from Johns Hopkins University–Carey School of Business. Bob has been an active PMI volunteer since 2000, including roles as the chair of the IT & Telecom Specific Interest Group and founding member of the Agile Community of Practice.

Preface

Since its first conceptualization in the early 1960s, organizational change management (OCM) has primarily been considered the responsibility of human resources, and, for the past 60 years, project managers have focused on the delivery of tangible results. This situation created a gap between product delivery and benefits realization, resulting in a shortfall in the anticipated value for change recipients and for the organization as a whole. This shortfall was documented and, over the past five years, has been recognized as a key obstacle to the adoption of organizational project management (OPM).

As organizational strategies become more fluid and are adjusted to context on a regular basis, the ability to change quickly and effectively has become an important part of any organization's capability to stay competitive. In 2012, the Project Management Institute (PMI) began developing a practice guide that provides practical advice on change management. The resulting publication, *Managing Change in Organizations: A Practice Guide* (2013), is considered to be a "must have" book for change management in organizations and demonstrates how effective change is delivered and implemented.

BRISK Business Inc., being a leader in organizational change management and having utilized portfolio, program, and project management for the purpose of delivering organizational change and executing organizational strategy, adopted *Managing Change in Organizations: A Practice Guide* (PMI, 2013) and integrated it into its practice. It was not long before we saw the opportunity to expand on the content of the guide, sharing our lessons learned, best practices, insights, and know-how with the organizational change management community. An internal project was quickly initiated, and after developing a vision for what this book should be and what it will achieve, we set out on a journey to bring together experts, academics, researchers, and practitioners who have come together as a team to develop *How Successful Organizations Implement Change*.

How Successful Organizations Implement Change builds on the information in PMI's practice guide by integrating organizational change management and organizational project management to consistently deliver benefits to a business in a complex and turbulent environment where strategies may be continually realigned to a transient business context. Practitioners will learn how to become more effective in delivering value to stakeholders in a change context that is in alignment with PMI's *Managing Change in Organizations: A Practice Guide*.

How Successful Organizations Implement Change is the collaborative effort of a team of respected and accomplished authors/practitioners writing about the interface and interdependency between organizational project management (OPM) and organizational change management (OCM). It is in alignment with PMI's *Managing Change in Organizations: A Practice Guide*.

Part I of *How Successful Organizations Implement Change* starts with the history of project management and how it has evolved to include organizational change. Understanding where a discipline comes from helps in understanding how the discipline got where it is today. Chapter 2 describes the complexities that surround the management of organizational change and that continue to be an inherent part of organizational change. Whenever people are involved, complexity increases. People do not like change, especially when they perceive that they will be negatively affected by it. Portfolio, program, and project management are mapped to implementing change in Chapter 3. Portfolio management drives the strategy of an organization that drives change. Programs are developed to drive strategic change that results in a better return on investment than could be achieved by managing each project individually. Projects drive all organizational change. Chapter 4 discusses the importance of organizational agility to help ignite organizational change. Those companies and organizations that are able to adapt to change in an efficient and short time will be well ahead of those organizations that are not as agile.

Part II begins with a discussion on the change process. Change does not occur easily for leadership and employees, and Chapter 5 discusses how change occurs. The next chapter describes the merits of using agile to implement change management. Chapter 6 describes how agile approaches to project management in certain situations can help implement change in a controlled fashion by seeing each sprint's success or changing what was done in a previous sprint. Organizational culture is addressed in Chapter 7. An organization's culture normally will predict a successful change, though a company's culture can hinder the company's ability to change. A company that supports innovation will most likely embrace change that pushes the organization in a positive direction. Stakeholders play a large role in successful organizational change, and this is discussed in Chapter 8. Key stakeholders have the ability to facilitate organizational change by providing the right message to employees. Understanding stakeholders is a must when introducing organizational change, and change cannot be implemented unless it can also be measured. Key measurements are discussed in Chapter 9. These measurements help project management practitioners provide leadership with information regarding how change is progressing. Chapter 10 discusses how to sustain organizational change once it has been implemented. Organizational change will not automatically be accepted after the project manager has left, but there are many ways to make sure the change becomes a part of the culture, and this chapter provides some good ideas.

Part III has four chapters that describe how to put together a change team, how to lead it, and the importance of sponsorship. When putting together a change team for a project or program, it is important to ensure that the essential parts of the organization are included. Chapter 11 further discusses the idea that unless key personnel in the organization are included, the employees will not consider the change credible. Not all project or program managers are ready to lead a change effort. Chapter 12 enlightens the reader that the person who is leading the organizational change must be able to communicate well and have the necessary soft skills, including leadership. Sponsors are an essential part of each organizational change effort. Chapter 13 highlights how the need for the correct sponsor is just as important as the project or program leader. Chapter 14 takes a peek into the future of portfolio, program, and project management and its importance to organizational change. There are discussions on how technology will drive change and how those companies that do not understand these new technologies and adapt to them may be left behind.

Every author who has contributed to *How Successful Organizations Implement Change* is highly regarded in the field of organizational change management; the disciplines of portfolio, program, and project management; and the huge intersection among them. They come with the experience, certifications, knowledge, and background that makes *How Successful Organizations Implement Change* a valuable resource for the leaders of change in tomorrow's organizations. BRISK Business Inc. wanted to ensure that *How Successful Organizations Implement Change* captured the best of the authors' experiences and remained aligned with PMI's *Managing Change in Organizations: A Practice Guide*, so it identified Wanda Curlee as the subject matter expert and chief editor to closely consult with all the authors. Wanda's experience and guidance proved to be priceless in making this work a reality, and creating synergies between each chapter of the book and the chapters that surround it.

CHAPTER 1

Change Management, Project Management, and the Project Management Profession: 1969–2015

By Ginger Levin, DPA, PMP, PgMP,
OPM3 Certified Professional

Abstract

Heraclitus, the Greek philosopher, stated approximately 2,000 years ago, "Change is the only constant." Project professionals, from team members to chief project officers, know that change is expected on portfolios, programs, and projects, and these people are often well versed in how to manage change in terms of changes to cost, schedule, quality, or scope, using proven methods such as configuration management and integrated change control. In this chapter, however, the term *change management* is defined in a broader way, as "a comprehensive, cyclic, and structured approach for transitioning individuals, groups, and organizations from a current state to a future state with intended business benefits" (Project Management Institute, 2013b, p. 119). This definition supports the approach of organizational project management (OPM) in which work is guided by the organization's strategic goals and vision and, in turn, serves as the basis for portfolio, program, and project work. along with operational activities. This OPM approach then emphasizes the overall benefits that will be delivered to promote business value. This chapter discusses project management, change management, and the work of the project professional from 1969 to January 2015.

The Importance of 1969

The concepts of change management and project management are not new. But the year 1969 is significant because that is when the Project Management Institute (PMI) was established by a group of five individuals. PMI's purpose was "to provide a means for project managers to associate, share information, and discuss common problems" (quotations without associated references in this chapter can be found at PMI.org).

Although PMI was established in 1969, it began with discussions by E. A. "Ned" Engman and three others in 1967 about forming a "project management organization." Mr. Engman wrote to five other individuals, and they met in 1968 to establish the Project Management Institute. By 1969, PMI was officially formed and incorporated, and 47 people became members.

At that time, literature in the project management field centered on tools and techniques, building from the Gantt chart in 1919 and focusing on scheduling methods, work breakdown structure, and earned value. Other literature discussed the need for matrix management and the use of teams to do the work on projects.

In the 1960s, the Southern Railway recognized the value of portfolio management, and established a group to implement it. The portfolio group's focus was to recommend the products and services that the railroad should offer to its customers to put the company in the best position to achieve its goals with an emphasis on return on investment and increased market share. Although there was no official standard available for guidance, The Southern Railway took an OPM approach, which supported some of the tenets later found in PMI's *Organizational Project Management: A Practice Guide* (PMI, 2014), with its emphasis on organizational strategies and priorities. Southern Railway disclosed little about this group to others, recognizing that a confidential approach could foster a competitive advantage.

Literature in organizational effectiveness began in the early 1900s, with Frederick W. Taylor's use of scientific management for greater quality control in 1911. Wanting to create a more efficient workplace, Taylor focused on the internal organization, as opposed to external variables. A leading founder of bureaucracy, Max Weber, contributed to this line of thinking with his work in 1946, writing about defined processes and procedures which lead to more stability in individual behavior. In 1957, Simon softened this approach to one with a focus on administrative control to best simplify complexity and decision making. Others such as Barnard (1938) stated that there were generic principles that could be applied to organizations, such as defining an organization's mission, purpose, and goals, and focusing on structuring, organizing, and designing the organization with established roles and lines of authority. Mayo (1945) noted that commitment and loyalty from the people within an organization were more important in determining the behavior of each person in the organization, and Likert (1961) focused on networks, with a linking pin concept to show how people fit into the organization's structure. The linking pin was a manager who would report back to the people who worked for him or her to inform them as to what was under way. This manager then learned about the organization's undertakings from his or her superiors and thus was the linking pin between the two groups, and people who were considered as linking pins existed throughout the organization.

Lewin (1947) was considered the first to focus specifically on change management. He prepared a change model of unfreezing, changing, and refreezing. During the unfreezing phase, stakeholders are prepared for change so everyone can see why change is needed. During the changing phase, the goal is to motivate stakeholders to change so they can see the importance of the change in their work. During refreezing, people have accepted the change, new ways of working are in place, people are following those new ways, and the change is reinforced and ingrained in the work people are doing.

By the time PMI was established in 1969, other work was under way in the areas of portfolio management, organizational project management, change management, organizational structures, and the importance of interpersonal skills to help set the stage for success in the next decade.

The 1970s

Beginning in April 1970, PMI published the first issue of *Project Management Quarterly (PMQ)*, which was continued until 1983, when it was renamed *Project Management Journal® (PMJ)*. As literature in the field was in its infancy, the first *PMQ* was only 27 pages.

PMI also held its first conference in St. Louis, Missouri, in 1970, which stressed, among other things, "the need to involve top executives in project management. New channels of *communication* to top management should replace the unsuccessful methods of the past decade." This conference further noted the need for a standard definition of project management and forecasted that project management concepts would be used extensively by line managers. Additionally, the conference emphasized engaging executives to support "the coming age of project management." The March 1971 *PMQ* included a bibliography of 89 items as a small sampling of the literature on project management to that date. By December 1971, the *PMQ* had increased in length to 51 pages. Houston, San Francisco, and Los Angeles formed PMI chapters in 1974, and PMI began to hold its Professional Awards Program. By the end of the decade, PMI membership totaled more than 2,000 individuals worldwide.

One example of the project field at that time was a Federal Railroad Administration (FRA) program known as the Freight Car Utilization Program. This was a consortium involving FRA, the Association of American Railroads, and the railroad industry, with the FRA providing US$43 million per year in funding. At the time, the once-dominant railroad industry in the United States was losing market share to the motor carrier and barge industries through a lack of emphasis on customer centricity. Recognizing that change was necessary, a consortium was established and led by the FRA to demonstrate that the railroad industry could begin a major initiative to cooperate at switching stations to decrease the time it took to change freight cars from one carrier to another, thereby decreasing delivery time of products to its customers. Rail industry representatives recognized that to remain competitive, they had to work collaboratively to provide benefits to customers, and several projects were part of this program as the change process ensued. This program tracked to research done by Baker and Wilemon (1977) on the management of complex programs. Barker and Wilemon noted, among other things, that project managers had to cope with numerous challenges, including organizational design and the relationship of projects to the organization, the client, and external groups.

Youker (1978) also published a paper to serve as a manager's guide to implementing change in organizations at the 1978 PMI® Seminars & Symposium, which discussed how best to implement change in organizations, described problems in implementing change so the change is not resisted, and explained how best to manage change to handle anticipated problems, drawing upon tools and concepts from behavioral sciences. Interest in the fields of change management and project management was converging, along with a focus on the impact on programs and projects to organizations and to customers.

As another example, the Policy Review Office of the Interstate Commerce Commission (ICC) was responsible for regulating the railroad and motor carrier industries. The office had four people, including a manager, and the team reported to the chairman of the ICC. This team also performed the rudimentary functions of a project management office (PMO), because it reviewed possible regulatory changes and other internal changes and made recommendations before they were forwarded to the commissioners for approval. The airline industry had already undergone deregulation with Congress's Airline Deregulation Act of 1978, and railroad and motor carrier regulations were next in line for possible deregulation, meaning there would be numerous changes in how work was done at the time and how it would be done in the future.

The decade ended with the publication of many papers and books in the field, including the first edition of Dr. Harold Kerzner's (1979) *Project Management: A Systems Approach to Planning, Scheduling, and Controlling.*

The 1980s

During the 1980s, PMI's membership, programs, and services continued to grow. In 1981, PMI published *Implementation of Project Management: The Professional's Handbook*, edited by Linn C. Stuckenbruck. The purpose of this book, a two-year undertaking by the PMI Southern California Chapter, was to further PMI's objectives, serving as a guide for project managers who were considering implementing project management in their organizations. Noting that the need to start a project correctly by establishing a roadmap was a stated goal to best ensure project success, Stuckenbruck (1981) wrote, "the most important of these actions is ensuring the organization is ready for project management" with executive commitment and follow-up by project managers with positive and continuous support (p. 11). Other chapters focused on the complexity of projects requiring multidisciplinary efforts, which project management could provide, focusing on its benefits; the necessity of an implementation plan for project management; desired actions by the project manager; best ways to organize to support project management; determining project strategy; and management involvement and values, along with an emphasis on which tools and techniques to use.

In 1982, the Federal Aviation Administration (FAA) formed a new PMO that reported to the FAA administrator. This PMO's role was to introduce project management to the silo-driven FAA as it began a major upgrade of the nation's airspace system. One team member in the five-person PMO lacked aviation expertise, but was offered the position because of her understanding of matrix management and experience with projects and programs. Stuckenbruck's (1981) book became extremely useful to this organization, along with other resources, and later, when a consulting company won a competitive contract to develop and conduct project management training at the New York City Transit Authority in the late 1980s, the client wanted a book by PMI to be given to each participant; Stuckenbruck's book met the criterion.

In 1981, PMI's Board of Directors established a project to develop procedures and concepts in three key areas: ethics, standards, and accreditation. The team involved was then known as the Ethics, Standards, and Accreditation Group. It had ten members assisted by 25 volunteers. Its results were published in the *PMQ* special summer issue in August 1983. It included a set of topic areas for the first body of knowledge in project management: human resources, scope, time, cost, quality, and communications management, providing the cornerstone for PMI's professional program. A code of ethics was also adopted and set forth in the same issue of *PMQ*. Western Carolina University was the first university accredited by PMI because it was the first to offer a master's degree in project management. Other universities around the world offered project management courses in master's degree programs or a concentration area within a master's degree in business administration.

With this "initial" project management guide in the 1983 issue of *PMQ*, work also was under way for a certification program in project management. The process for attaining the Project Management Professional (PMP)® certification was announced in March 1984, and in October 1984, 43 people attained their PMP certification.

During the 1980s, PMI also began to publish a series of monographs or short handbooks. One related to this chapter was *An Organization Development Approach to Project Management* (Adams, Bilbro, & Stockert, 1986). It set forth a change management strategy to implement project management so people accept it, focused on key leadership competencies to do so, and identified ways to both maintain and nurture a project management organization, with people recognizing the change process as being implemented through projects until project management became pervasive. This monograph bridged the gap between an organizational development approach and project management because project management, at that time, was primarily instituted in silo-driven, bureaucratic organizations. Numerous other project management, change management, and organizational development books were also published around this time, along with journal articles in *PMJ*. Other universities began to offer graduate-level courses in project management, including concentration areas and master's degrees in project management. Numerous project management training and consulting firms were also established.

In August 1986, a special issue of *PMJ* presented a detailed report on the *Project Management Body of Knowledge* under the direction of R. Max Wideman. There were more than 50 individuals identified as contributors to this effort, and many more participated in the numerous discussions that were an integral part of the process. The PMI Board of Directors accepted this standard on 1 September 1987. The first edition added risk management and contract/procurement management as Knowledge Areas to the work done in 1983. As noted by Wideman in the Foreword to the 1987 standard, formal recognition of project management was seen in a variety of industries and government agencies, but because project management meant different things to different people, including what was involved in it, the concepts in this standard can assist in improving how resources are used through this documented body of knowledge. Wideman further noted, "The essential feature of those projects, indeed of any project, is to bring about change" (PMI, 1987, p. 1-1). He explained that project management involves managing change, whereas general management is concerned with managing the status quo, and technical management focuses on managing technology.

In change management in 1986, Levy and Mary classified changes into two kinds: first order and second order. A first-order change was one characterized by "minor improvements and adjustments that do not change the system's core and occur as the system naturally grows and develops" (p. 5). Examples included changes in processes, organization structure technology, communication systems, recognition and rewards, and the decision-making process. On the other hand, a second-order change was one considered a multidimensional, radical change or a discontinuous, deep structural change that led to a new identity for the organization. These changes took at least a year to implement, because they were complex and dynamic, and were often met by resistance. There was a need to learn from experience with such changes because there was little to no experience in working with them.

Bartunek and Moch (1987) extended these concepts to identify a third-order change in which organizations change as events require. In a third-order change, the commitment is to the unexpected, boundaries are not set, negative impacts are to be avoided, and there is a commitment to continuous improvement, process improvement, and embracing change.

By the end of this decade, PMI had its first project management standard, and more people were involved in PMI activities. As well, change management literature was also increasing, building on the earlier initial work.

The 1990s

By 1990, PMI's members totaled more than 8,500 people, and by January 1990, 355 people had attained their PMP certifications. In 1991, PMI chapters began to actively promote the certification and prepared study materials for it; and in 1993, PMI published a study guide to help people prepare for the exam. The PMP exam was translated into other languages as interest increased globally. By 1995, there were 3,500 applications to take the PMP exam, and by that time, almost 5,000 people had attained the certification.

In 1991, to further the growth of the profession, PMI established specific interest groups (SIGs), known today as practice areas on ProjectManagement.com, with the first one in information systems. These SIGs held their own symposia and also established specific tracks for papers and presentations at PMI's National Symposium on Project Management. PMI also established Seminars USA, a series of educational programs on project management (later renamed SeminarsWorld®).

Also in 1991, PMI's director of standards initiated a project to update the 1987 standard on project management. Several drafts were prepared and, in 1994, a public exposure draft was developed, on which the approximate 10,000 PMI members were given the opportunity to comment. Then, in 1996, PMI published *A Guide to the Project Management Body of Knowledge (PMBOK® Guide)*, which superseded the 1987 document. It added a Knowledge Area on Integration Management and revised the definitions for the terms *project* and *project life cycle*. It pointed out that it was not the project management body of knowledge (PMBOK) *per se*, because no one document could contain the entire body of knowledge in the field. PMI issued a request for proposals to develop courses on each of these Knowledge Areas, along with questions to help people when taking the PMP exam.

Other initiatives were under way in change management. "The organization that never changes eventually loses synchronization with its environment, while the one that never stabilizes can produce no product or service efficiently" (Mintzberg & Westley, 1992, p. 46). Consultants now had opportunities to assist public and private sector organizations in change initiatives, including managing change as a project. For example, at the Center for Food Safety and Applied Nutrition of the Food and Drug Administration (FDA), a program was established to reorganize the organization to be less silo-based, and to develop strategic goals and a strategic plan so everyone could see how his or her work fit into these goals and the center's priorities. The program also set up advisory groups to oversee some of the work under way. This was a seven-year program that included numerous change projects.

Kotter (1995) published *Leading Change,* noting that change is implemented or sticks when it is embedded into the daily work of the professionals in an organization. He explained that new behaviors must be rooted within social norms and shared values. For best results, the pressure for change needs to be removed. He described a nine-step process to follow to overcome resistance by first establishing a sense of urgency and, at the end, anchoring the new approach to follow.

Wright and Schacht (1996) describe the transformation project at IBM that began in 1994 to change the culture to one driven by project management, moving from a pyramid structure to one that used integrated, cross-functional teams. IBM established a career path for its project managers, provided training and ongoing support through a Project Management Center of Competency, and created a virtual online community for project managers, along with defined project management processes and procedures. This cultural change required executives and managers to participate in the process, showing their commitment and their own responsibilities for project management success. In 1997, IBM established a Center of Excellence in Project Management. Similar transformational initiatives were under way at other organizations throughout the world.

Canterucci (1998) pointed to change management as the next step in project management, describing change projects as those that have a significant influence on one's life at work. He linked the change management literature with that of project management, noting that different procedures will be needed for change projects because the aspects of a job will change, including accessibility to data, a decentralized environment, and other intangible factors.

With the increased interest in project management during the 1990s, organizations wanted to understand the level of maturity of their project management processes. Interest in using project management increased because of the Software Engineering Institute's Capability Maturity Model for Software (CMM-SW), a leading model for increasing maturity in software projects. In a consulting project in 1995–1996, for example, with the National Finance Center of the U.S. Department of Agriculture, a consulting firm was asked to assess its project management processes. It became evident that the CMM-SW was lacking, with its emphasis on software projects, and a maturity model applicable to all projects was needed. Fincher and Levin presented a paper on the need for a generic project management maturity model that was not limited only to software projects at the 1997 PMI National Symposium in Chicago, noting the need for a maturity model that applied to all types of projects, and interest in this area was overwhelming; more than 200 people attended the session. Many others also were in the process of working on project management maturity models. Levin teamed with Ward and ESI International to develop one, and ProjectFramework™ was issued in 1999, which was modeled after the CMM-SW noted above, but covered all types of projects with the nine Knowledge Areas from the 1996 *PMBOK® Guide*, with specific examples to ascertain whether or not a specific level of maturity had been attained based on objectives at each level for each Knowledge Area. Recognizing the interest in this area, in 1998, PMI set up a core team of people who were working on or had prepared maturity models to develop the *Organizational Project Management Maturity Model* (*OPM3®*).

This decade also saw an increase in universities throughout the world offering master's degree programs in project management. In 1998, two universities, Western Carolina University and the University of Wisconsin-Platteville, began to offer these degrees online.

In 1998, PMI was accredited by the American National Standards Institute as a standards developer. At its 30th anniversary in 1999, there were more than 50,000 members of PMI, more than 150 chapters, and more than 25 SIGs. PMI's SeminarsWorld® had grown to 39 topics. The PMI website averaged 125,000 hits per month. At the PMI Symposium held in 1999 in Nashville, Tennessee, more than 100 vendors displayed their products and services. The exhibitors included software developers, educational organizations, and consulting groups.

To conclude the 1990s, PMI's book *The Future of Project Management*, released in July 1999, provided an overview of future scenarios and probable trends. Some of the trends identified in the book were the following:

- Project management is continuing to evolve from a set of skills into a profession, and the pace of evolution is increasing.
- Participation in the project management profession is growing very rapidly.
- The people aspects of project management are increasing significantly in importance in the successful management of projects.
- Technology continues to advance exponentially and greatly enhance the capability for positively aiding the management of projects.
- The complexity of all aspects of the life cycles of projects is increasing and placing greater demand on the capabilities of project managers and project personnel.

- The locations, compositions, cultures, and communications of project management teams are changing dramatically and also becoming increasingly complex.
- Overall, the world appears to be changing more dynamically in more areas than ever before in its history. (PMI, 1999)

From 2000 to January 2015

In 2000, PMI issued its *A Guide to the Project Management Body of Knowledge (PMBOK® Guide) – 2000 Edition*. This *PMBOK® Guide* noted that projects are managed to requirements, strengthened the link to organizational strategy, added more emphasis on progressive elaboration, referenced project management in developing economies, expanded the treatment of earned value, updated risk management with more processes, and broadened the "overall change control process" to become the "integrated change control process." The 39 processes in the *PMBOK Guide®* were mapped against the five Process Groups and the nine Project Management Knowledge Areas. This update showed that change was evident as the project management field expanded, and frequent updates of the *PMBOK® Guide* became the norm.

PMI subsequently adopted an approach in which it updated the *PMBOK® Guide* on a four-year basis; the third edition was issued in 2004, the fourth edition in 2008, and the fifth edition in 2013. The team is in the process of developing the sixth edition for a 2017 release. With each update, the project management coverage increased. For example, in the third edition, additional material was added to emphasize best practices. Process Groups were expanded, especially the treatment of integration and its importance to a project, along with the addition of the Initiating Process Group to focus more on the start of the project and each phase. The number of processes increased to 44 from 39 in 2000.

The *PMBOK® Guide – Fourth Edition* (PMI, 2008a) established standard approaches for organizational process assets, enterprise environmental factors, change requests, preventive and corrective actions, and defect repair. It also included greater clarity regarding the project management plan and the documents required to manage the processes, and the number of processes was decreased to 42 because of the greater focus on the Integration Knowledge Area and to avoid duplication. This edition included an appendix on interpersonal skills.

In September 2010, a *PMI PMP Examination Content Outline* (ECO) was issued, which changed the format of the PMP exam: Rather than receiving a numerical score based on the number of questions answered correctly, applicants were graded as proficient, moderately proficient, or below proficient in each of the five domains. This ECO showed the number of items per domain, with 25 of the 200 questions in the exam considered pretest questions, which were randomly dispersed but would not reflect one's score. The purpose was to use analytics to monitor applicants' performance on the questions.

In the *PMBOK® Guide* – Fifth Edition, changes included (PMI, 2013a):

- Harmonization with other PMI standards and the *PMI Lexicon of Project Management Terms*;
- Alignment with the International Standards Organization (ISO) 21500;
- Refining processes for greater clarity;
- Adding a Knowledge Area on stakeholder management;
- Refining the data model of work performance data, information, and reports;
- Enhancing the discussion on organizational strategy, the relationship between programs and portfolios, and PMOs;
- Expanding the information on interpersonal skills; and
- Providing broader coverage on organizational impacts.

This time period also saw an increase in other PMI standards documents. For example, to enhance the concepts in the *PMBOK® Guide*, PMI developed extensions to the publication in several areas beginning in 2002. These extensions were developed to supplement, but not replace, the *PMBOK® Guide*.

In 2006, the *Government Extension to the PMBOK® Guide Third Edition* was issued. Its purpose is to provide specific examples relevant to the unique characteristics of public-sector projects. It contains an overview of the key project governance processes used in most public sectors, defines key terms, describes the environment in which government projects operate, and follows the same structure as that of the *PMBOK® Guide*, with the same Knowledge Areas. The first edition was issued in 2002, based on work beginning in 1998 by the Government SIG, and it was the first application area extension applicable to government projects at the national, state/provincial, and local levels.

In 2007, the *Construction Extension to the PMBOK® Guide Third Edition* was issued to address additional knowledge and practices on construction projects. In addition to the Knowledge Areas in the *PMBOK® Guide*, the *Construction Extension* included Project Safety Management, Environmental Management, Financial Management, and Claims Management. It further addressed the "green" construction trend, along with required skills and resources unique to the industry.

In 2013, the *Software Extension to the PMBOK® Guide Fifth Edition* was issued with congruency with the *PMBOK® Guide* – Fifth Edition. This extension work was developed jointly by PMI and the IEEE Computer Society, with the goal of providing readers a balanced view of methods, tools, and techniques for managing software projects across the life cycle continuum, from highly predictive life cycles to highly adaptive life cycles.

Because of the widespread interest of project professionals throughout the world, practice standards on various areas were developed based on interest and approval from the PMI Board. They included:

- From 1999 to 2001, many participated in discussions about a practice standard on the work breakdown structure (WBS), which then was issued in 2001 as the *Practice Standard for Work Breakdown Structures*. It introduced WBS concepts, described its usefulness, and the steps required to complete one, with examples, and was consistent with the 2000 Edition of the *PMBOK® Guide*. The Second Edition, issued in 2006, refined this work and was consistent with the Third Edition of the *PMBOK® Guide*. The second edition added a section on WBS quality, added other appendices and methods to show a WBS, and included a CD-ROM with the standards and appendices. It provided new material to explain differences between a poorly-constructed WBS and a well-constructed one and added more detail as to the evolution of the WBS.
- The *Practice Standard for Scheduling*, issued in 2007 (with development beginning in 2003), aligned with the *PMBOK® Guide –* Third Edition. It clarified the term "schedule," and described the benefits of a schedule model, a scheduling method, and a scheduling tool. At that time, PMI supported "colleges" for specific areas, including the College of Scheduling. Its members participated actively in conferences over a three-year period while the standard was developed. The second edition was issued in 2011, in which the volunteers worked actively with PMI's scheduling community. In the second edition, there is additional information on earned value, resource application, risk management, and enhanced coverage of the schedule model and its assessment. This edition aligns with the fourth edition of the *PMBOK® Guide*. It led as well to a PMI Scheduling Professional (PMI-SP)® certification.
- In 2005, PMI published the *Practice Standard for Earned Value Management* supplementing the *PMBOK®* Guide – Third Edition to engender further understanding of earned value management (EVM). It covered an overview of EVM, its basic elements, use for analysis and forecasts, and guidance in using EVM practices for more effective schedule and cost management. Many participated in the development of this practice standard, and the then College of Performance Management took a leadership role in its development. This group had formed as a PMI college when the Performance Management Association joined PMI in 1999.
- In 2007, PMI published the *Practice Standard for Project Configuration Management*, consistent with the *PMBOK®* Guide – Third

Edition. Chartered in March 2002, the practice standard provides a guidance on project configuration management (PCM) and how to apply it throughout the project life cycle with a focus on configuration management and planning, configuration identification, configuration change management, configuration status accounting and metrics, and configuration verification and audits. This practice standard expanded the information covered in the *PMBOK® Guide* and provided sample processes and forms.

- In 2009, PMI published the *Practice Standard for Project Risk Management*, consistent with the *PMBOK® Guide* – Fourth Edition. The practice standard includes the principles that underlie the six processes in risk management included in the *PMBOK® Guide*. Each process is further described with its purpose and objectives, critical success factors, tools and techniques, and ways to document the results. The practice standard led to the PMI Risk Management Professional (PMI-RMP)® certification.

- In 2011, PMI published the *Practice Standard for Project Estimating*. Its objective was to apply sound estimating for projects and treat estimates as ongoing. The practice standard, then, is a guide and a reference to promote understanding of estimating and how best to apply it in projects. Included in this practice standard are principles and concepts of project estimating; how to best prepare to estimate and create an approach to do so; how to then create estimates for activity durations, resources, and costs; the ongoing maintenance and management of these estimates; and making improvements in estimating based on lessons learned. This standard is consistent with the *PMBOK® Guide* – Fourth Edition, and its development began in late 2006.

Recognizing the increasing importance of program and portfolio management, in 2006, PMI issued standards in each area. The purpose of *The Standard for Program Management* was to provide guidance for program managers comparable to what project managers received in the *PMBOK® Guide*. The standard focused on benefits management, stakeholder management, and program governance, and built on concepts in the *Organizational Project Management Maturity Model (OPM3®)*, to be discussed later in this chapter. This standard recognized that programs could result in more benefits, both to the organization and to its customers, than when projects and the ongoing work in them were managed as stand-alone projects. It further emphasized the usefulness of program management to organizational planning, such that work was aligned with organizational objectives and coordinated effectively with the best use of resources in the programs. Work on this standard began in 2003.

Similarly, work began in 2003 on *The Standard for Portfolio Management* and the standard was published in 2006. Although portfolio management had been practiced for years, this standard recognized its importance to the project management profession. The foreword noted that project management has multiple meanings, but that in the mid-1980s, project management began to include portfolio and program management. *The Standard for Portfolio Management* recognizes good practices, and it is directed to a higher-level audience, including senior managers. Its focus is on "doing the right work." The standard provided ways in which portfolio management could streamline overall operations, support corporate governance initiatives, support the organizational structure and its relationship to organizational strategy, and provide metrics to demonstrate and improve return on investment and portfolio management reporting.

Following the publication of *The Standard on Program Management* in 2006, PMI announced that it was initiating a new certification, the Program Management Professional (PgMP)®. About 100 people participated. This certification, in addition to including a difficult exam, also had a strict application process: Everyone who applied was audited, and, after passing the exam, went through a multi-rater assessment, similar to a 360-degree assessment, of actual experience as a program manager from peers, managers, and subordinates. At PMI® Global Congress 2007—North America, in October of that year, PMI honored the first 31 people who attained their Program Management Professional (PgMP) certification.

In 2008, both standards were updated to be consistent with the *PMBOK® Guide* – Fourth Edition and *OPM3®* – Second Edition. *The Standard for Program Management* was broadened significantly, adding Knowledge Areas rather than themes, including Governance, Financial, and Stakeholder Management, while benefits were incorporated throughout the document. However, this edition omitted cost, quality, and human resources, noting that they were more appropriate at the project levels. For each of the processes in the Knowledge Areas, inputs, tools and techniques, and outputs were added.

Knowledge Areas addressing portfolio governance and risk management were added to *The Standard for Portfolio Management* – Second Edition, along with a standard approach for discussing organizational process assets and enterprise environmental factors. These Knowledge Areas and their 14 related processes were mapped to two processes: (1) Aligning and (2) Monitoring and Controlling, with the inputs, tools and techniques, and outputs specific to portfolio management.

The third editions of both standards were published in 2013. Of interest was the decrease in the size of *The Standard for Program Management*. The core team members who led the development of this standard recognized the increased importance of program management and addressed differences between the program and project environments and approaches in managing a program versus a project. This standard returned to the domain nomenclature used in the first edition. There were five domains included in the third edition: program strategy, benefits, stakeholder engagement, governance, and life cycle. It enhanced the discussion of the relationship of program management to portfolio and operations management and organizational strategy, emphasized business value, and described the role of the program manager. Inputs, tools and techniques, and outputs were removed, with the life cycle focusing on program definition, program benefits delivery, and program closure. Competencies of program managers were detailed in an appendix, with change management as a core knowledge and skill area.

The Standard for Portfolio Management took a different approach, expanding the Knowledge Areas to add Portfolio Strategic Management, Performance Management, and Communications Management. The third edition added information on interactions between portfolio management and programs and projects, business value, the role of the portfolio manager and key knowledge and skills, and the functions of the portfolio management office. In 2014, PMI launched a Portfolio Management Professional (PfMP)® certification, and more than 100 pilot participants attained it.

The January 2015 issue of *PMI Today*® (p. 4) states the number of certification holders as follows:

- Certified Associate in Project Management (CAPM)®–26,771
- Project Management Professional (PMP)®–632,023
- Portfolio Management Professional (PfMP)®–168
- Program Management Professional (PgMP)®–1,131
- PMI Risk Management Professional (PMI-RMP)®–2,966
- PMI Scheduling Professional (PMI-SP)®–1,254
- PMI Professional in Business Analysis (PMI-PBA)®–192
- PMI Agile Certified Professional (PMI-ACP)®–6,987

It also lists more than 450,000 PMI members, and 273 chartered and 13 potential chapters in 105 countries and territories, with close to 5 million total copies of all editions of the *PMBOK® Guide* in circulation.

Organizational Project Management Maturity Model (OPM3®)

When the core team formed to develop this maturity model in 1998, there were 27 project management maturity models of varying degrees of complexity on the market. In 2003, the project was finished, and PMI published the *Organizational Project Management Maturity Model: Knowledge Foundation*. OPM3® was set up differently from other maturity models using best practices, which were listed in the standard, with the objective to provide a way for an organization to make its own informed decisions regarding potential initiatives for change. Other objectives were to enhance more predictable project outcomes and correlate them with organizational success, include program and portfolio management, and provide a way to measure maturity against best practices as organizational project management advances the strategic goals of the organization through individual projects. *OPM3®* is based on knowledge as described in the standard, which led to an assessment tool used to determine areas of strength and areas in need of improvement, where the capabilities required to achieve best practices were sequenced. It was considered the first PMI standard for organizations. Approximately 600 best practices were listed in the standard, along with lists for capabilities and improvement. Best practices were set forth for portfolios, programs, and projects, using a format of standardize, measure, control, and continuous improvement. The standard included a self-assessment for organizations to determine where they stand along a continuum of OPM, resulting in a list of best practices in place and ones that are needed.

In 2008, the *Organizational Project Management Maturity Model (OPM3®) – Second Edition* was published and, at the beginning of this publication, it stated: "Successful implementation of a new organizational strategy can turn a good organization into a great one . . . effective strategy execution is the responsibility of all levels of management, who must be involved actively and consistently to orchestrate required organizational changes" (2008b, p. 1). This standard was aligned with the *PMBOK® Guide* – Fourth Edition and the second editions of *The Standard for Portfolio Management* and *The Standard for Program Management*. However, the *OPM3®* – Second Edition included a new category, organizational enablers, underpinning the other best practices in the standard. Organizational enablers included areas such as competency management, sponsorship, success criteria, resource allocation, benchmarking, training, policy and vision, communities, management systems, knowledge management, strategic alignment, and metrics scattered across the project, program, and portfolio dimensions as well as those relevant to standardize, measure, control, and continuous improvement, which enabled maturity to be assessed in a variety of ways.

The *OPM3®* – Third Edition was issued in 2013, to expand, reinforce, and clarify concepts in the previous editions and to be consistent with the *PMBOK® Guide* – Fifth Edition, *The Standard for Portfolio Management* – Third Edition, *The Standard for Program Management* – Third Edition, the *PMI Lexicon of Project Management Terms*, and the *Project Manager Competency Development Framework* (see the next subsection). In terms of change, *OPM3®* – Third Edition states: "The increasing pace of change and the rising complexity of the economy and global competition requires executives to re-examine their strategy to fulfill stakeholder expectations and meet market needs" (p. 2). The focus was on organizational agility with a project-based approach. The standard emphasized best practices to achieve stated goals and objectives. Recognizing that no organization had all the needed capabilities to face future challenges, this standard noted steps to be taken to ensure that needed talent was available. It further noted organizational change management as a knowledge and skill area for an *OPM3®* practitioner to recognize how an OPM initiative impacts the organization. Although the same structure was retained, organizational change was emphasized with the requirement to assess change readiness, initiate the change, and manage it. Assessing change readiness was described in terms of required inputs, tools and techniques, and outputs. This change emphasis throughout this standard emphasized the evolving importance of change management to the profession.

Although extensive work had been done over the years on *OPM3®*, and a number of people had become certified in it, PMI announced in 2014 that it would be retired, effective September 2015. The future direction of PMI and an organizational maturity model remained unclear at the time this chapter was written.

The Importance of People

Though much of the discussion in this chapter has been about the growth of the project profession and the various PMI artifacts over the years, the importance of people cannot be overlooked or considered only within the Human Resource Management Knowledge Area of the *PMBOK® Guide* and its appendix.

Recognizing the need to ensure competency in project managers, PMI issued a *Project Manager Competency Development Framework* in 2002. First published in 1997, it was based on the theme of "Improving the Performance of Project Personnel" (p. ix). It defined competence, the units of competence, elements that comprised each unit, and performance and personal dimensions. It also outlined a recommended method to achieve competence as a project manager.

The Second Edition was issued in 2007. This edition placed increased emphasis on personal competences, included professional responsibility and ethics, and discussed how best to develop one's competences. *Competence* is defined as "the demonstrated ability to perform activities within a project environment that lead to expected outcomes based on defined and accepted standards" (p. 2). There are three key dimensions:

1. *Knowledge*—what a project manager knows about the best way to apply processes, tools, and activities to projects;
2. *Performance*—how the project manager applies knowledge of project management to meet requirements; and
3. *Personal*—how the project manager behaves as he or she performs activities on projects including attitudes and personal characteristics. (p. 2)

Of relevance to this book, element 4.2 in Monitoring and Controlling is "project change is managed"; however, it is a performance competency and relates more to integrated change control as covered in the *PMBOK® Guide – Fifth Edition*. The personal competence element, 10.3, refers to "changes at the required speed to meet project requirements" (p. 35), which applies to this book. Specific performance criteria include:

- Adapting to change in the project environment and minimizing adverse impacts;
- Being flexible when changes benefit the project;
- Taking action to maximize opportunities or resolve problems;
- Fostering an environment that emphasizes continuous learning by being change friendly; and
- Serving as a change agent.

These documents demonstrate commitment to talent development and how a project manager could assess his or her own competencies to see areas of strength and areas that are in need of improvement. It also supports efforts under way by project-oriented organizations that had adopted their own competency centers and competency frameworks.

Levin and Ward (2011) developed a competency model for program managers. It followed this same framework, but has a performance competency: "Element 5.6 program changes are implemented with established integrated change control procedures" (p. 52). They included a personal competency on change because it is so prevalent on programs as a stand-alone unit—8.0 Embracing Change—with four elements, each with performance criteria and evidence to assess whether one has met the criteria:

- Establishes an environment receptive to change;
- Influences factors that may result in change;
- Plans for change and its potential impact; and
- Manages changes when they do occur.

Exploiting and Adapting Change

The trend is to exploit and adapt to change rather than resist it. For example, in 2011, the *Harvard Business Review* published *On Change Management,* which featured ten articles (including that of Kotter, previously mentioned), eight of which were published between 2000 and 2011. PMI selected this book for review in the *Project Management Journal.*

Marge Combe and Lynn Crawford conducted a seminar on change management at PMI® Global Congress 2010—North America. Levin wrote and presented a paper titled "Embracing and Exploiting Change as a Program

Manager" at the PMI® Global Congress 2011—North America. PMI established a change management community; today it is known as a practice area. Five change management on-demand webinars are available for PMI members. Eight face-to-face professional development courses, two instructor-led e-learning seminars, nine e-learning on-demand seminars, and two quizzes on change management are also available. "Leading Change Management" was a theme at PMI's PMO Symposium® in 2013, held in San Diego, California.

These and many other initiatives led to the PMI publication *Managing Change in Organizations: A Practice Guide* in 2013, the first of several practice guides to be published, and will be discussed throughout the rest of this book.

However, PMI's *Pulse of the Profession®* reports show that the use of change management practices has been declining (71% in 2011; 65% in 2014). Change management at the organizational level remains a challenge. Building on its 2014 *Pulse of the Profession®*, PMI published an in-depth report in March 2014: *Enabling Organizational Change Through Strategic Initiatives.*

As Kerzner (2015) states, "Organizational change management mandates the use of transformational leadership where the goal is to transform the organization from one state to another . . . it is heavily focused on the people side of the change and is a method for managing the resistance to the change" (pp. 181–182).

The Future

Although we cannot predict the future, we know that as the project profession grows, change management in its various forms will play a significant role. Are we ready?

References

Adams, J. R., Bilbro, C. R., & Stockert, T. C. (1986). *An organization development approach to project management.* Upper Darby, PA: Project Management Institute.

Baker, B. N., & Wilemon, D. L. (1977). Managing complex programs: A review of major research findings. *R&D Management, 8*(1), 23–28.

Barnard, C. I. (1938). *The functions of the executive.* Cambridge, MA: Harvard University Press.

Bartunek, J. M., & Moch, M. K. (1987). First-order, second-order, and third-order change and organizational development interventions: A cognitive approach. *Journal of Applied Behavioral Science, 28*(4), 488–500.

Canterucci, J. (1998). Change project management (SM)—The next step. *Proceedings of the 29th Annual Project Management Institute 1998 Seminars & Symposium.* Long Beach, California. Upper Darby, PA: Project Management Institute.

Fincher A., & Levin, G. (1997). Project management maturity model. *Proceedings of the 28th Annual Project Management Institute 1997 Seminars & Symposium*. Project Management Institute, 1997, Chicago, IL.

Kerzner, H. (1979). *Project management: A systems approach to planning, scheduling and controlling*. New York, NY: Van Nostrand Reinhold.

Kerzner, H. (2015). *Project management 2.0: Leveraging tools, distributed collaboration, and metrics for project success*. Hoboken, NJ: Wiley.

Kotter, J. P. (1996). *Leading change*. Boston, MA: Harvard Business School Press.

Levin, G. (2011). Embracing and exploiting change as a program manager. *Proceedings of the Project Management Institute, Vancouver, Canada*. Newtown Square, PA: Author.

Levin, G., & Ward, J. L. (1999). *Project Framework™*. Arlington, VA: ESI International.

Levin, G., & Ward, J. L. (2011). *Program management complexity: A competency model*. Boca Raton, FL: CRC Press.

Levy, A., & Mary, U. (1986). *Organizational transformation*. New York, NY: Prager.

Lewin, K. (1947, June). Frontiers in group dynamics: Concept, method and reality in social science; social equilibria and social change. *Human Relations, 1*, 5–41.

Likert, R. (1961). *New patterns of management*. San Francisco, CA: Jossey-Bass.

Mayo, E. (1945). *The social problems of an industrial civilization*. Boston, MA: Graduate School of Business Administration, Harvard University.

Mintzberg, H., & Westley, F. (1992). Cycles of organizational change. *Journal of Strategic Management, 13*, 39–59.

Project Management Institute (PMI). (1987). *Project management body of knowledge (PMBOK) of the Project Management Institute*. Upper Darby, PA: Author.

Project Management Institute (PMI). (1996). *A guide to the project management body of knowledge (PMBOK® guide)*. Upper Darby, PA: Author.

Project Management Institute (PMI). (1999). *The future of project management body of knowledge: The first PMI forecast*. Newtown Square, PA: Author.

Project Management Institute (PMI). (2000). *A guide to the project management body of knowledge (PMBOK® guide) – 2000 Edition*. Newtown Square, PA: Author.

Project Management Institute (PMI). (2002). *Project manager competency development framework*. Newtown Square, PA: Author.

Project Management Institute (PMI). (2003). *Organizational project management maturity model (OPM3®): Knowledge foundation*. Newtown Square, PA: Author.

Project Management Institute (PMI). (2004). *A guide to the project management body of knowledge (PMBOK® guide) – Third edition*. Newtown Square, PA: Author.

Project Management Institute (PMI). (2006). *Organizational project management maturity model (OPM3®): Knowledge foundation* – Second edition. Newtown Square, PA: Author.

Project Management Institute (PMI). (2007). *Project manager competency development framework* – Second edition. Newtown Square, PA: Author.

Project Management Institute (PMI). (2008a). *A guide to the project management body of knowledge (PMBOK® guide)* – Fourth edition. Newtown Square, PA: Author.

Project Management Institute (PMI). (2008b). *Organizational project management maturity model (OPM3®): Knowledge foundation* – Third edition. Newtown Square, PA: Author.

Project Management Institute (PMI). (2013a). *A guide to the project management body of knowledge (PMBOK® guide)* – Fifth edition. Newtown Square, PA: Author.

Project Management Institute (PMI). (2013b). *Managing change in organizations: A practice guide.* Newtown Square, PA: Author.

Project Management Institute (PMI). (2013c). *Organizational project management maturity model (OPM3®): Knowledge foundation* – Third edition. Newtown Square, PA: Author.

Project Management Institute (PMI). (2014a, March). PMI Pulse of the Profession®: *Enabling organizational change through strategic initiatives.* Newtown Square, PA: Author.

Project Management Institute (PMI). (2014b). *Implementing organizational project management: A practice guide.* Newtown Square, PA: Author.

Project Management Institute (PMI). (2015, January). *PMI Today®*, 4.

Simon, H. A. (1957). *Administrative behavior.* New York, NY: Macmillan.

Stuckenbruck, L. C. (Ed.). (1981). *The implementation of project management: The professional's handbook.* Reading, MA: Addison-Wesley Publishing Company.

Taylor, F. W. (1911). *The principles of scientific management.* New York, NY: Harper.

Weber, M. (1946). In H. M. Mills & C. W. Mills (Eds.), *From Max Weber: Essays in sociology* (pp. 245–252). New York, NY: Oxford University Press.

Western Carolina University. Retrieved from https://www.wcu.edu/learn/programs/project-management-mpm/index.asp

Wright, C. L., & Schacht, N. R. (1996). Where the rubber meets the product development road: Institutionalizing project management in IBM's development community. *PM Network 10*, 17–20.

Youker, R. (1978). Implementing change in organizations: A manager's guide. *Proceedings of the Project Management Institute, 10th Annual Seminar/Symposium.* Los Angeles, California. Retrieved from http://www.pmi.org/learning/implementing-change-organizational-5728

Note: References to the history and early years of PMI are from PMI.org

CHAPTER 2

Complexity and Turbulence as Triggers for Change

By Dave Gunner, MSc, PMP, PfMP

Abstract

Change management is often viewed with trepidation. There are many documented accounts of failed change management initiatives, and the causes are attributed to complexity. However, it is easy to use complexity as a reason for failure in change initiatives and projects in general, but surely it is better to try to understand the causes and then deal with these complexities to help improve the chance of success. Traditional methods and means, although appropriate, are seldom sufficient on their own. There is an increased need to be perceptive and vigilant and to remember that what works in one situation may not work in another. This chapter intends to help project and program managers navigate their way through the complexity landscape, so that they will have some additional tools and techniques to help deal with their situation and increase the chances of a successful outcome.

Introduction and Background

Change initiatives are subject to varying degrees of complexity. Many, if not most, change initiatives can be classed as difficult. Difficult change initiatives usually involve individuals who have a natural propensity to want to avoid change. This reluctance, along with other human behavioral factors, can manifest itself as an example of complexity. The complexity can then adversely impact the success of change initiatives. For additional information regarding organizational change, refer to *Managing Change in Organizations: A Practice Guide* (PMI, 2013a).

There are many views regarding the meaning of complexity. It can be defined in a number of ways, backed up by research that has been done on the topic—especially on how to assess it. There is no single definition of what complexity is, and there is no single description of the types or classifications of complexity. However, for the purpose of this chapter, we will look at the definition and approach adopted by *Navigating Complexity: A Practice Guide* (PMI, 2014). Though not much has been done on how to cope with or navigate these complexities, it is worth stating up front that there is no single cause, answer, or approach for dealing with complexity. The first key step is to be aware and vigilant, and then to try to appreciate and understand the causes of the complexity. What may work for one situation and one individual may not work for another. Because of the multidimensional and multifaceted nature of complexity, it is ultimately up to individuals to find an approach and determine what works, based on personal experiences and acquired knowledge.

This chapter provides some ideas, techniques, and approaches that I hope will help readers recognize the complexity of a situation and navigate to a better outcome.

In accordance with PMI's *Navigating Complexity: A Practice Guide*, the causes of complexity are grouped under three main headings:

- **Human behavior.** This relates to the aspects that are, in general, associated with people.
- **Systems behavior.** This refers to the principle that different elements or components, when combined, can produce results or outputs that would otherwise not be possible.
- **Ambiguity.** This includes change that is unanticipated (emergence) and the lack of understanding or appreciation for a situation (uncertainty).

Much of the research that has been done on complexity points to the fact that human behaviors contribute to the majority of complexities, and this appears to be the case when managing internal change initiatives. Because the main focus of this chapter is on handling complexity in change initiatives, the causes of complexity that relate primarily to human behavior aspects are discussed herein. It is worth stating, however, that complexity is usually not attributable to a single cause, but rather results because of a combination of various causes that fall under all three of the main headings. Systems behavior and ambiguity may also be present, but as they are unlikely to be the main causes, they will not be covered here. However, when systems behavior and ambiguity are determined to be the primary cause of complexity for an initiative, project, or program being managed, the recommendation is to refer to *Navigating Complexity: A Practice Guide* and other sources and to conduct further research.

The Human Behavioral Aspect Causes of Complexity

Human behavioral aspects of complexity are underpinned by people, attitudes, demeanors, what people do and how they act, as well as other emotional aspects. The cause is usually not limited to one of these types of behaviors, but may involve a myriad of behavioral aspects. The list included here is not intended to be definitive; rather, it is hoped that it will provide an overview of some of the more common causes of complexity, which should help make readers aware of what to look for. Before appropriate actions can be taken, it is important to understand how to address these complexities. First and foremost, however, it helps to gain an appreciation of the various types of causes, either individual or group behaviors.

Individual Behaviors

Optimism Bias and Planning Fallacy

Optimism bias and planning fallacy is a common behavior in change initiatives. It usually arises at the outset, when the person initiating the change needs to sell the change and paints a positive picture, with little or no focus on the potential pitfalls that may arise. In many organizations, there are multiple potential change initiatives and projects competing for a share of the limited funds available. This often leads people to overstate benefits and understate the budget, time frame, and risk. Once these unrealistic expectations have been set, it is difficult to reset them. Once a commitment has been made, depending upon the organization in question, it may be difficult to report poor performance or any deviation from the original plan or schedule. Again, the sponsoring body or organization does not necessarily wish to hear such news, and the individual initiating the change feels pressure to meet what may be an unrealistic time frame and budget. By this time, the initiative is often over budget and is unlikely to be delivered within the original time frame, no matter what remedial action might be put into place. Once this mind-set has been established, it can grow because the complexity of the dependencies is not understood or appreciated. This can result in the project team's lack of awareness of the stakeholders and their needs and expectations. There are further ramifications, because from this point forward, it is likely that additional complexity will be generated.

It is easy to conclude that optimism is not a desired behavior; however, this is not always the case. Optimism is a major contributing factor in teams and projects that are performing at optimal levels. The project manager or change sponsor should carefully consider assumptions and adopt an approach in which they are able to perceive small signs in the project, program, or overall initiative that indicate deviation from the plan. This is supported by the lessons that have been learned from high-reliability organizations (Weick, 2007).

There are other reasons for optimism. These include (1) the natural bias toward being successful and (2) a "can-do" attitude, which in itself can mask issues and underlying problems. Overconfidence can override other evidence to the contrary. Kutsch (2011) refers to this sustained false optimism and makes an important point that this false optimism does not just occur at the outset. It is a common phenomenon that cannot be addressed by applying techniques such as earned value analysis, which can be used to justify and support any optimism bias and instill confidence in senior leadership. It is also worth remembering that good or optimistic news is easier than bad news to pass on. In many cases, a project manager may naïvely believe that the issues will be rectified and may choose not to inform senior leadership about any problems, because the leadership is likely to respond with unwanted additional attention and scrutiny.

This is just an example of how optimism bias and planning fallacy can manifest itself. As previously stated, this behavior can lead to further negative behaviors and may result in compounding and introducing further complexities.

Anchoring

In many ways, anchoring is linked to both optimism bias and planning fallacy. Early estimates in terms of effort and time frame for the initiative being proposed are likely to be positive and influenced either consciously or subconsciously by the desire to get the initiative approved. The project team or person submitting the business case is likely to be aware of critical constraints in terms of budget and time frame. Therefore, they know how to frame the project in order to gain approval. Once anchoring has been established, new information that comes to light in relation to any of the aspects of the project is often ignored. In some cases, even when the original business case or proposal includes realistic costs and time frames, many organizations have a tendency to set stretch targets for their projects. However, these targets can be unachievable, and the project or change manager may not have the confidence to refute them.

Framing

Information and progress may vary depending on who is presenting the information and to whom the information is being presented. This can lead to hidden agendas from the person presenting the information, and also from the original source of the information, whether it comes from a member of the project team, from stakeholders, or from another source. In effect, there is not a single version of the truth—everything relates to perception and positioning and is underpinned by many personal, motivational, and often hidden factors. Often, it is not a case of uncovering these, but rather accepting that these factors exist and ensuring that alternative perspectives and points of view are reviewed by looking at the project or change initiative from a holistic viewpoint.

Loss Aversion

Loss aversion, like optimism bias, is another human bias. It can arise following some of the previously mentioned tendencies, such as optimism bias, planning fallacy, and anchoring. When the project is no longer viable and is unlikely to be recovered, there is often a reluctance to accept this situation. This is especially prevalent when much time and effort have been invested in the project or change initiative, and the project team and/or project manager is reluctant to stop. People do not want to accept that the project cannot be recovered because that would mean they had wasted their time, usually involving a great deal of personal expense and sacrifice.

This situation may also arise when the business strategy and needs change, resulting in a reevaluation of priorities. The consequence of this reprioritization means that some projects will be terminated to make way for new initiatives that are in alignment with the evolving and changing needs of the business. When time, effort, and passion have been committed to a project, individuals on the project team who have been actively involved in the change are reluctant or hesitant to change.

Loss aversion can also occur in other stakeholder communities, such as those that may be the potential recipients of the change. In this case, the tendency is to look for reasons not to change and to focus on the downsides and risks of what could go wrong as opposed to any benefits or advantages that may be gained.

Resistance

Resistance to change is a recognized cause of complexity, though resistance itself can be attributed to other causes and reasons. Some of the fundamental causes behind this behavior, however, are grounded in science and, in particular, neuroscience. The findings from neuroscience research conclude that the brain is fundamentally averse to change. Obviously, it is important to understand and appreciate this fact when managing change programs. The brain's automatic or natural predisposition is to be wary of any change. This response is more sensitive and developed (and more easily set off) than the reward response. Anxiety and fear may be at the heart of resistance to change, so finding the underlying cause of the anxiety is a good first step in addressing or dispelling it. Actively looking for the positives and benefits at the individual level and helping address the "What's in it for me?" question is a good step to help reposition individuals' views of change.

The way individuals and organizations feel about change, in addition to the brain's natural response, can involve factors such as the following:

- Their previous experience with change—was it a good, bad, or indifferent?
- How much change has occurred recently?
- How fast is the change happening?
- Do people feel they are prepared for the change? Have they been trained and do they have the ability to do the new work?
- Will the change be likely to increase their workload beyond what they believe to be acceptable?

Resistance as a cause of complexity should not be ignored, nor should the organization readily assign specific causes or reasons. There will probably be more than one cause or reason, and each one will need to be given careful consideration.

Misrepresentation

It is easy to look at the behavior of misrepresentation as simply being unethical; in reality, however, there are many reasons for it. These can range from ignoring specific issues or risks to the over- or underestimation of costs and the ability to meet milestones. It may happen because of the fear of repercussions, especially when the organization in question takes a dim view of any bad news.

Group Behavior

Up to now, we have looked at some of the key individual behaviors and how they manifest themselves and contribute to complexity in change projects, programs, and initiatives. However, there are also some other human behavioral aspects related to groups and organizations. It is worth noting that these group behaviors can have a positive and constructive impact on the change, though this is more the exception than the rule.

Groupthink

Groupthink behavior occurs when a group or organizational unit's need to conform takes priority at the expense of logic and reasoned decision making. Even when a compelling argument for the change is presented, it can often be overridden by the groups' own needs. These associated behaviors and actions are also closely linked to another organizational behavior, called groupshift. The theory behind groupshift is that individuals, from within the safe confines of a group or team, may be more likely to take an extreme stance or action. This can adversely impact any change initiative, and prevent reasoned arguments from being given serious consideration.

Tribal Mind-Set

The tribal mind-set relates to rivalries between teams or groups and can lead to an "us versus them" way of thinking. In many cases, this results in unhealthy and irrational behavior, ranging from a healthy level of competitiveness to more negative behaviors. It is important to identify the presence of a tribal mind-set and its dynamics—for example, noting when it exists between different teams, groups, or projects. Such a mind-set can be compounded when there are competing change projects or programs and where organizational politics play a big part.

Self-Organization

There is a natural tendency for people to organize themselves and work together in groups. The manner in which this self-organization takes place does not take into account the needs of the change project or program. In some cases, this could lead to positive outcomes; however, whether self-organization manifests itself in a positive way or not toward the project or program is merely a matter of chance.

Stakeholder Commitment

This is one of the primary causes of complexity with change initiatives, because many do not have the appropriate level of engagement and commitment. There are several ways of dealing with this, which will be covered in more detail later.

Communication and Control

Many company-wide change initiatives and organizations operate across and in many countries with many different cultures. This can lead to challenges such as dealing with political and legal considerations—for example, what may be outlawed in one country may be perfectly acceptable in another. In addition, there are the cultural nuances that should not be ignored. Time spent understanding how to communicate and understand the cultures involved is time well spent.

Managing Stakeholders in Complex Situations

It is the stakeholders of the change initiative who experience or display these behaviors, which contribute to the complexity. Therefore, in this section, we will look at what activities we can include in our action plan to help understand the situation and, ultimately, improve it.

First, let's consider stakeholder management. Various techniques for analyzing and managing stakeholders have been published; some of these

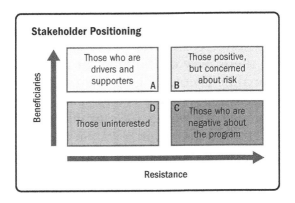

Figure 2-1.   Example of power/interest grid used for stakeholder positioning.

are described in *A Guide to the Project Management Body of Knowledge (PMBOK® Guide) – Fifth Edition* (PMI, 2013b). One technique in particular—the power/interest grid—can be used to plot and position identified stakeholders. However, this model only considers two dimensions (power and interest), whereas in change initiatives, which include elements of complexity, it is important to consider additional dimensions. As we have already discussed, there is a natural tendency toward resistance to change, even when individual stakeholders will benefit from the change initiative to varying degrees. These stakeholders can similarly be plotted onto another quadrant (see Figure 2-1).

Plotting the stakeholders onto a quadrant will help ascertain which stakeholders are particularly negative about the project and which stakeholders are fully supportive. The quadrant to which the stakeholders are assigned will determine how they need to be managed, although other factors should also be considered. Bear in mind that the position of stakeholders is not static; it is likely to change as the project progresses, not as a result of the project itself, but when other external factors are considered. For example, a stakeholder in quadrant B (essentially positive, but worried about some risks) could easily move into quadrant C when the stakeholder's own business priorities change. It is a good idea to assess the opinion of others on the change team. Remember, there is no absolute answer; the positioning is subjective and based on individuals' experience and engagement.

- **Quadrant A.** This quadrant includes the supporters and drivers of change. Although they are in this quadrant, these people should not be ignored. They can often be used to help influence and reposition others, depending on their sphere of influence. Usually, these are the stakeholders who will benefit most from the initiative.
- **Quadrant B.** These are the stakeholders that are generally positive (that is, they will benefit), though they may also appear to

be somewhat resistant. This resistance may be a result of the fact that these stakeholders are the ones who are impacted most—and who could be required to change the most or make the most effort. More often than not, these people need to be involved and (ideally) moved to quadrant A. For each of these stakeholders, their ideal position needs to be given careful consideration. If it is deemed that they need to reside in quadrant A, then the appropriate actions need to be considered to accomplish that. It is worth noting that this may not always be possible; however, if moving them to quadrant A is not possible, then actions may at least need to be put in place to prevent them from moving into quadrant C.

- **Quadrant C.** Usually, quadrant C includes the stakeholders who have the potential to cause the most disruption and have a negative impact on the overall change initiative. For each one of these, it is important to understand why they are negative resistors. Perhaps they are involved in conflicting initiatives or have other interests. Once this assessment has been done, it should be possible to determine whether it is worthwhile to try to move these stakeholders to another quadrant or, if not, to initiate damage control actions.
- **Quadrant D.** These are the stakeholders who are generally indifferent or uninterested. This may be fine; however, these people should not be taken for granted. If any of these stakeholders would ideally be in quadrant A or B, then the appropriate actions to achieve this need to be considered. Also, if these stakeholders are not managed appropriately, there may be a danger that they could adversely influence other stakeholders.

The Stakeholder Action Plan

Having completed the first stage in assessing the position of the stakeholders and identifying where they need to be, the next stage is to capture the appropriate actions to take for each one. See Table 2-1 for a mechanism to track the actions for each stakeholder.

Table 2-1.   Example of stakeholder action plan.

Stakeholder	Quadrant in which they reside (A, B, C, or D)	How they are impacted by the change	The stakeholder's perception	Their outward commitment (hostile, anti, neutral, assist, or drive)	Influence (High, Medium or Low)	Where they should be	Action to take to manage and "move" their commitment

Columns can be added or removed from the stakeholder action plan (Table 2-1) as necessary depending upon the particular initiative, for example:

- **Column A.** Stakeholder name.
- **Column B.** Quadrant in which stakeholder resides.
- **Column C.** How stakeholder will be impacted by the change is an important factor and consideration.
- **Column D.** The stakeholder's perception, which is always going to be a subjective measure. However, it is important to regularly monitor this because it could change and, in many cases, it will need to change. This will have a direct influence on which quadrant the stakeholder is placed in.
- **Column E.** Stakeholder commitment, which may be different from his or her perception. They can be categorized as hostile (aggressive and opposing), anti (against, but not actively hostile), neutral (no preference or interest), assist (helping when asked), or drive (proactively pushing things forward). Stakeholders will need careful handling, especially if they are openly hostile.
- **Column F.** Stakeholder influence, which has an impact on the priority of any actions that have been identified.
- **Column G.** Stakeholder's ideal quadrant position.
- **Column H.** Respective action to take. In many instances, it may be appropriate not to take any action at all or to deliberate on the most appropriate timing for the action.

Reflective Thinking

Reflective Thinking—The Benefits

Dealing with complexity requires the use of specific techniques and tools as well as learnings from high-reliability organizations about the idea of mindfulness (Weick, 2007). Mindfulness is about paying attention and being aware of a situation and doing so in a nonjudgmental fashion. Being cognizant and aware of a situation is the first step in considering what actions should be taken. Begin by looking at reflective thinking and how this can be applied when complexity is encountered.

The ideas behind reflective thinking are simple but effective. Reflective thinking is about individuals thinking about (or reflecting on) the actions that they have taken and what they have learned, and then assessing and considering what worked and what did not work, or what could have been changed or improved. This approach is often encouraged as a means to help with an individual's own personal development. However, when encountering complexity, it is important to be aware of the actions that may or may not work; otherwise, the situation could become even worse. Before we look at a process, let us review the benefits of reflective thinking, which include the following:

- Reflection on the actions taken helps put experiences and ideas into perspective.
- Reflection helps individuals recognize what they have learned.
- Reflection helps generate new ideas and enables plans to be put in place to test these ideas.
- Keeping a log or journal to capture the effectiveness of the actions that are taken is a great way to learn what works in certain circumstances and what does not.
- Reflection also helps with personal development and growth, including understanding an individual's strengths and weaknesses.

Reflective Thinking—The Process

The starting point for the exercise is not necessarily to understand all the causes of complexity, but rather to focus on one particular area and then take a view and appreciation of what can be done to address the causes of complexity. It is advisable to solicit others' views, because everyone may have a different viewpoint and complexity is usually a matter of perspective. When possible, gather input from the project or program team and use brainstorming techniques to capture ideas about the main complexities or challenges being faced. Here are some questions that can be used to start the discussion, though it is best not to restrict the discussion to these questions alone. Doing so may well prevent other important points from being raised:

- What is the situation being experienced or witnessed?
- Where is this situation being observed?
- When is this situation being observed?
- When did the situation first arise?
- What are the implications?
- Who is affected?
- What are the consequences?

Step 1

Capture all answers to the questions. It is best not to rule out any ideas or suggestions at this stage. All the ideas can be collated into a tabular format using the previous questions as headings. This will help evaluate and determine the main causes. The key is to select one challenge at a time and then to circle back and select the next one, in order of priority.

Step 2

Once one or some of the causes of complexity have been identified, the next step is to carefully consider what needs to change or be done differently. The key is to select a challenge, determine how to address it, and decide what actions to take. This requires some in-depth analysis into the triggers of the causes. Consider the following questions:

- What would make the most difference in improving the situation?
- What can be done? Make a list of options and then rate them. This is another opportunity to seek the ideas and thoughts of the project and program team.

PMI's *Navigating Complexity: A Practice Guide* refers to a number of useful practices, which also provide guidance on some useful sources to consider. Some of these may fall within the control of the project or program manager, though others may not. In many cases, the optimization of the organizational structure and governance are not necessarily factors that the project or program manager can influence; however, all options should be explored.

Some useful practices to consider from *Navigating Complexity: A Practice Guide* include the following:

- Optimize the organizational structure.
- Establish effective governance.
- Diligently research the program or project prior to approval.
- Match the manager and key team members to the program or project.
- Listen to the experts.
- Manage integration effectively.
- Focus on change management.
- Encourage a resilient mind-set.
- Pay attention to small signs that signify major changes.
- Avoid oversimplification.
- Encourage reflective thinking.

When managing complex change initiatives, some of these practices are going to be more relevant than others. Some of these will be covered in more detail elsewhere in this chapter.

Step 3

As part of Step 2, a number of activities may have been captured. For the next stage, the idea is to decide which are the most appropriate actions to take. Quite often, there is no right or wrong answer; deciding which action to take first will be a subjective decision. However, the important aspect is to be specific, which may involve breaking down the actions into a number of smaller tasks or activities. A key part of reflective thinking is to repeatedly step back and reflect on what you have decided and determine whether or not it is a suitable solution. Reflect on whether or not there are likely to be any unexpected consequences that could worsen the situation or cause additional challenges or issues.

These activities are unlikely to resolve all of the complexity in the situation. In many cases, complexity cannot be resolved or removed, though ideally, the aim is to reduce it and deal with it, whenever possible.

Step 4

After establishing a number of actions and activities, the next step is to ensure that the expected outcomes for these actions are clear. Ideally, there should be metrics of some sort, and these metrics need to be clear, concise, and unambiguous. They also need to be agreed upon up front, along with dates and time frames, to avoid perpetuating the same issues that caused the situation in the first place. In some cases, when it is not possible to establish suitable metrics and dates, this fact needs to be acknowledged and recorded.

Step 5

In Step 5, take the action or actions identified and monitor the results closely, again through the adoption of reflective practices. Be particularly vigilant for small signs of change in both outcomes and behaviors.

Step 6

This next step is to look at what was done. This is important, because sometimes what was planned is not the same as what was done. Before any further analysis, review what was done and compare this with the actions that were intended.

Step 7

Be critical when evaluating the results. Did all the actions work or did part or some of the actions work? At this point in the process, seek feedback from others in the project or program team or from other stakeholders who are likely to be affected by the actions. Capture as many comments and opinions as possible and compare the viewpoints. Also solicit opinions about whether there have been any unexpected consequences. On the surface, the actions may have appeared to have had a positive outcome, but sometimes they may also have unplanned or unexpected consequences. It is essential to capture and document any such occurrences.

Step 8

It is only at this point that the results from the actions taken are analyzed. This is a very important step in the overall process. Changes, improvements, or unexpected consequences are not always obvious. As a result, it is necessary to be sensitive to small changes and find those that could evolve into something more. Do not be deterred if there are either no improvements or if there is a minimal reduction in complexity. By their definition, complex situations are not easy to address. They may require a number of iterations of action and reflection.

Step 9

After the analysis has been performed, it is time to consider what has been learned from the entire exercise. Even when the results are not positive, there may be future situations where the actions taken could be effective. If the actions resulted in positive outcomes, do further analysis to understand the critical success factors as to why the approach worked.

Step 10

It is important to remember that the process is iterative. A key lesson from the success factors of high-reliability organizations is to develop resilience; accept up front that not all actions will result in a positive outcome or impact. The individual managing the change initiative needs to be prepared for potential failure and be ready to develop new plans when necessary.

The cycle should continue until it is determined that the major elements of complexity have been addressed or are being addressed in the most appropriate manner.

Figure 2-2 shows each of the process steps and how they relate to one another.

When to Use Reflective Thinking

Reflective thinking is generally considered good practice and is part of being mindful. However, it is not a replacement or substitute for normal project management good practices. Complexity in change management initiatives is a matter of perspective, which implies that there is no right or wrong answer—just the view of the individual. When considering when to start using the process, the recommendation would be to start as soon as there are any indications that complexity is present. Start by undertaking a complexity assessment, such as the one in PMI's *Navigating Complexity: A Practice Guide,* or one of many other assessments that are readily available. An assessment provides a starting point on where to focus and how to determine where the main areas of complexity are. Even when the assessment does not reveal any specific complexities, it is important to revisit this continually.

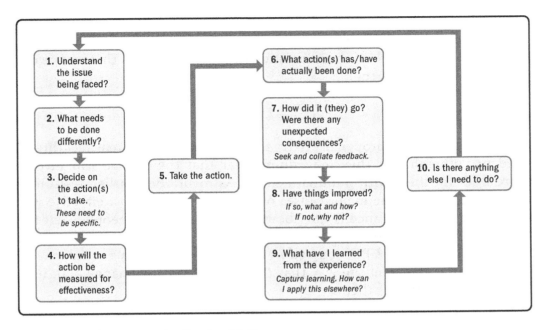

Figure 2-2. The process of reflective thinking.

At minimum, do a reassessment once the project or program is set up and being managed using the standard processes, life cycles, and methodologies of the organization. As for the reflective process, it can be commenced at any stage from initiation through to closure.

There are many variations to this process. Rather than start by asking the seven questions, another commonly used technique is to ask the "five whys." This will help get to the root cause of the problem. After each answer, ask another "why" (e.g., "Why is that the case?", etc.) five times or even more. However, bear in mind that for the one answering the question, this method can appear somewhat frustrating.

Influencing

The Importance of Being Able to Influence

As discussed previously, most change initiatives are likely to have complexity, and many of these initiatives are going to involve aspects associated with human behavior. As a result, being able to interact with, engage, and influence people effectively is a critical success factor in managing such projects and programs. There has been much research done on how best to influence others and which aspects of behavior are most important. Ultimately, it boils down to answering two questions:

- What is in it for me?
- Do I have the skills and ability to take on the change?

Being able to apply skills that address these questions and needs is the key to being able to successfully influence others.

We will look at each of these questions and the strategies that can be deployed to help address them.

What Is in It for Me?

People have a natural propensity to try to avoid change. They may feel threatened or vulnerable or they may simply fear that the change will involve more work for them with minimal benefit. As mentioned earlier, resistance to change is one of the major causes of complexity. The most effective way to deal with the resistance is not about trying to convince people what the higher-level benefits are; rather, it is about trying to establish empathy. What is important for them? Put yourself in their position and try to understand what and why they feel the way that they do toward the change and, ultimately, what motivates them.

The following five techniques and approaches can help address and answer the question: What is in it for me?

- **Who is doing whom a good turn?** This is the first step in being able to relate to others on their level and on their terms. Daniel Pink (2012) looks at how this can be classified as who is doing whom a favor. If the initiator of the change believes and acts as if he or she is the one doing the favor and this is not reciprocated by those who need to change, then problems arise. The solution is for the change initiator to act as if he or she is the one receiving the favor. In other words, behave as if you, the project or program manager, are the recipient of the favor—not the other way around. Being humble, thankful, and appreciative is more likely to win support for the change initiative. This is a behavior that initiators of change need to adopt.
- **The use of storytelling.** This is a key way to engage with people, especially those who are the recipients or the ones who need to change. Create and recount stories that those who are impacted or required to change can relate to. Make the stories personal to the individuals so they realize that the change is to their advantage and benefit.

  Once their hearts and minds have been won, they will be on board and supportive. Referring back to the stakeholder quadrants mentioned earlier, these individuals will more than likely be in quadrant A. They will have become supporters and drivers, or at worst, positive but concerned about risk (quadrant B). Tell them how their day-to-day work/life will be better, and try to get this message across by recounting stories that will engage them.

Basically, the project or program manager should treat everyone as if they are friends or family. It is worth noting that people generally remember stories, especially when they can relate to the stories. Ensure that these stories are accompanied by a memorable message, one that will stay with the individuals to whom you are reaching out. This will help get the change campaign off to a great start.

- **"Try before you buy."** It is far better for individuals to feel they have a say in whether the change will be adopted. Coercion rarely works, and will result in minimal compliance at best. Usually, coercion results in resentment, and behind the scenes, people will revert back to the way things were done before. Commitment through coercion is not commitment and is not sustainable, and those being coerced may try to find and uncover the disadvantages of the change initiative. Whenever possible, sell the benefits to individuals by demonstrating the change. Individuals will then have firsthand experience of the change and its benefits; but even more importantly, this will help remove the fear of the change, which is the primary reason for resistance.

- **The power in using visuals.** Using words to get the message across is a powerful tool, but it is not enough to rely on words alone. The use of simple visual cues, either in static form or through simple, short videos, can be extremely powerful. Ideally, visuals should also be used together with some of the other techniques discussed here, such as storytelling.

- **Find the right influencer.** The person initiating or managing the change is not necessarily the best person to be responsible for doing the convincing or influencing. This is especially true when there is no evidence of trust or respect. It is far better to reach out to someone who already has respect or is deemed to be a thought leader within the area that needs to adopt the change. This could be more than one person and may be a functional group within an organization. This becomes more important when there are numerous, different cultures involved. Find the right person who has the influence and also understands the cultural nuances, which may also be complex. There is no easy answer to deal with different cultures, but it is essential to communicate to them on their terms. Five dimensions that should be given serious consideration for each different culture that you are working with include:
  - How to communicate;
  - How to persuade;
  - How to gain trust;
  - What the attitude is toward learning; and
  - What the attitude is toward time, scheduling, and meeting dates.

Many change initiatives associated with global economies and global countries involve a multitude of different cultures. All of this is proportional to the amount of cultural complexity that the initiative may be experiencing. The key is to remember that there is no absolute rule for cultures—it is all about what Erin Meyer (2014) calls "cultural relativity." When you consider each dimension or aspect that relates to each culture, this needs to be thought of as a scale, where a particular culture or country resides is relative to another culture or country. Stakeholder management and communications need to be tailored to each culture and country. When an approach is formulated for a particular culture, remember that even within each culture, there is no absolute rule.

These approaches to the question "What's in it for me?" are not intended to be definitive; they contain ideas and suggestions of methods that have proven to be successful when managing change in complex situations. It is worth noting that other techniques can also be used, such as introducing healthy competition between the managers of peer groups. This may be especially useful when deploying or adopting new tools or processes within an organization. Reflective thinking (previously discussed) also plays a very important part here: Listen more than you talk. Do not just second-guess or believe that you know what influences or motivates people; instead, listen intently to what they say. More importantly, avoid the use of harassing and threatening behavior.

Do I Have the Right Skills and Ability?

Having started to answer "What is in it for me?", the next step, which can be done in parallel, is to consider what skills and knowledge are required. This can be determined by performing a skills inventory for all the stakeholders who will be impacted directly or indirectly by the change. Then, compare the results with the skills that will be required in the future mode of operation and analyze the differences to determine and address which skills are needed. This can be done by paying particular attention to the following:

- **Consider the work environment.** How much time has been allocated for training? Are there other competing priorities in terms of training and the current roles? Understand how conducive the environment is to learning. Even if you have convinced stakeholders that the change is beneficial, if they are not able to undertake the necessary training, then progress will be hampered. If there are time pressures, consider how these can be addressed by breaking down the work into smaller components, even going as far as delivering a series of 10-minute briefing sessions. Utilize available tools and learning resources.

- **Will people be able to understand the training?** It is possible that those who are being trained have not had to undergo such a major change for a long time and will be unfamiliar with the type of training involved. They may be wary and unsure about whether they have the ability to adapt to the new way of doing things. Being cognizant of this fact is very important; tactics need to be deployed to address this issue. These tactics may include continuous feedback on progress and constant reassurance. Breaking training down into smaller components can often make it easier to evaluate interim progress.
- **Provide the necessary support framework.** Training on its own is usually not enough. In today's virtual environment, much training is web-based, and individuals are expected to complete the training without adversely impacting their regular work. This is a recipe for disaster; people will do the training while they continue to multitask, doing other work at the same time. They may naïvely believe that they have completed the training and understood the message and learning; however, this is far from reality. A common mistake of those who provide training is that the training is an item that can be crossed off the to-do list. To address this, consider implementing a coaching and mentoring framework, with exercises that can assess and provide feedback on progress. One effective technique is to have individuals do the training in peer groups and set up train-the-trainer sessions. By doing this, you will have a network of experienced and accessible trainers. In today's work environment, social media should also be used. We have previously considered the cultural dimension, which is essential; however, there is another dimension to be concerned about—the generation dimension. What works for Generation X does not necessarily work for Generation Y.

Ultimately, everyone has different learning styles as well as different learning speeds—some people learn easier and more quickly than others. Training has changed somewhat from what it was in the past, and the norm is no longer attending an onsite course with an instructor. Much training is now performed on the job and through media such as communities of practice and self-directed learning.

Essential Soft Skills

In addition to the new technical skills that are likely to be needed, there are also many interpersonal and soft skills that are needed when managing changing initiatives. This applies not only to the individuals who are the recipients of the change, but also those who are managing the change. Below are 10 of the most essential soft skills that have been found to be beneficial when dealing with complexity in change management initiatives:

- Decision making;
- Leadership;
- Collaboration;
- Bravery and judgment;
- Resolving ambiguity;
- Innovation and change;
- Cultural and political awareness;
- Risk attitude;
- Delegation; and
- Communication.

Final Thoughts

This chapter was intended to provide insight into tools, techniques, and approaches that can be helpful in managing complex change initiatives. Some recent research looks at the psychology of change and a topic called neuroplasticity, which concerns how the brain can be molded and modeled in order to better adopt and adapt to change. Some of these findings include the following:

- The brain needs to be ready for the change.
- Training should not be too easy (the participant needs to feel a sense of having accomplished or achieved something).
- Human emotions strengthen the internal connections of the brain.
- Emotions linked to experiences and learning will strengthen the entire learning experience.
- Be aware that the brain can change in both a negative as well as a positive way.

There are many other methods and media to help successfully manage change initiatives and many of these will be covered in the other chapters in this book. However, it is important to always be on the lookout for how things can be done better. Trying to get people to influence, alter, or change human behavior and convincing them to do new things or do things differently is an art—there is no single right answer or approach. But it is never too late to change, and there are always ways in which things can be done better.

References

Kutsch, E., Maylor, H., Weyer, B., & Lupson, J. (2011). Performers, trackers, lemmings and the lost: Sustained false optimism in forecasting project outcomes—Evidence from a quasi-experiment. *International Journal of Project Management, 19*(8), 1070–1081.

Meyer, E. (2014). *The culture map.* New York, NY: Public Affairs Books.

Pink, D. (2012). *To sell is human.* London, England: Riverhead Books.

Project Management Institute (PMI). (2013a). *Managing change in organizations: A practice guide.* Newtown Square, PA: Author.

Project Management Institute (PMI). (2013b). *A guide to the project management body of knowledge (PMBOK® guide)* – Fifth edition. Newtown Square, PA: Author.

Project Management Institute (PMI). (2014). *Navigating Complexity: A practice guide.* Newtown Square, PA: Author.

Weick, K. E., & Sutcliffe, K. M. (2007). *Managing the unexpected.* San Francisco, CA: Jossey-Bass.

Review Questions

1. *How do I recognize complexity?*
2. *How is complexity different in change projects from other projects?*
3. *How will I know if the actions I take are the right ones?*
4. *How does knowing the causes of complexity help?*
5. *What is the difference between stakeholder communication and stakeholder engagement?*
6. *How does reflective thinking help manage complexity?*
7. *Why is influencing important?*
8. *What else do I need to know or do?*

CHAPTER 3

Organizational Agility: A Catalyst for Organizational Change

By Yves Cavarec, MBA, PMP

Abstract

Agility is not a quality for an organization; it's a strategic choice. Organizational agility defers to any strategy that an organization applies when facing uncertainty in business. It is the strategy that works best when the business environment is so turbulent that it seems to be a permanent crisis.

Being agile is not only about managing projects in an agile way; it also implies strategic portfolio, project, program, and operational agility. To be functional, agile organizations have chosen to decentralize decision making. Employees, who are selected because they share the values of the organization, are trusted rather than controlled. They take part in the choices the organization makes so that decisions are accurate and the level of commitment is high. In agile organizations, the role of managers includes creating strong cohesive teams, supporting their employees, and reminding employees of the short-term priorities of the organization. Organizational agility requires managers to excel in engaging people at work. An organizational agility assessment model can be used to help an organization identify its strengths and weaknesses among seven domains in order to be more agile.

Introduction

Strategy in a Permanently Changing Business Environment?

Strategy is about *orienting an organization in the long term* (Johnson, Whittington, Scholes, Angwin, & Regnér, 2014). It's about allocating resources in the long run in order to achieve a competitive advantage. Traditional strategic tools, including Porter's four strategic forces, SWOT analysis, BCG matrix, or experience curve work, assume that the future is quite predictable.

Since the beginning of the 20th century, we have progressively transitioned to a turbulent economic environment. Today, organizations face fast and unpredictable changes that affect their ability to create value. Nonconventional crises tend to be more and more frequent and unpredictable than in the past. Looking back at what has happened since the turn of the 21st century, we have faced a number of nonconventional crises, including the 9/11 attacks, the global financial crisis, Hurricane Katrina, the Ukraine crisis, the rise of the Islamic State (ISIS), terrorist attacks in Europe, and so on. The turbulence in business is so great that we are now in a permanent state of crisis.

Can an organization have a strategy in a turbulent world? When a company allocates human, technological, and industrial resources and it doesn't know what will happen tomorrow, isn't that called gambling? We expect strategists not to be gamblers. In fact, they are not. Strategists have learned to adapt and have invented five ways to face turbulence.

Agility as a Strategic Choice

Publicly and privately held businesses across all ranges of industries, as well as nonprofits, government organizations, and even countries, must be prepared to face change. For nonagile organizations, change is a reaction. It is essential for survival. Project, program, and portfolio managers who have to deal with unexpected change in business in a nonagile organization have to work under pressure because they are always short on time and resources for strategy execution. It's a case where something could have been done previously but wasn't, because no decisions were made.

On the contrary, being agile is a conscious, strategic choice. This chapter is about agile organizations. The first part of the chapter explains how organizational agility is different from traditional strategies that nonagile organizations apply to face uncertainty; organizational agility works best in the current permanent business crisis. The second part of the chapter describes agile organizations, showing that being agile is more than just managing projects in an agile way. It also describes how agile organizations work and how they defer from nonagile organizations in decision making and control, management, and leadership.

Organizational Agility to Face Turbulence

Uncertainty in business is not new. When businesses are faced with uncertainty and turbulence, traditional strategies no longer work in today's permanent crisis.

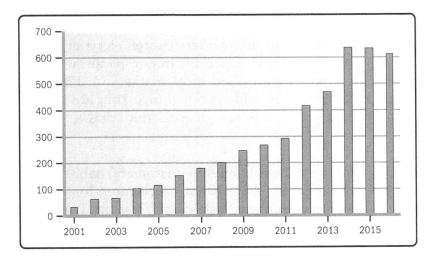

Figure 3-1. Number of scientific papers related to organizational agility published since 2001.

Organizational agility is still rising (see Figure 3-1). It is the strategy of choice in the current turbulent, economic environment, though it hasn't been broadly applied as a business strategy thus far. It is still expanding. Being agile (i.e., having organizational agility) is by far the best way to thrive when changes are permanent and massive.

The Five Possible Strategies for Facing Turbulence

There are five possible strategies to face a changing business environment. They are:

- Being bold;
- Copying;
- Identifying scenarios;
- Finding a blue ocean; and
- Organizational agility.

Strategy 1: Being Bold

What It Is

The first strategy to use when facing turbulence is to be strong enough to stay still, just like an oil platform facing bad weather. This approach assumes that the organization has the resources to face the variations of the environment.

Conditions

Being bold works well for organizations with a large market share; having a barrier to entry provides products or services that customers need and that are difficult for competitors to imitate.

Example of Bold Organizations

Bold organizations include utility markets (water, electricity, railway transportation, telecommunications), especially in Europe through the end of the 20th century. Monopolies controlled local markets in different countries. Governments are examples of bold organizations: They are strong enough to keep tax rates unchanged even in case of economic crisis.

Assumptions

As long as there are no major changes in customers' habits, bold organizations don't have to innovate. There is not much room for new competitors because organizations are well established and their size is a barrier to entry.

Relevance and Limit

Being bold works well when organizations are big enough to face turbulence—they have enough resources to get through the unknown. Corporations whose assets require long life cycles use this approach, which makes agility nearly impossible. Being a large monopoly in itself is a good strategy to escape the effect of competition. Because customers buy, there is no reason to change. Regulation can terminate such dominant positions. The free movement of goods, capital, and labor in Europe; and the authority given the Competition Commission to allow the free flow of goods, capital, and labor across borders inside the European Union, have had a major impact on local monopolies, including European governments. Organizations were forced to innovate to reduce costs or increase customer value to conquer new market shares. In the case of governments, people can move to other places to pay less tax or to receive better public services. In the long term, governments will change to adapt. Being bold is no longer an advantage when turbulence is so huge that it is better to be small and adaptable.

Impacts on Project and Change Management

An organization that has chosen to be bold in order to face a turbulent environment needs strong assets, just like an oil platform has to withstand the worst weather conditions. Project managers need to deliver results that will resist the perturbation of a changing economic environment. Among project management activities, requirement management and risk management are key success factors. Program management is another way to face the ambiguity that characterizes large organizations in a turbulent environment.

Strategy 2: Copying

What It Is

For a senior executive's career, it is not good to make the wrong decisions for an organization. But it does happen. Worse than making a wrong decision is being alone in making that wrong decision. Instead of taking the risk of being alone in making a wrong decision, an executive would rather make the same strategic decisions that the competitors make. If it happens to be a good idea, they made the same decision as others in order not to be decried. If it happens to be a wrong decision, it can be explained by circumstances. A financial market analyst would not blame a CEO for having made the same mistake as another CEO.

Conditions

There are not a lot of innovations on the market. When a competitor makes a decision, it can easily be copied by others. This is not a question of intellectual property or patent. For example, when a traditional retailer develops a new service like home delivery, online ordering service, or payment by installment, it is easily imitated by competitors.

Assumptions

From a career management perspective, it would be too risky for an executive to take the initiative to be a pioneer on the market when others are minimizing risks by doing the same thing as their competitors.

Relevance and Limit

With a copying strategy, a company will never change its position in the market. A new entrant on the market or a major innovation would ruin this strategy. For example, Amazon has completely changed the way to effectively market consumer goods; traditional retailers must now create new strategies to stay alive. For this same reason, Airbnb[1] is making a big impact on the hospitality industry.

Impacts on Project and Change Management

When an organization decides to copy a competitor's strategy, what counts is the ability to deliver results quickly in order to stay ahead of the competition.

Strategy 3: Identifying Scenarios

What It Is

The organization identifies what could happen and applies techniques such as Monte Carlo simulation or game theory to aid in making decisions.

---

[1] Airbnb is the community marketplace that connects travelers with the owners of vacant accommodations. It has become a cheap alternative to a hotel. In January 2015, Airbnb claims to have more than a million accommodations (rooms, apartments, houses, lodges, castles) in 190 countries, and 25 million guests.

Conditions

The environment can be simulated with a limited number of parameters. For example, if the parameters are the cost of raw materials and market demand, there are four major scenarios: increase in cost and increase in demand, increase in cost and decrease in demand, decrease in cost and increase in demand, and decrease in cost and decrease in demand.

Assumptions

Identifying scenarios works when the environment is simple and foreseeable (not complex) and remains still. For example, in the oil and gas industry, the main variable is the market price. Companies can develop scenarios based on market price variation.

Relevance and Limit

Scenarios no longer work when major changes are involved; for example, a major innovation like shale gas exploration, or a nonconventional crisis like the oil crisis in the 1970s or the invasion of Kuwait by Iraq. Because nonconventional crises have become more frequent and unpredictable, scenario-based strategies are less and less relevant.

Impacts on Project and Change Management

Scenarios seem like a great idea on paper, but they are often hard to put into practice, especially when they require investments. When competing to win a large public tender, companies have, generally, at least two scenarios: A) we win the contract; and B) we lose.

Scenario A includes making a series of investments that should not be made in case of scenario B. These investments are projects, programs, and changes that require time to be executed. And when the company knows the tender result, it is too late to start the projects, programs, and changes to be ready on time to start the new contract in good conditions.

The company could start projects, programs, and changes in advance to get ready to start the contract on time and in good conditions, in case of scenario A. But if scenario B happens, it will be a lot of money and energy spent for nothing.

Strategy 4: Finding a Blue Ocean

What It Is

A blue ocean strategy (BOS) refers to differentiating an organization from its competitors by focusing on delivering high-value products and services to customers. This is what Nintendo did with the Wii®. Instead of jumping into technological competition with Sony and Microsoft, Nintendo decided to attract new customers to the video game market. Nike also chose the option to offer running shoes to people in the street, instead of focusing only on athletes, the way former global leaders Adidas and Puma did prior to the 1970s.

Conditions

Competitors are not able to adapt and deliver competitive products and services because they are not necessarily ready for change in terms of their capacity or culture. When the vineyards in Chile, the United States, and Australia introduced new techniques to make wine, it was difficult for French wine producers to adapt because they had to ignore the know-how they had learned from their heritage—something that can be emotionally hard to do.

Assumptions

The firm is able to set new rules for the market, but competitors and new entrants are not. Cirque du Soleil proposed a new way of presenting a circus using sophisticated and elegant shows without animals. Although it is a circus, it is different. Cirque du Soleil realized lower costs (no animals) and higher prices (it is a luxury item). Though most traditional circuses are facing difficult economic times, they are unable to accomplish what Cirque du Soleil was able to do because of a cultural gap—the change is too big. In addition, it is complicated for new entrants because customers want the original Cirque du Soleil, not a pale copy.

Relevance and Limit

A blue ocean strategy is very close to what Porter (1980, p. 41) used to call differentiation strategy, as opposed to a low-cost strategy. BOS is easy on paper. Many leaders claim to use a blue ocean strategy, but few succeed in having their products accepted by customers. The more innovation there is on the market, the harder it is to sustain a leading position. For example, Microsoft used to be the reference on the IT market, but it is being replaced by Google, which uses cloud computing.

Impacts on Project and Change Management

In blue ocean strategies, creativity is key. Project managers must be able to lead their teams to think outside of the box and do things in a different way. Agile project management can support this strategy. Being too tight on risk management (avoiding risks) will usually kill creativity; therefore, project managers and sponsors need to be risk tolerant on the project and also be able to manage the people side of change.

Strategy 5: Organizational Agility

What It Is

By definition, agile organizations reallocate resources more easily than others, for example, in case of a change in the market. An example of this is the strong increase in demand for hospitality in the city of Paris, France. Hilton, Sheraton, and Marriott need time to find locations to build and open new hotels to offer new supply. Airbnb is able to provide more accommodations at no extra cost if there is an increase in demand. In the event that there is a decline in demand, Airbnb does not have to pay for empty accommodations, unlike a traditional hotel.

Conditions

Increases in production require heavy industrial investments, as in the gas industry, where more time is needed to reach the break-even point and to dismantle assets at the end of the life cycle. On the contrary, organizations from a sharing economy are more agile than in traditional business. Another factor of agility is the decision circuit, where small companies generally need less time to make a decision; this is one reason why they are able to be more agile. Large companies can be agile only when decisions are decentralized and when employees and small units are trusted to do their jobs.

Assumptions

Organizational agility means frequent change. To be agile, organizations must be change-ready in terms of capacity (they have the resources and the willingness to change), in terms of processes (they know how to change), in terms of commitment (people in the organization agree to change and are ready to make the effort), and in terms of culture (despite the changes, the organization manages to remain aligned with its values and mission).

Relevance and Limit

A bad way of becoming agile would be not to commit to any decision, which would mean having no strategy at all. Sometimes, executives are not ready to make a decision because they don't have all the information; they prefer to wait for more information. The temptation to not make a choice is real. The problem is that executives can have no certainty that more information will be enough. It's better to make a decision, even if the decision is temporary, than to avoid a decision entirely.

People in an organization must be prepared to make a decision. Once they commit to a decision, most people like to fulfill their commitment. But change is not natural, and it is a real challenge in terms of leadership. It is not easy for leaders to tell their people that there will be a change in strategy or direction. Leaders and other employees need to realize that they will be vulnerable in an agile organization. This is what Lencioni (2002, p. 195) calls "vulnerability-based trust": People can be vulnerable with a group only when they trust that the group won't use their vulnerability against them.

Impacts on Project and Change Management

Change management is the key success factor of organizational agility. Organizational change includes not only the people side of change, but also the processes, systems, and relations among people (culture).

Organizational Agility Is the Most Powerful Strategy Today

No single strategy fits all organizations. The best strategies come from a good strategic diagnosis, which includes a deep understanding of three things:

- Opportunities on the market;
- Organizational strengths, including the ability to rework the market; and
- Context.

The world today is turbulent, changing, and unpredictable, and organizational agility appears to be an option for all organizations to consider if not in the short term, then at least for the long term.

Today's Main Challenges

All organizations have faced, are facing, or will face at least one of the following three challenges:

- Draining of natural resources;
- Rise of the sharing economy; and
- Maintaining stakeholders' trust.

The Draining of Natural Resources

The planet today counts seven billion inhabitants. The demand on natural resources, including the following, will inevitably grow:

- **Water.** By 2025, 1.8 billion people will live in places with a scarcity of freshwater.
- **Oil.** We have enough proven oil resources only for the next 50 years.
- **Natural gas.** We have enough gas in proven reserves to face the next 60 years.
- **Phosphorus.** We will probably run out of reserves of this essential fertilizer for plant growth in less than 100 years.
- **Rare earth minerals.** These are used in any electronic engine or device; 97% of the world's current supply comes from China. The entire industry is dependent on China.

The Rise of the Sharing Economy

In a context where natural resources are becoming rare, controlling the resource supply is a good way to gain a sustainable competitive advantage. For those who can't control resources, the sharing economy may prove to be a better alternative.

The sharing economy has impacted the information industries. *Wikipedia*, for example, was created to compete with *Encyclopedia Britannica*. And we know now that any industry that is concerned with competition can create a better alternative: To compete with hotel chains worldwide, Airbnb was created in lieu of locating real estate and building hotels; to compete with taxi cabs and other transportation companies, Uber and car-sharing platforms (such as Blablacar) were invented.

Any organization knows that new entrants could affect the market with potentially zero marginal cost, which would be absolutely disruptive to the market.

Keeping Stakeholders' Trust over Time

Trust has always been a key economic factor. When trust is lacking, one needs to spend time and resources in setting rules and controlling their application, which automatically has a negative impact on business.[2]

In a stable environment, though, when an organization possesses a dominant position in the market (i.e., the strategy is *being bold*), trust is less of a problem in the short term because people have nothing but the choice to work with you (because there is a lack of competition). In turbulent environments, things could change rapidly and it is safer to belong to an ecosystem in which you trust your stakeholders for all of the following reasons:

- It is advantageous when employees are able to apply their thoughts instead of asking for authorization or for a solution to the hierarchy.
- Suppliers can help by providing their latest innovation instead of sharing it with the competitor.
- Customers may have cheaper opportunities, but when they are certain they are receiving the best, they will be loyal.

We used to believe that creating value for shareholders was the most important objective—and it still is. We are being reminded now that shareholder value in the long term depends on equilibrium among all the organization's stakeholders.

---

[2] The question of trust in the economy was at the core of the alternative between the administrated economy and the market economy in the 20th century. A caricature of controlling was the USSR's system: Resource allocation was supposed to be done by the government. But the administrated economy was so inefficient that the Soviet government had to tolerate the black market in order to allow people to have food and the basics they needed to survive. In China, the reform introduced by Deng Xiaoping, called the Four Modernizations and launched in 1978, was a bottom-up reform (contrary to top-down perestroika in the Soviet Union). It consisted of less centralized planning, less control, and more of a market. The notion that socialism and the market economy are not incompatible is the foundation of the Chinese market socialism.

In conclusion, regarding today's challenges, the current context is favorable to disruptive changes, which include both:

- The arrival of **new entrants** into markets, whatever the industry—potential threats come not only from competitors, but also from outsiders; and
- The **change of uses and practices**—ownership used to be the norm, but sharing is the new trend.

Organizational Agility Best Fits This Context

Consider the five strategic options in light of today's challenges.

Being Bold

Being bold is no longer an option. Whether or not the organization controls the resources that it needs (and gaining control is easier said than done), the organization may be threatened by a disruption in the market—at least in the long run.

Copying

Copying is not enough. It helps an organization stay at the level of its competitors; however, the organization will never be protected from new entrants.

Identifying Scenarios

Scenarios are based on a short list of parameters. The current context is probably too open for most organizations; identifying a limited number of parameters is not easy. How would anyone have imagined a few years ago that the main competitor of Hilton Worldwide (hotels) would not be Marriott International or any other hotel group, but Airbnb? New entrants to the market sometimes bring disruption.

Finding a Blue Ocean

Blue ocean strategies are good options for new entrants to a market. Imagining new products and services or new ways of conducting business is always difficult for insiders because they are anchored within the existing framework. Finding a blue ocean is not impossible, but it is probably more difficult for existing companies in the market. It will also not protect the organization from future turbulence in the market.

Being Agile

Postmortem analysis of crises has always shown that there were warning signs—information that, if we had paid attention, would have served to prevent crises. This information is referred to as weak signals. Any organization should watch weak signals and use them to react promptly by initiating changes when needed. Being agile is probably the only option for most organizations that want to continue conducting business within their market. For any existing organization, agility is the best strategy to use and potentially thrive in a context when turbulence is the new norm. Let's see now what it means for an organization to be agile.

What an Agile Organization Looks Like

Definition of Organizational Agility

Key Figures

Business leaders believe that organizations need to be agile in order to succeed. They must be able to change tactics or direction quickly. That is what recent research proves.

A survey conducted by McKinsey (2006) collected 1,562 responses from a representative worldwide sample of executives at publicly and privately held businesses across a full range of industries, including nonprofits and government organizations. Nine out of 10 executives considered organizational agility critical for business success, and this belief is gaining importance over time.

The Project Management Institute (PMI) conducts annual global research called *Pulse of the Profession®*. In 2012, the research was about agility (PMI, 2012). According to this survey, the benefits of agility include:

- 71% faster response to changing market conditions;
- 55% overall improved organizational efficiency;
- 54% improved customer satisfaction;
- 44% more profitable business results; and
- 38% organizational changes made more quickly or efficiently.

In the same survey, CEOs described organizational agility as resulting in:

- 75% quicker response to strategic opportunity;
- 64% shorter decision/production/review cycles;
- 59% focus on change management;
- 54% integrating voice of the customer; and
- 53% elimination of organizational silos (PMI, 2012).

Last but not least, the PMI survey showed a clear correlation between change management–performing organizations and agile organizations. Approximately 92% of organizations that were highly effective at change management reported high or moderate agility (PMI, 2012).

Agility as a Strategy

PMI (2013, p. 121) defines organizational agility as "the capability of a business to proactively seize and take advantage of business environment changes while demonstrating resilience resulting from unforeseen changes." Taking this one step further, Sull (2009) broke down organizational agility into:

- Strategic agility,
- Portfolio agility,
- Project and program agility, and
- Operational agility.

Agility is a way for organizations to embed change within their strategy and to cascade it down to their operations, as shown in Figure 3-2.

Strategic Agility

Strategic agility is an organization's ability to stay in the game until it is able to seize an opportunity. For example, Apple's stock price remained flat for 20 years until in 2004, when the price rose after the launch of the iPod. An organization must be able to wait for the right moment before acting, like a predator patiently waiting for its prey. The difficulty is aligning all stakeholders on that principle, especially over a long period of time. Shareholders, for example, might not be willing to wait so long and may pressure the CEO to make a risky investment. From this perspective, turbulent economic

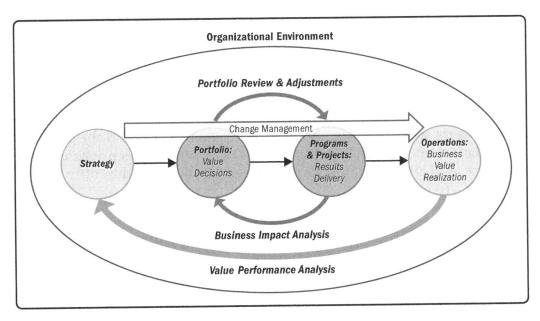

Figure 3-2. Driving achievement with change management and OPM.
Source: *Managing Change in Organizations: A Practice Guide* (PMI, 2013, p. 25).

environments are an opportunity, because they bring many opportunities to "predators."

Portfolio Agility

Portfolio agility is the ability to shift resources from low-potential businesses to high-potential ones. This is easier said than done. For example, when an executive sponsors the development of a business, it is hard for the same person to disengage the company at a moment when demand is decreasing on the market. This is a well-known cognitive bias; it comes from the feeling of not being consistent (and even in contradiction) with oneself when making a decision that is opposite to a previous decision.

Program and Project Agility

Program and project agility refer to the ability to take into account market evolutions and to seize opportunities between the beginning and the end of a program or project. For example, the program or project should support changes to its requirements. The organization should be allowed to terminate the program or project if it appears that there is no longer a business case for it. From a higher perspective, an agile organization does not necessarily apply agile project management approaches in the meaning of the Agile Manifesto, or any specific methodologies, such as Scrum or extreme programming. Only 50% of CEOs believe organizational agility implies the use of iterative project management practices (PMI, 2012). Both waterfall and agile project management are compliant with organizational agility as long as they facilitate response to changes in the business environment.

Operational Agility

Operational agility is the ability to seize revenue-enhancing and cost-cutting opportunities faster and more effectively than competitors do. No one knows in advance the scale and the timing of these opportunities. The retail industry has put systems in place to determine in real time what is being sold in stores so as to make their supply chain more reactive. To avoid the deluge of contradictory operational information, it is necessary to filter priorities at the executive level and communicate them clearly throughout the entire organization on a frequent basis.

Operational Agility: Centralized Versus Decentralized Decision Making

Throughout history, there have been periods of centralization and decentralization in societies worldwide. Most of the literature on agility today implicitly refers to centralized decision making. After considering both centralization (Figure 3-3) and decentralization (Figure 3-4), organizations have a higher potential to become agile when they decentralize decisions.

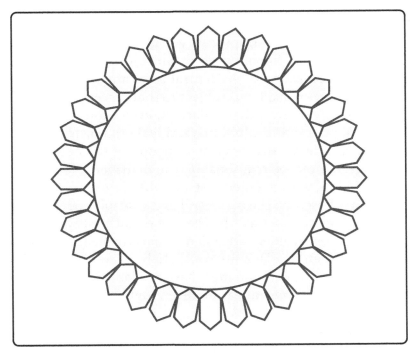

Figure 3-3. The sunflower with small petals symbolizes centralization.

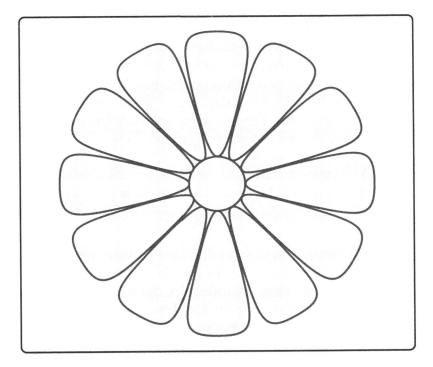

Figure 3-4. The large petals of the daisy symbolize decentralization.

Centralization

Centralization corresponds to any process where plans and decisions are made by a small group of people. In politics, centralization is the concentration of a government power. For example, the central government has the most power and local authorities are considered subject to that power. In a centralized corporation, decisions are made at headquarters, even though the decisions are applicable to local subsidiaries. In a hierarchical organization, decisions are made at the top. Few initiatives are given to people at the bottom of the pyramid. In a manager-employee relationship, the manager gives the employee a clear process to follow, with detailed instructions on how to do the job.

Centralization is based on the command and control model, which the U.S. Department of Defense defines as "the exercise of authority and direction by a properly designated commander over assigned and attached forces in the accomplishment of the mission" (DoD, 2010, p.40). To be effective and make the right decisions, the center of the decision must have a reliable information system.

Those who want more centralization often highlight the following:

- *Cost savings:* The organization is more consistent and economy of scale is made possible in procurement, production, and marketing.
- *Fraud reduction:* The risk of fraud is low because local employees have to refer to headquarters for decisions, or even before making a decision, and the internal control system is able to detect scams.

These arguments ignore the following:

- Businesses are not made from cost savings but from value creation, and centralization by nature disengages employees.
- Every massive fraud since the year 2000, including Enron, WorldCom, Fanny Mae, Freddie Mac, Lehman Brothers, and AIG, has occurred at the headquarters level by CEOs.

The main risk of centralization is to strengthen the power of a few and to put their achievement above the benefit of the whole organization.

Decentralization

Decentralization is the distribution of decision-making authority. In a headquarters-subsidiary model, subsidiaries have a lot of autonomy in decision making. In a manager-employee relationship, the manager gives freedom to the employees to do their job their way. Employees are also given clear guidelines, and they are accountable. Freedom without accountability would lead to anarchy.

With decentralization, local employees, who know their customers best, make decisions to serve their clients. They do this because they are accountable for their business results—no matter how much they spend. What counts is the value created (that is, the difference between sales and expenses).

In conclusion, decentralized decision making helps operational agility because employees are prompt to respond quickly to operational changes.

Commitment and Culture for Organizational Agility

Trust Rather Than Control

When decisions are centralized, the control system is part of the command and control system. Instructions are given and are executed according to the plan. Response to a change in the environment implies that the decision center identifies the change, determines a new plan, and executes the new plan. This process is not agile: It takes time.

In 1939, the French army, which was supposed to be the strongest in the world at that time, expected an attack from the German army. All the French troops were getting ready for the battle along the German border in the east when, on 10 May 1940, the German Wehrmacht cut through Belgium and the Netherlands to invade France in the north. The French troops received instructions to move from the German border only on 12 June. On 21 June, the French were defeated. The Nazis occupied France until the success of the Western Allied Operation Overlord in Normandy on 6 June 1944.

An agile organization is, by definition, quick to respond to changes, unlike the French army in 1939–1940. Reactivity increases with the decentralization of the control system. Instead of waiting for instructions, people are accountable for their results and they are given freedom to take initiative to solve problems or face new situations. For many years, Nordstrom, the U.S. upscale fashion retailer, used to provide new hires with an employee handbook that was a model of empowerment. It was a single, five-by-eight-inch gray card that contained the following words:

> *Welcome to Nordstrom. We're glad to have you with our company. Our number one goal is to provide outstanding customer service. Set both your personal and professional goals high. We have great confidence in your ability to achieve them. So our employee handbook is very simple. We have only one rule. Our only rule:*
>
> Use good judgment in all situations.
>
> *Please feel free to ask your Department Manager, Store Manager, or Human Resource office any question at any time.*

Build the Team Before Defining the Objective

When applying strategic planning principles, start by planning, then identify the required resources, and finally, execute the plan. This process works well with resources in general, but not with people.

When applying strategic planning to organizational change, the result is always the same: People are resistant to change. When we try to sell a plan without listening to the team's experience, ideas, and solutions, we disengage people. We don't let people weigh in on decisions. And when people don't weigh in on decisions, there is no buy-in for solutions. This is how resistance emerges.

Most people think an employee's resistance is the basis of the problem. People look for solutions to overcome the issue—for example, setting up change management programs dedicated to helping people transition to the future state. This is why project management is used, on the one hand, to define the future processes and the future systems; and change management, on the other hand, is used to handle the people side of change. Organizations spend time and energy trying to prove to employees that they have the best processes (at least on paper) and the best software to support the processes. When organizations operate in this way, their priority is internal negotiation and compromising—not solving the client's problem. So who cares about their customers? Competitors always do!

Agile organizations avoid change resistance and politics (See Figure 3-5). Patrick Lencioni (2012) calls them "healthy organizations." A healthy organization must follow these four disciplines:

1. **Build a cohesive leadership team.** Team building is the first step, and it is based on trust. It starts with the leadership team at the top of the organization and then cascades down.

2. **Create clarity.** Clarity is about sharing the same purpose, the same value, the same strategy, and the same short-term priority list. It is essential to build clarity from discussions and conflicting ideas so that employees have an opportunity to be heard. Then, a decision must be made and the employees must commit to the decision; at this point, there is no longer room for discussion.

3. **Overcommunication clarity.** Most executives and managers underestimate the communication effort. People only receive a

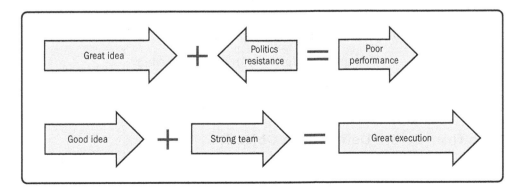

Figure 3-5. Start with team building rather than with a great idea.

message when they get it at least seven times in seven ways, including meetings, discussions with managers, emails, intranet, and so on. Repeating the message is a key success factor.

4. **Reinforce clarity.** Clarity is not only about words. It is also about setting an example. Reinforcing clarity includes, for instance, aligning the recruitment process (hiring employees based on the organization's values), the management system (setting goals that are consistent with clarity), and the reward system (formulating it with clarity).

Attitude over Skills

Henry Stewart, who founded Happy Computer in the United Kingdom in the 1990s, explains that a core value of the company is having employees who are positive and supportive of others. This is required of all staff members. It is not enough for employees to have a strong set of skills. The company adapted its recruitment process to put people in groups to see if they are supportive and to observe the way they interact with others. Stewart (2012, p. 75) explains that there are challenges in recruiting someone with less technical expertise, but says, "We found greater challenges in having somebody on board who wasn't supportive of others." It is even threatening for the whole culture "with the message that you could be as nasty as you wanted if your core expertise was strong enough" (p. 75).

The example of Happy Computer is an illustration of Lencioni's (2012) fourth discipline (reinforce clarity) in which the values of the company must be applied during recruitment. Employees' attitudes make the organization more (or less) agile, not only at the operational level, but also in projects and program management, portfolio management, and at the executive level. If employees don't have all the skills, they can be trained; however, if they don't have the attitude, there is nothing that can be done, no matter how skilled they are.

Management Skills in an Agile Organization

Because organizational agility requires employees to be able to take initiative, the skills of managers (including executives, senior managers, line managers, and project managers) in agile organizations are different from those of managers in centralized, decision-based organizations. What is specific to an agile organization is that leaders should have the ability to enable their team.

Tolerance to Turbulence

Organizations are agile because the world is changing and becoming more turbulent. Good managers will tolerate turbulence and change. A manager who needs certainty in order to make decisions will not feel comfortable in a turbulent world.

Creating Trust

To perform well in a team, team members must trust one another. Being agile implies that people change the way they do things; otherwise, they keep doing what they used to do and the organization does not change. When people jump into the unknown and try new things, they sometimes make mistakes. This is all right because that's how people learn. Employees must be willing to take the risk of being wrong, ask for help, and communicate when there is a problem. In an agile organization, managers must be able to build trust, which means creating a workplace where people can be vulnerable with one another.

Letting Go

Organizational agility is possible when people take initiatives. It is important for managers to provide their team members with the freedom to do their jobs. Letting go instead of controlling is a good quality for leaders in agile organizations.

Supporting

Instead of making all the decisions, managers should encourage people to weigh in. Managers cannot have all the information they need to make the best decisions in a world that is always getting more and more complex. Rather than trying to collect all the information to make decisions themselves, managers should learn how to coach and support their team in making collective, great decisions.

Creating and Communicating Clarity

Being agile also requires knowledge of the immediate priorities. Managers must be clear about what the priority is for the short term and should communicate the priority to the team. Clarity takes time and requires that a message be repeated. People really pay attention to information once they get the message seven times in different contexts. So, all executives should take on the role of "chief repeating officer" and other managers should support the executives in repeating the information.

How to Engage Employees into Agility

WIIFM Is the Only Radio That Counts

Organizational agility implies a highly engaging organization. When it is time to engage people in a change or a project, the key question is whether people will help (or resist) you. The sales and marketing acronym *WIIFM* stands for "What's in it for me?" The intention behind it is to involve and engage people. It is essential to make them understand why they are impacted and why the project is important for them. It starts from understanding what is important. A good way to start is to understand that money is not the only motivation for people; we all need to give meaning to what we do. We all need to help someone. It is crucial to help employees understand who they are helping by doing their job.

The Size of the Cake Counts

An organization is always more agile when stakeholders are concerned with the challenge. There are two types of organizational changes:

- Increase-the-cake changes; and
- Give-me-a-bigger-piece-of-cake changes.

Increase-the-Cake Changes

Changes that ought to increase the resources of the organization are *increase-the-cake* changes (Cavarec, 2014). *Managing Change in Organizations: A Practice Guide* (PMI, 2013) gives examples of change initiatives that require change management. These are all intended to make a bigger cake:

- A pharmaceutical company decides to enter a new drug category.
- A passenger rail organization decides to initiate high-speed rail service.
- A university decides to add distance learning to its traditional classroom offerings.
- A software company decides to begin offering hardware that runs its software.
- A telecom company decides to outsource its facilities function.
- A federal agency decides to consolidate all regional planning on a central server.
- A trucking company acquires its largest competitor.
- A hospital needs to comply with rapidly emerging federal regulations.
- A country needs to reform and modernize a major agency.

These examples all focus on improving what organizations do; for example, entering a new market, selling more products, improving products, and reaching out to new customers. The common aim is to make the organization grow. Only this type of change is compliant with agility.

Give-Me-a-Bigger-Piece-of-Cake Changes

The second type of change aims to increase the resources of one particular stakeholder: I call these *"give-me-a-bigger-piece-of-cake"* changes (Cavarec, 2014). From the moment that these changes could introduce tension and politics among stakeholders in the organization, they are not compliant with agility. Examples of these types of change include the following strategic initiatives:

- *Launching an employee social program:* This could have a positive impact on the organization only if the program would increase good employee retention or bring the organization up to the market standard.

- *Increase shareholder value:* Focusing on a single stakeholder leads to a dead end because the organization also needs customers to buy its products, employees to solve customers' problems, and suppliers to provide the best ideas to differentiate the organization from competitors.
- *Cost cutting:* Cost cutting per se does not create value for customers—it is just about taking from a stakeholder.

Sustainable changes help the entire organization grow. This is why increase-the-cake changes tend to be much more engaging. People will commit to a change when they know that it serves all stakeholders' benefits, including their own. Stakeholders (including employees and suppliers) are willing to help an organization when they know that they are working for their own interests.

Employees Are the Goal, Not the Means

Another way to engage people to help the organization be more reactive and more agile is to put employees at the core of the organization. Many believe team building is a means to a higher stock price or some other organizational result. DaVita's Kent Thiry says he just realized after a couple of years that the means and the end had flipped. At DaVita, the means is to have adequate profit and shareholder value in order to support the end of creating a fulfilling and rewarding workplace for a thousand people. At a conference given at Stanford University in 2010, Kent Thiry pointed out that, "People can smell your intentionality." People know when you care about them because you are sincere or when you just want to manipulate them.

At DaVita, people want to be a community first and a company second. They behave as a community. They call it the DaVita village and view Kent Thiry as the mayor. This makes a huge difference because people really trust their colleagues as members of the same community.

When the organization is being challenged, employees may substantially behave in a more coherent way if they are a true community rather than if they are just colleagues. Once they commit to a decision, they will make the organization change faster.

Organizational Agility Assessment

Based on the previous description and the characteristics of agile organizations, one can assess how agile organizations are. Organizational agility assessment gives an indication of how prepared an organization is for turbulence.

An agility assessment is determined by assessing the seven following domains:

- Strategic agility;
- Portfolio agility;

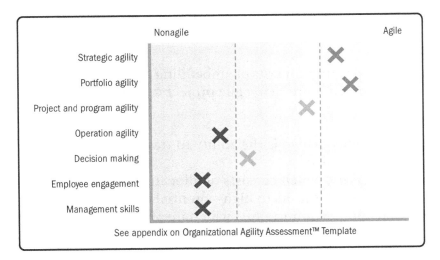

Figure 3-6. Example of agility assessment results.

- Project and program agility;
- Operational agility;
- Decision making;
- Employee engagement; and
- Management skills.

Results show what can be done to prepare the organization for a highly changing environment. Figure 3-6 indicates that the organization is highly agile in strategic agility and portfolio agility. More efforts could be made in project and program management and in decision making. Finally, it indicates that operational agility, employee engagement, and management skills are the major weaknesses of the organization.

Detailed instructions to rate the seven criteria are available in Appendix: Organizational Agility Assessment™ Template.

Summary

To protect themselves from uncertainty, organizations have developed several strategies:

- Most of these strategies, including being bold, copying, identifying scenarios, and finding a blue ocean, consist of trying to avoid change. Unfortunately, these strategies are temporary and don't protect organizations from the current turbulence of the economic environment. Instead, they can give the impression that one can escape change, which opens up opportunities for new entrants to the market.

- Being agile (organizational agility) is the only sustainable strategy in a turbulent world. Agile organizations embrace change.

Organizational agility consists of embedding change at all levels of the organization. It is much more than agile project management. Organizational agility includes:

- Strategic agility, which is the ability to stay in the market until an opportunity arises;
- Portfolio agility, which consists of allocating resources from low-potential business units to high-potential ones;
- Program and portfolio agility, which involves taking into account new opportunities and risks when they arise between the beginning and the end of a project; and
- Operational agility, which is about finding new revenue opportunities and new cost savings at any time faster than competitors.

Employee engagement is at the core of agile organizations. Employees are trusted for their initiatives. They are given clear guidelines and freedom to do their job their way. They take part in decision making. Executives and managers are enablers and supporters rather than deciders and controllers. Making an organization agile is not about adding features to existing organizations. It is not about changing a method or a technology. It is about changing the system, changing the management style. To make an organization more agile, start with management.

References

Cavarec, Y. (2014). Increase your organization readiness to change. *Proceedings of the 2014 PMI Global Congress*, Phoenix, Arizona.

Department of Defense. (2010). *Dictionary of military and associated terms.* Washington, D.C.: Author.

Johnson, G., Whittington, R., Scholes, K., Angwin, D., & Regnér, P. (2014). *Exploring strategy text & cases* (10th ed.). New York, NY: Pearson.

Lencioni, P. (2002). *The five dysfunctions of a team.* Hoboken, NJ: John Wiley & Sons.

Lencioni, P. (2012). *The advantage: Why organizational health trumps everything else in business.* Hoboken, NJ: John Wiley & Sons.

McKinsey. (2006, July). *Building a nimble organization: A McKinsey global survey.* New York, NY: The McKinsey Quarterly.

Porter, M. E. (1980). *Competitive strategy: Techniques for analyzing industries and competitors.* New York, NY: Free Press.

Project Management Institute (PMI). (2012). *PMI's pulse of the profession® in-depth report: Organizational agility.* Newtown Square, PA: Author.

Project Management Institute (PMI). (2013). *Managing change in organizations: A practice guide*. Newtown Square, PA: Author.

Stewart, H. (2012). *The Happy manifesto: Make your organization a great place to work—now*. London, England: Happy.

Sull, D. N. (2009). *The upside of turbulence: Seizing opportunities in an uncertain world*. New York, NY: Harper Business.

Definitions

Organizational agility. The capability of a business to proactively seize and take advantage of business environment changes while demonstrating resilience resulting from unforeseen changes (PMI, 2013).

Turbulence. Fast and unpredictable changes that affect an organization's ability to create value.

Review Questions

1. What indicates that the economic environment today is more turbulent than it used to be?
2. Why is organizational agility a good strategy in a turbulent economic environment?
3. What is the risk for an organization to avoid change in the long term?
4. Is organizational agility the same as agile project management?
5. What are the risks of centralized decision making for an organization that needs agility?
6. What is the purpose of team building for agile organizations?
7. What are the specific skills required to lead an agile organization?
8. How can employees be engaged and help make the organization more agile?

Appendix: Organizational Agility Assessment™ Template

The purpose of the organizational agility assessment™ tool is to

- evaluate how agile an organization is
- identify its agility strengths
- collect ideas to make the organization more agile in the future

The organizational agility assessment™ result can be put in a chart such as the following. The following template gives instructions to rate the seven criteria.

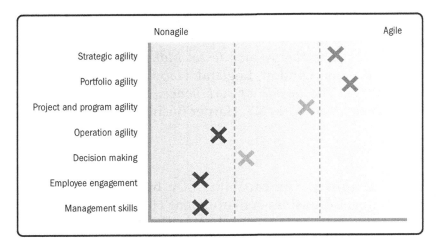

Example of organizational agility assessment™ result.

1. Strategic agility

Is your organization allowed to wait for an opportunity for a long period before acting, like a predator waiting for its prey? Or is any stakeholder pressuring the organization to make a risky investment or launch a new product before any opportunity arises?

Strategic agility rating scale

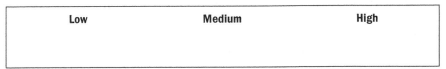

Explain your choice:

What could be done to improve your strategic agility?

2. Portfolio agility

Can your organization reallocate resources from low-potential businesses to high-potential ones? Does it happen that projects are terminated after discovering that the expected benefits no longer correspond to expectations (e.g., because of complexity or ambiguity)? Can resources and people easily be reallocated from one business to another when needed?

Portfolio agility rating scale

Low	Medium	High

Explain your choice:

What could be done to improve your portfolio agility?

3. Project and program agility

Project and program agility include, but are not limited to, agile project management. Is your organization able to take into account market evolution, complexity, and ambiguity by supporting changes to the requirements in the midst of a project or program?

Portfolio agility rating scale

Low	Medium	High

Explain your choice:

What could be done to improve your project and program agility?

4. Operation agility

Compared to your competitors, is your organization able to seize revenue-enhancing and cost-cutting opportunities faster than your competitors? Do you have a process to collect, filter, prioritize, and use operation information in order to make the best and fastest decisions?

Operation agility rating scale

Low	Medium	High

Explain your choice:

What could be done to improve your operation agility?

5. Decision making

Is decision making fast? Has anything been done in the last decade to improve decision-making speed? How is it compared to competitors and other industries?

Decision-making agility rating scale

Low	Medium	High

Explain your choice:

What could be done to improve your decision-making agility?

6. Employee engagement

There are many tools to measure employee engagement. Gallup's Q12 is a tool that is being used by thousands of organizations throughout the world for almost 20 years. Use Q12 or other engagement assessment tools.

Employee engagement rating scale

Actively disengaged	Not engaged	Engaged

Explain here why your organization is good at engaging employees:

What could be done to improve employee engagement?

7. Management skills

How do managers feel about turbulence and change? Are they good at creating trust? Do managers need to control everything in detail? Do they need to make all decisions by themselves? Or do they support their team in making decisions? Are they good at creating clarity about the goal, the priorities, and the values of the organization?

Management skills agility scale

Low	Medium	High

Explain your choice:

What could be done to improve management skills in order to make your organization more agile?

CHAPTER 4

The Role of Portfolio, Program, and Project Management in Organizational Change

By Bryan R. Shelby, BA, CSM, PMP, PgMP, PfMP

Abstract

Each of the separate disciplines of portfolio, program, and project management has a key role in effecting change in organizations. This chapter starts with a quick review of these three disciplines, explores how they relate to one another, provides an example for organizational change used throughout the chapter, and then gives an in-depth discussion of the contribution of each discipline to each of the five phases of the change life cycle: formulating, planning, implementing, managing the transition of, and sustaining change in organizations, relating each one to the example.

Portfolio Management

In the project management context, a portfolio (sometimes called a project portfolio to differentiate it from a financial portfolio) is "a component collection of programs, projects, or operations managed as a group to achieve strategic objectives," as defined in *The Standard for Portfolio Management* (PMI, 2013a, Section 1.2). Thus, every organization has at least one portfolio because every organization has a collection of efforts that it has undertaken to achieve its objectives. See Figure 4-1 for an example of the components of a portfolio.

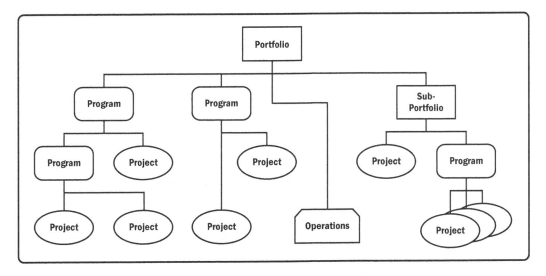

Figure 4-1. Sample portfolio structure.

Portfolio management "is the coordinated management of one or more portfolios to achieve organizational strategies and objectives" (PMI, 2013a, Section 1.3). Clearly, if the strategies and objectives of the organization include specific organizational changes, then portfolio management will be a key factor in that process. Table 4-1 shows the 10 underlying principles and practices of portfolio management.

The portfolio manager is "responsible for the execution of the portfolio management process" (PMI, 2013a, Section 1.8), receiving reports from the portfolio components, communicating with portfolio governance on strategic alignment, recommending options for action, maintaining the portfolio timetable, and communicating with component managers and portfolio stakeholders. (Note that stakeholders include any individual or group who may affect, be affected by, or think they might be affected by the portfolio activities.) Portfolio managers focus on "doing the right work," allowing the component managers to focus solely on "doing the work right."

Program Management

The word *program*, in our context, means "a group of related projects, subprograms, and program activities that are managed in a coordinated way to obtain benefits not available from managing them individually" (PMI, 2013c, Section 1.2). It is important to understand that a program is not just another term for a large project with a number of different moving parts. The components of a program (i.e., the projects and subprograms that make up the program) are separate from one another, with their own deliverables, but they are related by a common thread.

Table 4-1. The 10 underlying principles and practices of portfolio management.

Principle/Practice	Description
1. Strategic Focus	Portfolio management is the coordinated management of one or more portfolios to achieve the strategies and objectives of the organization. It includes related organizational processes and change initiatives by which an organization evaluates, selects, prioritizes, and allocates its limited internal resources to best accomplish organizational strategies consistent with its vision, mission, and values.
2. Strategic Initiatives	Organizations execute their strategies through the creation of strategic initiatives, comprising portfolios of programs and projects to achieve a future state. The portfolio components may not necessarily be interdependent or have related objectives. An organization may have more than one portfolio, each addressing unique organizational strategies and objectives. Proposed initiatives are structured as portfolios and components are identified, evaluated, selected, and authorized. Managing the necessary changes should be an integral part of planning initiatives.
3. Portfolio Components	As shown in Figure 4-1, a portfolio is a component collection of related programs, projects, and/or operations managed as a group to achieve strategic objectives. A portfolio exists to achieve one or more organizational strategies or objectives and may consist of a set of past, current, and planned or future portfolio components.
4. Quantifiable Components	The portfolio components are quantifiable, that is, they can be measured, ranked, and prioritized.
5. Time Horizon	Portfolios and programs have the potential to be longer term, with new projects rotating into the portfolios, unlike projects, which have a defined beginning and end.
6. Portfolio Snapshot	At any given moment, a portfolio represents a snapshot of its selected portfolio components and reflects the organizational strategy and objectives—even when specific programs or projects within the portfolio are not interdependent or do not have related objectives.
7. Portfolio Management Activities	By reflecting upon the investments made or planned by an organization, portfolio management includes activities for identifying and aligning the organizational priorities, determining governance and the portfolio management framework, measuring value/benefit, making investment decisions, and managing risk, communications, and resources.
8. Aligned with Organizational Strategy	When elements of the portfolio are not aligned with organizational strategy, the organization should question why the work is being undertaken. A portfolio should be representative of an organization's intent, direction, and progress. It is possible to undertake essential projects that do not strictly align with the strategic portfolio. However, when these projects cannot be justified as essential, the portfolio manager should remove them from the portfolio of activities for reconsideration at a later date.
9. Governance	Portfolio management requires a governing body to make decisions that control or influence the direction of a group of portfolio components as they work to achieve specific outcomes. The governing body needs to be particularly sensitive to the degree of change required to achieve the portfolio initiatives.
10. Balancing Conflicting Demands	Portfolio management balances conflicting demands among portfolio components, allocates resources (e.g., people and funding) based on organizational priorities and capacity, and manages resources in order to achieve the benefits identified.

Adapted from *Managing Change in Organizations: A Practice Guide* (PMI, 2013b).

Unlike a portfolio, a program has a specific beginning, middle, and end. Conceptually, the life cycle of a program has three phases: program definition, program benefits delivery, and program closure. In program definition, the program team expands on the organization's strategic objectives, turns them into specific program outcomes (i.e., organizational benefits), and then

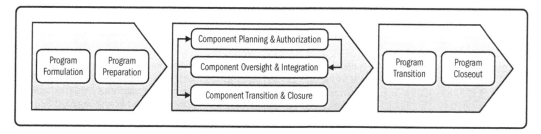

Figure 4-2.   A representative program life cycle.
Source: *The Standard for Program Management* (PMI, 2013c).

seeks approval from the appropriate governance body to execute the program. The benefits delivery phase of the program is self-explanatory—it is the execution phase, in which the defined organizational benefits will be realized by planning, authorizing, and overseeing the program components (projects and subprograms) that will deliver these benefits. Finally, in program closure, the program team receives approval to close the program, transitions the organizational benefits to the appropriate operational areas, completes all final reports, closes out all contracts related to the program, disposes of or reassigns all program resources, documents all lessons learned, archives all program records, and, so to speak, turns out the lights (PMI, 2013c, Sections 8.3.6 and 8.3.7). See Figure 4-2 for an example of a program life cycle.

Program management "is the application of knowledge, skills, tools, and techniques to a program to meet the program requirements and to obtain benefits and control not available by managing projects individually. It involves aligning multiple components to achieve the program goals and allows for optimized or integrated cost, schedule, and effort" (PMI, 2013c, Section 1.3). In other words, it consists of overseeing the interrelationships among a number of different but related projects and subprograms to ensure that they do not interfere with one another, that resources are properly shared across them if needed, that they remain aware of the positive or negative impact that they may have on one another (for example, as a result of predecessor/successor relationships or shared resources), and that their status is tracked, reviewed, and reported to the management of the organization (i.e., governance) and other interested stakeholders.

The program manager must do all of the following (PMI, 2013c, Section 1.7):

- Coordinate across the program components, that is, the projects and subprograms that make up the overall program.
- Communicate with the component managers to track their problems and deal with escalated issues that must be handled at the program level.

- Track component progress and monitor their deliverables to ensure that they are delivering the expected program benefits, and take corrective action if they should fall behind or fail to deliver.
- Provide the support infrastructure needed to assist the component managers in the successful execution of their projects and programs. This support may include:
  - Establishing templates and standards;
  - Setting up a program management information system (PMIS) to facilitate communication across components as well as to stakeholders and governance; and
  - Providing additional management assistance and guidance if needed to help the component managers handle particularly difficult issues.

Project Management

The official definition of the word *project* is "a temporary endeavor undertaken to provide a unique product, service, or result," according to *A Guide to the Project Management Body of Knowledge (PMBOK® Guide)* – Fifth Edition (PMI, 2013d, Section 1.2). The key concepts in this definition are that a project is temporary and that its deliverable is unique. This differentiates a project, such as designing and building an automobile factory—a temporary effort—from the process of building cars once the factory is operational, which is an ongoing process. The factory is, presumably, unique, but the cars are not.

There are many separate activities that go into a successful project. The *PMBOK® Guide* lists 47 different processes, but they are grouped into five main categories called Process Groups (PMI, 2013d). These groups are called Initiating, Planning, Executing, Monitoring and Controlling, and Closing. Their interaction is usually shown in a diagram such as Figure 4-3.

As can be seen, the Planning/Executing Process Groups are cyclical: As one executes a project, circumstances can change, which can mean another cycle of Planning is required, followed by more Executing, and so on. In addition, the Monitoring and Controlling processes occur throughout the project.

Project management is the job of making sure that all this happens as it should, and that the project delivers as promised. Specifically, it "is the application of knowledge, skills, tools, and techniques to project activities to meet the project requirements" (PMI, 2013d, Section 1.3). It includes responsibilities such as:

- Identifying project requirements and defining project scope;
- Managing the needs and expectations of the project stakeholders through properly established communications;

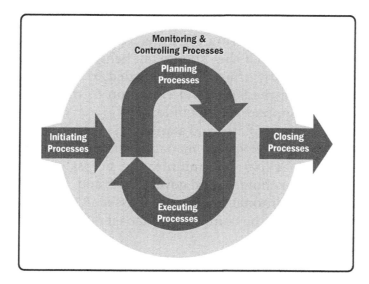

Figure 4-3.   Project Management Process Groups.
Source: *PMBOK® Guide* (PMI, 2013d).

- Managing the main aspects of the project, including:
  - Scope,
  - Schedule,
  - Cost and budget,
  - Resources, and
  - Quality.
- Planning and managing project risks; and
- Planning and managing requested or required changes to any of the above.

The project manager "is the person assigned by the performing organization to lead the team that is responsible for achieving the project objectives" (PMI, 2013d, Section 1.7). This means that the project manager is the person responsible for the tasks in the bulleted list above, whether the project manager performs them personally or ensures that they are adequately covered by another member of the project team.

Similarities, Differences, and Interactions

As can be seen in the previous descriptions, there are many similarities and differences among portfolio, program, and project management. Table 4-2 summarizes these.

In the following sections, we will describe how each of the three disciplines—portfolio, program, and project management—participates in effecting organizational change, discussing its contribution to each of the

Table 4-2.   Similarities among projects, programs, and portfolios.

Topic	Projects	Programs	Portfolios
Scope	Projects have defined objectives. Scope is progressively elaborated throughout the project life cycle.	Programs have a larger scope and provide more significant benefits.	Portfolios have an organizational scope that changes with the strategic objectives of the organization.
Change	Project managers expect change and implement processes to keep change managed and controlled.	Program managers expect change from both inside and outside the program and are prepared to manage it.	Portfolio managers continuously monitor changes in the broader internal and external environment.
Planning	Project managers progressively elaborate high-level information into detailed plans throughout the project life cycle.	Program managers develop the overall program plan and create high-level plans to guide detailed planning at the component level.	Portfolio managers create and maintain necessary processes and communication relative to the aggregate portfolio.
Management	Project managers manage the team to meet the project objectives.	Program managers manage the program staff and the project managers; they provide vision and overall leadership.	Portfolio managers may manage or coordinate portfolio management staff, or program and project staff that may have reporting responsibilities into the aggregate portfolio.
Success	Success is measured by product and project quality, timeliness, budget compliance, and degree of customer satisfaction.	Success is measured by the degree to which the program satisfies the needs and benefits for which it was undertaken.	Success is measured in terms of the aggregate investment performance and benefit realization of the portfolio.
Monitoring	Project managers monitor and control the work of producing the products, services, or results that the project was undertaken to produce.	Program managers monitor the progress of program components to ensure that the overall goals, schedules, budget, and benefits of the program will be met.	Portfolio managers monitor strategic changes and aggregate resource allocation, performance results, and risk of the portfolio.

Source: *The Standard for Portfolio Management* (PMI 2013a).

five phases of the change life cycle framework: formulating, planning, implementing, transitioning, and sustaining. Throughout these sections, we will use the example outlined below to show how the different disciplines support these processes.

Example

Mammoth Manufacturing is in trouble. Its many divisions have a wide variety of consumer products and good relationships with the retail stores that are their primary customers, but these divisions also operate as if they were separate companies, which, in many cases, they once were. They have their own inventory systems, their own warehouses, their own product databases and customer relationship management systems, their own management structures, and their own financial reporting systems. The divisions assert that this makes them more nimble and able to react quickly to market changes. However, their primary competitor, Upstart Products, is steadily gaining in market share, and Mammoth's board of directors is concerned about the future of the company. The previous CEO recently retired for health reasons, and the board, recognizing the need for organizational change, hired a new CEO with a mandate to reverse this decline and turn the company around.

After consultation with the board and the division heads; after discussions with employees, customers, and former customers; and after reviewing the existing financial, marketing, and strategic plans, the new CEO announces ACT, the acronym summarizing his vision of Mammoth's new strategic direction: *Availability, Communication,* and *Transparency* for information and products. If implemented successfully, this strategy will have many positive consequences for the company—but first it needs to be made real.

The Role of the Portfolio Manager in Organizational Change

Note: The term *portfolio manager* may refer either to a specific individual or to an entire team charged with portfolio management responsibilities.

Formulating Change

In order to turn this strategic direction into reality, the CEO in the example turns to the Mammoth's portfolio management function. The strategy is clearly summarized in the CEO's acronym, ACT, and so the portfolio manager's next step is to translate this strategy "into tangible objectives that are aligned with stakeholders' needs and expectations." (PMI, 2013b, Section 2.4.1). This is what portfolio management is all about: developing a portfolio of components that are aligned with the organizational strategy. In our example, that strategy is focused on massive organizational change.

In formulating organizational change, the first step is to identify/clarify the need for change. In our example—and, indeed, in general—this step will have already been accomplished by the time the portfolio manager gets involved. It is the identification and clarification of the need for change that drives the establishment of the organizational strategy, that is, the changes that the organization's leadership (in this case, the CEO) wants to accomplish.

The next step in formulating change is to assess the organization's readiness for change. This is a key focus for the portfolio manager. In the case of a massive structural change such as the ACT initiative in our example, there is a real danger that the initiative could fail if it is not embraced by the company. The portfolio manager, therefore, needs to structure the program so that:

- The right, enthusiastic, senior executives will be overseeing the initiative and sponsoring the programs and projects, and experienced, competent component managers are identified to run them;
- Accountability for the success of the component programs and projects is clear and well understood;

- Sufficient resources are or will be made available to the initiative as needed;
- The business case has been clearly stated and the critical success factors for the program and project managers are accurately defined, measurable, and achievable;
- The initiative communicates that the future of Mammoth Manufacturing is at stake so that all stakeholders will give the effort the support it needs for success; and
- As the components are completed, the organization is positioned to incorporate their deliverables into sustained operational activities.

In our example, all of this will definitely require significant preparation because of the massive nature of the changes being made. Therefore, the portfolio manager determines that the first component of the portfolio must be educational, communicating the value of the initiative to all stakeholders and explaining how it will improve operations and save the company. The key facets of the education process will be to communicate and reinforce the following:

- Employees need to understand and accept that the result of the initiative will improve their daily jobs by eliminating duplication and streamlining bureaucracy.
- Shareholders need to understand that, although the initiative will be expensive, the resulting return on investment (ROI) will be significant and the future of the company will be much stronger.
- Customers need to understand that, though their interactions with Mammoth will be different, these changes will make it easier to deal with the company and will simplify their own ordering processes.
- Other stakeholders, such as auditors, regulators, and so forth, may also need to be brought into this education process, as determined by the project team.

See *Checklist: Communicating Change* in the Appendix at the end of the chapter for more details on what and with whom to communicate.

The final step is to delineate the scope of the change. The first action in this process is to assess the impact of the change. This assessment has two activities, a gap analysis and a change readiness assessment. The gap analysis analyzes the current portfolio in the context of the new strategic direction and identifies the required components that are missing and must be added to achieve the desired organizational changes. Once these gaps have been identified, the next actions are to develop the list of portfolio components needed to bridge these gaps and assess how ready the organization is to execute these programs and projects.

Some of these gaps have already been identified in our example—the lack of communication across divisions, the separation of customer and product data, and so on. In this phase of the change life cycle, it is the job of the portfolio manager to pull together the complete list of issues to address and present them in a portfolio scope document. This document, once approved and accepted, will form the basis of the readiness assessment. The portfolio manager can, point by point, go over the scope with the affected stakeholders and determine:

- What the impact of the changes will be on their structure, people, systems, and processes;
- If they are ready to accept the changes;
- If not, when could they be ready and what would be necessary to get them to that state;
- How to implement the changes in a way that will gain their support; and
- Whether there are any obstacles to implementation specific to each group that must be taken into account (regulatory, environmental, political, etc.).

See *Checklist: Assessing Organizational Readiness for Change* in the Appendix at the end of the chapter for more details.

Planning Change

This is the central task of what portfolio managers do. When given a strategic direction, they work with governance and senior management to determine how best to accomplish this strategy. They define the approach, identify and work with the affected stakeholders to achieve acceptance of the goals and objectives of the portfolio, and develop the plan to execute the strategy and transition the result to normal business operations.

To that end, a portfolio manager has three deliverables: the portfolio strategic plan, the portfolio charter, and the portfolio road map. The portfolio strategic plan translates the overall strategy into more concrete goals and objectives. The portfolio charter is the key document here. It identifies the portfolio components (i.e., the programs and projects) that are necessary to achieve the strategic objectives of massive organizational change. The portfolio charter not only lists the components, but also describes how these components will deliver value to the organization. Finally, the portfolio road map provides the list of components and subcomponents and identifies the cross-component dependencies that largely define the order in which the components are implemented.

Example

In our example, the resulting set of programs and projects might look something like Figure 4-4.

As you can see, this diagram presents four main areas of focus consisting of one project and three programs:

- First is the readiness and communication project. This is the key effort for the entire initiative and is essential to the success of the entire portfolio. It is here that the portfolio management team will communicate the importance of the initiative, explain how it will improve Mammoth Manufacturing and its interactions with all its stakeholders, and ultimately generate the enthusiasm necessary for success.
- In addition to the stand-alone project above, there are also three programs in the portfolio. One program will focus on systems and technology, a second program will deal with modernizing the warehouses, and the third program deals with the organizational consolidations that will be needed to the corporate structure to unify key departments across the divisions and ensure that Mammoth is positioned to successfully take advantage of all the other efforts.

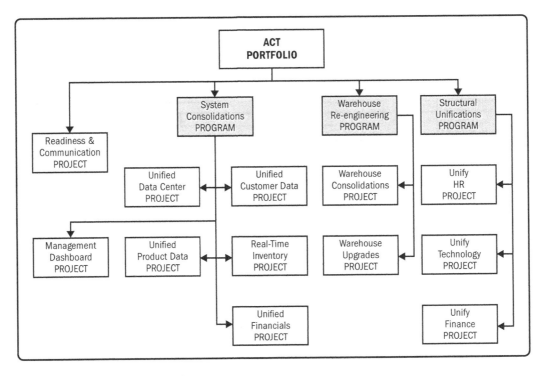

Figure 4-4.   Portfolio hierarchy.

The portfolio manager has determined that the human resources (HR) function should be consolidated first, pulling together the teams from all divisions into one central group. The idea is that this should provide a strong foundation for the rest of the changes to the corporate structure. The technology teams would be next, to enable Mammoth to get started on the system consolidations, and so on. Taking all this into account, the resulting road map, which defines the predecessor/successor relationships among these components, might look something like Figure 4-5.

Tracing through the arrows, you can see the order of the projects within the programs that the portfolio manager established, starting with the readiness and communication project and eventually ending with the management dashboard. There could certainly be other ways to accomplish the corporate strategy, and other sequences that could be defined to sequence the steps, but this is what the portfolio manager presented to governance and this is what was approved. It is important to note that there are definite cross-program dependencies, and these dependencies need to be managed at the portfolio level.

See *Template: The Portfolio Plan for Organizational Change* in the Appendix at the end of the chapter for a sample outline to use when planning for organizational change.

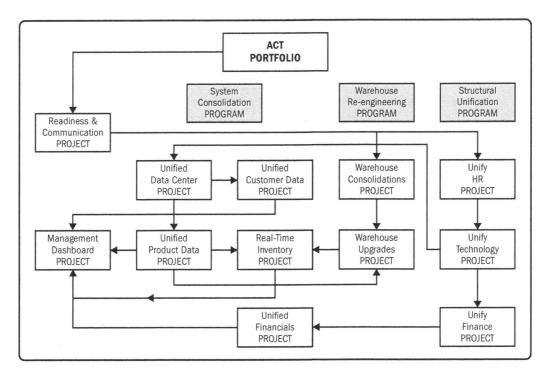

Figure 4-5. Example portfolio road map.

Implementing Change

Once the organizational change initiative is under way, the role of the portfolio manager is essentially the same as for any other portfolio. The key functions in this context are the following:

- **Manage strategic change.** This includes monitoring organizational strategy for possible changes, assessing their possible impact, and making any necessary adjustments. For example, if Mammoth decided to sell off one of its divisions, that would affect the scope of the various consolidation efforts.
- **Authorize portfolio.** This involves activating selected portfolio components by allocating resources to develop component proposals or begin execution.
- **Optimize portfolio/manage portfolio value/provide portfolio oversight.** This refers to monitoring portfolio component performance and adjusting or rebalancing resources accordingly to maximize portfolio business benefits. For example, if the unified product data project was falling behind and had greater business benefits than the unified financials project, the portfolio manager might recommend shifting resources to assist the unified product data component.
- **Manage supply and demand.** This involves managing the portfolio resources (funding, staffing, equipment, space, etc.), ensuring that each component can deliver the maximum organizational benefit. For example, if a warehouse scheduled to be renovated was discovered to have an environmental contamination problem, the portfolio manager could authorize additional funding to hire a team of specialists to address this issue.
- **Manage portfolio information.** This includes collecting, analyzing, storing, and delivering *portfolio-level* information to the stakeholders in accordance with their requirements and in a timely manner (PMI, 2013a, Section 7.2). For example, the portfolio manager may provide the CEO or board of directors with reports or even a real-time dashboard on the health of the portfolio and its individual components.
- **Manage portfolio risks.** This aspect involves identifying *portfolio-level* risks, analyzing their probability and severity, developing responses to them, and monitoring them. For example, because some of Mammoth's divisions are international, there is a risk that currency swings could significantly affect the ROI of some portfolio components—either up or down. The portfolio-level risk management plan should identify that risk and the portfolio

manager should track it, with plans in place to lock in any benefits or mitigate any problems.

- **Measure benefits realization.** This refers to tracking the success of the change initiative by measuring the benefits realized by the underlying portfolio components. Expected benefits and their measures of success are established at the formulating change stage. Each benefit should be aligned with the strategic vision of the change initiative and its contribution measured at the organizational level.

Managing Transition and Sustaining Change

With respect to these two phases of the change life cycle, most of these activities occur in the components within the portfolio and not at the portfolio level itself. It is the job of the portfolio manager to ensure that the component plans properly reflect the needs of these areas and that these plans have been carried out. At the end of the life cycle of an individual component, whether program or project, the component manager must apply for component closure. During this process, the portfolio manager and the appropriate governance group review the component's deliverables and resulting business benefits, and at this point, also review their transition to operational status and the provisions made for ongoing sustainment of these changes.

Summary: Portfolio Management and Organizational Change

Portfolio management has a central role to play in organizational change. The portfolio manager must assess the impact of the new organizational strategy on the existing portfolio, propose and obtain acceptance of a new component structure to achieve the new strategic vision, and then monitor the execution of these new components by measuring benefits realization as the components transition into the operational areas. These tasks are accomplished by:

- Ongoing timely communication with senior stakeholders on component status and overall portfolio health;
- Participation in component reviews to represent the portfolio and to reflect the interests of senior management; and
- Oversight of portfolio execution through strong portfolio management processes.

The Role of the Program Manager in Organizational Change

Note: The term *program manager* may refer either to a specific individual or to an entire team charged with management responsibilities for a specific program.

Introduction

Because most organizational change occurs through programs targeted to achieve specific change-related organizational benefits, it is not surprising that their life cycles have a number of similarities, cross-referenced below in Table 4-3 (PMI, 2013b).

Example

In our example, we identified three programs required to implement the CEO's ACT initiative:

- System consolidation;
- Warehouse re-engineering; and
- Structural unification.

In the next sections, we will describe how programs like these can and should be organized to implement organizational change.

Formulating Change

An organizational benefit "is an outcome of actions and behaviors that provide utility, value, or a positive change to the intended recipient. . . . Programs and projects deliver benefits by enhancing current capabilities or developing new capabilities that support the sponsoring organization's strategic goals and objectives" (PMI, 2013c, Section 4, Introduction). In our context, these goals and objectives will implement the planned organizational change that is the reason for the portfolio.

Thus, in an organizational change initiative, the need for change has been established at the portfolio level. Now, the program manager must clarify that strategic vision, turn it into tangible objectives that define the program scope, ensure that this scope fulfills the needs and expectations of the many stakeholders that will be affected by the program, and assess their readiness to accept and support the changes that the program introduces. In formulating the program to implement organizational change, the program manager needs to be aware of the importance of pacing the change introduced by the program. Change that moves too quickly may be resisted by certain stakeholders, but on the other hand, delays in benefits delivery because of change that moves too slowly may be taken by resistant stakeholders as evidence that the program is ineffective.

Finally, the program manager needs to define the scope of the change as it will be implemented by the program. The key process here is benefits identification (PMI, 2013c, Section 4.1), and the program manager's key tasks are to:

- Focus on the specific objectives of the change initiative;
- Assess stakeholder needs and readiness to accept change;

Table 4-3.   Similarities between program and change life cycles.

Program Life Cycle Phases	Change Life Cycle	Specific Change Activities
Program Definition	**Formulate Change**	
Program formulation	Identify/clarify need for change	Analyze internal and external pressures Define purpose/vision Identify and classify stakeholders
	Assess readiness for change	Assess impact of change on organization Assess organizational capabilities and staff receptivity Map stakeholders (positive or negative interest and power) Identify potential agents
	Delineate scope of change	Agree on critical success factors and key performance indicators Prepare benefits map and benefits register
	Plan Change	
Program preparation	Define the change approach	Choose a change process adapted to organizational structures and culture
	Plan stakeholder engagement	Prepare for sense-making activities Identify specific activities to mobilize and engage stakeholders
	Plan transition and integration	Identify transition and integration needs and activities
Program Benefits Delivery	**Implement Change**	
Component planning and authorization	Prepare organization for change	Initiate sense-making activities Identify areas of resistance and support Initiate transition and integration activities Initiate support activities and components
(Continuous stakeholder engagement)[A]	Mobilize stakeholders	Empower agents and recipients Conduct sense-making activities
Component oversight and integration	Deliver project outputs	Ensure that project results are fit for purpose and well transitioned
Component transition and closure		Assess fit for purpose Assess results integration into business as usual
Program Closure	**Manage Transition**	
Benefits transition	Transition outputs into organization	Assess delivery of organizational benefits and value Take corrective or realignment action, if necessary
	Measure adoption rates and outcomes/benefits	Assess rate of change integration
Adaptive change[B] **(at all phases)**	Adjust plan to address discrepancies	Assess internal and external changes in content Readjust pace of change according to needs Initiate corrective actions, if needed

(continued)

Table 4-3. Similarities between program and change life cycles. *(continued)*

Program Life Cycle Phases	Change Life Cycle	Specific Change Activities
	Sustain Change	
Benefits sustainment	Ongoing communication with, consultation with, and representation of stakeholders	Identify external and internal influences Define change management approaches Monitor for resistance or apathy Respond to resistance or apathy
	Conduct sense-making activities	Implement specific sense-making activities
	Measure benefits realization	Assess integration of change Identify realized benefits Market the program
Program closeout	Not applicable	Not applicable

A Stakeholder engagement is not strictly a program life cycle phase; it is a continuous program activity and a key responsibility of the program manager throughout the program.
B Adaptive change consists of all the activities required as the program adapts in response to environmental pressures, based on plan changes initiated by the program manager and authorized by the program governance board.

Source: *Managing Change in Organizations: A Practice Guide* (PMI, 2013b).

- Involve stakeholders in benefits definition so that they become program supporters;
- Manage stakeholder expectations regarding delivery of the program benefits; and
- Develop a detailed program scope definition.

To describe the benefits that will implement the program's portion of the strategic initiative, the key deliverables are:

- The business case, defining the organizational changes that will come from the program and justifying the allocation of resources to the program; and
- The benefits register, formally describing the planned program benefits, mapping these benefits to the program components, and describing how their successful implementation will be tracked and measured.

Example

In the warehouse re-engineering program:

- The business case would describe:
  - The tangible savings from consolidating a large number of partially empty warehouses with outdated infrastructures into fewer, larger, more fully stocked, centrally located, and

technologically sophisticated structures that will support further automation; and
  - The more intangible benefit of improved customer satisfaction through better inventory control and faster delivery.
- The benefits register would list at least these benefits:
  - Better use of warehouse capacity through consolidation;
  - Faster delivery to customers by relocating closer to major shipping centers;
  - Better inventory control through automation such as bar codes and tablet access to the inventory database;
  - Online ordering capability once the inventory is accurately tracked; and
  - Job enrichment for warehouse personnel as a result of exposure to improved technology.

Planning Change

For a program manager, planning for change is different from planning for more typical product-oriented programs such as constructing a building or developing a computer application. "Programs that deal with change are required to consider people and cultural issues as essential elements of the planning process. Based on the analysis of the need and readiness for change, the program team sets the pace of delivery for the change. The pace of the change is based on the progressive delivery of intermediate benefits until the ultimate purpose is achieved" (PMI, 2013b, Section 5.3.2).

So, although any program needs to include stakeholder management as a key practice, this area is particularly important in the context of a change program. If the stakeholders are not receptive to or are actively resisting the change, the program will probably not be successful. Thus, the change must be carefully planned to ensure the widest (and deepest) possible stakeholder acceptance. The key process here is benefits analysis and planning (PMI, 2013c, Section 4.2) and key considerations include the following:

- **Matching the complexity of the plan to the needs of the stakeholders.** Stakeholders who are already receptive to the plan will accept a more generic, high-level plan. Concerned stakeholders, on the other hand, will require more detailed plans or they will not be convinced. In either case, it is important to involve key stakeholders at all levels in the planning process so that they feel the plan is their own and will be more likely to support it.
- **Matching the leadership style to the culture of the organization and the needs of the program.** Leadership styles can range from autocratic to democratic to *laissez-faire*. These styles will resonate differently in different organizational and cultural contexts.

- **Matching the method of introduction to the type of change being introduced.** Smaller incremental changes can be introduced with minimum fanfare, whereas larger, more disruptive changes will require more stakeholder interaction and acceptance. Frequent small changes may be more appropriate for complex and turbulent environments, while larger, less frequent changes might be better for a more stable environment that can support greater incremental change.

The key deliverables are the:

- **Benefits Realization Plan**, documenting the activities needed to achieve the organizational change under the program and to ensure that the changes are fully accepted and sustained; and the
- **Program Road Map**, defining the components necessary to achieve the organizational change under the program, the sequencing of these components, their approximate implementation schedules, and the degree to which they interact and/or are interdependent.

Example

Take the structural unification program as an example. This program has the potential for massive resistance from stakeholders. Its mission is to centralize several major support functions, effectively removing the human resources, technology, and finance teams from the various divisions and moving them all to a central corporate administration division. Management stakeholders may fear for the loss of their empires; staff will probably fear for the loss of their jobs. There may be geographical relocations as people have to move from division headquarters to corporate headquarters. Longstanding relationships will be severed as new organizational charts are established. Familiar divisional processes will be replaced by new corporate-level standards. New accounting and financial systems will be introduced, different from those previously used at the divisional level. It sounds like, and has the potential to become, a human resources nightmare.

This is why the change must be very carefully planned. The program manager has determined that the human resources unification must take place first. Furthermore, this initial project will have to work carefully with human resources staff at all levels to address their concerns. Key questions in any such change include the following:

- Why do we have to do this? Weren't things just fine as they were?
- How will this affect me, my daily work, and my career, both immediately and in the longer term?

- This seems really complicated—how can you tell whether it is going well or badly?
- If part of it does go badly, what are you going to do then?

Recall that the first component in this portfolio is the readiness and communication project. This project team will have already considered all these questions, prepared materials to address these and other concerns, set up hotlines and focus groups to ensure that people have both a place to express these concerns and a forum to offer suggestions, and developed a communications rollout plan that provides all this on a schedule that fits the needs of the divisional groups that are merging as part of this project.

In this context, a detailed plan is needed to reassure all stakeholders that the process has been carefully and thoroughly planned. A flexible management style will be needed to be able to accept reasonable suggestions from the stakeholders and modify the plan accordingly. And finally, the program manager determined that this environment lends itself more to incremental change than to a "Big Bang" approach, so the best method of introduction of these changes will be to start with the two biggest divisions and consolidate them, and then move down the list according to size until they are all consolidated into one large corporate human resources team for all of Mammoth Manufacturing. The program plan to implement the structural unification change has therefore been constructed accordingly.

Once the human resources team members have had the opportunity to voice their concerns and have their feedback included in the resulting benefits realization plan and program road map, and once they start to see their own ideas and suggestions being implemented, the plan predicts that they will go from resisting the change initiative to embracing it and will become advocates for the change. When the time comes for the other teams to unify and consolidate, the program manager expects that human resources staff will be right there to support the process. They will be able to say that they have been through this already, and can tell the other teams that it will be okay.

Implementing Change

In understanding the role of the program manager in implementing organizational change, remember that the baseline of the change plan itself is expected to evolve as the programs within the change initiative adjust to the reaction of the organization to the changes. For this reason, the planning, implementing, and transitioning processes are iterative, overlapping, and cycling back upon one another. Thus, while implementing change, the program manager is also very likely to be re-planning and re-executing existing or new components as well as reviewing and revising the transition of others.

The key process here is benefits delivery (PMI, 2013c, Section 4.3), and the key considerations include the following:

- **Prepare organization for change.** The program manager must ensure that the plan will enable the stakeholders to understand, make sense of, and accept the organizational change.
- **Mobilize stakeholders.** This is important in any program, but is particularly crucial in effecting organizational change. The program manager must bring the stakeholders into the process, work with them to maintain their support as the organizational change begins to take hold, and respond quickly to resistance or apathy on the part of the stakeholders, or to management pressure to increase the rate of change when the organization is not ready for it.
- **Deliver project outputs.** The central activity in any program, of course, is to deliver the results of the program's components. These results must be evaluated on their contribution to the organizational change, corresponding organizational benefits, and stakeholder satisfaction.

The key deliverables are:

- **Program component authorization**, creating new governance structures to oversee program component requests for authorization to begin and to commit organizational resources to its execution;
- **Program component deliverables**, that is, the organizational changes implemented by the program components—this, of course, is the fundamental deliverable of the entire initiative; and
- **Stakeholder support**, as described previously, so that the program component deliverables are embraced and supported by the stakeholders.

Example

Taking the system consolidation program as an example, you can see from the program road map in Figure 4-5 that the first component in the program is the consolidation of the divisional data centers. If a new centralized data center is planned, then it is logical for all system consolidations to happen in that new environment. In that way, the upgraded equipment and system software needs to be installed only once, not once per division. However, this component dependency can also be used to prepare the organization for change and to mobilize the stakeholders to support the initiative.

During the stakeholder discussions preparing the organization for change, the program manager can start with the chief technology officers within the various divisions and with the heads of their system infrastructure and data center operations teams. It is likely that these groups are, or feel that they are, underfunded, under-resourced, and using outdated equipment and systems. If the program is carefully represented by the program manager, these divisional managers can be brought to see it as their salvation—a shiny new data center, upgraded operating systems and database software, 24/7 hot backup for disaster recovery, and so forth. In this way, the foundation has been laid to prepare the organization for the changes to come, and the stakeholders who might have resisted the change have instead become advocates for it.

Similarly, it is likely that some (perhaps many) of the application support teams also feel under-resourced, holding together antiquated systems with the digital equivalent of duct tape and chewing gum. If the program manager can identify these disaffected managers, persuade them that the consolidated systems will be state of the art, provide training in the new technologies, and otherwise make the change appealing, then these managers (and their teams who will be the main beneficiaries of this job enrichment) will also become advocates for the change initiative.

The systems consolidation program is the largest and most complex of the four components of the ACT initiative's portfolio. In order to monitor and control all the components and their interactions, both within the program and with the components of other programs, the program manager will want to set up a program management office (PMO). This group will be given the resources and systems needed to oversee a multifaceted effort like this, helping to ensure a successful delivery of program benefits to support the overall strategic goal of massive organizational change. Within the PMO, there will be subteams to track the status of the individual projects, allocate resources across them, monitor the progress of the other programs on which these projects depend, and prepare status reports to all the stakeholders to communicate the progress of the program components. Note that other, smaller programs may not need this level of oversight and may be fine with just an individual as program manager.

Managing Transition

In this context, *transition* means the transfer of the component deliverables and resulting organizational benefits to operational status, enabling the organization to sustain the changes introduced by the program—an essential part of program success. Once transitioned, the benefits must continue to be monitored and measured to ensure that the changes have been fully adopted and incorporated into the operation. Where issues arise and adjustments prove necessary, the program will develop and implement a plan to address these discrepancies.

The key process here is benefits transition (PMI, 2013c, Section 4.4) and the key considerations are whether:

- The benefit realization criteria have been met or exceeded by the program's deliverables;
- The program has developed and implemented a transition plan to support the realization of the organizational changes after they are turned over to the affected operational areas; and
- There is a plan in place to measure the adoption of the changes after the transition.

In this process, "the scope of the transition is defined, the stakeholders in the receiving organizations or functions are identified and participate in the planning, the program benefits are measured and sustainment plans are developed, and the transition is executed" (PMI, 2013, Section 4.4). Of course, a successful transition is not only the responsibility of the program; the receiving organization must prepare its own plan to accept the organizational changes implemented by the program and incorporate these changes into its standard processes.

The key deliverables are the successful transition of the desired organizational changes into normal business operation and the ability to measure their ongoing contribution. The transitioning of organizational changes delivered by program components may include a review and evaluation of:

- The effectiveness of the program and the program components in delivering the desired operational changes;
- The acceptability of these operational changes;
- Documentation associated with these operational changes, including training and maintenance materials where applicable; and
- The level of acceptance and integration of these changes by the receiving organization, including activities intended to facilitate their adoption.

Example

Continuing with our example of Mammoth Manufacturing and the data center consolidation component of the system consolidation program, the transition of the component benefits will occur when the divisional systems complete their migration from the old divisional data centers to the new corporate environment and are successfully operating there without any service disruptions to critical business functions or users of the migrated applications. The effectiveness of the change introduced by the component can be tracked by metrics such as:

- The duration of system downtime, if any, as they migrated to the new environment;
- Any change in the frequency or type of user complaints or calls to the help desk;
- System performance metrics on response time, duration of offline jobs, and so on; and
- The level of user satisfaction with the affected systems, measured by user polls both before and after the migration.

With the exception of the duration of migration-related downtime, these metrics can and should continue to be monitored long after the initial migration to ensure that there is no decline in the quality of the service provided by the new data center. If any of the metrics start trending in the wrong direction, further action by the program manager will be required to get things back on track.

Sustaining Change

The activities required to sustain organizational change do not start only when the transition is complete. In a well-run organizational change initiative, these activities will probably start as soon as the portfolio scope is defined and the need for change is accepted. At that point, the portfolio and program managers should initiate communication programs and sense-making activities that will help the organization understand and support the need for, and value of, the proposed initiative.

The key process here is benefits sustainment (PMI, 2013c, Section 4.5) and the key considerations are as follows:

- **Ongoing communication and consultation with, and representation of, stakeholders.** This involves implementing and continuously improving the stakeholder communication plan developed in the planning change stage of the effort; in this activity, the program manager must also actively engage the stakeholders, getting them to provide input and participate in decisions about the program's future.
- **Conducting sense-making activities.** This refers to providing opportunities for targeted official and untargeted unofficial communications to help stakeholders and affected groups make sense of the program deliverables. "These activities are related to the engagement and mobilization of stakeholders during a

change process and include both management approaches and specific activities" (PMI, 2013b, Section 5.3.5.2).

- **Measuring benefits realization.** "The ultimate purpose of change is to contribute to the organization's continued growth and to sustain its competitive advantage. Successful execution of the change can only be measured through benefits realization, which is an assessment of the successful integration of the change into business as usual" (PMI 2013b, Section 5.3.5.3). This assessment typically is implemented through a benefits register that supports the measurement of and reporting on both the progress of the implementation and the adoption of the change.

The key deliverables, of course, are the organizational changes delivered by the program components:

- Sustainable changes, having the resources and plan required to support them;
- Changes that are readily accepted by the receiving organization;
- Changes that can be measured and tracked; and
- Changes that can be adjusted, as necessary, going forward.

All these characteristics are typical of good program management, but they become particularly important in the context of organizational change because the disruptions are potentially much more extreme. As a result, even more attention than usual should be paid to ensure a smooth and successful transition from full program/project mode to operational readiness and usage.

Example

Continuing one more time with our example of Mammoth Manufacturing and the data center consolidation component of the system consolidation program, once the migration is complete there is a risk that the separate divisions might start up their own small centers of technology expertise, possibly using cloud-based services instead of the corporate data center. The corporate data center group would have the means to monitor network traffic and so would be very much aware of any unauthorized sidestepping of the consolidated data center. If they were to suspect or be able to demonstrate that this was either being contemplated or even had been implemented, their solution must be to demonstrate that there is greater organizational value to their solution than to the divisional detour. If the division has specific needs that are not being addressed, then it is the responsibility of the management of the corporate data center to understand these needs and initiate measures to resolve their issues.

Summary: Program Management and Organizational Change

Of the three disciplines, program management is the closest to the practice of organizational change management. Both programs and organizational change initiatives are defined by their strategic direction, subject to change as they evolve, require a high degree of stakeholder engagement, contain a number of components that are all different and yet related, and complete their work by transitioning the results to the operational areas and ensuring that these results are sustained. In both cases, the key to success is "to integrate and align people, processes, structures, culture, and strategy" (PMI, 2013b, Section 5.5).

The Role of the Project Manager in Organizational Change

There is a fundamental dissonance between the disciplines of project management and organizational change. Projects are subject to the well-known triple constraint of schedule, scope, and cost, and are, literally by definition, limited in time and in scope. Change management, on the other hand, is subject to continuous change. As circumstances evolve, the change initiative will be modified iteratively, forcing the underlying components to change accordingly. Thus, there is a basic conflict when a project manager manages projects that are part of a change initiative. On the one hand, the project manager must define the expected scope, schedule, and cost of the effort and manage the team to execute the resulting plan. On the other hand, however, the project manager must also stand ready to up-end that plan if the changing needs of the initiative require it.

Whereas a project focuses on delivering the (very tangible) product, service, or result that it was created to provide, change management can focus on much less tangible and less bounded deliverables, shifting the project to a more iterative mode of operation. "When change is viewed as a predictable part of the project environment, a change management plan shifts from an emphasis on control to an emphasis on continued, cyclic review and adaptation" (PMI, 2013b, Section 6.2). The emerging discipline of agile project management has this same iterative orientation and so, may be more appropriate in an organizational change context than more traditional project management approaches.

In any case, the only way for the change programs to deliver organizational benefits is through component projects. Thus, projects and the project manager remain the foundation of any change management initiative. The *PMBOK® Guide* divides the activities of a project into 10 Knowledge Areas, and it is worth taking a look at these within the context of organizational change management to see how they need to be refocused for this particular purpose. This summary is provided in Table 4-4.

Table 4-4.　The project management Knowledge Areas and organizational change.

Knowledge Area	Project Management Emphasis	Extension Implied in Organizational Change Management
Project Integration Management	Managing interdependencies and unifying project components	• Managing and unifying interdependencies with change management activities performed in program management • Ensuring transition of project deliverables into operations for ultimate achievement of project, program, and strategic benefits
Project Scope Management	Clarity and limitation of scope	• Soliciting input into scope before agreeing to limitations • Replanning scope as new information or challenges develop
Project Time Management	Completion of the project on schedule	• Building adaptive and iterative processes into the schedule
Project Cost Management	Estimating, funding, and controlling project costs	• Ensuring realization of expected organizational benefits with project deliverables having reasonable cost structures
Project Quality Management	Ensuring the quality of the project deliverables	• Ensuring that high-quality deliverables result in expected organizational benefits
Project Human Resources Management	Organizing, leading, and managing the project team	• Ensuring and coordinating change management resources and activities
Project Communications Management	Communicating project information to stakeholders	• Seeking participation of stakeholders in communication • Delivering extensive two-way communication
Project Risk Management	Planning for and controlling project risks to scope, schedule, and budget	• Planning for and monitoring risks, particularly those posed by people's actions and reactions • Adapting project deliverables and outcomes as necessary to ensure realization of expected organizational benefits
Project Procurement Management	Planning for, securing, and controlling contracts for products or services necessary to complete the project	• Planning for, securing, and controlling contracts for services necessary to ensure change adoption and ultimate realization of expected business benefits • Obtaining professional expertise in areas such as process design, organizational design, and (when applicable) knowledge transfer
Project Stakeholder Management	Engaging stakeholders in defining, analyzing, negotiating, and managing expectations	• Engaging a broad range of stakeholders when defining expectations • Seeking stakeholder participation in decision making • Testing stakeholder assumptions

Adapted from *Managing Change in Organizations: A Practice Guide* (PMI, 2013b).

Formulating Change

Generally, this step of the change life cycle does not include input from, or participation by, project managers. In fact, in this phase of the life cycle, it is not even clear yet who the project managers are because we don't yet even know how many programs and components will be needed to execute the initiative!

The only context in which this might arise for a project would be if it was part of the change portfolio directly and not part of a component program. In that case, the project will take on many of the aspects that would normally have been handled by the program, as described previously (PMI, 2013b, Section 5.3.1).

Planning Change

In planning projects within an organizational change initiative, the project manager performs the same duties as on any other project, but focuses more on stakeholder management and the impact of the project deliverables on those affected by these deliverables. For the project manager, the key activities in planning change are the following (PMI, 2013b, Table 6-2):

- Identify the appropriate project resources.
- Identify the stakeholders affected by the change and their vested interests in either supporting or opposing the change.
- Coordinate the project change management activities with their program-level equivalents; if the project is not part of a program, then coordinate with the portfolio-level equivalents.
- Collect the project requirements that will deliver the specified change and define the resulting scope.
- Define the activities to deliver the changes, sequence these activities, specify the resources needed to perform these activities, obtain these resources, and develop the budget to execute them.
- Identify the metrics that will evaluate the effectiveness of the change in providing the organizational benefits.
- Clarify the positive and negative project risks, related both to the delivery of the changes and to the acceptance and adoption of these changes, and plan the risk monitoring and response activities accordingly.
- Develop the communications management plan, paying particular attention to the issues and sensitivities around organizational change—a higher-than-normal level of communication is necessary.
- Develop the human resource management plan and quality management plan, both in support of the implementation of the organizational changes.

In the planning change phase of the change life cycle, the key Process Groups for the project manager are Initiating and Planning. Their key deliverables are the:

- **Project Charter**, documenting the organizational change that the project is created to deliver and the associated high-level requirements, as well as additional aspects of the project such as constraints, assumptions, stakeholder list, and other project initiation information (refer to Section 4.2.3.1 of the *PMBOK® Guide* [PMI, 2013d]); and the

- **Project Management Plan**, describing how the project will be executed, monitored, and controlled, to deliver the required organizational change, among many other subsidiary plans and baselines (refer to Section 4.2.3.1 of the *PMBOK® Guide* [PMI, 2013d]).

Example

Continuing with our example of Mammoth Manufacturing, let's focus this time on the unified customer data project. At the program level, the project deliverable has already been defined. In brief, the organizational change that is the goal of the project is to unify all the divisional customer lists, databases, and spreadsheets into one available and transparent system that is readily communicated to all divisions, their systems, and their marketing and sales departments. The high-level plan is also relatively straightforward and includes the following:

- Define the new system's functional requirements.
- Find and implement the best alternative vendor package.
- Work with the stakeholders and the vendor to enhance the package to bridge any significant functional gaps.
- Migrate all the divisional marketing and sales teams to the new system.
- Turn off and archive the old systems.

Of course, each of these broad activities contains a great deal of complexity as well as the need to carefully handle the particular sensitivities specific to a change initiative. For example, to define the functional requirements, the project team must interview all the different divisional groups—not just the marketing and sales teams, but anyone who either makes updates to or inquires against the current divisional customer information systems. Then, the project team must pull together all these different requirements into a single document. This document will necessarily be a compromise, because the new system will almost certainly not look or operate like the divisional system, and will therefore be suspect to anyone who is inclined to mistrust change. The project team will need to be sure that all stakeholders feel their concerns have been heard and that their needs will be addressed as the project proceeds.

Implementing Change

As discussed previously, when implementing projects within an organizational change initiative, the project manager performs essentially the same duties as on any other project, but focuses more on stakeholder management and the impact of the project deliverables on those affected by them. For the project manager, the key activities in implementing change are as follows (PMI, 2013b, Table 6-2):

- Acquire and organize the project/change management team, procuring outside resources if/when needed.
- Manage change communications even more carefully than usual, being mindful of the sensitive nature of organizational change and the importance of a clear and positive message to affected stakeholders—they will need more than the customary dashboard and "stoplight" status updates.
- Deliver the defined organizational changes—this is, of course, the meat of the project and, in fact, of the whole initiative; it is here that the changes actually happen.
- Assess change acceptance thoroughly, using metrics that are readily understandable at all levels, and reporting not only acceptance but also on the results of that acceptance.
- Manage project risk to maximize acceptance of the change and to minimize resistance.
- Review and modify change management scope, activities, schedule, and budget based on the resulting feedback. As has been noted earlier, a change initiative is an iterative process, and this is where the project may need to iterate a bit in order to achieve its objectives.

In this phase of the change life cycle, the key Process Groups and activities for the project manager are listed below.

- **Executing:**
  - Direct and Manage Project Work, delivering the desired change.
  - Manage Communications, ensuring that stakeholders understand the project status.
  - Manage Stakeholder Engagement, keeping the stakeholders positive about the change.
- **Monitoring and Controlling:**
  - Monitor and Control Project Work, keeping all the activities on track.
  - Control Stakeholder Engagement, adjusting plans as needed to maximize acceptance.
  - Control Communications, ensuring the effectiveness of change communications.
  - Control Scope, Schedule, Costs, Quality, and Risk, monitoring the project's effectiveness.
  - Perform Integrated Change Control, controlling change within the project itself.

In these phases of the project life cycle, the key deliverables are:

- First and foremost, the organizational change created by the project deliverables;
- Second, the positive and enthusiastic acceptance of the organizational change; and
- Third, the updated plans and reports created and modified over the course of the project.

Example

In our example, the unified customer data project team assembled a focus group of key owners and users of the various divisional customer information systems. Some were enthusiastic about the change to the new system, and others were deeply concerned. The enthusiastic stakeholders were tired of having to support an old and technologically fragile system and looked forward to working with something new. On the other hand, the concerned stakeholders knew the old system and all its quirks and shortcomings, were comfortable with it, and saw no pressing need to change. Through the research in the vendor selection process, even the concerned group of stakeholders became convinced that there were better options out there, and by the end of the evaluation and proof of concept, the project team had to hold a lottery to decide which group would be the first to migrate to the new system. Through careful stakeholder engagement and communications management, those who were initially the most resistant to change became its greatest advocates.

Managing Transition and Sustaining Change

In the context of these phases of the change life cycle, the project manager does have additional deliverables that are not necessarily always present in other projects. These deliverables are more generally found at the program level, but in an organizational change project, it is important to keep them in mind at the project level as well. Specifically, these deliverables are as a result of the need to (PMI, 2013b, Table 6-2):

- Measure the acceptance/adoption of the change against predefined, established measures of success;
- Identify, plan, and execute the activities needed to transition the change into organizational operations—this includes the creation and execution of a transition plan;
- Develop and execute a plan for operational sustainability of the implemented changes, including ongoing stakeholder involvement through continued sense-making activities; and
- Close out the project and report the results to the program manager or portfolio manager.

The key Process Group for the project manager is Closing (i.e., Close Project) and the key deliverables are:

- Documented acceptance by the stakeholders that the change is acceptable, that the transition plan was executed successfully, and that the change will be sustainable using the plan for operational sustainability;
- The usual post-project review, lessons learned, archiving, reports of changes, or enhancements to standard project processes, and so on;
- Formal application to, and acceptance by, the project sponsors that all objectives have been met and the project can be officially closed; and
- Release of all project resources to other components within the initiative or possibly to other initiatives.

Example

In our example, after the package has been installed and enhanced and a few months after the last division was migrated to the new system, the project team distributed a customer satisfaction survey to the original focus group and to all the other users of the former systems who moved to the new system. The results were very positive and a significant improvement over the scores when the same survey was given at the start of the project. Overall satisfaction was higher, there were fewer complaints and many fewer system outages and data errors, and in general the user community was pleased with the availability of the data and the speed of the system. However, there were also some substantive comments regarding system shortcomings and requests for very worthwhile enhancements. The project team assembled these suggestions into a proposal for a Phase 2 effort, and will be presenting this proposal to the portfolio manager; they expect that it will be approved and they will continue to improve this system for their stakeholders.

Two years into the ACT initiative, Mammoth completed all the organization's structural changes, consolidated many warehouses into a few that are geographically dispersed to enable faster deliveries, and completed the warehouse upgrades that were part of that consolidation. They improved their inventory controls and can tell their customers exactly what is available, when it can ship, and how quickly it can be delivered. Furthermore, they reorganized their marketing and sales so each customer has one, and only one, marketing representative for all of Mammoth instead of one per division, saving time and effort for both Mammoth and its customers. Sales and repeat sales are up, costs are down, and as a result, Mammoth's stock is at a five-year high. The company still has a long way to go, but the ACT initiative has more than paid for itself.

Chapter Summary: Portfolio, Program, and Project Management in the Context of Organizational Change

In one sense, the roles of the portfolio, program, and project manager in an organizational change initiative are much the same as they are in any other context: Determine what needs to be done, figure out the best way to do it, and then execute to that plan, adjusting as necessary along the way. There are, of course, substantial differences among the three disciplines and in the skills and competences needed to be effective in these roles, but this is the fundamental and central theme for all three.

However, the context of organizational change adds another whole level of complexity because of the nature of the initiative—it is a much riskier effort, there is much greater sensitivity among stakeholders, and there is likely to be greater polarization of their positions relative to the initiative. When dealing with organizational change, the key considerations are:

- At the portfolio level, the assessment of the organization's readiness for change is critical. If the organization is not ready for change, then the first task of the portfolio must be to get it ready.
- At the program level, it remains critical to work closely with the stakeholders to ensure that they stay supportive (or can be convinced to become supportive) of the change initiative. In addition, it is also very important to carefully plan the transition of the organizational benefits (i.e., the change) into the operational areas. The program manager must also ensure that the operational area is prepared to receive the change and that the processes are in place to sustain that acceptance after the transition is complete. Again, communication is even more important than usual, and it is critical to closely monitor adoption and acceptance of the results of programs and program components.
- Finally, at the project level, the project manager (as always!) must deliver the product, service, or result. However, because of the context of the project, there must be increased focus on stakeholder engagement, communication management, and on managing risks related to possible stakeholder resistance to change.

Thus, the keys to success at all three levels are:

- Carefully managing, and even nurturing, stakeholder involvement and enthusiasm;
- Establishing detailed metrics and key performance indicators that will enable managers at all three levels to measure acceptance of the change and effectiveness after the change has been adopted;

- Incorporating flexibility into planning and execution—important in any portfolio, program, or project, but even more so in this context; and
- Ensuring a smooth transition to sustainable organizational benefits, realized through the delivered changes.

References

Note: In most of the citations for these references, section, table, and figure numbers are provided instead of page numbers.

Project Management Institute (PMI). (2013a). *The standard for portfolio management* – Third edition. Newtown Square, PA: Author.

Project Management Institute (PMI). (2013b). *Managing change in organizations: A practice guide.* Newtown Square, PA: Author.

Project Management Institute (PMI). (2013c). *The standard for program management* – Third edition. Newtown Square, PA: Author.

Project Management Institute (PMI). (2013d). *A guide to the project management body of knowledge (PMBOK® guide)* – Fifth edition. Newtown Square, PA: Author.

Review Questions

1. Of the three disciplines, which is the most similar to the practice of organizational change management, and why?
2. Of the three disciplines, which is the most different from the practice of organizational change management, and why?
3. With respect to the roles of the portfolio, program, and project managers, what are the key differences between initiatives that are part of an organizational change and those that are not?
4. What is the most important consideration for a portfolio manager to keep in mind when setting up and running an organizational change portfolio?
5. What is the most important consideration for a program manager to keep in mind when planning and executing an organizational change program?
6. What are the most important considerations for a project manager to keep in mind when running an organizational change project?
7. In which of the five phases of the change life cycle does the portfolio manager make the greatest contribution? The least contribution? Explain.

8. In which of the five phases of the change life cycle does the program manager make the greatest contribution? The least contribution? Explain.

9. In which of the five phases of the change life cycle does the project manager make the greatest contribution? The least contribution? Explain.

Appendix

Checklist: Communicating Change

In order to communicate change effectively and win over stakeholders at all levels, there are a number of stakeholder concerns that need to be addressed. The communication does not have to follow this format; in fact, it will probably be more effective if it does not. However, whatever the form of the communication, it should provide the answers to these questions.

1. **Why do we need to do this? (Or, more directly, why do *you* want to do this?)**

   It is a false truism that people resist change. Most people do not resist change—they resist *change that they do not understand*. If they can understand the reasons behind the change, it appears less arbitrary, more rational, and therefore more acceptable.

2. **What is the extent of the change?**

   Understanding the full scope of the change helps in this acceptance. If they are going to be adversely affected by the change, it's probably best to put that in front of them as well, because the unknown is worse than the known. Be sure to describe both what will be changing and what will not be changing.

3. **How is it going to affect me?**

   Clearly the most important consideration for most people, and one that should be easy to communicate.

4. **When is this going to happen? (How soon is it going to start, and when will it all be over?)**

   If the change will not happen for a while, people can grow to accept it over time. If it is going to happen soon, it is best to let them know it is coming so as not to surprise them.

5. **How will we know if it worked?**

People can become cynical about the "flavor of the month" nature of change in some organizations, and are more likely to accept change if they know that its impact will be measured. They are likely to feel more comfortable that those proposing and implementing the change will be sure it goes smoothly if the results will be measured and evaluated.

6. **Who is responsible? (Or more directly, who do I go to with questions, comments, suggestions, and/or complaints?)**

Change becomes more effective and more acceptable if the change agents are known to the stakeholders rather than being just "the central office" or "those people at headquarters."

Checklist: Assessing Organizational Readiness for Change

In order to affect change, it is critical to be sure that the organization is ready for the change. This is a checklist for the portfolio, program, or project manager to assess the organizational readiness for change and, if the organization is not ready, to assist the manager in turning that situation around.

Assessing the People

1. **Who are the advocates (potential or actual) for change?**

Current advocates for change can be enlisted to help persuade others that the change will be positive. The manager should try to find these advocates at all levels. Resistance to change can happen at all levels, and is most effectively countered by peers, not by management.

2. **Who are the ones (likely to be or actually) opposing change and how can we change their minds?**

Similarly, it is important to find the naysayers, determine their specific issues, and try to address their concerns if at all possible. One of the most effective arguments for change starts with: "I used to think this was a really bad idea, but then I realized that . . ." It is best for this change of heart to occur before the initiative gets under way to avoid negative comments in the critical early stages of the effort. Converts are almost always the most effective advocates.

3. **Who will be responsible for making the change happen in the organization?**

Does the organization have the right portfolio, program, and project managers to be able to affect the organizational change and, if not, is it prepared to do what will be needed to acquire these critical people?

Assessing the Resources

4. **What resources will be needed to affect the organizational changes?**

   Is the organization prepared to provide the portfolio, program, and project managers with the necessary people, equipment, technology, and other resources that will be needed to affect the organizational change? In order to make that determination, high-level estimates will be needed to define these required resources.

5. **Is adequate funding available?**

   Is the organization prepared to expend the funds needed to supply the portfolio, program, and project managers with these resources? If not, the case will need to be made and accepted for such expenditures well in advance of initiating the effort.

Checklist: Assessing Organizational Readiness for Change

Assessing the Plan

6. **Are the objectives clear for those planning and implementing the organizational changes?**

   Clear objectives are, of course, essential to the success of any undertaking. They are particularly important in the context of organizational change initiatives because of the need to communicate these objectives in order to overcome anticipated resistance.

7. **Does the road map clearly define the cross-component interdependencies within the organizational change portfolio?**

   Organizational change initiatives typically are far-reaching with numerous components across many, if not all, parts of the affected organization. Thus, it is critically important for the component interdependencies to be fully understood and well-documented to ensure smooth execution.

8. **Are the lines of communication clear and operating so that all stakeholders are informed on the progress of the initiative relative to the overall organizational strategy?**

   Once again, it is important to note that clear communications and effective stakeholder engagement are essential to the success of any initiative, but are particularly important in the context of organizational change.

9. **Are the measures of success clear so that all teams know when their objectives have been met and the resulting benefits have been realized?**

   As always, it is important to be able to define when the job is done. Otherwise, a change initiative (or, indeed, any initiative) can continue on well past its usefulness.

10. **Is there a clear plan to incorporate the component deliverables into sustained operational activities?**

    Any change initiative must, from the start, define how these changes will become woven into the fabric of the organization and integrated into ongoing operations. Otherwise, the initiative runs the risk of creating new processes or products that cannot be sustained.

Template: The Portfolio Plan for Organizational Change

This template summarizes the critical sections of the portfolio strategic plan, portfolio charter, and portfolio road map that are most important when dealing with organizational change. Other sections can be added, of course, but none of these should be omitted.

Making the Case for Organizational Change

11. **Vision and Objectives**

    Describe the challenges faced by the organization that created the need for the change and explain how the proposed change initiative will enable the organization to meet these challenges. This section should not be more than a half a page typed. It should summarize the challenges in the first paragraph and summarize the resulting objectives of the initiative in separate bullets or paragraphs of one to three sentences each.

12. **Organizational Benefits**

    Describe the benefits that will come from the organizational change.

    - "Hard" (i.e., immediately objectively measurable) benefits such as reduction in square footage, occupancy costs through relocation, or the need for certain raw materials
    - "Soft" benefits that depend on projections and can only be measured after the fact, such as a reduction in projected headcount increase due to increased efficiency
    - "Intangible" benefits that cannot be measured, such as improved controls or reduction in operational risk

13. Organizational Structure

Describe the current organizational structure and the desired end state after the change initiative has completed; include interim states if they are likely to persist for any length of time. Use no more than one page for each stage of the change.

14. Finances

Develop a high-level analysis of the value of the organizational benefits described in #2 above. Estimate the resources needed to plan, manage, implement, and sustain the organizational change—separately if possible, and adding whatever reserves are appropriate to ensure a realistic cost picture. Project both benefits and costs on a year-by-year basis and calculate whatever financial metrics are appropriate to the organization: return on investment (ROI), internal rate of return (IRR), net present value (NPV), and so on. The complexity of this analysis will depend on the size of the change initiative and the extent to which it is well-defined. Do not seek a level of accuracy in your projections that is greater than the level of accuracy in your inputs.

Template: The Portfolio Plan for Organizational Change

Describing the Plan for Organizational Change

15. High-Level Road Map and Time Line

Through a network-type chart if at all possible, show the predecessor/successor relationships within the components of the organizational change portfolio, explaining the reasons for the dependencies within the chart or in an associated narrative.

Through a high-level Gantt chart or equivalent time line, show the progression of these components through time to give your audience an idea of what will be happening and when. This will also assist in the projection of benefits and costs for the financial analysis above.

16. Governance

Again, through a chart if possible (in this case, probably an org-chart type of presentation), describe the hierarchy of governance within the portfolio, programs, and projects. Explain the roles and responsibilities at each level.

17. Responsibility

To the extent possible, identify each role in the governance section above with the corresponding named individuals or organizational titles who will fulfill those responsibilities. It is critical that the portfolio managers, program managers, and project managers be empowered by this section to help them be able to fulfill their responsibilities. It is also very important that the business owners, sponsors, and/or members of the various governance boards understand their roles and be publicly connected with them to ensure that they give these roles the attention that they require.

Template: The Portfolio Plan for Organizational Change
Other Considerations in Organizational Changes
18. Planning and Managing Risk

As with any initiative, large or small, risks must be identified, assessed, planned for, monitored, and responded to when necessary. In this section, identify the potential high-level risks to the organizational change initiative (both positive and negative as appropriate), their probability and impact, and so on. It is, of course, important not just to list the risks but, as the initiative proceeds, to continue to monitor them and respond as needed. Note that this section applies to the overall initiative—the individual components will have their own risk management plans.

19. Planning and Executing Change Communications

Once again, it is important to note that clear communications and effective stakeholder engagement are essential to the success of any initiative, but are particularly important in the context of organizational change. In this section, describe the levels of stakeholders, the frequency, and method through which they will receive communications on the organizational change initiative, and the type of information that will be contained in these communications. Since this is assumed to be a publicly available document, it is *not* the place for a stakeholder register, influence assessment, and so on.

20. Assumptions and Constraints

Describe the assumptions and constraints that the organizational change initiative is operating under. Recall that assumptions are the factors that are *considered* to be true, real, or certain, without proof or demonstration, while constraints, on the other hand, are *real* limiting factors that affect the execution of the initiative.

CHAPTER 5

The Change Process in Practice

By James Marion, PhD, PMP

Abstract

The field of change management has, as its basis, theoretical models for leading, implementing, and managing change. Such models tend to agree that organizations need to be readied for change, changed, and then reach a state whereupon change becomes institutionalized. The practice of change management, however, has been known to deviate from theory when the attempt is made to actually implement it. Theoretical change models may minimize the importance of the unique contexts in which change is implemented. Further, other topics such as the role of project management techniques in organizational change management (OCM), the effectiveness of organizational preparation and communication, as well as specific techniques that arise empirically in practical change efforts may be overlooked. This chapter examines change management as a practice and provides recommendations for the advancement of OCM practices. The examination of OCM field practice as described in the literature is expected to complement, as well as advance, the theoretical basis of the OCM discipline.

Where Does Change Begin?

Executives seek to change organizations for a reason. In many cases, organizations exhibiting poor financial or operational performance would appear to be prime candidates for change. Other organizations may find themselves producing acceptable results and may lead in their respective markets—yet they also embark on managed change initiatives. The literature of organizational change management (OCM) offers a range of recommendations for what to change as well as tools and techniques for implementing change (Brown, Waterhouse, & Flynn, 2003; Buller, 1988; Tan, 2006). Regardless of what or how to change, from the perspective of change management practice, organizational leadership must clearly know and be able to articulate the fundamental purpose, or the "why," of change as well as the "when" change must be undertaken. Regardless of the process, the methodology, the timing, or the theoretical lens used, change begins as a practical matter with a clear rationale for the change as well as a clear articulation of that rationale. It is expected that the rationale will be forthcoming from the change agent or team leading the change. OCM and organizational development (OD) research informs change managers regarding how this is best achieved; however, change initiatives in practice tend to draw upon a wide array of techniques and methodologies employed in industry (Sullivan, Rothwell, & Balasi, 2013).

Change Triggers

Change in organizations is often a response to a trigger. Events may trigger change and such triggers may arise both internally and external to the company. Although change is said to be triggered, how a company responds to triggers may or may not follow theorized change processes (PMI, 2013a). For example, the decline of IBM triggered the board of directors to bring in an outsider, Lou Gerstner, in 1993. In this example, action immediately follows a trigger, and that action, in turn, was followed by change led from the vision of the executive (DiCarlo, 2002). On the other hand, some companies face change triggers but do not recognize them as such. For example, the introduction and success of the first touchscreen phone offered by Apple would appear to be an obvious trigger for legacy companies offering smartphones that their product lineups would be in dire need of change in order to react to this new type of product. As is often the case, the trigger was apparently dismissed by most legacy companies and was not acted upon until it was too late. The literature of change management focuses on the leadership and implementation of change, but apparently does not emphasize the importance of management sensitivity to change triggers or how to recognize such triggers (Manuele, 2012).

Change as Problem Solving

One of the most longstanding models of organizational change is Lewin's model of change management (Lewin, 1947). The model is prescriptive in that it suggests that managers need to "unfreeze," change, and then "refreeze" in order to institute the changes made (Buller, 1988). In practice, change is often thrust upon the manager as well as the organization as a result of events that range from a series of quarters of poor financial performance, to a major shift in the competitive landscape or a major leadership change.

In such instances, the presence of problems is widely acknowledged. Further, the need for changes in order to address such problems is recognized. What may not be immediately obvious is the exact nature of the underlying problems. Managers who find themselves at the helm when change is necessary typically have little time to waste. Change is required for survival, and this requires movement. But what moves should be taken? This can only be determined by developing a deep understanding of the root cause or causes of the underlying problems. Often, these causes are complex and cannot be gained by cursory inspection. In practice, the manager leading change will likely encounter a range of opinion and hearsay as employees and managers present their respective views about "what is going on" and what went wrong. It is at this moment that the manager leading the change must step back, resist the urge to take action, and instead collect data as the first phase of a problem-solving change initiative (Brown et al., 2003).

Change and Data Collection

The data collection process in OD terms is referred to as diagnosis. In practical terms, it involves acquiring an in-depth understanding of the problem developed by the collection of supporting evidence. Unfortunately, change managers receive mixed signals from data that may be at times contradictory. This is because the problems that OCM attempts to address are not well-structured problems. They are often ambiguous, and they resist facile troubleshooting by change practitioners (Connor, 2011). For this reason, the change management professional will likely structure or frame the problem in a way that makes most sense based on his or her experience and know-how. Unfortunately, this manner of viewing the problem, although convenient, may miss key elements of the reality of the underlying problem or situation. If this is the case, the proposed change solution that results may not solve the intended problem. In fact, in the worst case, it may increase the problems faced by the organization, and even in the best case, it may result in unintended consequences. Change managers in this scenario often experience changed processes or methodologies going unused because the proposed solution either does not solve the problem, is inconvenient for those expected to use it, or causes other problems that make the solution not worth the cost of acceptance and implementation. The fields of problem solving and decision making, therefore, both begin with the identification or framing of the problem (Jansson, 2013). The framing of the problem to be diagnosed is likely to be difficult for managers of change because it is not always easy to view a problem in a different way, or through a different practical or theoretical lens. Practitioner-oriented approaches that borrow from project management include various methods of brainstorming and collaborative problem solving. Structured practical methods also exist, such as the "six thinking hats" methodology, which is a powerful tool that facilitates critical thinking, collaboration, communication, and creativity. All of these methods are intended to aid the change manager in viewing the world in different ways so that essential causes of organizational problems are not missed. The early stages of change management, when used to correct organizational problems or dysfunction, is therefore said to be little different from traditional problem solving (Mento, Jones, & Dirndorfer, 2002).

Finding the Root Cause

How, then, do practitioners "get to the bottom of things" and make sure they are solving the right problem? The first step in accomplishing data analysis is for the practitioner to recognize that all data sources within the organization are imperfect measures. Different employees may see the same thing, but report different phenomena. The true picture may emerge only if all of those who see the phenomena are queried. This suggests that in practice, managers of change talk to employees—many employees at all levels and functions. On the other hand, although the input of large numbers of employees may well help uncover the "wisdom of crowds," the collection of opinion may not capture the entire story. Research suggests that human memory is imperfect, so qualitative interview data of employee opinion are best validated by comparison with hard data from sources such as budgets, business metrics, meeting minutes, documented plans, and company presentations. The resulting comparison and conclusions may then be validated in a facilitated group meeting of key employees selected from multiple functions and levels. Such ongoing comparison and validation of data using multiple imperfect sources is referred to as "triangulation" (Miles & Huberman, 1994). Because the term *triangulation* is used in pathfinding and distance estimation, the term appears to be particularly appropriate in change management settings. The saying, "if you don't know where you are going, you may end up somewhere else," would appear to apply in this context. Above all, successful practitioners embarking upon a journey of change determine clearly what the issue is, prior to setting the direction for change.

The Importance of Context

Chaos theory informs us that the beating of the wings of a butterfly in one part of the world may lead to storms in another part of the world. This view into chaotic systems speaks to the importance of initial conditions. It could be argued that organizations have elements of chaos, in the sense that the events faced by managers on a day-to-day basis tend to be unpredictable. Further, some have proposed that results obtained by a business are not related to the skill of any particular manager at all, but instead are the result of random and fundamentally indeterminate events (Singh & Singh, 2002). Imagine the difficulty faced by change managers who seek to diagnose the issues that have led to the need for change and seek to embark on change initiatives that will eventually produce improved results. This cannot be done without a deep understanding of the context in which the change is being initiated. To continue with the analogy with chaotic systems, the initial conditions in a system are key; likewise, the context in which change is proposed informs the means by which change is undertaken. This intuitive view of change at the level of practice would appear to argue against prescriptive methodologies for initiating and managing change. For this reason, change practice would suggest that an understanding of the context of the organization is an important predecessor to understanding the underlying cause of the problem. Further, any proposed solution in the form of organizational change that is divorced from the context of the history, culture, and market conditions faced by the firm is less likely to succeed. Exceptions to this rule of thumb do exist, but when changes outside the context of the firm are implemented successfully, they do so under extraordinary leadership circumstances (Sturdy & Grey, 2003).

Leadership Change and Context

For example, Nissan sought to change the way the company managed itself and made decisions in order to remain competitive with the global market. For this reason, the company brought in Carlos Ghosn from Renault as part of the Nissan-Renault alliance. In 2001, Ghosn, as CEO of Nissan, led the Nissan revival plan and took steps that were considered extraordinary from the perspective of the staid, corporate cultural context. Ghosn laid off thousands of employees, closed plants, reduced suppliers, and sold off expensive nonproductive assets (Tierney & Gerber, 2005). Nissan returned to profitability in short order, and has enjoyed relative success since the advent of this leader of change from outside the fold of its culture. The success of Ghosn at Nissan is in contrast to a similar change experiment undertaken by Sony with Howard Stringer. Although Sony was traditionally a manufacturer of electronic hardware products such as the Sony Walkman® and flat-screen televisions, Stringer rose through the ranks of Sony by means of the media industry and Sony in the United States. Sony in Japan long believed that the media and content business would be a natural complement and growth engine for Sony's many content-driven hardware products such as TVs, the Blu-Ray DVD player, and video games. Further, the need to compete with faster-moving Western companies led Sony to bring Stringer to Japan as its CEO. Unlike the success experienced at Nissan, Sony did not become profitable after Stringer took the helm. Also, the internal difficulties in driving changes in the slow, consensus-based decision-making systems in place at Sony ensured that, unlike Nissan, much of the status quo management practice remained in place at Sony (McIntyre, 2013).

Understanding the Actual Context in Change

When Nissan and Sony are compared with respect to the context and the management of change, it is tempting to assume that in one case, extraordinary leadership led to success, whereas in another case, the fresh approach to leadership at the top level was not sufficient to overcome the organizational inertia at Sony. On the other hand, a closer examination of the actual nature of the proposed changes at the respective companies and how each was or was not consistent with the underlying context of the culture of each company is revealing. It is clear that the degree of change deviated from the context of the company far more in the unsuccessful change. In the case of Nissan, the proposed changes did not involve a completely new category of business. Rather, the existing business (automobiles) was optimized by seeking to make the business more efficient and to add new product categories. In the case of Sony, Stringer was promoted as a means of fundamentally shifting the company from being a traditional electronics manufacturing business to a media and content-centric enterprise that utilized hardware as an enabler of content delivery. Unlike the change effort at Nissan, the change pursued by Sony deviated from the traditional corporate culture on many levels. In terms of the basic mind-set, companies generally adopt an inductive or bottom-up manner of thinking based upon tangible businesses such as hardware overlaid with a manufacturing culture of continuous improvement. It is for this reason that many companies are said to lack strategy. Given this context, it is conceivable that a drive for efficiency involving force reductions and supplier cutbacks would not be completely outside of the experience and cultural context of a company that employed continuous improvement as its philosophical foundation. Understanding the context of the Nissan change management in this way may provide a deeper appreciation of the relatedness of the proposed changes to the fundamental context of the company. On the other hand, the shift to a more abstract business model that was outside the bounds of the experience base of most Sony employees would represent a far larger conceptual leap. A high-level comparison of these cases, therefore, informs change management practice with respect to the importance of context in determining the nature and direction of change (Weiner, 2009).

Context and the Iterative Approach

Although traditional views of change management would appear to have little to say about the role of context, more recent literature does address the importance of change practitioners learning about the organization and its background in depth prior to initiating specific change. The Viplan methodology (Harwood, 2012) is one such practice that involves an iterative approach to becoming aware of the issues that are in need of addressing in the change effort. This iterative learning approach would appear to have much in common with iterative and phased project management life cycle methodologies (Harwood, 2012). Given that a change initiative is, in essence, a project with a unique and temporary nature, the diagnosis of the organization to be changed could well be viewed as analogous to the requirements-gathering phase of a project. A project gathers requirements in order to define the deliverables, whereas a change initiative diagnoses, collects data, and learns the context of the firm in order to implement and ultimately deliver the change. Further, some product, software, and information systems life cycle approaches are iterative in their orientation. Borrowing from these life cycle management techniques, therefore, would appear to have much to offer change practitioners (Hornstein, 2012).

Change in a Successful Company

Kodak is often cited as an example of a company that should have changed, did not change, and as a result, ultimately failed. The practice of change in terms of the methodology employed is never the issue of focus in case studies of Kodak's history. The primary area of concern is the fact that Kodak failed to anticipate the end of a market life cycle and to capture the beginning of the next. Because of this, Kodak failed to initiate the process of change (Das, Nair, & Baker, 2012). The problem of the failure to recognize the need for change is not unique. For example, companies that once dominated the wireless industry, such as Nokia, Motorola, and Research in Motion (Blackberry), have either exited the industry, have been acquired by other companies, or are struggling to reposition themselves. It is of interest to consider why the initiation of change appears to be more difficult for successful companies than it is for companies that are experiencing obvious problems. From the perspective of practice, successful companies often appear to lack the trigger for change. In light of strong revenues and profits, the need to "unfreeze" or "diagnose" may appear to be unnecessary. As an example, in 1996, Kodak peaked with revenues of US$16 billion with two-thirds of the global market and US$31 billion of market capitalization. However, Kodak steadily declined until it declared bankruptcy less than 20 years later in 2012 (Das et al., 2012).

Failing to See Triggers

Why do highly successful companies often fail to see the need for a major change? Change practitioners face a number of management dilemmas that are unique to successful companies. Change of the scope and scale of a company such as Kodak likely involves innovation that positions the company into combinations of new product lines and markets. The difficulty associated with such large-scale change is multidimensional. Funding new product development projects costs money, as does the promotion of products into new markets. Further, products involving new technologies, such as digital photography in Kodak's case, tend to offer smaller profit margins compared to mature "cash-cow" products (Das et al., 2012). Change of this scale, therefore, involves more than simply following a prescribed process, understanding the underlying context of the company environment, or being able to identify the root cause of the problem. Unlike the case of an organization with a known problem, the challenge of change in a successful company is not finding the root cause of the underlying problem, but rather recognizing the fact that a problem exists and it is out there on the company's future horizon. This lack of recognition tends to sap the will of the company CEO or potential change agent to face shareholders with proposals that increase expenses, reduce margins, and generally impede earnings. Further, the uncertainty of the result of the change is likely to reduce the attractiveness of such change proposals. Finally, new product ideas raise the concern that the company will potentially be competing against its own successful product lines (Weiner, 2009).

Change in Response to Future Problems

Change within a successful company may, therefore, be viewed as change that is initiated in order to solve a problem that has not yet materialized. This situation may naturally lead to resistance to change, but—unlike traditional prescriptive change management models—such resistance is not merely a reluctance to adopt something new or do something different. Rather, this form of resistance in practice is linked to legitimate concerns over the productivity and profitability of the overall business (Clarke & Garside, 1997).

Although the prospect of reduced earnings often leads to resistance to changing that which is not apparently broken, change becomes progressively difficult when companies fail to recognize key opportunities to change and begin to decline. Funding required for initiating change projects or new product feasibility efforts is less available than that which existed during years of high profit. Further, the fundamental management bandwidth and overall energy of the company is often preoccupied with resisting the decline in revenues. The irony is that by the time the need for fundamental change is recognized, in practice, it may be too late to initiate change and, later still, to implement it. Given the noted importance of the need to understand the rationale for change and to effectively communicate it, change in a successful company is often observed to fail in this fundamental requirement.

Systematic Commitment to Change

What, then, is the solution to finding a trigger for change when the rationale for change is not clearly recognized? One practical approach is to commit to an ongoing regime of change initiatives. An organization dedicated to ongoing, continuous improvement is more likely to view change as essential and, in viewing change this way, will fund it accordingly with a percentage of expense or revenues. Another practical approach taken to change in the context of a successful company is to employ practices drawn from the management of innovation. The very term *innovation* implies something new, and new things correspond to change. Companies that implement innovation management systems to govern the new product development pipeline seek to produce a regular stream of new products and experiment with new markets as a means to continually advance and strengthen their respective positions. It is of interest to note that one of the key processes introduced into IBM by Lou Gerstner in the 1990s was an innovation management system known as Product and Cycle Time Excellence, pioneered by the consulting firm PRTM and now championed in various forms by the Product Development Management Association (PRTM, 2001). This system is said to have improved the process of converting IBM's know-how into consulting services and using these to initiate new lines of business and new markets. The improved bottom line of IBM was a testament to the improved performance brought about by innovation and change. Another measure of the ability of a company to innovate and change is by establishing metrics that effectively monitor the progress of innovative change. One simple metric is the percentage of annual revenues derived from new products or services. A company that adopts such a metric has no choice but to continuously attempt change in this arena. It is not inconceivable to consider that a company like Kodak might have pursued digital photography sooner and more extensively when governing its management and advancement of change using such metrics (Das et al., 2012).

The Implementation of Change

When adopted formally, change is often implemented by strategic initiatives. A strategic initiative is a temporary endeavor undertaken to achieve specific goals. For this reason, the practice of change is often implemented using practices and terminology adopted from project management and the product development or system development life cycle. Instead of following the formulaic process methodology promoted by OD theorists, a company initiating change within the context of a fast-moving and highly competitive industry may simply perceive the need to act, authorize an initiative to address the specific issue, and then monitor progress. The practice of change, therefore, is consistent with project management practice that operates at the level of strategic implementation. Researchers also note that project management and organizational change management have traditionally existed in two different domains, in spite of the fact that both offer methodologies for implementing change (Hornstein, 2012). Whereas change management focuses on the human element of the organization, including alignment, the project management Human Resource Knowledge Area is limited to the narrower focus of acquiring, leading, and managing project teams. It has been suggested that a synthesis of both disciplines would likely provide an effective method for carrying out organizational change. Practices from OD and OCM would focus on the macro level of human resources, while project management would employ the Human Resource Knowledge Area to acquire and manage the teams leading the change implementation effort (Hornstein, 2012).

Change Governance

An organization with an ongoing commitment to continuous improvement may be likely to sponsor an ongoing stream of change initiatives. Given that the focus of such projects is internal—with the possible exception of experimental efforts to deliver new products, technologies, or reach new markets—it is unlikely that the sponsorship of such projects flows from an external client. Who, then, as a matter of practice, sponsors change projects? The field of OD emphasizes the importance of the executive team in leading change efforts (Balogun, 2007). Likewise, the field of product development and innovation management suggests that a cross-functional senior executive group or committee of sponsors provides the optimal point of focus for organization-wide project sponsorship. The project approval committee (PAC), given that it represents all executive functions in the company, approves and charters all change initiatives and further initiates many of them as a means to drive improvement and major changes throughout the organization. The CEO would then have ultimate responsibility for the PAC, with oversight by the company board of directors. The board of directors would likely get involved in reviewing initiatives that are associated with high risk or are considered of material concern because of the financial impact of the initiative (McGrath, 1996).

The Change Project Life Cycle

It has been observed that the practices of change management and project management are seen to overlap with respect to the management of human resources. Additionally, the disciplines of project management and product development and innovation management overlap in the domain of project governance. In the field of product development and innovation management, the governance of the product life cycle is the key area of focus. Given that funding and resources within an organization are constrained, it is essential that funding be funneled only to those projects that are most likely to succeed within the marketplace. Therefore, all product development proposals are thoroughly vetted with the goal of weeding out proposals that fail tests of assumptions about markets, technologies, internal capabilities, and business models. Within the field of product development and innovation management, the PAC makes these go/no-go vetting determinations at each phase of the life cycle (McGrath, 1996).

The Project Office and OCM

In the field of project management, the project office, in concert with clients and executive sponsorship, assesses the ongoing viability of the project. In OD and OCM, the change agent and the executive team govern the change initiative and make necessary course corrections. Given the need to infuse the organization with the culture of ongoing change and improvement, the need for process consistency, and finally, the need to provide an efficient means to consolidate and harmonize project governance structures, it is suggested that in practice, change management may be managed and governed using the same practices that have been so successful in project management and product development and innovation management. In this manner, change initiatives are proposed and governed using the same processes as projects. Likewise, they are adopted, funded, and managed using a common project life cycle that begins with the initial proposal and ends with the launch of the change initiative (Hornstein, 2012).

Concept/Proposal

It has been observed that companies with obvious problems may be likely to sense the need to change, and therefore proceed with change initiatives, whereas companies that are doing well may be less likely to observe the need for change. A change life cycle provides the infrastructure to either address perceived problems, advance new product or market ideas, or act on suggestions for process improvement. In such a governance structure, anyone in the organization may put forward a change proposal to be reviewed by the committee of sponsors or PAC. Such proposals may be rejected with explanation, returned for feedback, or result in the request for a full presentation meeting before the PAC. In a manner similar to a CEO presenting to a board of directors for the approval of strategic initiatives, the author of the change proposal or product concept presents the justification for the proposal, including the funding and resource requirements, the underlying assumptions and rationale, the specific outcomes of the initiative, and finally, the proposed time frame. Consistent with decisions resulting from an innovation management governance system, the PAC either authorizes the funding, resources, and time line for the initiative to proceed to the next phase; redirects the proposal for further information; or does not approve the proposal. Approved proposals do not represent a total commitment to the overall initiative, but rather a commitment only to the next stage of the life cycle—in this case, the feasibility assessment (McGrath, 1996).

Feasibility

Many proposed change initiatives may be deemed worthy of further effort and consideration, but not all such proposals can actually be achieved by the organization. The feasibility phase of the change life cycle exists to carefully evaluate the degree to which the company is both ready and capable of achieving the stated goals. The feasibility phase of the change life cycle is, in effect, a project authorized to answer a number of questions regarding the proposed initiative. Such questions include the following:

- Do we have the required skill sets?
- Do we have the resources in sufficient numbers?
- Are any specific technologies required, and do we have access to them?
- What opportunity costs will we face by proceeding with this initiative?
- What assumptions do we have regarding the internal and external environment in which this project executes?
- Do we have the funding for the project?
- What specific resources and funding are required for the next project phase?
- What is the proposed time line of the next project phase?
- What benefits are expected from completing this project?
- What return on investment can be expected?

As can be observed in this series of questions, change initiative feasibility is little different from the feasibility analysis associated with any project, including a product development project. The initial change proposal, therefore, advances to the feasibility phase once the organization is able to answer, in the affirmative, the question "Should we do it?" The change initiative successfully exits the feasibility phase when the answer to the question "Are we able to do it?" is yes. Successful proposals then proceed to the planning phase of the change life cycle (McGrath, 1996).

Planning

A Guide to the Project Management Body of Knowledge (PMBOK Guide®) – Fifth Edition (PMI, 2013b) provides extensive guidelines for planning work. Because change management involves accomplishing work and completing activities, the use of the Planning Process Group in the *PMBOK Guide®* would appear to be a natural fit for change initiatives. The planning phase begins with a consideration of scope, both from the perspective of the totality of what the change initiative will deliver and how the scope of the initiative will be managed. The scope of the planning phase itself, and what this phase of the change initiative will deliver is, also developed as part of this first step. In all cases, the evaluation of scope is primarily concerned with what the change initiative will deliver. In the case of a proposed new product development, the initiative may result in tangible products. However, in the case of a change initiative, such as a process improvement or an organizational structure change, the scope may result only in the delivery of documented processes or policies and procedures. As described in the Planning Process Group, once the deliverables are determined, the change project team proceeds to capture all activities, arranges the activities in logical order, adds resources to the activities, and finally, uses the resources assigned to all activities to develop a baseline project budget and schedule (Hornstein, 2012). Once the plan for the change initiative is complete, the change project team leader presents the plan to the PAC. The PAC then reviews each element of the plan and rechecks all assumptions made and questions asked during the concept/proposal phase meeting. The planning PAC meeting is critical. Beyond this point, the change initiative will require significantly more funding and resources. The overall company at this point will be fully committed to the endeavor. If the plan is approved, the PAC then charters the change team to proceed to the implementation phase. The team is authorized to proceed until the end of the implementation phase and is allocated a given budget, schedule, and deliverables requirements. Should the change team determine that it will go beyond any of the commitments made to the PAC, it is required to request an ad hoc PAC approval session in order to receive either a revised authorization or face possible cancellation (McGrath, 1996).

Change Implementation

The implementation of change is a topic of interest among change management and OD theorists. Change at the level of the organization is never easy and often faces resistance. In OD terms, driving forces exist—some for and some against the proposed change. Prescribed change management methodology places the responsibility for organizational motivation and alignment with the team of executives sponsoring and leading the change (Connor, 2011). Frequent communication framing the change actions for the organization with the aim of providing motivation and garnering support are issued frequently. The *PMBOK Guide*® places responsibility for such leadership communications with the project team. When adopting project management practices in change management, communication begins with "knowing the audience." This is done by identifying all parties that have an interest in the outcome of the change. The parties' interest may be positive from those who support the change, or negative from the perspective of those who are said to resist the change. Communication is thereby tailored to fit all stakeholder groups with the goal of fostering an environment of support and minimizing resistance. Resistance is addressed and managed on an ongoing basis through stakeholder engagement in the form of face-to-face meetings, presentations, and both formal and informal communications. This process is of key interest to the change project because resistance is often cited as one of the most difficult aspects of managing change (Hornstein, 2012).

Resources Required for Change

Central to the success of the change is the actual completion of the tasks associated with the scope of the change initiative. As in the case of work organized as projects, the work of the change initiative is not completed by the project team alone, but by resources loaned to the project team from functional groups. At this point, the organization of change management implemented in the form of a project may deviate from projects that produce deliverables for paying clients (Zou & Lee, 2009). At issue is who will pay for the loaned resources and how functional managers will cope with the loss of resources that are not dedicated to revenue-generating deliverables. Firms that dedicate an annual budget to continuous process improvement and use change life cycle methods are able to solve this problem by providing internal funding as well as an overall database of resources throughout the organization. A role still remains for project leadership to promote the change activity and create a unique identity that creates a draw for key internal resources. OD and change management research highlight the importance of influence within the change management process. This is no different in change management organized and driven by project management and innovation management methodologies. Possible avenues for fostering such an attractive environment for key employee resources include newsletters, an intranet site, open status review meetings, and periodic progress reports. Given that the change initiative is organized as a project, each of these communication methods would normally be outlined in the communications plan as part of a comprehensive communications strategy (Van de Ven & Poole, 1995).

Project Change Management

The understanding of the implementation of organizational change using project management techniques would not be complete without a review of project change management techniques (Zou & Lee, 2009). Unlike permanent organizations, projects are temporary endeavors. However, projects also face change throughout the project life cycle and have structured processes designed to deal with change in the same manner as permanent organizations. Because projects are temporary organizations, the approach to managed change may be informed by theories of temporary organizations. The primary goal of a permanent organization is long-term success and survival. Change is, therefore, something new that is proposed in order to depart from the status quo. Projects, on the other hand, exist to produce deliverables. Change in the project context is directed at project deliverables and the associated budget and schedule associated with such deliverables (Zou & Sang-Hoon Lee, 2008).

OCM and the Baseline

The original plan set by the project is said to be the baseline commitment of the project, and change requests or proposals are evaluated in terms of their impact upon the project baseline. What, then, is the baseline of the permanent organization? It could be said that the baseline is the annual plan and budget commitment presented to the shareholders of the company. Any action that materially deviates from such a plan could be considered a change. On the other hand, as has been observed, an annual budget that sets aside funding for continuous improvement and change initiatives could be said to be a part of the baseline commitment. Regardless of what is in or outside of the scope of the baseline—however it is defined—the importance of project change management lies in how it is used to evaluate proposed change. For example, in the course of evaluating a project change proposal, the project Change Control Board (CCB) asks a number of important questions such as the following (Zou & Sang-Hoon Lee, 2008):

- Does the proposed change involve additional resources or funding?
- Does the change proposed in one functional group or technology impact other groups or technologies?
- What is the overall scope, scale, and expected time line to complete the proposed change?
- How much does the change cost?
- What impact does the proposed change have on the morale of the project team and associated stakeholders?

Ultimately, project change management processes result in a thoughtful approach to change. Changes are not undertaken in an ad hoc manner. Rather, they are carefully evaluated prior to implementation. Further, changes are not implemented without associated plans for doing so. Finally, change management considers the overall culture and macro environment of the extended team and the stakeholders with which the team interacts. In short, the overall physical, resource, cultural, and monetary cost of the change is evaluated prior to the change taking place. The underlying philosophy is, therefore, akin to quality management, with its Plan-Do-Check cycle. The lesson for organizational change management is that in spite of being triggered, change agents would be wise to plan first, then do (Hornstein, 2012).

Launching Change

One of the more common forms of implementing change in an organization in practice is the implementation of an enterprise resource planning (ERP) system. ERP systems consist of hardware and software systems that support the processes of the firm. ERP suppliers work with a number of different firms across multiple industries. Because of this, ERP vendors are able to develop significant insights into the best practices for any given business process. Companies that are triggered to change the way they do business may draw upon the collective wisdom and experience embodied in the embedded processes of an ERP system. Such a change could be viewed as a packaged change because all processes of the business must be altered to fit how they are organized and governed in the ERP system. The cutover to a new ERP system in an ERP implementation project is one method of launching change. However, as in the case of change initiatives that are outside the scope of an ERP implementation, the launch of new processes as a result of change often presents significant management difficulty. Problems arise for many reasons, including the need to train those who will implement the processes and the need to garner acceptance and buy-in from the overall stakeholder community. Further, it is at the launch of change when resistance to the change is often at its highest level (Hornstein, 2012).

The Status Quo and Vested Interests

Those stakeholders with a vested interest in the status quo are said to be more likely to point to problems in the new system and promote the virtues of the legacy system. Stakeholders who have been with the firm for an extended period of time are likely to have significant expertise in the legacy system. Because of this, a change to a new system has the potential to significantly detract from a significant source of power among such stakeholders. Newer employees tend to be more willing to adopt something new in order to develop a source of expertise and demonstrate their contribution and commitment to the company. Also, regardless of the amount of preparation and training prior to the launch of new processes or a new system, the attention paid to the details of the operation of the system is likely to be far stronger after launch than it was before the launch. This is because, in the post-launch environment, employees have little choice but to make the new system work (Weiner, 2009).

Change Management and ERP Implementation

The ERP system implementation is, therefore, an apt analogy for the launch of change in general. In both cases, employees are faced with doing something new or doing the same thing in a new way. Both situations involve new processes and procedures, and perhaps a shift in the power structure of the organization. In each case, resistance to change peaks at launch, and the expected realization of positive results occurs only after an extended period as the new methods become inculcated into the day-to-day routine of the employees. Change agents or project managers leading the ERP implementation who are expecting quick results are likely to be disappointed. Immediately after the launch, productivity and company performance overall tends to decrease rather than increase. In short, things get worse before they get better. It is at this stage of change that visionary leadership is essential. The change agent leading the project team must be aware of what successful change will ultimately look like and promote this vision to the stakeholders of the company. Further, the leader of the effort should likely possess a mental toughness that allows him or her to stay focused and to exhibit the tenacity needed to stay with the change effort until the results are realized (Raineri, 2011).

Failure to Change

Not all change initiatives are successful. In fact, research shows that many, if not most, efforts are not. Researchers point to many possible reasons for failure, and most indicate a lack of strong leadership or executive sponsorship as opposed to the failure to execute against a prescribed process. Success or failure in change management and implementation appears to be strongly linked to context. The actions and adjustments taken by leaders who successfully lead change are often subtle, difficult to recreate in different contexts, and resistant to formulas. It is for this reason that change practice produces both unexpected successes and failures as it navigates the specific contexts in which it is undertaken.

Critique of Change Management Theory

Practitioners and theorists work hand in hand through the evaluation and implementation of best practices in change management. Researchers identify best practices by making note of change methodologies that are observed to work in many cases. Such best practices may then be adopted by change agents who are seeking the same outcomes as those experienced by companies that utilize such practices in other contexts. It has been observed, however, that practice divorced from context may not be universally applicable. Although the principles derived from such research may be informative and may provide possible tools and techniques for the practitioner, evidence suggests that best practices, when utilized, require the application of judgment and may be adjusted as needed in order to enhance the probability of success. The collection of best practices could be viewed as the collection of multiple observations of a phenomenon—in this case, change practice—that produces success. The observations associated with this inductive mode of research could then be used not only to produce suggested practices, but to build a generalized theory or model or change management practice. A model derived from this approach could be tested in deductive research to confirm its merits. However, beyond statistical generalization, the relationship of the context to successful practice suggests that a generalized theory or model that produces change success in all cases is unlikely to be practicable (Brown et al., 2003; Clarke & Garside, 1997; Connor, 2011; Van de Ven & Poole, 1995).

Examples of Change Models

In spite of this observation, a few models do exist in the literature that outline the sequence of steps recommended for change practitioners. Three models of interest include Kotter's strategic model for transforming organizations, Jick's 10 steps for implementing change, and GE's change model (Mento et al., 2002). A comparison of these three models reveals a fundamental similarity among the approaches. The three models could be characterized by the initiation of change, the change itself, and the sustainment of the implemented change. In each model, the leader is identified as the impetus for change. The leader analyzes the need for change and, presumably, is able to interpret perceived triggers for change. The leader also demonstrates commitment to the change and fosters a sense of importance and priority for it. Finally, in each model, the leader is the change agent who is able to influence others so that the stakeholders in the organization are able to view the proposed change in the same manner as that framed by the leader. The Jick 10-step model departs from the Kotter and GE models by making explicit reference to the need to break or separate from the past. Given the short-term difficulty that even successful change initiatives encounter upon launch, the focus on moving beyond the processes, structure, and thought patterns of the past appears uniquely suited to sustaining the results of the change initiative. The separation from the past could, therefore, be viewed in a manner similar to Kotter's consolidation of improvements and GE's focus on making change last. Though Jick and Kotter both appear to view change as emanating from the change agent or leader of the company, both also see the need for a group to drive change rather than just a single individual. Kotter identifies this group as the "coalition," whereas Jick points to the need for political sponsorship. GE presents a similar, yet broader, view by highlighting the importance of a shared vision and need along with the mobilization of commitment. All three methods are, therefore, not inconsistent with change initiated, led, and managed by project teams. The project team drives change while it influences stakeholders using the communication plan of the project. Further, a project-led organization will have a sponsor, or committee of sponsors, authorizing the work of the team. The mobilization of change in a project-led change initiative occurs through the Human Resource Knowledge Area, with its guidance associated with acquiring and managing resources. As previously described, the mobilization of stakeholders is funded by budget allocations for ongoing change initiatives. Finally, each model suggests a means for institutionalizing the idea that the change is warranted. Kotter points to the need to institutionalize change, while Jick describes the need to "reinforce and institutionalize." GE captures a similar idea by identifying the need for changing systems. Presumably, the change of systems in this model could be linked to a change in culture. Therefore, when systems and culture change, the long-term support for acceptance of the change is likely to remain in place, thereby institutionalizing the change. It is of interest to see that this change life cycle pattern roughly follows Lewin's model of "unfreeze-change-freeze" as a means for preparing for change, implementing it, and then institutionalizing it. If Lewin's OD model is viewed as descriptive at a high level as well as metaphorical in nature, it has the potential to be generally informative regarding the overall process of change, while other models, including Kotter, Jick, GE, and project management-led and -governed change, fill in the specific details (Mento et al., 2002).

Understanding the Change Models

What are we to make of these change management models? A comparison of three significant models illustrates that they may be generic enough to be made to fit into a range of contexts (see Table 5-1). Further, it can also be seen that each of the models is not dissimilar from change led by a project team—the differences being primarily in terminology. Although change models follow a life cycle in the same way project management does, initiating and

Table 5-1. Comparison of change models.

Kotter Strategic Model	Jick 10-Step Model	GE Change Model
Urgency	Analyze need for change	Leader behavior
Coalition	Create a shared vision	Create shared need
Create vision	Separate from the past	Shaping a vision
Communicate vision	Create urgency	Mobilizing commitment
Empower others to act	Support a strong leader role	Making change last
Consolidating improvements	Political sponsorship	Monitoring progress
Institutionalizing	Implementation plan	Changing systems
	Enabling structures	
	Communicate and involve	
	Reinforce and institutionalize	

implementing change in organizations is likely to present far more difficulty for project leaders than the production of product-related deliverables. Processes associated with change are less tangible, and deliverables produced for a paying client do not produce the same level of organizational resistance. For this reason, the emphasis on the commitment of the change leader and the focus on communication for the purpose of developing a shared vision necessarily tend to go above and beyond that of typical project management practice (Benchmarking study issued on change management practices, 2000).

Is Change Necessary in Practice?

Do all companies need change? Jim Collins (2001) in *Good to Great* points out that the most successful companies are those that "stick to their knitting" and, as a result, benefit from the flywheel effect that companies are said to enjoy as their business grows in success as they improve their ability over time to serve the customers in their respective markets. In Collins's study, companies that enjoyed sustained returns over and above stock market returns tended to promote CEOs from the ranks of those who had worked for the company throughout their careers. In short, the companies succeeded not because they changed, but because they did *not* change (Collins, 2001). Is change, then, always necessary or even desirable? Some researchers do not see change as inevitable. Further, this is supported by empirical research. This reflects the risk and difficulty of promoting and advancing change at the senior management level. The resistance of the status quo is tangible and the data supporting change success are mixed. Change leads both the company and senior management into uncharted territory of risk and uncertainty. It should not be surprising that many successful companies are observed to ignore apparently obvious triggers for change.

Measuring Change Effectiveness

Companies that do change effectively make an investment in risk and uncertainty with the expectation of reward. But how is the success of the change measured? Obvious measures include improvements to revenue and the rate of the bottom line's growth over time. The overall financial returns would likely be considered confirmation of success if the returns were commensurate with the level of investment in the change as well as the level of risk undertaken. However, such financial improvements may take time to develop. This suggests that intermediate measures in the form of metrics that serve as key performance indicators (KPIs) may need to be adopted in order to track the success of the change initiative. Drucker informs us, "You cannot manage what you cannot measure," and research suggests that the management of change is no different in this respect (Lavinsky, 2013). Metrics can inform management of the progress of change initiatives, but such metrics do not necessarily inform management regarding the degree of effectiveness of the change to the degree that bottom line measures are able to. Also, metrics may not speak to the level of acceptance by the stakeholder population and the overall impact to morale (Raineri, 2011).

The Importance of Change Preparation

Regardless of the model or underlying theoretical framework used to implement change, some firms are more responsive to change than others. One recurring theme in the literature supporting this idea is the importance of readiness for change and the role of the leader in preparing the organization for change. One aspect of preparation is the organizational structure itself (Weiner, 2009). For example, it is said that hierarchical, functional organizations are based on command and control governance and are fundamentally designed to be highly stable. Such structures are common in traditional industries that developed during periods of highly stable markets and low uncertainty. Stability is the antithesis of change, so it is not surprising that a functional, hierarchical, mechanistic, command and control organizational architecture would not easily lend itself to change. On the other hand, the literature does point to the need for different organizational structures in order to better deal with rapidly changing markets and the resulting high level of uncertainty. Organizations that are said to be a better fit with these conditions include team-based organizations such as project organizations as well as organizations that are said to be self-governing, organic, and flat rather than hierarchical. Organizations that are viewed as better prepared for uncertainty may naturally be perceived to be more prepared to change because uncertainty requires constant organizational adjustment (Weiner, 2009).

Organizational Structure and Change Readiness

The implication for change managers is that a possible preparation for change is to first shift a hierarchical organization to one that is more organic in structure or, at minimum, to implement horizontal, organic structures within the organization. A project organization would appear to be an ideal candidate (Hornstein, 2012). Although moving from a purely functional organization to a project team/matrix organization could itself be considered a change initiative, starting small by initially running projects and then building upon the success would appear to be prudent. Further, the establishment of a small project office to promote project management and offer support through the means of training, certification, and tools would likely sustain the transition. Once project management becomes established in an organization, any change initiative will simply be another project—albeit a special category of project. A change initiative introduced without context or existing internal support structure would, therefore, likely meet more resistance than change introduced by means of internal mechanisms that are already established.

Stakeholder Capacity for Change

Structure, however, is not the only element of an organization that must be prepared for change. Readiness for change is also said to be related to the capacity for change among the organization's employees. How do agents of change achieve this state of readiness in employees in practice? Change in organizations produces uncertainty, and uncertainty tends to breed fear. Fear of the unknown is said to be linked to resistance. Because preparation for change involves reducing resistance, one avenue for change agents in reducing resistance is to decrease the fundamental, underlying fear of the unknown within the organization (Mento et al., 2002). Tom Peters is a thought leader in this regard, as an author of a series of books addressing the need to succeed within the context of rapid change, chaos, and continuous disruption. A key theme within these seminal works is that chaos and disruption are facts of life in the Information Age in which we live, and that managers should accept the reality of the situation while seeking ways to leverage disruption and make it work for them. Another key factor driving disruption and the need for organizational change in order to thrive is the fact that firms operate within a highly technology-centric world (Peters & Waterman, 2012).

Change and Technology Disruption

Technology disruption is said to be a phenomenon that all firms continually face. Christensen of the Harvard Business School has long promoted the theory of technology trajectories and the disruption in markets that tends to result (Christensen, Raynor, & McDonald, 2015). A classic example of disruption associated with the trajectory of technology is the comparison of sailing ship and steamship technologies. Sailing ships were increasingly optimized so that they made the Atlantic crossing faster and faster. Steamships initially were not able to match the longstanding success of sailing ships, but firms that did not shift to the new technology were eventually overtaken when steam technology eventually surpassed the capability of sails. This example illustrates how the reluctance to change may bring on more risk to a company than the acceptance of change. The Atlantic sailing ship transport business is long dead—and so is steamship transportation. However, companies that continually sought to leverage improvements in technology into their products and organizations ultimately survived. Therefore, although change and uncertainty are often feared, accepting them may be less risky in the long run than the failure to change (Clayton Christiansen Institute, 2012).

Summary

A review of change management theory drawn from OD, OCM, and long-standing practice provides evidence that all tend to converge in their perspective of life cycle. They all see the need to prepare the organization in some way, to lead the change initiative in an influential way, and to take steps to ensure that the implemented change remains in place long after the change initiative is complete. Although the way each phase of the life cycle is implemented may differ significantly within any particular organization given the differing contexts of change, the overall high-level steps provided for in change management models appear generic enough to be modified so that they may be of use within unique contexts. Change is the result of triggers—some of which are tangible and present, and some of which are by no means obvious. In practice, some companies are observed to succeed because they did change, whereas other research, such as that pioneered by Collins (2001), suggests that some companies succeed precisely because they do not change. Context, therefore, is an essential consideration for change management practice. It is because of context that an ongoing process improvement effort managed using governing processes drawn from innovation management is observed to be a potentially effective means for setting the stage for change as well as managing it. Such methods rely on project teams reporting to a committee of sponsors who are actively involved in the organization and have high visibility of current and future needs for change. Change initiatives are, therefore, rolled out to the organization in a manner similar to other project work within the organization, thereby reducing uncertainty and fear-related employee resistance. Given the relentless disruption associated with the fast pace of markets and technological change, an ongoing change system would appear to provide a more rapid and ongoing response, along with less need for organizational preparation for change.

References

Balogun, J. (2007). The practice of organizational restructuring: From design to reality. *European Management Journal, 25*(2), 81–91.

Benchmarking study issued on change management practices. (2000). *Quality Progress, 33*(10), 24. Retrieved from http://search.proquest.com.ezproxy.libproxy.db.erau.edu/docview/214772600?accountid=27203

Brown, K., Waterhouse, J., & Flynn, C. (2003). Change management practices. *International Journal of Public Sector Management, 16*(3), 230–241.

Buller, P. F. (1988). For successful strategic change: Blend OD practices with strategic management. *Organizational Dynamics, 16*(3), 42–55.

Christiensen, C., Raynor, M., & McDonald, R. (2015, December). What is disruptive innovation? *Harvard Business Review.* Retrieved from https://hbr.org/2015/12/what-is-disruptive-innovation.

Clarke, A., & Garside, J. (1997). The development of a best practice model for change management. *European Management Journal, 15*(5), 537–545.

Clayton Christiansen Institute. (2012). *Disruptive innovation.* Retrieved from http://www.christenseninstitute.org/key-concepts/disruptive-innovation-2/?gclid=CjwKEAiAhIejBRCKm_fTxIWyyXcSJABXY0XYrg9GRhVkq0rF-8w6yS8Z8AezED_lxYp1lKjwcnhaWyBoCY7Pw_wcB

Collins, J. (2001). *Good to great.* New York, NY: HarperCollins.

Connor, R. (2011). Changing change management. *Strategic HR Review, 10*(5), 35–36. Retrieved from http://search.proquest.com.ezproxy.libproxy.db.erau.edu/docview/894860616?accountid=27203

Das, K. N., Nair, U., & Baker, L. (2012, January 19). Timeline: The Kodak moment fades. *Reuters.* Retrieved from http://www.reuters.com/article/2012/01/19/us-kodak-timeline-idUSTRE80I1XN20120119

DiCarlo, L. (2002, November 11). How Lou Gerstner got IBM to dance. *Forbes.* Retrieved from http://www.forbes.com/2002/11/11/cx_ld_1112gerstner.html

Harwood, S. A. (2012). The management of change and the Viplan methodology in practice. *The Journal of the Operational Research Society, 63*(6), 748–761.

Hornstein, H. (2012). The need to integrate project management and organizational change. *Ivey Business Journal Online.* Retrieved from http://search.proquest.com.ezproxy.libproxy.db.erau.edu/docview/1038945133?accountid=27203

Jansson, N. (2013). Organizational change as practice: A critical analysis. *Journal of Organizational Change Management, 26*(6), 1003–1019.

Lavinsky, D. (2013, June 25). The two most important quotes in business. *Growthink.* Retrieved from http://www.growthink.com/content/two-most-important-quotes-business

Lewin, K. (1947, June). Frontiers in group dynamics: Concept, method and reality in social science; social equilibria and social change. *Human Relations, 1,* 5–41.

Manuele, F. A. (2012). Management of change: Examples from practice. *Professional Safety, 57*(7), 35–43. Retrieved from http://search.proquest.com.ezproxy.libproxy.db.erau.edu/docview/1118446644?accountid=27203

McGrath, M. (1996). *Setting the PACE in product development a guide to product and cycle-time excellence.* Boston, MA: Butterworth-Heinemann.

McIntyre, D. A. (2013). Howard Stringer, who ruined Sony, retires. *24/7 Wall St.* Retrieved from http://247wallst.com/investing/2013/03/11/howard-stringer-who-ruined-sony-retires/

Mento, A. J., Jones, R. M., & Dirndorfer, W. (2002). A change management process: Grounded in both theory and practice. *Journal of Change Management, 3*(1), 45. Retrieved from http://search.ebscohost.com/login.aspx?direct=true&db=bth&AN=7329277&site=ehost-live

Miles, M. B., & Huberman, A. M. (1994). *Qualitative data analysis: An expanded sourcebook.* Thousand Oaks, CA: Sage Publications.

Peters, T., & Waterman, R. (2012). *In search of excellence: Lessons from America's best run companies.* New York, NY: HarperCollins.

Project Management Institute (PMI). (2013a). *Managing change in organizations: A practice guide.* Newtown Square, PA: Author.

Project Management Institute (PMI). (2013b). *A guide to the project management body of knowledge (PMBOK® guide)* – Fifth edition. Newtown Square, PA: Author.

Raineri, A. B. (2011). Change management practices: Impact on perceived change results. *Journal of Business Research, 64*(3), 266–272.

Singh, H., & Singh, A. (2002). Principles of complexity and chaos theory in project execution: A new approach to management. *Cost Engineering, 44*(12), 23–32. Retrieved from http://search.proquest.com.ezproxy.libproxy.db.erau.edu/docview/220447111?accountid=27203

Sturdy, A., & Grey, C. (2003). Beneath and beyond organizational change management: Exploring alternatives. *Organization, 10*(4), 651–662. Retrieved from http://search.proquest.com.ezproxy.libproxy.db.erau.edu/docview/218617574?accountid=27203

Sullivan, R. L., Rothwell, W. J., & Balasi, J. B. (2013). Organization development (OD) and change management (CM): Whole system transformation. *Development and Learning in Organizations, 27*(6), 18–23.

Tan, C. C. (2006). The theory and practice of change management. *Asian Business & Management, 5*(1), 153–155.

Tierney, C., & Gerber, C. (2005, February 27). Nissan CEO: The making of a superstar. *TITANtalk.com.* Retrieved from http://www.titantalk.com/forums/nissan-titan-news/21966-nissan-ceo-making-superstar.html

Van de Ven, A. H., & Poole, M. S. (1995). Explaining development and change in organizations. *The Academy of Management Review, 20*(3), 510. Retrieved from http://search.proquest.com.ezproxy.libproxy.db.erau.edu/docview/210967560?accountid=27203

Weiner, B. (2009). A theory of organizational readiness for change. *Implementation Science, 4*(1), 67. Retrieved from http://www.implementation-science.com/content/4/1/67

Zou, Y., & Lee, S. (2008). The impacts of change management practices on project change cost performance. *Construction Management & Economics, 26*(4), 387–393.

Zou, Y., & Lee, S. (2009). Implementation of project change management best practice in different project environments. *Canadian Journal of Civil Engineering, 36*(3), 439–448.

Review Questions

1. What is a change trigger? Identify a trigger for organizational change and describe a best practice for responding to the trigger.

2. Describe the importance of framing the problem as it relates to organizational diagnosis and data collection.

3. Define *triangulation* as it applies to root cause analysis in change management. Explain how it relates to the concept of "the wisdom of crowds."

4. Compare and contrast the concept of "context" in change management versus "initial conditions" in chaos theory. Discuss the validity of this analogy.

5. Identify reasons (if any) why companies might seek to initiate change in the absence of obvious triggers.

CHAPTER 6

Applying Agile Techniques to Change Management Projects

By Bob Tarne, CSM, PMI-ACP, PMP

Abstract

Agile project management techniques continue to gain more widespread acceptance. Once used primarily for software projects, these techniques are now being applied to many other areas. This chapter looks at how agile techniques can apply to change management projects.

Change management is a comprehensive, cyclic, and structured approach for transitioning individuals, groups, and organizations from a current state to a future state with intended business benefits, as discussed in *Managing Change in Organizations: A Practice Guide* (PMI, 2013).

Agile project techniques use short iterations, where more detailed planning occurs at the start of the iteration and not at the beginning of the project itself. There are other aspects as well, including an emphasis on open, honest communication; respect for the team members; and, most important, responding to change rather than trying to follow a plan that may no longer move the team in the right direction.

What Is Agile?

Agile project management has evolved from a number of areas, including lean manufacturing and the software industry, primarily in the 1980s and 1990s. The *Manifesto for Agile Software Development* (Beck et al., 2001) is often cited as the basis for how agile is approached. The Agile Manifesto, as it is commonly called, is a formal proclamation of key values and principles that promotes an iterative, people-centric approach to software development. The four key values are found at agilemanifesto.org:

- Individuals and interactions over processes and tools;
- Working software over comprehensive documentation;
- Customer collaboration over contract negotiation; and
- Responding to change over following a plan.

As shown in Figure 6-1, responding to change is one of the basic principles of agile. In order to understand how change management is approached in an agile project, which is a general understanding of agile is required. Figure 6-1 illustrates the key points of agile.

Like any project, an agile project begins with a vision of the desired outcome of the project. This vision guides the team as it starts to create the product backlog, which is a list of features that may be included in the project. These features may be expressed as user stories or simple statements describing a capability. When developing the product backlog, it is important to keep the items at a high level. This approach applies to any project using agile principles, whether it is the implementation of a new website or a complex software product with a challenging delivery date.

A user story is a one-sentence description of a feature from an end user's standpoint. For example, if the project is to create a website for selling T-shirts, user stories might include "As a customer, I want to be able to search for T-shirts by size" or "As a project manager, I want a list of key stakeholders so I can develop a communications matrix." Although the user story may seem like a requirement, it is really just the representation of the requirements, which is a key distinction when it comes to change management.

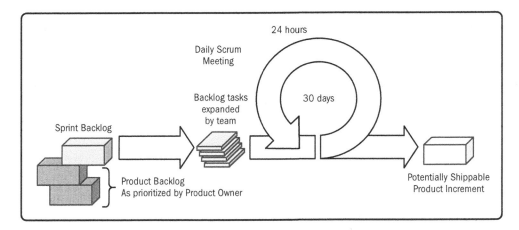

Figure 6-1. A simple view of agile.
Adapted from Schwaber & Beedle, 2002.

The user story is meant as a placeholder, a reminder about some work that may need to be done later. As an example, let's take the user story mentioned previously: the project manager developing a communications matrix. This user story would be reviewed later in the project and, after discussing it, the team may decide that a communications matrix is not necessary. In this case, the list of stakeholders is also not necessary; therefore, the user story would be discarded. This could be the case for a small project where a communications matrix may be additional documentation that doesn't provide additional value.

Using an initiate/plan/execute/close model, the product backlog may not be complete at the start of the "execute" phase of the project, but that is common. As any project progresses, the team thinks of other things it wants to include in the scope. However, during planning, the team will capture enough user stories to start the work, which means planning for the first iteration. The first step in planning is to prioritize the product backlog; the most important features should be at the top of the list. This activity is often called grooming the backlog.

One important role is that of the product owner. This is the person responsible for what is in the backlog. The product owner prioritizes the list of features and may even decide whether a feature is in or out. This role should be filled from the business side, by someone who understands the business reasons for the project and defines the vision that guides the project team.

The second step is to develop a high-level effort estimate for each item in the backlog. At this point, the goal is not to develop a budget—it is simply to capture information that will be used for iteration planning. More detailed estimates will come later. The team members perform this task. Each item is evaluated in comparison to the rest of the backlog in order to assign an estimate. It is less important for the team members to come up with an exact estimate of how long each user story will take than it is for them to gain an understanding of how complex each story is in relation to the other stories. For this reason, the estimate may be made in story points rather than in hours or days.

A story point can be thought of as an imprecise quantity (for now). By using relative estimates rather than absolute estimates, the team will be more accurate in the long run. As part of the story point technique, the points are assigned on a Fibonacci sequence, where each new number in the sequence is the sum of the previous two numbers (1, 2, 3, 5, 8, and so on). This sequence can be seen in naturally occurring objects such as the branching pattern of a tree.

The Fibonacci sequence facilitates the process and may be used, for example, when the team is estimating a story. Without the Fibonacci sequence, the team may get distracted by trying to decide whether a story is an 8 or a 9, which in reality, is about the same thing when compared to a 5. The Fibonacci scale keeps the team from trying to be too precise.

Now that the team has assigned story points to each story, the team looks at the highest-priority work and estimates how many stories can be completed during the first iteration. The product owner is important to this discussion; he or she provides the priority. The team may have a situation where the next story on the list is too large to include in the current iteration, but a smaller story further down the list could be included. The product owner is the one to make this decision, not the team members. Once the stories for the iteration are selected, the team plans out those specific stories in more detail and can begin development.

This is when the real requirements for each story are captured. The team works closely with the users to understand the story. The team may create a design or just begin the development, but only for one story at a time. When the team members are done, they review the work with the user, and when the user is satisfied, the story is considered closed.

To aid in the final step, the user may write acceptance criteria after the user story is written but before development starts. This can be thought of as a checklist that will be used to accept the story at the end. The acceptance criteria are the "what" the user wants, but not the "how." The "how" is the design, which is up to the developer. So, a properly worded acceptance criterion could be "I want to be able to submit the request for approval."

The developer and user will review the completed work, using the acceptance criteria as a guide. When all the acceptance criteria have been fulfilled, the story is considered completed. In some cases, the user may ask for additional work, which could be something as simple as changing the location of a button or other, more complex changes. The developer and user must agree whether this is an easy enough change to complete within the iteration or whether it is a new requirement that requires a new user story. If they cannot agree, then the product owner and project manager are brought into the discussion.

At the end of the iteration, the team reviews all the completed work. The team members may have selected five stories to complete and only finished four, or may have found they had extra time and placed a sixth story into the iteration. This is where story points come into play. The team looks at how many story points were completed in the iteration. This becomes the velocity; now the team members have an idea as to how many points they can complete in each subsequent iteration. At this point, the team can come up with a ratio between story points and actual hours; however, this is not required. The project manager will determine what the ratio is, because it may be required for budgeting.

With the velocity established, the team, led by the project manager and product owner, develops a more detailed schedule for the remainder of the project. The team may be on a fixed calendar and may need to complete the project before a certain date. Going back to the example of the T-shirt website, the deadline for the website completion may be prior to 30 November.

The product owner is responsible for setting this date and it would only be changed under extenuating circumstances.

With the end date, the velocity, and the list of estimated/prioritized stories in place, the team can plan out the rest of the work by assigning stories into iterations until the velocity is full for each iteration; then the team can begin to complete the work. The product owner continues to update the backlog, adding new stories when required, prioritizing the stories, and removing stories that may no longer be required.

Because stories can be added to the backlog throughout the project, the question arises as to what happens if all the work cannot be completed. The product owner is faced with two options: either stick with the original date and not complete all the work or push the date out to incorporate additional work. Many factors can influence this decision, such as getting a product to market ahead of the competition, ensuring that key features are in the product, or meeting external deadlines that may be imposed by the market or even government regulations. For example, teams working on Y2K projects in 1999 did not have any flexibility in the date; however, a team working on the next version of an existing product may decide to take the extra time for a key feature in order to create a better product.

This approach is good for an organizational change project because it allows the product owner (the person driving the change) to effectively organize the work that needs to be accomplished via the backlog. The product owner is able to assemble a list of the work that needs to be completed through detailed planning. The product owner has the flexibility to respond and update the backlog as changes are being implemented when priorities change based on new information.

For example, the first iteration of work may include a change readiness assessment. The outcome of that assessment may indicate that the organization is not as ready to change as originally thought. This could result in a new backlog item being added for the next iteration to create a list of "champions" to help with the change effort.

Changes in Agile Projects

Now that the components of an iterative agile project have been described, we need to address how agile accommodates changes. As discussed at the beginning of the chapter, an agile project should embrace change. The authors of the *Manifesto for Agile Software Development* knew that changes happen all the time. People do not always know what they want at the beginning of a project. As the project progresses, when they see what is being built, they have a better idea of what it is they really want.

Let's return to the backlog. This is where changes can be managed. There is a nice list of features. We have estimated all features and planned which iteration each feature will be developed in. Then someone comes up with a new idea, and it is a really good one. In a project being managed with more traditional tools, the response may be "Sorry, we've already written the requirements—that will have to wait until Phase 2."

This is not the case with agile. In an agile project, the product owner steps in again. As mentioned earlier, the product owner decides what is in the backlog. When a new feature is identified (and anyone can write a new user story), the product owner will decide if it belongs in the backlog. The development team estimates the feature, which may help the product owner's decision. A great idea that does not take much effort is easier to consider than a great idea that takes a lot of effort.

If the product owner decides that the new feature is valuable, the next decision is to determine how valuable it is. The product owner decides where to place the new feature in the backlog, and everything below that on the backlog moves down in priority. This results in some feature at the bottom of the project's backlog getting pushed out and no longer being included in the project.

Keep in mind that at the beginning of the project, the focus is not on capturing all the detailed requirements. The details are not captured until the particular user story or feature has been selected for an iteration and development begins. There has not been a lot of time spent on the details; therefore, when one story is pushed out and another story is pulled in, the impact is small. This effective technique is referred to as deferring detail.

There are times, however, when more structure may be in order. One example would be when there is a large pool of stakeholders. There may be one product owner who represents multiple business areas. A more formal approach will ensure that all stakeholders are aware and approve of a proposed change.

Kanban

Now that we have looked at an iterative approach to agile, we will briefly look at another agile technique—Kanban. Kanban does not use iterations. Work flows in a continuous method. As one task is finished, the next task is pulled from the top of the prioritized backlog.

Kanban does not use many formal practices—just some principles. One key principle is to limit the work in progress (WIP); in other words, do not try to do too much at once. The idea is that by focusing on one thing at a time, you are more effective in getting it done. However, as we will see later, Kanban also plays an important role at the program and portfolio levels.

When following Kanban, you should limit how many tasks you are working on at one time—your WIP. In part, this is associated with change management. For example, imagine you are working on 10 different features at once. You are not making much progress on any one of them because you keep switching back and forth from one feature to the next and then to the next. Your product owner then requests a change to one of those features. The time you spent on that feature has been wasted. Had you focused on one feature at a time, when the request for change came along, it would most likely be on a feature you had not yet started—so there would be no time lost on rework.

Case Study

A major U.S. bank was implementing a new business process around how a specific type of account was opened. The existing process was not followed in a consistent manner, key documents were not filed on time, and other errors impacted customer satisfaction.

The new process also involved new software, which created a barrier to the change. The team implementing the new process had to be able to get past this barrier in order for the new process to be accepted and, therefore, be considered successful.

A team of external consultants was brought in to handle the software development process. This team also brought in an agile methodology, which it knew could help overcome the resistance to change.

At the beginning of the project, the team met with the key stakeholders at the bank and explained how the agile approach would work. The consultants were not surprised that there would be resistance to change, and now they had an answer.

The project was planned around four-week iterations. At the end of each of these iterations, a demonstration of the completed work was planned. The team, however, took this one step further. Rather than having the team members run the demonstration, they identified one of the business experts to play this role. This business expert had worked with the other users, understood their job, and more importantly, knew why people were resisting the new process.

The approach was very effective. The end users did not see the new process as something a vendor had built and management was forcing them to use. In each demonstration, they saw one of their colleagues using the new application, talking with them about how this would help their problems and make their work easier.

When it came time to pilot the application, people were eager to jump in. The new process was quickly adopted and became a stepping-stone for other process improvements.

Agile in Change Management Projects

Now that we have gained an understanding of the basics of agile, let us look at how this approach can be applied to our change management project.

As mentioned previously, one of the initial steps is to create a product backlog. Let us start with a few user stories that we might see on a change management project:

- The project team wants a change management vision statement to provide direction during the project.
- The project sponsor wants to have a change readiness audit conducted so that he or she can understand how large the barriers to change may be.
- The project manager needs a stakeholder analysis so that he or she can effectively reach out to all stakeholders of the project.
- The project team wants a change management work plan to understand the time lines and deliverables of the project.

Regardless of whether we are following agile or a more traditional approach, we have the same objective and the same deliverables. What changes is how we approach those deliverables.

Once the user stories are captured, the next step is grooming the backlog. The product owner may see some dependencies when looking over the stories. For example, the vision statement is important to have in place from the beginning of the project. Based on that, the product owner puts the vision statement on the top of the backlog. Likewise, it would be good to have the stakeholder analysis done before the change readiness audit, so that the audit gets to all the key stakeholders.

The product owner continues to review the user stories in this fashion, identifying both dependencies and high-priority items to move to the top of the list.

The question the product owner needs to answer is whether to use an iterative/agile approach as described at the beginning of the chapter or the Kanban approach described later in the chapter. Because the items in the backlog will vary in the effort they require, it may be difficult to squeeze them into fixed-length iterations. For this reason, Kanban may be a more effective approach.

Agility at the Program and Portfolio Levels

Now that we have discussed how agile can be applied at the project level, both from a general perspective and as a technique in change management projects, let's look at how agile techniques can be applied at the program and portfolio levels to facilitate an agile organization. This topic is important when an organization is implementing a strategic change, which may first start out at the portfolio level before the change is implemented at the program and portfolio levels.

In *Managing Change in Organizations: A Practice Guide* (PMI, 2013, p.8), strategic agility is defined as "the capability of a business to proactively seize and take advantage of business environment changes while demonstrating resilience resulting from unforeseen changes." Being able to execute projects following agile principles is not enough. It is also important to have a framework at the program and portfolio level that allows for agility.

There are several models for scaling agile to the program and portfolio levels. One model is the Scaled Agile Framework (SAFe®). The developer of SAFe®, Dean Leffingwell (n.d.), describes it as "an interactive knowledge base for implanting agile practices as enterprise scale."

It is at the portfolio level where the differences between traditional portfolio management and the SAFe® model can be seen. The SAFe® model calls for lightweight business cases rather than detailed plans. The agile estimating techniques described earlier in this chapter are used in lieu of more detailed work breakdown structures. This allows for decentralized decision making, such as deciding which features from the backlog will be included in the next iteration. However, at the portfolio level, a vision guides how these decisions are made.

One important element of the SAFe® model at the portfolio level is a portfolio backlog being managed using Kanban. At the portfolio level, the backlog is composed of epics. Leffingwell (n.d.) describes epics as "large-scale development initiatives that realize value of investment themes." Each epic will have a set of features (described below) at the program level and user stories at the project level, at which the project team works.

The principle of limiting work in progress that comes from Kanban is very important at the portfolio level as well. When organizations do too many projects at once, it causes all the projects to be completed later than would be the case if only a limited number of projects was undertaken.

Example

Imagine that you work in a shipyard unloading ships. You have five ships come in on Monday morning. Each takes five person-days to unload and you have five dock workers. Here is how the work could be accomplished:

- An organization not limiting WIP would work on all five ships at once. With this approach, everything gets done on Friday.
- But what if you took the limited WIP approach and had everyone work on one ship? That ship would get done on Monday. Everyone would then work on the second ship (project) and get that done on Tuesday, and so on until all five ships were finished.
- By taking the second approach, you would deliver some value early and continue delivering value throughout the week. If the ships were full of cars, you would be able to start selling cars on Monday, instead of Friday if you used the other approach (Tarne, 2014).

It is important for there to be alignment between the teams working on user stories and the program and portfolio levels.

At the program level, the view is toward features, which can be thought of as a group of user stories that together deliver a coherent set of capabilities. For example, at the user story level, there may be stories related to a specific user interface. Take the following examples:

- As a job seeker, I want to be able to search for a job by location.
- As a job seeker, I want to be able to search for a job by pay range.
- As a job seeker, I want to be able to search for a job by title.

These user stories could all be part of a feature called "job search." At the program level, features are prioritized and scheduled within releases. At the project level, the user stories that make up the feature are prioritized and scheduled within specific iterations.

The implication here is that at the program level, an agile approach must be used to maintain the prioritized list of features. This backlog is not just created once and finalized. Each release is an opportunity to review and update the program backlog.

How is organizational change handled at the program level? If the program backlog is updated frequently, the implication is that the stakeholders are kept aware of these changes.

At the program and portfolio levels, the responsibilities are the same whether or not an organization uses agile techniques. The key duties include aligning projects and programs to strategy, funding, program management, and governance.

However, the techniques used to implement these responsibilities differ in a lean/agile environment. Control and decision making are decentralized. Budgeting is performed through a more agile and lightweight approach. Planning is done following a rolling-wave approach.

So, where do epics and features fall when performing an organizational change management initiative? A change initiative would have to be very significant to reach the portfolio level. This would be a major strategic change that impacts the entire company.

The first step for an initiative like this would be to define the vision. This would set the stage to define epics, which may be major changes that impact departments. For example, if a large software company was changing the way it delivered products, each product line would have an epic describing the work that had to be done to align to the new vision, where each product line aligned to its own department.

At the program level, the epic would break into features that described the work being done in the department. One department may have a program to replace hardware components, while another department may need to realign and close office space. The change management aspect becomes more apparent at this level. Though there are tasks associated with closing an office, there will also be change management tasks.

Finally, at the project level, the features are broken down into user stories that describe the specific work being done, which includes specific change management tasks such as sending out a communication to the department or holding a "town hall" to discuss the changes.

Summary

This chapter covered the following aspects of an agile approach:

- Agile approaches projects in short iterations without heavy analysis and upfront planning.
- Planning in short iterations facilitates changes in requirements.
- Agile techniques can also be used on projects that involve organizational changes.
- Agile approaches can also be used at the program and portfolio levels.

References

Beck, K., et al. (2001). *Manifesto for agile project management.* Retrieved from www.agilemanifesto.org

Leffingwell, D. (n.d.). *Scaled agile framework.* Retrieved from http://scaledAgileframework.com

Project Management Institute (PMI). (2013). *Managing change in organizations: A practice guide.* Newtown Square, PA: Author.

Schwaber, K., & Beedle, M. (2002.) *Agile software development with scrum.* Landisville, PA: Pearson.

Tarne, R. J. (2014). *Principles of agile, part 1.* Retrieved from http://zen-pm .blogspot.com/2014/05/principles-of-agile-part-1.html

Review Questions

1. Why can agile be more accommodating of changes in a project than a more traditional approach?
2. How does the product owner manage changes to the project?
3. How can agile be used in an organizational change project?
4. Does agile work at the program and portfolio levels?
5. Can agile and traditional approaches be combined on a program?

CHAPTER **7**

The Role of Organizational Culture in Successful Change

By Robert Gordon, DM

Introduction

Culture has often mystified organizational leadership, for unlike all the other planned aspects of an organization, culture can develop spontaneously and without direction by management (PMI, 2013a). Unlike an organizational chart defined by leadership and implemented by all involved, culture becomes a wild-card element in an organization. Culture transcends the employee handbook and, in most organizations, offers clearer guidance than any manual. Furthermore, during times of change, culture becomes something that will aid or debilitate the organization. To this end, the leadership of any organization must seek to understand all aspects of the culture to shape it in the direction of the change. Success is achieved only when the culture embodies the change. Excluding culture courts disaster for organizational change. The equation of organizational change needs to include culture because, without it, the likelihood that a change will remain permanent is low.

Given this introduction to change, leaders need a directional map that will guide them to successful change by leveraging organizational culture. A successful plan involves taking the following actions (see Figure 7-1):

- Understand the culture of the organization.
- Build the foundation for successful organizational change.
- Launch the change with organizational culture.

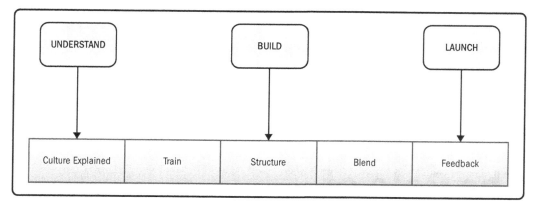

Figure 7-1.   Understand-Build-Launch model of successful organizational change.

A successful change includes all three of these elements. First-order change is often described as incremental change. Second-order change is when the organization changes and adapts, while third-order change happens when the organization uses a system to implement change. In practice, third-order change comes from the successful change that moves the culture to a new and often better place (PMI, 2013a). When these elements are not employed, the organization will fall short of a successful change, which will lead to a first-order or, possibly, a second-order change. Second-order change could motivate some and have some impact, but eventually something will supersede it. Other organizational priorities will arise, and the temporary change will disappear. Also, falling short in any of these areas will lead to only a temporary first- or second-order change (PMI, 2013a).

Understanding Culture

To harness organizational culture, it is important to understand what culture is (see Appendix). Schein (1992) defines *culture* as "a pattern of shared basic assumptions that the group learned as it solved its problems of external adaptation and internal integration that has worked well enough to be considered valid and, therefore, to be taught to new members as the correct way to perceive, think, and feel in relation to those problems" (p. 12). This has been the traditional definition found in business manuals; however, this definition has begun to shift with changes in how people interact today. Given the year Schein defined culture, one can see that his definition had not yet seen the information revolution that came with new technologies and the internet.

No doubt, Schein's definition fit the time; however, his definition only explains the importance of shared assumptions by a group. Schein falls short of offering more details about the experiential nature of culture. Although Schein (2004) updated his ideas on organizational culture, he still maintained his basic definition. Clearly, the definition helps organizations understand the basic premise of culture; however, there needs to be more to this definition to apply it correctly to organizational change. In this regard, going beyond this definition of culture, one important way to perceive organizational culture is to view culture as a fabric.

The Fabric of Culture Defined

Looking at culture as a fabric of experiences allows one to consider how each thread helps make up the organizational culture as a whole. Each simple thread is woven together in a manner that allows the fabric to become more than the individual threads alone. A fabric is a discrete item that people understand to be the combination of different threads; however, each thread is important to the overall fabric. When too many threads are damaged, the fabric begins to unravel. When enough unraveling occurs, the fabric will cease to exist.

If one were to view each thread as a simple binary thought, one could see how these binary thoughts can be brought together to create a culture. Culture exists as simple concepts brought together and held by the group. Cultural constructs could be as basic as the concept that people need to show up to meetings on time. Managers may fear that missing a deadline could result in reassignment to a less desirable project.

Organizational Culture

With culture explained, one must understand the role of the manager concerning change. Management's complex role in organizing human capital on behalf of the organization is essential for the management of change. Handling several roles challenges management, and this becomes even more difficult when coupled with the needs of the organization. Managers must be adaptable to go from being organizational visionaries to being politically perceptive in the organization (Verzuh, 2011). These critical adaptations to the culture are necessary for leaders. The needs of the organization often drive the need to change. The manager struggles with the undefined expectations of change. Vague directives provide less detailed information to managers regarding the procedures to use for various tasks. This rift causes managers to try to determine the best interests of the organization. This does not always work out in the best interest of the organization, as managers may interpret these directives differently.

Humans create cultural systems because humans seek context for their existence. People desire a culture to give organizational life a sense of order. Groups need barriers of differentiation to feel apart from others. Groups desire differentiation from others in the group as well as from other individuals.

Therefore, managers must understand the foundation of culture and the desire of people to differentiate themselves from one another. Managers of programs and projects need to implement change as part of their organization's unique methodology (PMI, 2013a). Without differentiation, there is no feeling of connection to others in the group. However, three specific factors create culture:

- Morale;
- Investment; and
- Indoctrination.

Morale is the lifeblood of any organization. Maintaining the morale of an organization should be a top priority for the leadership of the organization. Trying to overcome morale issues and change issues becomes a consuming task. Morale will rise and fall with the degree of change. Part of morale is communication, because communication explains current happenings. Good communication tools and events will improve cultural awareness and will allow people to correct any misunderstandings. Poor communication will weaken the culture and reduce organizational morale. In many ways, leadership creates the morale of the organization. Organizational leadership should create an environment that is supportive and conducive toward change (PMI, 2013a).

Investment is where the organization expends resources to improve its employees. A successful organization must invest in training, mentoring programs, recognition programs, and awards to show people they are valued. The culture must support the investment and show that the expenditures are available to everyone in need. The organization must show that it is willing to spend money on training people. This training must be applicable and useful to make the workforce as valued and as educated as possible.

Indoctrination is the term for the knowledge transfer of the organization's culture. In many ways, it is part of training and mentoring; however, indoctrination requires a greater immersion into the culture. The culture must require compliance of those who are part of the culture. Indoctrination reinforces the culture in the minds of individuals.

Figure 7-2 offers a graphical understanding of how these three elements interact with one another. One can see how the three elements connect to the organizational culture. Organizational culture is at the heart of change, because only when one can move the culture can one create the momentum for third-order change (PMI, 2013a).

Excellent organizational leaders understand that they can bring about change. Research has shown that transformational leaders are successful change agents. In this regard, anyone interested in managing change should move to become more of a transformational leader. Effective transformational

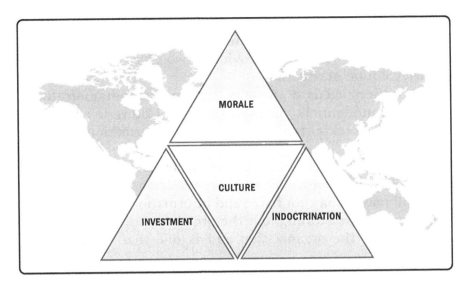

Figure 7-2. Cultural pyramid.

leaders need to have their own personal leadership philosophy. This philosophy should articulate values that support the goals of the organization. A continuously communicated individual leadership philosophy supports the organizational vision. A leader must understand the cultural implications of the business. Leaders must learn to stand out in a crowd by understanding the business culture while supporting the organization's business goals and objectives. Also, leaders have to seek new ideas and education to help improve themselves and their organization.

Limitations of Culture

In many organizations, there is only so much of the culture that the manager will be able to control. When the culture is positive, it may be easier to allow the culture to define the style of the manager; however, there are some weaknesses with this approach. In some cases, the manager will need to cope with the culture to survive within the organization. This does not mean that the only path is to cope with the change, but it is one way to get better results from the people in the organization. A manager must also accept that any group can become dysfunctional. Dysfunctional organizations are less efficient and less organized and are usually not a great place to work.

A common thread across dysfunctional organizations is a lack of rituals. An example of a ritual would be the annual company holiday party, which allows people to gather together in a festive setting. Without rituals, there is no sense of community to bind the employees together. Sometimes, management needs to drive these rituals, because they do not always happen spontaneously. In some cases, management can help create a mechanism to install new rituals. The desired method for change-minded organizations would be to create a mechanism providing two types of communication to support the evolution of rituals.

An organization needs a two-way system for communications while preserving the confidentiality of the employee. Failure to achieve this will lead employees to seek alternative sources of information. Solid two-way communications assist management in controlling the rumor mill. When employees do not believe that management is being honest, they will turn to the rumor mill as their source of "real" organizational information. Though the rumor mill may or may not have valid information, fear, uncertainty, and doubt will run rampant throughout the organization. This situation would be detrimental for the organization and is one that management needs to avoid.

Another method to foster improved communication is the use of symbols and stories. A common organizational symbol is the company logo, and if the logo apparel is popular in the company it shows that people have an affiliation for the organization. Furthermore, the retelling of great actions done by company members can help explain expectations to others, while highlighting great results in a project. These can be an important tool in internal communication, especially in projecting the organization's long-term vision. Often, an image or symbol communicates a concept quite effectively and quickly. This symbol can then become a rallying point, which will help instill a sense of pride in the company. Symbols and images become powerful tools when combined with organizational training materials to identify with these core organizational values.

Building the Foundation for Successful Organizational Change

To build permanent change, an organization needs to invest in four critical areas: training, structure, leadership, and project management. Each of these areas requires specific instructions and will be discussed below. However, organizations must realize that all these elements are required for successful change. The lack of any one element will lead to temporary change that does not improve the organization in the long term.

Training for Change

Whenever one anticipates rapid change, there is a great need for training. Training becomes necessary to address the knowledge gaps that come with change. Insufficient training yields workers who are dejected and who perpetuate mistakes and the poor habits of the past. Restricting training because it is ineffective leads to a downward spiral of skills within the organization. Leaders need to make sure that the right training comes at the right time.

Training increases efficiency when workers know what is expected of them. When there are no clear expectations, workers have the opportunity to be empowered; however, because of the dysfunctional culture within some organizations, workers lack the desire to succeed. This leads to reduced performance because the workers did not see any rewards for taking chances—they may only see risks that they are not willing to assume (Susser, 2012). Furthermore, a promise for training means that a lack of training will negatively affect morale. Negatively influencing morale will lead to organizational distrust and a lack of enthusiasm for future change.

The lack of formal training can be a frightening revelation. In one organizational review of employee training records, more than 90% of the employees had not attended professional training within the past 18 months (Bolman & Deal, 1997). The company's promise and commitment had been for two weeks of professional training per year. This promise placed the company in an awkward position. The company either needed to implement a change immediately and follow through on its promise or its employees would have yet another example of the company failing to deliver.

Structuring Processes for Change

Effective managers should structure their processes to ensure maximum productivity. For example, if an organization has little competition in an area, managers will seek out improvements in productivity. Frequently, managers are given vague directives for making things more efficient, but no one provides them with clear guidance. The simple relationship between labor, materials, and output describes the typical manufacturing relationship. An effective manager is one who can decrease either labor or materials *and* maintain or increase output (Krajewski & Ritzman, 2001). The problem becomes that these improvements hide some management-driven factors such as turnover, increased labor complaints, absenteeism, and burnout. If one does not maintain a global perspective regarding productivity, these problems may remain hidden from organizational leaders.

Visionary managers who understand the culture and change management will structure their organizations toward maximum flexibility. Organizations with an understood vision will grow; however, these organizations must have some structure to address day-to-day tasks. Another critical component is the communication of the vision (PMI, 2013a). Leaders need to continually communicate and reinforce the vision. Otherwise, that vision will never become part of the organizational culture.

One must remain leery of the fact that politics drives some managers. Human organizations are not mechanisms like cars or computers. People can always choose to make a difference or to be a roadblock, depending upon their political disposition. A machine has no free will, and will always perform its assigned duty unless it is broken. Unlike the cog that is either working and productive or broken and nonproductive, people have a wide variety of productive ranges.

Also, there are many challenges with international culture. When one works internationally, nothing should be taken for granted. This is especially true for managers whose title and presence lend credibility to their actions or inactions. Some managers forget that the world is watching them; however, it is important for them to remain culturally sensitive, but fair. For example, some people believe that some cultures do not understand deadlines as well as cultures in nations like the United States do. No one wants to wait, so why accept any excuse? The hard part is to make others accountable, and that often becomes even more difficult while trying to remain culturally sensitive. Therefore, some managers will not hold another person accountable, and then it becomes a problem of treating people differently.

Leadership

True transformational leaders understand the value of blending the culture of the organization with their distinct philosophy (PMI, 2013a). Culture is a construct that contains all the norms of the tribe. Transformational leaders must remain current about the business culture norms if they hope to perform their duties. Understanding the changing cultural forces that influence customers, employees, and stakeholders is critically important for change management. Companies that understand the evolving expectations of employees, customers, and stakeholders will flourish. Those companies that can change to meet these requirements will be the ones that will become successful in the future.

Leaders also need to master clear communication. A common way that leaders perform this goal is through public proclamation. A transformational leader must not only memorize the company vision, but must model it at every opportunity. Leaders who persuade individuals to attain greater productivity will always lead corporations that offer stakeholders greater value.

All of these issues will create communication challenges that do not occur in a traditional office environment. Face-to-face communication today has been replaced by different methods of communication in a virtual office. Telephones and electronic mail have replaced much face-to-face communication in dispersed organizations. Despite this transition, the spoken word continues to be important. However, stories have become a method for explaining the culture and values of an organization.

An example of the need for clear leadership and clear cultural expectations can be seen during a merger. In these cases, leadership and the organizational cultural factors weigh even more heavily than usual. The role of leadership and organizational culture is more predictive of a successful long-term merger than a review of the other available indicators. First, one must examine leadership and its effect on a merger; and second, one must examine culture as it evolves during a merger. Both of these elements are decisive in offering a potential solution to understand what makes for a long-term successful organizational change.

In a typical merger, leadership and organizational culture may be considered; however, these factors become secondary to the other necessities of the merger. Conflicting cultures can also lead to the fracturing of newly merged groups as individuals attain a culturally evolutionary focus. Businesses and corporations are living organisms that need to adapt to changes, and leaders must take the leading role in meeting this challenge. When groups are able to adapt during times of change, they will prove capable in the present as well as in the future.

To predict the success of a merger, it becomes important to analyze the leadership style and culture that exist. A transformational leader focuses on the many synergies that come with the combined organizational resources (Bolman & Deal, 1997). Leadership and culture play a role in the strategy and use of resources, and subsequent organizational success or failure.

Culture clash can lead to conflict. Transformational leaders understand the value of blending the culture of the organization with their distinct philosophy (Gordon & Curlee, 2011). Leaders are those in the organization who get things done, even when they are not the ones doing the work. A transformational leader must learn to value individuals while instilling a successful philosophy in them. Leaders must learn to adapt, adjust, or fit their behavior while harnessing the available resources to meet the different contingencies of the realities of business.

However, being a good follower is just as important as being a good leader. Leaders must manage the paradox of being both homogeneous and unique in the same instance. The difficulty can be found in formulating uniqueness while modeling the company culture. This runs contrary to the opinion that leaders are trailblazing individuals with a guiding vision. Leaders must avoid the mediocrity of poor leadership, and transformational leaders must strive toward a balance of following both the company culture and their inner voice (Curlee & Gordon, 2010).

Applying Project Management to Control Organizational Change

Every project has client-imposed deadlines, making a skilled project manager essential for a successful project. Achieving the project deadline requires time management, regardless of the requirements or challenges encountered in the project (PMI, 2013b). Project managers understand that project time management includes the processes required to manage time. Ultimately, managers must recognize time management as a must-have skill, and they will practice good time management throughout the project. Although project time management encompasses many different practices and skills, this research is limited to time management regarding the areas of developing and controlling a schedule.

Change management is a controllable element within a project. The project scope needs to align with the needs of sponsors (PMI, 2013a). A scope statement may begin to fulfill a certain task; however, one needs to make sure that the change charter addresses the overarching needs of the organization. The scope statement and the change charter can be used to control change, allowing the manager to be better equipped to address the needs of the organization.

Many projects have frequent client changes that a manager needs to organize. The client may feel entitled to ask and change things around once the project is in motion. After all, the client is paying for the project and for the project team's time. To counter the client's feeling of entitlement, the project manager needs to develop the project with the project sponsors as the focus. Part of this focus should include a communication plan that keeps sponsors informed about the status of the project.

At certain times, people want to change things to better suit their own needs, but that may not suit the needs of the organization. For example, a process that lacks any checks and balances will be faster and more efficient than one that has checks and balances. This does not mean that the organization should move to eliminate checks and balances. Instead, the organization should find a balance between efficiency and checks and balances. For example, the project manager should speak to the project sponsors to ensure that they are in agreement with any changes. Efficiency might be one of the reasons for the project, but that does not mean that the project sponsors want to lose control.

The project charter should identify the high-level requirements and risks. When lower-order requirements are in conflict with high-level requirements, the project manager needs to address this with the client and the project sponsors. This makes change difficult because of the conflicting information.

The people authorized to enact project changes need to be knowledgeable about the project charter. When changes are requested, one should alert the project stakeholders about the change request because the change may not work for everyone involved (PMI, 2013b). This means making sure that the project stakeholders want the requested change.

Thus, the organizational change charter is an important tool in change management and helps keep the higher needs of the organization in focus. The project scope statement should cover the tasks and lower-level needs for the project, but the project charter should identify the organizational needs to keep the project on track. This allows the project to fill the needs of project sponsors while still meeting the needs of the other stakeholders involved.

Launching the Change with Organizational Culture

The first step in launching change is schedule development. All change needs a plan, and a schedule is an ideal vehicle to communicate the change. Schedule development accounts for the various activities that relate to sequences, durations, and resources. To start, the project manager should have a detailed understanding of the project inputs and project outputs. Grasping the importance and relationship of project inputs and outputs gives the project manager a picture of possible delay points. Schedule development may also require the use of scheduling tools such as software programs. These scheduling tools will help the project manager understand the degree of accomplishments as compared to the targeted change. Using a tool can assist the project manager in developing a means to track and gauge the progress of the project. An automated tool can track multiple metrics or offer a more flexible system of tracking through the evaluation of decisions.

Controlling a schedule requires a baseline to maintain it (PMI, 2013b). The project manager cannot address deadlines in a vacuum. There needs to be defined starting and ending points so that there can be an assessment and understanding of what is on target and what is late. This is essential for any controls because there needs to be a way to gauge either success or failure of the controls. If there is no assessment, there is no way to be sure that the controls in place are effective.

Schedule controls come in the following three varieties:

- Environmental controls, such as the project manager requiring status reports;
- Project controls, where the project has a set system of change orders that takes into account both positive and negative impacts of changes made from the base project; and
- Contingency controls, or what-if scenarios that help control the project when it comes to risk.

The most traditional schedule controls are environmental controls. A project manager should regularly monitor the project baseline to determine the project status compared to the anticipated time that a project would take. Also, this schedule control reviews any modified baseline time line as the project changes. These traditional controls allow the tracking of progress and allow the project manager to understand what is happening when a project falls behind.

Traditionally, a project manager accomplishes this with a Gantt chart or time line. This visual project representation allows the project manager to understand the status of a project through visual elements (PMI, 2013b). Many sources of project management knowledge recommend using a tracking tool to monitor the time line. This is because, traditionally, the project manager would tend to ignore tasks that are on track. This means that attention becomes focused only once a task has fallen behind schedule. Although this allows for involvement by the project manager, it means that the project needs to be derailed before the project manager takes notice.

This traditional method has benefits to the project manager, but it should not be the only tool in the project manager's toolbox. For the project to be successful, there needs to be an assortment of proactive and reactive tools. A successful project manager does not wait for failure before determining status. This system certainly has its advantages, though it is not infallible. Such a system could be subject to groupthink: When intelligent people collaborate, it can lead to some of the worst possible decisions because people become more entrenched with meeting the needs of the group than finding the best decision. Using a group of experts offers a reliable method to find the best decision; however, this does not always happen when the group strives to reach consensus rather than determining the best possible solution.

Although organizations should operate with change as the goal, it is clear that many organizations are motivated instead by individual agendas and political divisions that are encouraged by management. These negatives do not eliminate much of the value that is gained by utilizing the input, but they do offer some cautionary statements regarding what is the best practice. Nonetheless, it is clear that there are some shortcomings to consider. It also means that human input needs to be qualified to ensure that the information being passed along is accurate and not merely information that the manager wants to hear.

Implementing Organizational Change

Implementing new organizational culture takes time, and managers need to infuse the culture with the vision of what the organization will look like in the future (Curlee & Gordon, 2010) (see Appendix). Merging the vision with the culture and combining them to become one allows the entire organization to move forward in unison. In shaping culture, a manager could confront a significant number of lines of communication because of the sheer size of the organization; this can lead to a lot of additional administration. From a cultural perspective, managers of large organizations may be dealing with language barriers, technology dilemmas, cultural tensions, and other sources of conflict. Organizations need to consider the impact of globalization upon their organizational culture. One should not expect the headquarters of an organization to disseminate the culture of the organization. The culture must involve everyone in the organization. Hence, it is more important to reflect the organizational culture through individuals' communication. Managers should also ensure that the top organizational performers are delivering results within the parameters of the organizational culture. Failure to do this allows certain individuals to operate above the culture, which can negatively influence the organization, deteriorating the effectiveness of the culture, as individuals would have to choose between following the culture and following the modeled behaviors of the top performers. Having to make a choice like this will confuse individuals and create greater problems for the leaders of the organization.

Any organizational change needs to consider several organizational elements. A leader must consider these elements as part of a greater cultural understanding, but starting with a review of these essential elements will assist any leader with implementing change. Not all of the following elements may be important for the implementation of a specific change, but they should all be considered, and as many as possible should be used together in order to implement the change:

- **Language.** Leaders should use language to transform the organization. Two of the most powerful cultural tools within language are myths and metaphors. By combining these with indices, icons, symbols, slogans, and other relevant codes, the transformational leader can drive the team beyond the typical achievements. This use of complex myths and metaphors goes beyond a contingency-based deterministic and mechanical model of projects and elevates it toward a fully developed cultural model. An example of this would be for the leader to always use positive and leading language, such as "when the project is over," or "we have a long road ahead, but I know that everyone will do their best work to make this project a great success."

- **Myths and metaphors.** Beyond language, the manager should consider using other imagery to shape the organization. Both myths and metaphors are expressions of how complex these human constructs can be. When used correctly, myths and metaphors can move organizations toward success. Myths and metaphors leverage any group toward a higher level of change.

  An organizational myth can become a central theme to help transform the organization. There are common myths about people and actions that transform deeds into acts of greatness. From the history of the early United States comes the myth of John Henry, the man who raced against a steam-powered machine to drive steel drills into the rock for the explosives that would be used to blast the rock for constructing railroad tunnels. It is unclear if John Henry was supposed to be a person or group of people. However, the myth creates a character that transcends reality and moves toward immortality through ordinary actions. Therefore, given the longevity and messages of this myth, one can relate this back to transformational leadership by asking if there is room for another person who is greater than a machine. It may not be possible in every circumstance; however, there is always room for one more mythical clash between a person and a machine. Ultimately, leaders can bring about positive change at many different levels (PMI, 2013a). One must consider how a culturally positive and value-driven myth can be communicated in a way that benefits the organization and highlights the actions of something ordinary in a manner that transcends to the extraordinary.

- **Success celebrations.** An important method of solidifying cultures is through periodic success meetings, where the organization's leaders, through personal testimony and charisma, relate various scenarios that recognize heroes and winners. These meetings should have members from every stratum of the organization, from the top to the bottom. A mixture of people from different levels of the organization is required because without buy-in from all levels, change is doomed to failure. This kind of cultural celebration helps show the cultural priorities that the organization values most. A leader should always make sure at the completion of a major milestone to recognize the great work with a celebration. It does not take much, for example, buy everyone pizza for lunch and talk about the project to ensure that everyone gets recognized for the accomplishment.

- **Leadership.** A transformational leader constructs the important details of the story to communicate it while retaining the right organizational values. People are social—they are not machines. So, if a leader can look to social systems to help manage change, then the leader can be more effective with larger changes that would normally be beyond reach.

  There is no doubt that culture can affect leadership, as good leadership will mold itself around the leader's style in a way that keeps individuals focused. Any leadership style can be successful as long as it incorporates the different elements of the culture; however, transformational leadership is one of the most successful leadership styles associated with change (Curlee & Gordon, 2010). A successful culture and a successful leader occur when the two blend to achieve a level of transparency. The leader embodies the culture to magnify the effectiveness of the team. For example, the leader should have a short narrative of the successes of the project to bring up to all the stakeholders. The leader needs to identify the starting point and the progress that has been made to ensure that people can see the transformation.

- **Quality.** Quality is important in organizations because a culture of quality can pay dividends as a result of fewer defects. Every organization has a level of acceptable defects. However, given effort and leadership, culture can reduce a number of errors. Organizations may not achieve Six Sigma levels of defect-free results, but the organization may reduce defects to a point where it can become significant.

  Quality is very specific to an organization, so this element needs to be considered carefully. Every organization has a particular strategy and the quality consideration must be consistent with the organizational message about quality. Many organizations already have a culture of quality, and so leaders must use their knowledge about the organization's culture to help support the change. For example, a company can put up a chart showing the progress and reductions of errors over time. This type of recognition can help show everyone the success of quality in the project.

- **Globalization.** Globalization has affected organizational culture rapidly. Organizations will succeed or fail based upon their ability to harness culture and the global village. Technology has made the world a smaller place to the point that we are all living in a global village. For example, people in Peoria are ordering items from China with the click of a mouse. Organizations need to adapt to the changing requirements of global involvement. An organization must understand that they are no longer just competing in the local area, the organization needs to think about competition worldwide because products and services can be purchased from many different locations. An example of this is that China has been more competitive in the U.S. market by leveraging global postal rates. By using the post, a company in China can send items inexpensively to global customers.

To understand how these elements relate to change, one should view these issues as petals on a flower, as shown in Figure 7-3. Without the petals, there is no flower. However, the flower could be recognized even if it had only a few petals. Similarly, unsuccessful change is recognized, but it does not bloom and take root. The beauty of the flower does not occur without all the petals present. Each petal plays an important role in the overall blooming of the flower; therefore, a leader must keep all elements in mind to make sure that the projected change blooms within the organization.

The lack of participation by those affected by the change will result in ultimate failure of the change. There are always problems when those most

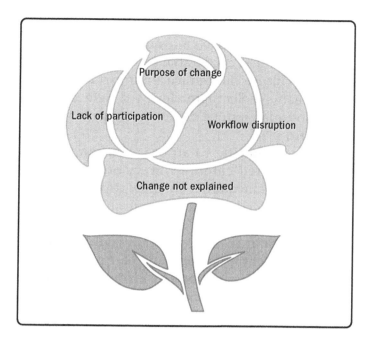

Figure 7-3.   Flower of change.

impacted by the change are not given a voice in the decision-making process. Disenfranchised employees may feel helpless when they are not convinced that the change is permanent; they will struggle against it even more. Conversely, the more that people are involved in the planning of change, the less likely they are to resist it.

Failure looms when changes are not explained. People will resist change more if they did not participate in the changes and then are forced to perform their role in a different manner. Many people will try to circumvent change to resist new methods in hope that the change will not last and the organization will return to the old ways.

When there is no understanding of the purpose of the change, people will resist it. The leader must take the time to explain the purpose for the change in detail. Otherwise, individuals will not see the long-term vision for the change. This creates an atmosphere of experimental change, where individuals will not fully embrace the change because they anticipate even more changes ahead.

Finally, the disruption to workflow makes all change unsettling. When people have become used to performing functions in a certain manner, and then things change, it is very difficult to make this leap without support. Successful training and other considerations create a more trusting environment without too much disruption to the work environment. Change will always happen, but avoiding these factors that cause people to resist change are some of the best tools of leadership.

Measuring Change

Once a change has been implemented, the organization needs to start measuring its impact. The goal is always to create an irreversible, third-order change (PMI, 2013a). Without this measurement, no success can be recognized or understood. Each organization is different, however, so milestones and benchmarks are needed to define success. In many cases, this is simply measured by evaluating whether the change worked and if it lasted.

How an organization chooses to measure change will often determine the overall success of the changes it implements. If the organization does not create a valid implementation plan, with various checkpoints that include some feedback, it will be difficult to determine whether the changes have been effective. This process should align with accepted management processes. There are several key focus areas to use in the management-change approach. Focus areas include milestones, success factors, being prepared, and review (see Figure 7-4).

- **Milestones.** The organization must establish definite periods for tasks and milestones. Milestones allow the organization to chart the progress of the change and the impacts (see Figure 7-4).
- **Success Factors.** An organization must establish key success factors. Identifying success factors allows the organization to know whether the results were achieved or not. The organization can then know if they have arrived at their expected destination (see Figure 7-4).

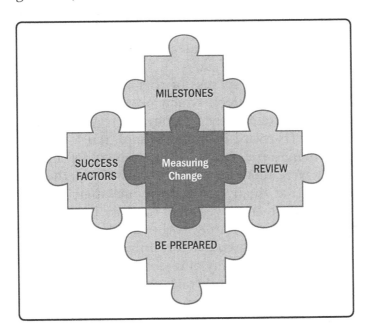

Figure 7-4. Measuring change.

- **Be prepared.** On organization must understand that change will happen and that the organization must prepare to make adjustments to accommodate the change. In any complex process that has an extended duration, the environment will be changing, and the organization should document all changes (see Figure 7-4).
- **Review.** The organization must review changes after they have been implemented. Holding a review meeting after the change has been implemented can make sure that the change is still valid, or if it is not. This change review can measure and reflect on the successes and failures. If the change is not having the desired impact, the organization should consider implementing a new change to make it successful (see Figure 7-4).

In addition to key focus areas, performance metrics may be used in a variety of ways to impact organizational change. In many cases, performance metrics push organizations toward change. When things are not improving, and everyone knows it, people will have the incentive to try something new. Making the success of the change visible to all will encourage people to continue to change (PMI, 2013a). There is a sizable body of work promoting the use of economic metrics to move an organization toward greater economic success; however, the same metrics can be applied to change (Schonberger, 2013).

Given that there are always deadlines looming, when an organization can make time management an organizational priority, it will allow for greater success in shorter amounts of time. This practice has wide application and a great deal of potential, and tracking these elements of time management can be done while also tracking economic elements. This modification would allow an organization to become more effective in change management.

Part of the reason for the success of this tracking method could be attributed to the Hawthorne effect, which postulates that monitoring people causes them to behave differently from the way they do when they are not being monitored (Harvard Business School, n.d.). When factory workers know they are being observed for a research study, they work more diligently. When they were unaware of the observations, they do not work as hard. It seems likely that the use of performance metrics benefits from the Hawthorne effect because employees feel they are being monitored and, in turn, will behave more appropriately. Although the Hawthorne effect could explain some of the improvement, it certainly does not detract in any way from applying this practice to many different organizations.

One should always monitor and track change to understand the results. Without such monitoring, there is no way to know if the change is successful in the long term. Just because people may have changed a bit in the short term does not mean that there will be a long-term cultural change.

Conclusion

In closing, any organizational leader who is about to embark on a significant change needs to consider the Understand–Build–Launch model of successful third-order organizational change. Not addressing all three of these elements within the culture will likely lead to a failure in implementing the change. Too many organizations spend considerable effort and time making changes that do not last because they never account for their organizational culture. Organizations need to understand that edicts from above last only as long as management is watching. As soon as any persecution of those who are non-compliant ends, the organization will tend to move back to its old ways. Only when leaders deliberately change the culture to support these new changes will the leaders and the changes become a successful force within an organization. For change to remain a part of the organization, the change needs to become entwined with the culture of the organization.

References

Bolman, L. G., & Deal, T. E. (1997). *Reframing organizations: Artistry, choice, and leadership* (2nd ed.). San Francisco, CA: Jossey-Bass.

Curlee, W., & Gordon, R. (2010). *Complexity theory and project management.* Hoboken, NJ: Wiley.

Gordon, R., & Curlee, W. (2011). *The virtual project management office: Best practices, proven methods.* Vienna, VA: Management Concepts.

Harvard Business School. (n.d.). *The Hawthorne effect.* Retrieved from http://www.library.hbs.edu/hc/hawthorne/09.html

Krajewski, L., & Ritzman, L. (2001). *Operations management, strategy and analysis* (5th ed.). Reading, MA: Addison-Wesley Publishing Company.

Project Management Institute (PMI). (2013a). *Managing change in organizations: A practice guide.* Newtown Square, PA: Author.

Project Management Institute (PMI). (2013b). *A guide to the project management body of knowledge (PMBOK® guide)* – Fifth edition. Newtown Square, PA: Author.

Schein, E. H. (1992). *Organizational culture and leadership* (2nd ed.). San Francisco, CA: Jossey-Bass.

Schein, E. H. (2004). *Organizational culture and leadership* (3rd ed.). San Francisco, CA: Jossey-Bass.

Schonberger, R. (2013). Time relevant metrics in an era of continuous process improvement: The balanced scorecard revisited. *Quality Management Journal*, 10–18.

Susser, B. (2012). How to effectively manage IT project risks. *Journal of Management & Business Research*, 41–67.

Verzuh, E. (2011). *The fast forward MBA in project management.* Hoboken, NJ: Wiley.

Review Questions

1. What model will support organizational change by leveraging culture?
2. Why is monitoring and measuring change so important?
3. Explain the Hawthorne effect.
4. How is implementing change like a blooming flower?

Appendix: Using the Understanding Culture Checklist

In the understanding phase of cultural change, the Understanding Culture Checklist can assist the leader in determining the baseline of the culture by examining different critical areas. Understanding critical areas allows the leader to better understand the strengths and weaknesses of the culture and the organization. This tool allows the leader and anyone else involved in the organization to offer feedback and reflection upon the culture. By looking at these eight key factors of culture, the leader can better grasp the culture in the preliminary understanding phase.

The leader can use this tool in one of three ways.

1. (High Trust) The leader can use the tool along with others in the organization to come to a mutual consensus of the strengths and weaknesses of the culture of the organization.
2. (Medium Trust) The leader can use the tool to determine personal observations and reflections to better understand the strengths and weaknesses of the culture.
3. (Low Trust) The leader can use this tool in an anonymous format to allow individuals in the organization to offer their feedback about the culture.

Each method can offer feedback to the leader regarding the culture. The uses are listed in order of high to low.

UNDERSTANDING CULTURE CHECKLIST

UNDERSTAND   BUILD   LAUNCH

Culture Explained	Train	Structure	Blend	Feedback

Name of Project being reviewed:_____

Score from 10 (highest) to 1 (lowest) regarding each aspect of culture described below. Note that this can be done by the project manager or it can be distributed to stakeholders for completion.

MORALE	Score: <table><tr><td>10</td><td>9</td><td>8</td><td>7</td><td>6</td></tr><tr><td>5</td><td>4</td><td>3</td><td>2</td><td>1</td></tr></table> Notes: _____
INVESTMENT	Score: <table><tr><td>10</td><td>9</td><td>8</td><td>7</td><td>6</td></tr><tr><td>5</td><td>4</td><td>3</td><td>2</td><td>1</td></tr></table> Notes: _____
INDOCTRINATION	Score: <table><tr><td>10</td><td>9</td><td>8</td><td>7</td><td>6</td></tr><tr><td>5</td><td>4</td><td>3</td><td>2</td><td>1</td></tr></table> Notes: _____
TRAINING	Score: <table><tr><td>10</td><td>9</td><td>8</td><td>7</td><td>6</td></tr><tr><td>5</td><td>4</td><td>3</td><td>2</td><td>1</td></tr></table> Notes: _____
PROCESSES	Score: <table><tr><td>10</td><td>9</td><td>8</td><td>7</td><td>6</td></tr><tr><td>5</td><td>4</td><td>3</td><td>2</td><td>1</td></tr></table> Notes: _____
CHANGE MANAGEMENT	Score: <table><tr><td>10</td><td>9</td><td>8</td><td>7</td><td>6</td></tr><tr><td>5</td><td>4</td><td>3</td><td>2</td><td>1</td></tr></table> Notes: _____
PROJECT MANAGEMENT	Score: <table><tr><td>10</td><td>9</td><td>8</td><td>7</td><td>6</td></tr><tr><td>5</td><td>4</td><td>3</td><td>2</td><td>1</td></tr></table> Notes: _____
FEEDBACK	Score: <table><tr><td>10</td><td>9</td><td>8</td><td>7</td><td>6</td></tr><tr><td>5</td><td>4</td><td>3</td><td>2</td><td>1</td></tr></table> Notes: _____

Name: **Date:**

CHAPTER 8

The Importance of Stakeholder Engagement

By Barbara Porter, MSc, MBA, CSM, PMP

Abstract

Stakeholder support is the key to ensuring that good changes are made in an organization—and that they last. Stockholders and management want growth and better financial performance. Employees want to feel good about the work they do and how they contribute to their organization's success. Customers want newer, better, faster, and less expensive goods and services. The public wants to know that the companies in their neighborhoods are being good neighbors who treat employees fairly and don't damage the environment or their quality of life. Organizations that don't understand all the forces affecting their stakeholders may experience friction with these stakeholders—from simple complaints to substantial business disruptions. Understanding what each stakeholder wants, needs, and expects is key; meaningful stakeholder engagement is the best way to achieve that understanding in the form of an ongoing dialogue of needs, perceptions, and expectations.

Introduction

Organizations need to change if they want to survive, and those that don't execute change well may not yield better results than those that choose not to try to change at all. The business landscape is littered with examples of companies that didn't properly size up the changing world around them and eventually became corporate dinosaurs. Companies such as Polaroid, Kodak, Borders, Blockbuster, Tower Records, Digital Equipment Corporation (DEC), Marconi, Amstrad, Nortel, and One.Tel all fell victim to this oversight. None of these organizations anticipated the shift in consumer demand and preferences or the strength of competitors well enough to survive the technological advances of the past 20 years. These companies ultimately folded, were forced to abandon certain lines of business, or the remnants of their existence were scooped up by another entity for purposes other than their "innovative" products.

Some companies eventually see the proverbial writing on the wall but react to it too late. For example, many Kodak executives discussed the likely shift in consumer trends from print to digital photography as early as the late 1970s, but the organization failed to significantly change its business model in time to survive that shift in tastes. Being reactive is not the answer—the world moves too fast now. Anticipating change needs and proactively meeting them is becoming a competitive advantage and marketplace differentiator for organizations.

Other companies embraced change—but changed in the wrong direction. Blockbuster Video launched Blockbuster.com in 2004. In 2007, the company named James Keyes as CEO. Keyes, former president and CEO of 7-Eleven, decided to shift the company's focus from growing its online business in favor of building its brick-and-mortar business. A company that had been making the shift to digital (a strategy that would have likely saved the company) began to change, but it changed back to what it had been doing in the past. Change is good, but it must be the *right* change. As an ironic footnote, Blockbuster passed on the opportunity to purchase Netflix in 2000. One can only imagine what level of success that combined company could have achieved.

Change is not easy. If it were, you wouldn't be reading this book. Although most organizations recognize the need to change and understand the strategic and competitive advantage of changing, they often struggle with how to execute the desired change because they fail to recognize that the single most crucial ingredient in their success is, quite often, people. According to *Inc.* magazine (n.d.), "Almost always, people changes are the most difficult and important part of the overall change process."

These people, referred to as stakeholders, have different relationships with the organization (see Figure 8-1). There are the owners or shareholders, who want to maximize their investment in both the short and long term. There are the managers of the company, who want to contribute to the organization's success because this directly impacts their own career growth and success. There are "front-line" employees, who want to feel that they are doing meaningful work, contributing toward a worthy goal, and earning an honest day's wage for a reasonable amount of effort. There are customers, who want to believe that they are getting a good product or service at a fair price. There are vendors and suppliers, who want to have a good long-term relationship with the organization, with smooth transactions that are free from hassle. There are citizens, who want to be sure that the organization is not selling or doing things that hurt people or the environment. There are government organizations that want to make sure the safety and well-being of their constituents

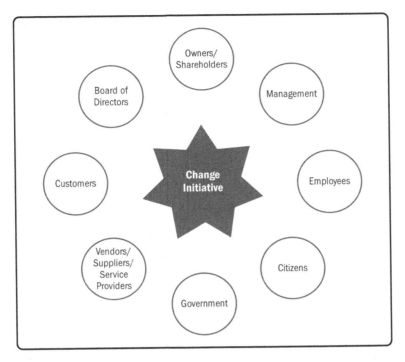

Figure 8-1. Change stakeholders in an organization.

is ensured. Any one of these stakeholder groups has the ability to disrupt a company's change efforts if they are not managed well. Trying to find a balance among all these wants and needs is challenging. Trying to maintain this balance through times of change requires a strong combination of respect, trust, and goodwill among all stakeholders and the organization.

It was so much easier when the owner of a company just demanded change—or was it? "Resistance to change is normal; people cling to habits and to the status quo. To be sure, managerial actions can minimize or arouse resistance" (Inc., n.d.). When it comes to employees, "change can make employees feel like victims, like the change is happening 'to' them" (Nelson, 2011, p. 1). Think back to the Industrial Age. The heads of companies would make decisions based on what suited them best (usually in order to maximize profits). In extreme cases, there was disregard for other stakeholders, physically abusive treatment of employees, and reckless treatment of the environment, with no regard for the impact of the organization's actions on local citizens or future generations. Organizations such as trade unions and increasing governmental involvement in environmental regulations arose in reaction to these trends.

So, assuming the change you want to promote is not violating any laws or human rights—how do you execute it well with regard to people? How do you make sure people work with you and not against you? How do you make sure you're considering various viewpoints to come up with the best solution? How do you earn that respect, trust, and goodwill? It all starts with conversations.

Change recipients (those who are affected by the change in some way) need to feel good about the change that is being made. If they don't support the change, the risk of failure increases substantially. There are several things an organization can do to better ensure the support of change recipients during the change process.

Help Change Recipients Understand How Change Will Affect Them

Think back to your first "real" job. You were young, bright-eyed, full of enthusiasm (hopefully), and wanted to do a good job so you could advance in your career. You were also likely very low down in your organization's hierarchy, and probably not privy to the strategy set by the executive team. Then you started hearing rumblings from coworkers, in the break room or (more recently) by email or text, or at a social gathering after work. Rumor said the executives were planning major changes, and things were going to be very different very soon—but little more was known than that. You had to wonder: What does this mean? Will people be laid off? Will those left behind have to take on additional work? Will the company move to a new location? Will the work become harder? Is this being done just to line the pockets of the owners?

From the time the first person speaks of this rumor until formal and detailed communication about a change is made by the organization, all sorts of wild theories are created by people, based on their own individual fears and biases. "People have different views on change. The most common issue is the fact that change creates discomfort. This discomfort is mainly stemming from fear. This could be a fear of having to relearn things, get accustomed to different ways of doing work, possible loss of control, or even of a job. In most instances, this fear comes from the lack of information" (Zeitoun & Potts, 2005). At best, productivity goes down in the short term. In some cultures, good people may begin looking for employment elsewhere, and those who stay behind are more likely to resist change once it arrives. How does this benefit the organization?

After an organization identifies the changes to be made and has performed a thorough stakeholder analysis to determine who will be affected, the next step that should be taken is to begin conversations with all of the impacted change recipients to explain what the change really means to them. The amount of effort put into preparing change recipients for change should be proportionate to the size and impact of the change initiative. For minor changes with little impact, change recipients may need little or no preparation. Larger initiatives with a significant impact should see significant planning and time invested into preparing the various categories of change recipients.

For those change recipients who are outside of the company (such as customers, investors, the community at large), legal, marketing, investor relations, and public relations teams are well suited to explain the change. But what about internal stakeholders?

An organization's internal change recipients need to understand how the change will affect them and the jobs they do. You need to help them understand why the change is necessary and what it will look like from their perspective. "If the future after the change comes to be perceived positively, resistance will be less. Education and communication are therefore key ingredients in minimizing negative reactions" (Inc., n.d.). Internal change recipients need to see the vision, understand what the goal is, and appreciate why it is an important goal to achieve:

> Employees are willing when they are motivated to work in new ways. They're willing when their job has been redesigned and they see how it fits into the new plan. They're willing when they are recognized and rewarded for adopting the new ways of working, not the old ways, and when they are evaluated based on the new business goals and measures. (Nelson, 2011, p. 2)

Despite best efforts, "legacy thinking" (thinking the old way) and politics may still obstruct full buy-in from change recipients. As outlined in *OCM—The Missed Connection* (Zeitoun & Potts, 2005), communication is essential to managing organizational politics, and it is crucial to tailor the message to those affected by the change. Project management must be finely attuned to the wants and needs of the key stakeholders in order to find a common ground between what management and stakeholders want. In an information-deprived environment, where nothing is discussed with stakeholders, political gamesmanship can quickly cause turmoil and stress employees. Some people seem to enjoy watching other people grow agitated and concerned by the stories they fabricate. Theories about what kind of change is coming, what it will look like, and what the motives are behind the change will circle. People may begin to spend more time thinking about the coming change than doing their actual work. Workers may begin to show signs of stress—acting disrespectful to others, exhibiting impatience and anger. Nothing good comes out of this type of environment, and it should be avoided at all costs.

Let's imagine that a company decided to implement additional metrics gathering with its warehouse workforce. This was clearly being done in an attempt to increase productivity and control costs. But how would the workers react? The managers explained to the employees that the belief was that some people performed consistently well, while others performed consistently poorly—and those in the middle without consistent results may need retraining to do their roles better. The managers also explained that salaries would be increased for the better performers once the underperformers were identified and removed from the salary pool. Employees who knew they were doing a good job accepted the change with some hesitation until the results showed that they were performing in alignment with their self-perception. Some of those who performed consistently poorly tried to find ways to subvert the measurement systems, either by not following protocol or, in some cases, by actually attempting to tamper with the measurement devices. Some of those who just could not seem to do the job well, but not for a lack of trying, were evaluated for transfer to another type of work within the organization. Few things can be as demotivating as feeling that you are being compensated the same as an employee who is only working half as hard or effectively as you are. When the underperformers were removed or reassigned, those remaining saw further productivity gains as their morale increased, having being recognized both systemically and financially for their better performance.

As another example, consider the different approaches of two boards that decided their companies should be put up for sale. In both organizations, there were months' worth of financial due diligence as external auditors and accountants studied the operations and reviewed the financial reporting and controls. One of the organizations told its employees that the company was for sale because it was attempting to borrow money in order to grow its operations. Only at the very end of the process, when a sale was finally announced, did the employees realize that they had not been told the truth—the goal all along had been to sell to another organization and cease local operations. This created a level of hostility in the workers that was unnecessary. Those workers focused on the "injustice" that had transpired instead of doing their work. They came to see the new owners as "the enemy," and many of them left during or shortly after the takeover transition.

In the other organization, the management team was open and honest regarding the sales process, and explained the reasoning behind it to all employees. A sense of mourning could be felt among employees, which certainly had an impact on productivity. But it was certainly better than the "hostile" environment that arose in the other organization, and employees seemed much more willing to try to do things better in the second organization, while in the first one they lost their motivation to try anything new.

Effecting Change in the Organization

When you want to change an organization, there are two options: bring in new talent from the outside or change the behaviors of the people currently on the inside. Neither is easy, and neither is without pros and cons.

Bringing in New Talent from the Outside

Especially for leadership or other key roles, it often seems like an easy answer to find someone who has the behaviors and track record you desire to see on your team. It seems like the easy answer, but there are several challenges to consider, such as the following:

- Often, too much is expected from new talent right off the bat. Until they've had the proper time to acclimate to their new organization's culture and ways of doing things, they likely will not perform at their previous levels.
- Members of the existing team may resent the action and work to foil the new team member's integration into the team. Although this team member may have enjoyed relationships that facilitated them getting things done in their previous organization, members of the new organization may actually be causing friction to dampen the results of the new team member in an effort to not be "outdone" by the new arrival.
- Some people don't perform well under pressure. Think about the people who started off in an organization and, step by step, worked their way up. They have a known track record, they have relationships with others, and they know how to get things done. Each step up the corporate ladder was relatively small for them, and with prior track records and relationships in place, they only had to adapt to the particulars of their new role. Now, compare this to team members who are coming in at similar levels from the outside. Their track records may not be known, they likely don't have many (or any) relationships in the new organization, and in fact, those people already in the organization may not like the fact that these new arrivals were chosen for specific roles. All of this results in many more factors for the new talent to juggle while trying to learn their new role!

Boris Groysberg (2010) of the Harvard Business School discusses these challenges in *Chasing Stars: The Myth of Talent and the Portability of Performance*. One example he gives is not from the business world, but from Major League Baseball. He cites the example of the 2011 Boston Red Sox. After getting eliminated in the 2009 playoffs, the Red Sox set out to sign superstars from other teams. By 2011, they had signed nearly US$400 million in contracts to bring three key players to Boston. These three players—pitcher John Lack, first baseman Adrian Gonzalez, and outfielder Carl Crawfield (all-star performers for three different teams in 2009)—either had horrible seasons in 2011 or fell apart in the playoffs. They were unable to withstand the pressures of playing in a championship-hungry city for impatient fans who demanded instant results, not a gradual transformation. Adding to the challenge was the management style of the team's manager, who used certain players to deliver messages to the team—an awkward style when dealing with superstar (and high-priced) players.

Groysberg (2010) cites a 2001 study that examines various player trades from 1900 to 1992 and the effect they had on player productivity (Glenn, McGarrity, & Weller, 2001). Interestingly, the study finds that certain positions that interact closely with other players as a part of their role (specifically pitchers, catchers, and shortstops) are more dependent on organization-specific knowledge, whereas other, more autonomous roles (like the outfield, where players have the least interaction with others on the field during the normal course of play) are the least dependent on organization-specific knowledge. The autonomous roles tend to perform equally well for their new team after being traded—unlike pitchers, catchers, and shortstops, who require more of an adjustment period to learn the ways of their new team in order to be successful.

It is not hard to think of this same paradigm in business organizations. Roles that are more dependent on organization-specific knowledge aren't as easy to "fill from the outside" as those with less organization-specific knowledge. For instance, roles that depend on knowledge of an organization's evolution in order to create a strategy for the future are either better filled from the inside (if possible) or by someone who is given a sufficient transition period to get up to speed before making significant changes in how the organization does business.

Take the example of Ron Johnson, former CEO of retailer JC Penney. JC Penney was known for being a mid-range department store, selling everything from clothing to housewares, electronics, and jewelry. The U.S. market at the time was used to heavy couponing tactics by JC Penney and competitors such as Sears and Target. Ron Johnson, without understanding the culture of the organization or the customer, discontinued coupons and sales and instead promoted an "everyday low price" policy. Johnson did not understand the impact that sales and coupons had on customers, creating hype and a sense of urgency. As a result, sales plummeted—dropping 28.4% in the year after the new pricing strategy was implemented (McGee, 2013).

Change the Behaviors of Those on the Inside

A great example of where an organization's leadership worked to change things from the inside is Aetna. In 2000, newly hired (from the outside) John Rowe, MD, determined that the organization's culture was its biggest impediment to growth. The long history of the company, which took a conservative approach in most matters, had developed a strongly risk-averse culture. This risk aversion was exhibited in all levels of the organization, and the result was that Aetna was not taking calculated risks that could have a tremendous positive impact on the company's future and bottom line. After spending some time "in the trenches," Rowe identified that containing costs had become the primary focus of the organization, to the detriment of its relationships with patients and physicians. This was an unsustainable model that left Aetna vulnerable to healthcare providers and customers who put more emphasis on patient care than the bottom line. Rowe knew that by changing the company's focus to patient care and patient satisfaction over profits, most employees would find greater meaning and satisfaction in their work. However, this change in focus, coupled with the fact that some employees would not be willing or able to shift their mind-set, would necessitate the elimination of 5,000 jobs.

Increased Accountability and Ownership

General George Patton once said, "Never tell people how to do things. Tell them what to do and they will surprise you with their ingenuity." Wise project and program managers know that successful deliverable adoption depends on engaging the hearts and minds, as well as the bodies, of the people facing a changed condition. We need to engage the energy and enthusiasm that comes from people having their own insights, for this is where true commitment to change comes from, and where the ownership of results is truly developed (Gilbert, 2008).

It is well known that engaging people in a dialogue about change and allowing them to take part in how that change is made is a key ingredient to change initiative success. "Perform change 'with' rather than 'to' people . . . When stakeholders are not part of the research and selection, they may be resistant to the solution" (PMI, 2013, p. 32).

So how do you perform change with people? You talk to them and understand their wants, needs, and concerns. There are good reasons for having a dialogue with change recipients about the changes that need to take place. Often, those doing the work are closer to the details of how things are done and the reasons why, and they may find critical pain points that were overlooked by the higher-ups who decided on the change without considering these details. They may also see opportunities that were missed by others. Sometimes, they might just have a different perspective on things altogether. During a team-building exercise many years ago, my peers and I were all directed to look into a file storage box that had 50 random items in it. For 60 seconds, we each looked into the box without saying a word. Afterward, we had another 60 seconds to quietly write down each thing we remembered individually. After that, we had three minutes to combine our lists into one final list for the team. The interesting thing was, although nobody remembered more than 25 items individually, as a team, we remembered more than 40 items. We each brought our own interests and perspective, and in the end, the solution (in this case, the team's list) was better than any individual's list.

Another good reason for engaging change recipients in designing the change solution is that they are more likely to support it if they are involved. How often have we heard of companies implementing a change that the change recipients knew would be unsuccessful before it even started? Usually, change recipients voice concerns throughout the implementation, and when the initiative eventually fails, they are quick to say, "I could have told them that was never going to work!" Alternatively, in cultures where critical feedback from lower-level employees is not embraced or encouraged, recipients may not say a word about the change, and management assumes all is well until it undeniably is not. Engaging change recipients in dialogue early and encouraging them to be active participants can help minimize resistance or passive disagreement and increase the chances for success.

Increasing accountability is an important way to make sure that an implemented change is sustainable. Without defining and measuring key data points to ensure that the change is having the desired impact, it is all too easy for old habits to creep back in, because they are either easier or more "comfortable" for employees. In such cases, the benefits of the change are quickly lost. "When a company's goals for new behavior are not reinforced, employees are less likely to adopt it consistently" (Lawson & Price, 2003, p. 33). Engage your change recipients in conversation not only about how to design the change, but also how to measure it to ensure that it lives on as intended. Building in a reward structure for compliance with changed behaviors and goals will send the message that the change is important, and that people will benefit by doing things the new way.

Not everyone will embrace the changes you are making. Some employees may have a hard time accepting change. Perhaps they feel threatened—fearing they will be made redundant and that their jobs will be eliminated. In this age of quickly evolving technology, that is a very real threat. Some employees will embrace the change, realizing that they must evolve in order to survive, and understanding that if they embrace the change, the company will help them expand their skill set, which, in turn, will make them more marketable should they need or want to find another job at some point. However, others will feel that resisting change is their best means for career survival. They feel that if they monopolize information, hide things from others, and make themselves seem indispensable, the company will have no choice but to work around them, which will extend their tenure. This attitude creates a tremendous amount of dysfunction within an organization. Such employees need to be dealt with swiftly, either with a retraining plan or a plan to transition them to another role in the organization where their skills are better suited.

In the warehouse example discussed earlier, employees were measured on how long it took them to perform a certain task. Their time to complete that task was then compared to the time it took their peers to perform a similar task. The work consisted of going to a bin to get the instruction sheet for the next task, scanning the barcode on that task sheet and their badge into the monitoring system, performing the task, and then returning to the monitoring system to scan the task sheet and badge to indicate that the work was done. There would then be a small gap in time where they would get the next instruction sheet and then scan it and their badge into the monitoring system to begin the next task.

What the data later showed was that some workers were doing the work; however, once completed, they would scan their badges in to "start" and "complete" their task within a few seconds (when, in reality, the task took several minutes). The workers thought that the speed with which they performed the task was the only important factor. We began seeing data, as shown in Table 8-1.

Though these workers had amazing task durations (averaging around 30 seconds each), they had very poor measures for the gap time between tasks. The worker profiled in Table 8-1 seems to be "unaccounted for" for 16.5 minutes out of the 18.5 minutes between the first start time and the last end time. When this trend was identified, we started monitoring *both* duration and gap time to get a true reading on the performance of the worker. Had we discussed the measurement approach with the workers early in the process, we might have uncovered this deficiency in our monitoring approach, and workers may have been less likely to attempt to work this way in an attempt to "look good."

Unfortunately, sometimes it is necessary to let employees go. Jack Welch, iconic CEO of General Electric (GE), was not one to shy away from making necessary firing decisions. According to Ron Ashkenas (2011), "The real turning point for GE's transformation came when Jack Welch publicly announced to his senior managers that he had fired two business leaders for not demonstrating the new behaviors of the company—despite having achieved

Table 8-1.   A worker's task durations and gap time between tasks.

Task	Start Time	End Time	Duration	Gap Time Between Tasks
Task 1	8:01:53 a.m.	8:02:30 a.m.	0:00:37	
Task 2	8:06:15 a.m.	8:06:45 a.m.	0:00:30	0:03:45
Task 3	8:12:43 a.m.	8:13:11 a.m.	0:00:28	0:05:58
Task 4	8:20:00 a.m.	8:20:23 a.m.	0:00:23	0:06:49
		Totals	0:01:58	0:16:32

exceptional financial results. This made it very clear that the culture was not just a soft concept—instead, it had tangible outcomes and consequences." Jack Welch was aggressive in his need to drive change within the organization, and though that helped GE achieve great things from both innovation and financial performance perspectives, it was a notoriously difficult environment in which to work. The top 20% of performers were given bonuses. The bottom 10% of performers were fired. The middle 70% spent the next year wondering if they were so close to the bottom that they might easily be in the new bottom 10% for the next year. Although this approach clearly "cleans house" of the underperformers in an organization, it sets up an artificial target. What if a company has 50% underperformers? Should you only cut 10% per year? What if a company only has 5% underperformers? If you cut 10%, you're terminating good people.

There is a common adage in management circles: Hire slow and fire fast. Hiring slowly is a good tactic. It is important to understand not only the technical abilities of the people you want to add to the team, but also what motivates them and what their wants and needs are as these relate to their career, in order to know if they will be a good fit for the organization.

Once hired, however, firing fast should not be an option. You saw something in the person initially that made you think he or she was the right candidate for the job. If you now think otherwise, you should ask yourself, "What did I miss during the interview and how could I have prevented this situation?" Depending on what is causing an employee to underperform, there are many options such as retraining and reinforcement that can help get an employee back on track. If the problems are rooted in a disregard or distrust for the mission of the organization, however, firing fast may be the only option.

Positive Peer Pressure

We would all love to work an environment where everyone is happy, does their fair share, and is motivated to perform better every day. This is one of the reasons the atmosphere in start-ups can be so infectious and appealing to employees. There are many reasons environments like this are not necessarily the norm. You have to hire people with the right skills. You have to hire people with the right attitude. You have to hire people who have the ability and willingness not only to adapt to change, but also to effect change. When hiring for management, you have to hire people who can drive and sustain change. Often, when change to an organization's culture is proving difficult to achieve, one or more of these elements was missed when people were added to the environment.

So, what do you do? In the extreme case, people who cannot be transitioned into a more positive way of thinking and behaving may have to be removed from the environment. This could be moving them to a role that is better suited for their skills and where their attitude has less of an impact on the organization achieving its change goals, or it may mean the person must be removed from the organization completely. Sometimes, this simply cannot be helped and is the necessary action to ensure the ongoing health and growth of the organization.

Others can be brought, possibly unwillingly at first, into a more positive place. Team-building exercises, cross-training, role-playing, and ongoing education give people the tools to see and do things in new ways. Ultimately, that is what you need to do if people are going to adapt to change. There are good reasons for helping your employees adapt to change. According to Gallup (2013, p. 9), "Organizations with an average of 9.3 engaged employees for every actively disengaged employee in 2010–2011 experienced 147% higher earnings per share (EPS) compared with their competition in 2011–2012. In contrast, those with an average of 2.6 engaged employees for every actively disengaged employee experienced 2% lower EPS compared with their competition during that same time period."

Once you've invested time in educating and training people, set clear targets and expectations for performance for both the individual and team. Measure performance routinely. Communicate results often—initially with additional support when needed, and eventually with rewards for those exceeding their targets. For team targets, this creates a self-policing environment, where other members of the team will not stand for certain behaviors of others that may prevent them from achieving their goals. The key is for management to ensure that it is measuring the right metrics and rewarding the right goals that are in alignment with the change initiative and the organization's strategy overall.

Change Collateral

One of the tenets of the agile methodology is that organizations must be prepared to change often and change well. Those that routinely execute change well win! They beat their competitors to market, they cut costs, and they adapt to changing market conditions and customer tastes. "In order for an organization to succeed in the future, it needs to have a robust change process—one that can continuously retune an organization's processes to support the management's vision and react quickly to changes in the business environment" (PMI, 2013, p. 7).

A robust change process sounds great. You might ask where you can buy one! Sadly, you can't. A change process is something that needs to evolve within an organization. Like a snowball rolling downhill, it picks up speed as it goes, getting larger and faster as it evolves. One way to allow the momentum to build is to eliminate resistance to change within the organization.

Cargill, the international food conglomerate based in Minnetonka, Minnesota, tackles employee resistance to change through a three-pronged communication methodology, as outlined by Jeff Schott (2013) of CBE:

- **Highlight contrasting behaviors.** Cargill explains to employees what behaviors it expects from them, giving them examples of "what it should look like" and "what it should not look like." Giving practical examples helps employees understand the nuances behind the change directives.
- **Enable group reflection.** Promote discussion within teams about the change directives. This allows the group to surface any questions that need clarification, while also allowing members of the group to demonstrate their understanding and support of the directives.
- **Prompt group commitment to action.** Now that the expectations have been communicated and the team has had a chance to reflect upon them, prompt the team to identify how they will implement the directives in specific steps. By committing to this plan of action as a team, positive peer pressure is created, whereby employees are less likely to passively abandon the agreed-upon plan because they have made a commitment to support it not only to the company, but also to their coworkers. It is one thing to forget a promise made to a faceless entity (an organization); it is much harder to forget a promise made to the people you work with every day.

As mentioned above, it is important to make sure you have the right people influencing the organization's environment. A sound change management methodology will support the organization to develop and hone its ability to change over time, until larger change initiatives can be taken on at a faster rate. As change recipients witness the increasing number of successfully completed change initiatives within an organization, they will tend to adopt a more positive outlook on future initiatives, and become less fearful of change. Organizations in which this happens are said to have "change collateral"—enough confidence in the change process within the culture that resistance to change in the organization is low.

Organizations must ensure that they guard against "change fatigue" when an organization is running in sprint mode for an extended period of time with no end in sight. Change recipients tire of this type of environment. Eventually, it feels like they are stuck running in a race that will never end. It feels like all management cares about are results and lining their own pockets, and that they don't care about the well-being of their employees. To prevent change fatigue, change initiatives should have a ramp-up and ramp-down time, with a measurable gap between major changes as the organization collectively "catches its breath" and gathers its strength for the next change cycle. Change initiatives should have a clear focus on objectives with measurable goals. Individuals expected to support the change initiative should understand what role they will play during and after the change process, how their adherence will be measured, and, if possible, how they will benefit from the change once it is complete.

The Role of the Change/Project Manager

Good change managers (who are often project managers) are networked throughout all layers of an organization and are in the best position to understand its goals, the requirements of the executive team, and the pain points of workers. Early in the life of a change initiative, the change manager should conduct a thorough stakeholder analysis and risk register. Understanding who is impacted, how they are impacted, and what the critical factors are to ensure that stakeholders will support the initiative must all be identified. "A main question on the mind of the project manager is who the potential allies are. This also includes a proper understanding of the potential allies' worlds. It also includes knowledge of what is important to them in business as well as their personal life" (Zeitoun & Potts, 2005). It's also important to understand who your enemies are—who are the people who will not support the change initiative? Will they try to subvert it or merely complain about it? Can they be won over through a discussion of the reasons for and benefits of the change? Understanding what is important to the stakeholders is imperative. Unhappy stakeholders have a tendency to disrupt (or even derail) change initiatives. What are their fears and concerns? What would make them happier or more likely to embrace the change? What could be done to overcome their fears and concerns? All of these factors (and risks) should be explored and planned for.

One of the best recent examples of an organization that mismanaged nearly every one of its stakeholders is Hershey. In the early 2000s, several trustees of the company voted to sell it. All decision making about the sale occurred at the highest levels of management, with zero engagement of any other stakeholder group. As discussed in *The Triple Bottom Line* (Savitz & Weber, 2006), because senior management did not engage any other stakeholder groups, they were unprepared for the strong objections voiced by those groups. Within hours of the news about the sale breaking in a *Wall Street Journal* article, the public outcry began. Employees and unions were concerned about the financial stability of workers. Local citizens were concerned about what would happen to their town and their own livelihoods—would a new owner move operations elsewhere? Suppliers were concerned that new owners may prefer other suppliers over their own. Former management was upset that the great organization that they had worked so hard to build was being valued for its profit measure only, and not for the good it did in so many other areas, including the Milton S. Hershey School for lower-income students, an initiative that was not a money maker, but provided immeasurable goodwill to the community. After sufficient uproar from these groups, the state of Pennsylvania got involved, seeking to protect the sales and payroll tax income it enjoyed while trying to secure the financial stability of all the groups mentioned above. After 55 days of constant media coverage and stakeholder protests, the sale was abandoned and 10 of the 17 trustees of the organization who had recommended the sale were forced to step down. Clearly, the days of companies looking to serve the interests of the privileged few are over, and organizations need to consider the "voice of the many" when setting corporate strategy with significant stakeholder impact.

Once the stakeholders (change recipients) and their needs, wants, and drivers are known, action plans tailored to each group can be defined to help prepare them for and support them through the change to better ensure the success of the change initiative.

How Do I Begin?

Identify who your stakeholders are (Figure 8-1 is a good reference to use). Identify every person who may have something to say (good or bad) about the change. Then, talk to them! Find out how they would be impacted, what they think about the change, and if they have any recommendations about what the change should look like. One effective way of doing this is to ask them how *they* would change things if it were their company. Not every idea you get will be actionable, but you will certainly learn a lot about what people want and need in the process. Once you've made changes, measure how successful they were and how well they are being accepted by the organization. Make adjustments when changes have not been acceptable or have not been sustained.

One important thing to keep in mind is that stakeholder conversations shouldn't end when an organization deems a change "complete." Once you're done with one change, there will always be another ahead. There will always be something to improve, either thanks to advances in technology, changing consumer tastes, changes in the competitive behaviors of other organizations, or economic changes in the world. There's always something that can and should be done better, and if you find yourself in an organization that doesn't embrace this concept of continuous improvement, it's a sign that it's probably time to improve your résumé.

References

Ashkenas, R. (2011, June 21). You can influence it. *Harvard Business Review.* Retrieved from https://hbr.org/2011/06/you-cant-dictate-culture-but-y/

Gallup. (2013). *State of the American workplace.* Washington, D. C.: Gallup, Inc.

Gilbert, J. (2008). Every team's captain: Leading the organizational change game. *PMI® Global Congress.* Denver, Colorado.

Glenn, A., McGarrity, J. P., & Weller, J. (2001, January). Firm-specific human capital, job matching and turnover: Evidence from major league baseball 1900–1992. *Economic Inquiry*, 86–93.

Groysberg, B. (2010). *Chasing stars: The myth of talent and the portability of performance.* Princeton, NJ: Princeton University Press.

Inc. (n.d.). Managing organizational change. *Inc.* Retrieved from http://www.inc.com/encyclopedia/managing-organizational-change.html

Lawson, E., & Price, C. (2003). *The psychology of change management.* London, England: McKinsey & Co.

McGee, S. (2013, March 4). How to ruin a retail giant in one easy step. *The Fiscal Times.* Retrieved from http://www.thefiscaltimes.com/Columns/2013/03/04/How-to-Ruin-a-Retail-Giant-in-One-Easy-Step#page1/

Nelson, K. (2011). Change management: Understanding the human dynamics of change. *PMI® Global Congress*, 1–2, 5, 6. Dallas, TX.

Project Management Institute (PMI). (2013). *Managing change in organizations: A practice guide.* Newtown Square, PA: Author.

Savitz, A. W., & Weber, K. (2006). *The triple bottom line.* San Francisco, CA: Wiley.

Schott, J. (2013, October 2). How Cargill conquers the impossible: Change employee behavior. *CBE.* Retrieved from https://www.executiveboard.com/blogs/how-cargill-conquers-the-impossible-change-employee-behavior/

Zeitoun, A., & Potts, W. (2005). OCM—The missed connection. *PMI® Global Congress.* Edinburgh, Scotland.

Review Questions

1. Why is change good for organizations?
2. Should outside consultants be brought in to help identify and implement changes in order to ensure the success of the business?
3. Who are the organization's stakeholders?
4. Should leaders consider how employees "feel" about the proposed changes?
5. What is "legacy thinking" and why is it dangerous to an organization?
6. What is "change collateral"?

CHAPTER 9

How to Structure, Plan, and Measure Organizational Change Management

By Jack Ferraro, CSM, PMI-ACP, PMP

Abstract

Portfolio management plays a unique role in increasing an organization's strategic agility. This chapter explores how portfolio management enhances certain organizational behaviors by embedding change processes and activities into portfolio management processes and portfolio initiatives. These processes and behaviors are the linking pins between strategy and execution teams. These processes enable portfolio managers, executive leadership, and program and project teams to increase their organization's ability to react effectively to change in environments that are challenged by resource constraints and conflicting executive priorities.

This chapter discusses a common-sense approach to effective structuring, planning, and measuring change management efforts across programs and projects. The reader will gain strategic and tactical insight from practical examples in leading and directing strategic programs for organizations using real artifacts and case studies. Readers will take away practical, usable examples to assimilate organizational change management into everyday projects and strategic initiatives for their organization's future.

The Role of Change Management in Portfolio Management

A portfolio is a collection of programs, projects, or operations managed as a group to achieve strategic objectives (PMI, 2012). Portfolio management is the coordinated management of one or more portfolios to achieve strategies and objectives. It includes how an organization evaluates, selects, prioritizes, and allocates its constrained, limited resources to best accomplish organizational strategies consistent with its vision, mission, and values (PMI, 2012).

Change management is a comprehensive, repeatable, structured approach to transitioning individuals, groups, and organizations from their current state to a future state with intended business benefits. Organizations require the ability to continue to react to external change events through strategic agility (the capability to seize and take advantage of business environment changes and demonstrate resilience from unforeseen changes). This enables organizations to achieve strategic objectives by developing a change management capability in their portfolio, program, and project management processes (PMI, 2013).

In order to aggressively reshape its culture and business practices, it is essential for an organization to have a rigorous change management process to better adapt to changing market conditions, a collaborative and structured risk management process, and increased use of portfolio, program, and project management best practices.

Portfolio Management and Change Management—The Connection

The smallest component of a portfolio is a project, which is the creation of a product, service, or result. The act of creating causes change. Programs and projects are the tools that organizations use to drive change; these tools are organized into portfolios to ensure that they align to and facilitate strategies. As strategies evolve and change, portfolios and the way in which organizations manage them also need to change. In particular, the resources executing a portfolio's components must be able to react quickly and effectively. Change management is an integral part of organizational project management—especially portfolio management—and requires a coordinated management of portfolios to achieve strategies and objectives. Figure 9-1 depicts the integration of change activities as strategies transition to portfolio management activities and then to program implementation activities.

Translating Changes in Strategy into Portfolio Changes—Management Role

Executives and boards are continually reviewing and tailoring strategies to maximize shareholder value. Portfolios are managed either formally or informally. When managed formally, resources are designated, empowered, and qualified to evaluate, select, prioritize, authorize, and control the portfolio's components. When managed informally, which occurs more often than not, portfolios are managed by an informal group of resources—perhaps a combination of executives, a CIO, and operations managers. In either case, as

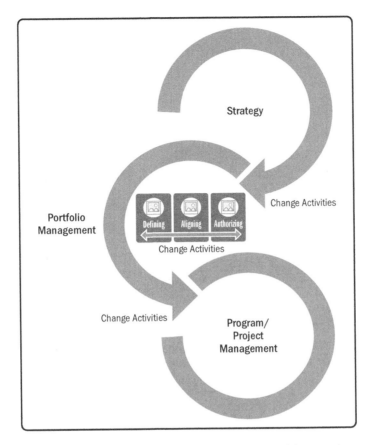

Figure 9-1. Integration of change activities with organizational project management.

strategy changes, a new partnership is formed, product lines change, and new technologies emerge. The translation of this strategy to the portfolio manager(s) is critical to organizational agility.

The role of change management is to consistently transition the changes in strategy to portfolio managers to allow them to make sense of the changes, buy in to them, and provide the authority to act on the changes (see Figure 9-2). Effective communications, sense-making activities, and personal and organizational impact assessments are some areas in which change activities should be targeted. This will provide portfolio managers with the ability to act decisively regarding their portfolio management activities. Without decisive, confident actions from portfolio managers (particularly those who are loosely organized), program and project resources will be less likely to understand the shift in priorities. This can degrade program and project performance. Or, even worse, strategy changes may result in simply adding more components to the portfolio, creating more chaos for constrained resources, and increasing task switching and multitasking. This can destroy the portfolio's value.

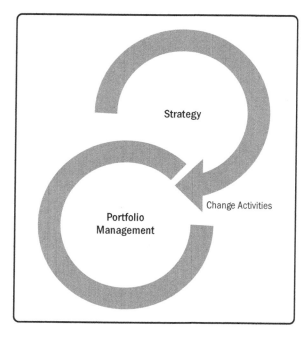

Figure 9-2. Relationship of change activities between organizational strategy and portfolio management.

Defining, Aligning, and Authorizing Portfolio Changes—Change Management Role

When strategy and portfolio managers properly execute change management, portfolio managers are able to execute and effectively manage changes to the portfolio components. Changing portfolio components is difficult—reprioritizing projects and shifting resources away from one executive's projects to another executive's projects can be a career-limiting decision. In order to transfer the changes in strategy reflected in portfolio changes to program and project resources or project management offices (PMOs), portfolio managers should execute change management activities in the definition, alignment, and authorization of these changes (see Figure 9-3). These activities should be aimed at the goal of gaining consensus through the stakeholder community and achieving a sequenced, prioritized portfolio component list.

When defining new portfolio components, portfolio managers need to ensure that certain change management activities (such as assessments of readiness, the crafting of need and vision statements, and the definition of done) are conducted to allow executives to properly assimilate and validate new components, to allow program resources to conduct high-level planning activities, and to allow other impacted stakeholders to assess

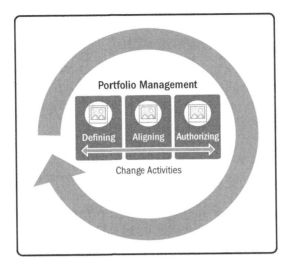

Figure 9-3. Portfolio management change activities occur across process groups.

feasibility and readiness. Without these activities and artifacts, alignment of the new component is unlikely. If a key stakeholder asks, "Why are we doing this?" it is likely that appropriate change management activities did not occur. This leads to improper alignment with strategy and, ultimately, the premature authorization of portfolio components—or no authorization at all.

The alignment of a component also requires change activities, including justifying (measuring the value of the component's impact on strategy), indemnifying (aligning resources to support the component), and building (a coalition of support). The vetting of a component through frank discussions about impacts on other components and positive and negative risks is a critical change activity that has to occur with executives and their direct reports. They must accept the tradeoffs inherent in portfolio changes.

When change activities are ingrained in the defining and aligning activities of portfolio managers, then the authorization of the component is a matter of excellent communication through the repurposing of previous artifacts (vision statements, readiness assessments, and so forth) into mediums that can be communicated to employees, business partners, and other stakeholders. These communication activities may include town hall meetings, posters, email newsletters, and updates to internal and external web portals. The initiative's credibility will be judged ruthlessly by stakeholders who are already dealing with many other responsibilities. Communications must answer basic questions, such as why the initiative is taking place and what needs to be done to have a successful outcome.

Facilitating Resource Prioritization and Optimization in the PMO—Change Management Role

Portfolio changes flow down to the PMOs and execution teams that will need to adjust their processes and procedures to allow for the shifting priorities. When the portfolio manager executes the proper change activities in the defining, aligning, and authorizing processes, the PMO and its project managers, Scrum masters, and delivery managers will be able to make sense of the change, and will need to be empowered to execute the change. During the transition to the PMO, the most important change activity portfolio managers need to execute is the turnover of the proper artifacts to the PMO along with the clear prioritization of the new component. The quality of portfolio change activities will determine the level of change activities that the execution teams need to apply in order to achieve buy-in and support from the stakeholders who are not involved in the portfolio management activities.

To avoid the devastating impacts that multitasking has on productivity, workers should be able to prioritize tasks to increase throughput given their fixed capacity. The focus of the previous change activities should have been on gaining stakeholder consensus, leading to a sequenced, prioritized portfolio component list. If the portfolio manager cannot provide such a definitive list, then the PMO will not be able to optimize resources using either critical chain or agile methodologies. A component may have a set of dedicated resources, but components more commonly rely on shared, matrix resources from other project teams or operations. In order to optimize portfolio performance, the portfolio managers will need to provide the PMO with a clear prioritization of all components so that component task-level resource conflicts can be resolved against the prioritized list (see Figure 9-4).

Organizational Behavior—Recognizing the Absence of Strategic Agility

Often, portfolio managers recognize the lack of strategic agility or the inability of their organization to react to new strategies. Some organizations simply do not have a strategy and latch onto whatever opportunities come their way, or the organization's executives promote personal agendas that increase their individual gain or reduce their own personal risk. Portfolio management change activities should address such a lack of a strategy by monetizing the impact of having no strategy.

Strategic agility is crippled when organizations have conflicting strategies set up by boards or CEOs to incentivize their senior executives to accomplish something strategic. The problem is that these senior executives have management business objectives (MBOs) tied to their compensation plans. The MBOs are aligned with the strategy and vision of the organization, but

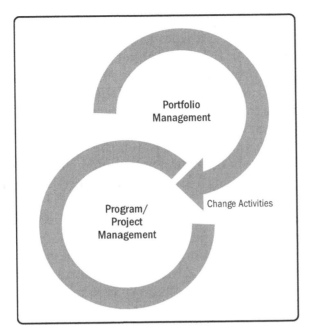

Figure 9-4. Portfolio management to execution change activities.

unfortunately, they often compete against one another at the resource level and sometimes at the strategy level. For instance, one executive may have an MBO to improve the quality of a product, while another executive has an MBO to increase throughput and reduce cost per unit of the product. Each of these executives marches forward to the portfolio manager, gaining authorization for his or her programs and projects, but then both stall at the execution level when the delivery teams are confronted with obvious conflicts in execution details and serious resource conflicts. The resource allocation problem can be solved through organizational project management maturity, but resolving the conflicting strategy at the execution level is more difficult to fix and requires effective decision making. This problem requires more than the prioritization of components; it involves a systems-thinking approach to designing business and product processes. Portfolio change activities should address these conflicts by making execution-level conflicts transparent in the portfolio risk analysis and reporting, and by providing execution teams with the ability and authority to resolve resource conflicts without fear of executive punishment.

Lack of realism is another symptom that needs to be addressed through change activities within the portfolio. The inability to define a change leads to a lack of realism about what the change will actually require. For example, executives may want the change to happen in four months when it really requires nine months. Seemingly simple changes can create unintended consequences that are never imagined or even understood until it is too late. Executives who are far removed from the day-to-day work or those who are too emotionally invested in the outcomes can oversimplify the impact of the change on people and processes. These executives may have allocated sufficient resources to execute the program, but the stakeholders need to be able to make sense of the program and realize a certain level of control. Without knowledge and appreciation for the impact of the change, an undercurrent of resistance can build, which will threaten the objectives. A portfolio manager's ability to educate sponsors and stakeholders and to facilitate the crucial dialogue in order to bring realism to the effort is a subtle, but critical, change activity.

Strategic agility is harmed when organizations become too risk averse. A risk-averse culture can have numerous root causes, including previous expensive and embarrassing program failures or an "if it isn't broken, don't fix it" mentality. Executives who are paid to execute on strategy become reluctant to allocate the necessary financial and human resources to initiate critical new programs and products. They may fund the new programs inadequately to keep costs low and personal risk at a minimum, resulting in the programs being carried out by teams of people with limited bandwidth or without the proper qualifications. The critical change activity for portfolio managers is to ensure that the execution team's project plans are able to show timely, incremental, and measurable progress in order to build the confidence of the organization. A fundamental principle to successful change management is to build on small wins, consolidate them into management systems, and move on to the next win. Structuring components to achieve momentum builds the stakeholder confidence necessary to survive the valleys that precede the peaks of organizational change. Portfolio managers can greatly influence the structure of large, complex programs and products to avoid long lead times and escalating costs before showing any measurable progress.

Portfolio Management's Role in Influencing Organizational Change Competencies

Portfolio managers (or teams) inherit the role of change maker from executives and are responsible for influencing organizational behaviors to increase organizational project management maturity. To attract agents or early adopters, portfolio managers and portfolio teams need to demonstrate competencies in portfolio, program, and project management that are based on knowledge, skill, and experience. They must also demonstrate competencies within change management and be comfortable with complexity and ambiguity. At the same time, they must exhibit subject matter expertise in the organization's business operations, portfolio components, organizational politics, and communications management. Their ability to develop trust within the organization is paramount—both vertically, with executives and program and project teams, and horizontally, with peers. Because they have no direct authority to develop or execute strategy, portfolio managers need to be able to influence those around them through consultative leadership. All this requires personal courage and resilience, particularly when strategy changes create portfolio components that necessitate second- and third-order changes requiring employees to think differently about their work and learn new skills.

Portfolio managers are in a unique position to influence organizational behaviors that enhance organizational project management maturity. Linking strategy to execution by defining, aligning, and authorizing portfolio components, portfolio managers have an advantage in that they are close to strategy development and understand why portfolios are being created or refined. They often have risen out of the PMO or program and project management ranks; therefore, portfolio managers are able to consult on program resources used to carry out the change, make sense of the changes, and guide/provide recipients with a feeling of mastery.

To capitalize on this unique position, portfolio managers should adopt a service-based portfolio leader's competency pyramid, as shown in Figure 9-5.

The base of the pyramid is a portfolio manager's organizational project management knowledge, skill, and experience. These three elements exist in the form of certifications and experience on various types of enterprises with a range of tools, methodologies, organizational knowledge, and systems. Knowledge, skill, and experience are tightly integrated. Turning knowledge into tangible skills requires action, and building experience requires the execution of those skills. The presence of a certification is not the completion of the base—the base must continually expand if the pyramid is to grow

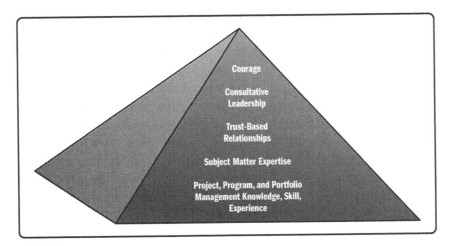

Figure 9-5. Service-based portfolio leader's competency pyramid.

wider and taller. From this base, portfolio managers can launch successful careers as service-based leaders who influence and grow organizational change competencies.

The second layer of the pyramid is subject matter expertise. This refers to domain expertise, with a knowledge of particular industries, applications, or processes that are needed to guide and transition strategic, transformational portfolios from strategy to realistic programs and projects. Understanding change management and having a solid understanding of an organization's business operations, portfolio components, internal politics, and effective communications management are important to portfolio managers if they hope to gain credibility with executives, project resources, and functional managers who are acting as change integrators.

Service-based portfolio leaders' customer focus and transformational intent requires that they understand the business of their customers—all of their customers. Complexity and compressing time frames require that they gain credibility quickly. In order to influence the organizational behaviors that inhibit strategic agility, a command of the subject matter at hand is critical. This requires portfolio leaders to continually learn and inquire about the environment around them and be able to put it into its proper context.

The third component of the pyramid is trust-based relationships, which is a cornerstone for leadership. People tend to trust less when more is at stake. Converting strategy to action is an organizational lifeline that requires trust within the surrounding environment. Trust allows portfolio managers to increase their sphere of influence. By enhancing credibility, reliability, and intimacy with sponsors, early adopters, integrators, and recipients, trust will increase with the adoption of changes and will ease the transition to future-state models.

The fourth layer of the pyramid is consultative leadership, which emerges directly out of trust-based relationships. Consultative leadership is the ability to lead others without direct authority. Also rooted in servant leadership, consultative leadership combines strong advisory skills with compassion and service to enable portfolio managers to achieve meaningful results through others. The demands of stakeholder management in change initiatives require a mixture of advisory and consultative skills to keep everyone moving forward of their own free will toward strategic objectives. Converting strategy into portfolio components that may be ambiguous and difficult to visualize and define, the service-based portfolio leader provides consultative assistance that aligns the growth of the organization with the desired results.

Service-based portfolio leaders are dedicated to giving of themselves to others in order to achieve something greater. Courage is the mortar in the service-based portfolio leader's competency model. The higher the level in the pyramid, the more courage is required. Trust-based relationships require the courage to know oneself better and to speak articulately and passionately about subject matter in front of executives and program resources. It takes courage to develop a relationship that reaches beyond the safe, rational level to the less predictable, emotional one. A service-based portfolio leader's behavior demonstrates honesty and sincerity through a commitment to improving the organization's health. Turning promises into actions requires courage. Portfolio leaders need courage to simultaneously transform themselves and to create and sustain change in the environment around them.

For all change efforts, the following three high-level factors are crucial to success:

- Executive leadership, such as visible and sustained support from the sponsor and other executives, and protection of the project from pressures such as time, budgeting, and resources;
- Employee needs, including fair treatment, clear communication, and defined expectations; and
- Project management, including capability, staffing, planning, and communicating the change and project progress (Mourier & Smith, 2001).

The value that service-based portfolio managers provide to their organization comes through using the competency pyramid to guide the conversion of strategy to viable change initiatives by eliminating conflicts in execution strategy, driving the appropriate risk analysis, and instilling realistic expectations with management before unrealistic deadlines are mandated to execution teams.

Structuring Project-Oriented Organizational Change—Roles and Responsibilities

When it's time for a project to bring change throughout an organization, the structure of the initiative is critical (see Figure 9-6). The structure begins with the organization's resources rallying around a *need* to change—the "why." The response to that need is the *vision*. Together, the need and vision are critical for properly aligning the project organization with the change. Out of the vision, the project or program organization *structure* arises. This structure has key roles, each with important responsibilities and skills that help facilitate the recognition of benefits and move the organization permanently in new directions. Out of the structure, specific *project mission* statements crystallize how each project associated with the larger change initiative facilitates this change.

Importance of a Real Need

An organization that wants to initiate change should take time to understand what its real needs are. What changes are required and why? Which people,

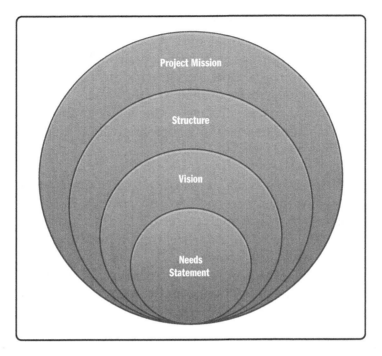

Figure 9-6. Structuring project-oriented organizational change.

systems, and processes are needed to make this change? Change begins with the collective organizational resources and willingness to adopt new attitudes and behaviors.

Understanding the real need of the change effort and its stakeholders is a discovery process that involves continual dialogue and collaboration. This implies that a relationship must exist among the program manager, project manager, change leader, and/or stakeholders. Conducting diligent research and investigation of similar projects are practical ways of beginning this process.

The leader of the change initiative can justify the importance of the needs identification and articulation process by asking such questions as the following:

- Why does capacity need to increase or cost need to decrease?
- Why do we need to embrace agile?
- Why do we need to restructure and realign resources?
- What if this need is not met? What happens? Who is at risk?
- Who ultimately benefits from having these needs met?

In order for everyone to comprehend and buy in to the project mission, these questions should be pursued vigorously.

Once these truths about real need are discovered and defined, the change initiative team can articulate the need accurately and in a meaningful manner so that stakeholders are able to understand it and so that the team can generate a sense of urgency. The skill of articulation takes practice, a strong command of the language, business acumen, and project management knowledge. Although the portfolio manager may have started these change activities, the change leader should continue them with integrators and recipients in order to drive adoption down to the lowest level of the organization necessary for the change to be successful. This level is often beyond the manager or supervisor level for second- and third-order change initiatives.

Developing a needs statement begins by validating the articulated need with the primary and secondary stakeholders and by gaining agreement with the needs statement. The needs statement should be truthful, specific, and eye-opening. It should articulate what is needed and why.

The following is an example of a needs statement that will allow a response or a vision to be generated:

> Our company needs to significantly reduce operating costs in order to stay competitive with our competition and provide our employees with long-term career growth opportunities. These needs, critical to securing the future health of our organization, will require an unprecedented commitment, collaboration, and innovation from our employees and partners.

This needs statement does not identify a group or an organization that is responsible for accomplishing the need; thus, it avoids having stakeholders adopt a "not my problem" mentality. It encourages inclusiveness while building urgency. A good needs statement is honest, transparent, and forward looking, and does not place blame on previous management or decisions. It aligns with stakeholders' long-term interests rather than short-term personal goals. It acknowledges the challenges and risks associated with the undertaking and recognizes the potential sacrifices that the organization may need to incur in order to satisfy the need. This is especially important because many people will take on additional duties beyond their normal jobs to accomplish it. Not all organizational change is enterprise-wide; some change initiatives are more tactical and align with larger organizational strategic goals.

Importance of a Compelling Vision

Vision is a "picture of the future with some implicit or explicit commentary on why people should strive to create that future" (Kotter, 1996, p. 68). In other words, a vision is a picture of the future *and* the need—it contains both aspects. Too often, organizations jump straight to the picture of the future without articulating the need, thus creating a change initiative that is not well structured.

Vision is critical to effective change. Driven by the identified need, it directs the stakeholders' actions and aligns them with objectives, avoiding problem-solving and conflict-resolution approaches that do not support lasting results. Instead, vision inspires the act of creating, which leads to permanent results. The creative project leader and team follow the vision to address underlying issues and tensions to create new solutions rather than to temporarily adjust to the same old situations. The vision statement should flow down from the portfolio managers; however, sometimes strategic initiatives start without the necessary portfolio management change activities. Even when passed down, these vision statements need to be discussed, reviewed, and possibly refined to ensure that they are assimilated by program stakeholders.

When vision and creativity are lacking in change efforts, project teams tend to recycle previous problems or move from one version of a problem to another. Without a project vision, they focus on solving the current problem. A strong vision is necessary to bring changes of attitudes, behaviors, and processes. Without a strong vision, the change effort can easily drift into a list of confusing, incompatible, and resource-consuming projects that go in the wrong direction or nowhere at all (Kotter, 1996).

Change leaders must be able to articulate the essence of the change that the organization is trying to create. An organization that is honest with itself has a healthy tension between reality and the future. A change leader's task is to define the current reality as truthfully as possible, and then create a compelling vision for where the organization wants to go or what it wants to become.

When articulating a vision, leaders can make use of pictures, graphs, and diagrams to begin with the end in mind. The creation of mental images and shared visions inspires the energy and hope that precedes the physical creation. This process requires project leaders to work closely with sponsors and key stakeholders to assist them in resolving ambiguity and conflicts. A good vision accomplishes the following:

- Clarifies the general direction for change,
- Motivates action in the right direction, and
- Provides a shared sense of direction that coordinates the actions of many people (Kotter, 1996).

A complete vision statement fully addresses the needs statement and expresses an outcome that is imaginable, desirable, and feasible. The plan is focused, allows for flexibility, and can be readily communicated to stakeholders (Kotter, 1996).

Developing this vision statement requires several iterations and feedback from key stakeholders and often needs time to evolve. The following is an example of how a financial organization's vision statement evolved over a period of a few weeks during the initiation of the change initiative.

Iteration one. The operations division will become a leader in lean manufacturing in our industry over the next five years by identifying, through a best-practices approach, methods to reduce costs while continuing to improve our customers' satisfaction. This will be accomplished through the endless pursuit of excellence—specifically, the definition and implementation of the most efficient best practices, processes, and procedures consistently used in our manufacturing facilities across the world. We will utilize the best-of-breed technology wherever possible and by continually measuring and monitoring our vital manufacturing metrics.

Stakeholder feedback indicated that this version of the vision statement was too long. Several stakeholders also wanted the term *supply chain* mentioned in the vision statement. The next iteration was simplified as follows:

Iteration two. We will become a recognized leader in supply chain management and lean manufacturing in the industry by continuously reducing our costs while improving our customer satisfaction.

Stakeholders liked this shortened vision statement, but executives thought it was not impactful and allowed stakeholders too much freedom to interpret the language.

After a few more iterations and survey of key stakeholders, including managers who would be critical to driving and implementing the change, the following version of the vision statement was approved.

Final iteration. We will become a recognized leader in lean manufacturing in the industry by reducing costs while improving customer satisfaction. To remain competitive in a global market, we will make our global supply chain and manufacturing facilities best in class within the next five years. We will invest in our people and technology to achieve this, and our success will be measured by continually monitoring our vital business metrics.

Although *best in class* may sound too abstract, trade groups in this particular industry define and measure the rating.

Structuring Change Management Initiatives

A seasoned change leader understands a basic law of nature that often drives organizational behavior: the path of least resistance. Slowly pour a glass of water on a driveway and watch how gravity moves the water through the crevices of the pavement. The water is following the path of least resistance. The law is that energy will travel along the path of least resistance determined by its underlying structure. When organizations or teams are not structured properly, they will likewise take the easy, familiar path, often failing to achieve their desired results (Fritz, 1999).

Two main structures drive organizational behavior: a conflict-resolution system that tends to oscillate, producing temporary results but ultimately failing to achieve lasting results, and a tension-resolution system that tends to produce success and permanent results (Fritz, 1999).

Problem-solving efforts in organizations often employ a conflict-resolution system. The desire for change yields initial results, but because the underlying structure does not support these results, instability occurs, and the structure seeks stability by resisting the change. Anyone who has tried to stop smoking or drinking realizes the potential to replace one vice with another: One may give up cigarettes, but wind up overeating instead. The same is true in organizations and project teams. Organizational problems may be temporarily "solved," but in reality, they are dispersed to other areas. A process-improvement effort to reduce the cost of operations may create customer satisfaction problems for sales and marketing; the result may cost the organization more in the long run. Executing strategic change requires the proper structure, including organizational structure, program team structure, and project team structure. In other words, great care should be taken to determine which actors will participate in this change and what roles they will play, starting with the identification of a basic provider/customer model.

Organizational Structure

Creating the right project organization structure is crucial to the success of an organization's change initiatives. The structure shown previously in Figure 9-6 is a temporary one that is unique to a specific program or project and it comprises three teams—the customer team, the advisory team, and the project team, as shown in Figure 9-7.

The teams work closely and balance one another, each with specific responsibilities and objectives to ensure that the effort achieves the desired outcomes. This type of project organization produces benefits, is likely to establish trust, helps team members to work in a more cohesive manner, and ultimately, increases project performance.

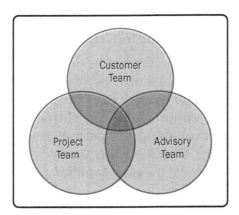

Figure 9-7. Three components of program organization for effective change management.

Customer team. Individuals representing those who will consume the deliverables and achieve the defined benefits make up the *customer team*. A functional manager (integrator) or team of functional managers typically leads this team and has significant responsibility for ensuring that users comply with new processes and adopt systems that are delivered. Members of this team also must be early adopters and provide thought leadership on the change's impacts on other aspects of the organization.

Project team. Members of the project team, led by the project leader, are responsible for ultimately producing the project deliverables that enable change. This includes deliverables related to change management, which are addressed later in this chapter. All customer-facing project team members are critical to creating a lasting organizational change. Their interactions with the customer team generate feedback and assimilation of the change on the part of the customer. The organization should structure the project team to be focused on the customer, which ensures that the project team understands the business need. Members of the project team should be able to see the big picture and understand how their work affects the organization's overall long-term goals. Project teams enhance the change process by focusing on how customers desire to experience the consumption of critical deliverables. To have an experience is to be rationally and emotionally involved.

Integrating a project team within an organization can prove to be difficult. Too often, this temporary team is unable to work closely with the overall organization in order to successfully deliver project results. Project teams may be disconnected from the real project need when they lack the understanding of a customer's business or work remotely from other users. They may use a vernacular in meetings and documents that customers and users do not understand. The size of the intersection of these three teams should be significant if these teams are to succeed in driving change.

Advisory team. This team comprises individuals with whom the project team and customer team are required to consult to ensure that the change being introduced by the project is acceptable, does not create unintended consequences, and, more importantly, will be accepted by the end users. Members of this team may include executives, regulatory advisors, legal experts, and other managers whose processes are affected by the change initiative.

Business, technical, and political subject matter experts (SMEs) are imperative for the project organization when implementing a change initiative. A strong advisory team is especially important for large organizational change initiatives; subject matter expertise and guidance will act as a significant risk management measure. This team's members are important stakeholders, even though they are not end users of the deliverables, responsible for benefits, or working on the project team. These experts provide essential insight into how a change in one department may impact other factors that might not be perceptible to the project or customer teams.

The project team will not understand every nuance of the organization or be experts in each aspect of the change initiative. However, they should have business process knowledge and financial operational knowledge, articulating this knowledge in a manner that quickly enhances credibility. Such business knowledge is essential for developing trust and gaining the necessary information from individuals on the customer and advisory teams.

Maximizing Organizational Change Management Through Deliverables

Once the correct structure is in place, change management should be displayed prominently in project planning, execution, and control. All too often, change management components are buried in the project's work breakdown structure (WBS) as broad communication plans or training efforts. For change initiatives to achieve benefits, the project team needs to elevate change management activities to a level of visibility that warrants measurement and produces accountability. Deliverables—including change management deliverables—inherently require acceptance criteria and success measures. Change management deliverables do not simply start with training activities, fancy newsletters, and project-branded polo shirts. Rather, they begin with measuring urgency, attitudes, and capabilities, then address what those measurements have revealed.

The project plan includes all change management components, starting with the WBS at level one or two. Change management deliverables can include:

- A clear vision statement for the project;
- Structure of the project organization with project team and customer team;
- Customer workshops with documented feedback;
- Assessments to measure organizational agility and attitudes; and
- Communication of best practices methodology.

The creation of project deliverables that enable change brings these three teams together in an organization for success. Deliverables drive the much-needed interaction and shared experiences between the customer team and project team, and this maximizes the project organization's agility to adjust and react to emergent needs in the organization and new requirements from the change initiative.

If these crucial change management elements are not visible in the project plan and do not have the accountability of measures, the change initiative is likely to fail. As schedule pressures increase as a result of typical project modification, uncertainty, and resource contention, change management efforts often are the first to get cut in order to meet a deliverable date. Organizational thinking needs to move away from a sole focus on meeting critical delivery dates to a focus on when benefits will accrue. When stakeholders and sponsors focus their discussions on benefits, better decisions are made during project execution, which will benefit all stakeholders.

The customers are the ones who realize benefits; thus, customers need to be actively engaged in the project. And the project team needs to be focused on customers' needs. This is accomplished by driving deliverables, such as prototypes, that users can test and experience, begin to understand, and begin to assimilate. When change management is given visibility and considered critical, its deliverables will dramatically influence the project plan. The plan needs to address factors such as how many iterations the project team will provide to the customers and how to receive their feedback. Feedback leads to interaction, and greater interaction means greater understanding between the teams as the project moves from the abstract to the actual.

Roles and Responsibilities

On a project that will bring about change throughout an organization, virtually everyone involved contributes to the outcome. Certain roles are critical to the completion of the project, of course, but other roles also have a significant impact on ensuring that the change is lasting and successful.

Project Leader

Leading the project team, the project leader is required to understand organizational change management. This individual may assist in creating the vision and project mission statements and should believe in them so that the effort required to achieve the change is sustained. A crucial task of the project leader is enabling active involvement of the sponsor and nurturing trust between the project team and customer and advisory teams.

The project leader assesses the change activities conducted at the portfolio level and ensures that change management deliverables are incorporated in the project plan. The creation of a detailed, written plan is a critical step. Such a plan may prevent discrepancies in the expectations of the different teams, ensures that critical requirements (such as training) are adequately addressed, and helps keep the change effort on schedule. The plan should include:

- A definition of each deliverable and a statement of its purpose;
- A schedule with milestones;
- A statement of accountabilities that outlines who will do what, and by when;
- A communications outline for the sharing of change information with the relevant stakeholders; and
- Measurements to evaluate the success and impact of the effort (Mourier & Smith, 2001).

Sponsor

The sponsor is the link between the project team and the organization's executive leadership. This person helps facilitate the necessary organizational support, which includes establishing the proper structure for the project organization. The sponsor helps keep the project aligned with the organization's strategy and vision. The sponsor should be actively engaged with the project, have a sense of ownership for the project, and ultimately be responsible for realizing the project's intended benefits and implementing the desired change (Bourne, 2012).

The sponsor's responsibilities include communicating with others in senior management regarding the project, gaining their commitment, and ensuring that the necessary resources are allocated to sustain the change. The sponsor supports the project leader and makes sure that any escalated issues are resolved effectively (Bourne, 2012).

Customer-Facing Analysts

Those analysts who interact directly with customers contribute first to the understanding of the organization's current state and its desired future state. Their ability to define these states communicates the discrepancies that the project and change management efforts are designed to address. Customer-facing analysts also provide necessary subject matter expertise that contributes to building trust-based relationships and effective planning.

Change Management Leader/Change Leader

Central to change management success is the change management leader. Seasoned project leaders often assume this role because they understand the necessity for change management on second- and third-order change initiatives.

The leader needs to understand what the future will look like, assess change indicators, align people with the vision, and inspire them to make it happen in spite of any obstacles (Kotter, 1996). The change management leader should have significant authority to build a coalition of leadership that continues to grow and sustain the energy of the change and its adoption by all within the organization. Hiring a mid-level public relations expert to develop fancy communications and brand the initiative is often insufficient. This person must have the right attitude to be the point person for change, which requires persistence, determination, and stamina. The change management leader should commit fully to seeing the project through to completion. And this leader must act as a voice of conscience, with the ability to tactfully and diplomatically raise issues with sponsors when necessary (Tan & Kaufmann, n.d.). The change management leader is also the one who listens to the fears of other stakeholders and identifies the root causes of any resistance.

From the first iteration of the change initiative idea, before beginning to put a plan down on paper, the change management leader ensures that change management is given visibility and recognized as being critical to the initiative's success. As plan development continues, the change management leader is responsible for making certain that change management deliverables are in place, with a means to measure their acceptance and/or implementation.

Functional Managers/Integrators

The functional manager leads the group that will receive the direct benefits of the change. This individual is a partner with the project leader in the process of implementing change. The functional manager engages with the project team and provides input for requirements. Another important responsibility of this role is to help align goals and objectives with organizational vision, as is the identification of potential unintended or unforeseen consequences. The functional manager provides the project team with the needed resources to complete the project and, with the project leader, shepherds the change within the environment (Ferraro, 2012).

During the course of a change effort, sponsors may be somewhat removed from the project process, especially regarding day-to-day matters. The functional manager continues to support the organizational vision, acting as a source of truth for requirements, validating the project team's business process analysis, and serving as a source of authority on measuring benefits.

To succeed, the functional manager and project leader should share the same goals, have mutual respect for each other, and have a common understanding of how to achieve the project's objectives (Ferraro, 2012).

Advisory Team Members

The project team engages with the advisory team members regarding the change that is being introduced by the project, in order to gain input on the requirements and identify unintended consequences and impacts. Members of this team may include executives, regulatory advisors, legal experts, and other managers whose processes are affected by the project. The project team needs their support to gain the insights needed for implementing the change successfully, including which staff members need which information and when. For example, for legal, HR, or operations, what are the implications for changing a particular policy?

Responding to the Need—Developing Project Mission Statements

A strategic organizational need is met by action—a project mission. This mission attempts to resolve some or all of the needs expressed in the needs statement and aligns with the broader vision statement of the change initiative. A project mission statement should be specific to the project objectives and should be short, precise, and bold. It should follow this format: "This project will create deliverables to be used by a customer(s) to achieve specific objectives." Specific project objective statements address the need by explicitly stating what the project is creating, who is using it, and what benefit they hope to achieve. Early attempts at a project mission statement provide a basis for scrutiny, which is needed for the change project to succeed. The project mission statement provides alignment between the project and the change initiative's vision statement. The mission statement clearly identifies the product, service, and result of the project; which stakeholders are using or consuming it; and which objectives, stated as measurable benefits, arise from its use. These benefits should be logically aligned with organization's vision for change.

Within the project life cycle, different customers will have different needs. The project may expand beyond technology to encompass new processes and possible changes to contracts or compliance aspects. The challenge is trying to capture all of this in one clear, concise project mission statement that identifies potential competing interests of primary and secondary stakeholders. This is not easy; nor should it be shortchanged. This statement should convey real meaning and imagery to the project team and stakeholders.

For example, one company has this need statement: "XYZ Associates is facing new regulations, which go into effect in four months; these regulations require changes to how credit card data are protected. Failure to comply will result in substantial fines, negative publicity, and loss of customers."

A mission statement that addresses the issues described above, including the competing needs of stakeholders, may look something like this: "The Customer Data Security Project will create new business processes and technology to manage customer information, including credit card data (the project's main deliverable), to be used by our website customers and e-commerce partners (primary customers) to comply with new federal security standards, eliminate existing supply chain data vulnerabilities, and reduce e-commerce operations maintenance and support by 3% as of 31 December (specific, timed objectives)."

The project manager should work closely with primary and secondary stakeholders to refine this mission statement until everyone understands it. It is not science; it is art.

When stakeholders are not clear about what the intent of a project is, they will likely resist it or be neutral. When it's done correctly, the project mission statement clearly states what the project team is creating; who consumes the product, service, or result; and what benefits are to be attained. This statement becomes an elevator pitch for project leaders, a consistent message to bring new stakeholders on board to the project, and a tool to quickly and articulately express sense-making statements to wary stakeholders.

Measuring Organizational Change Management on Programs and Projects

Delivery of the defined project outputs enables organizations to realize objectives and benefits. However, the successful delivery of project results—according to specifications, budgets, and schedules—does not ensure that benefits will be achieved. For this, key stakeholders have to be ready to use the project deliverables to achieve benefits. Effective change management prepares stakeholders to assimilate deliverables in their environment. Change management allows change to occur in a manner that accomplishes strategic objectives and realizes and accelerates expected benefits. Any project that drives recognizable change requires that change management be ingrained in all aspects of the project. To increase the likelihood of realizing benefits, these change management deliverables need to be measured accordingly.

Will a project actually realize the benefits for which it was begun? So many aspects of an organization can affect project results and the achievement of the project's desired benefits. These aspects can include the organization's preparedness; leadership capability, history, and experience of previous initiatives; resource availability and expertise to change readiness; motivations and attitudes; people's understanding of the change initiative; and their willingness to accept a change.

Change management aims to address these factors, but without measurement before, during, and after the change, leaders of change initiatives don't truly know their starting points and can't identify and reduce the barriers that prevent benefit realization. Without change management measurement, project risks increase, including cost escalation, schedule slippage, and the lack of customer acceptance. Without measurement, organizations risk failing to achieve the very benefits that drove the initiative. Project teams should execute projects in a manner that enables benefit recognition and not settle for only the acceptance of a final product, service, or result.

Measuring change management efforts within projects allows the project team and the organization to address critical barriers and increase the probability of recognizing the project's expected benefits. Measurement helps clarify what has to happen within the organization to accelerate both adoption rates of the changes that the project brings and the benefits of those changes.

Among the many examples of change failures, some projects have delivered high-quality results only to have the organization dismantle the project results within weeks or months, making the entire effort obsolete. Managers and users reworked new processes back to the old processes and modified performance reports to convince superiors that the new process or technology was not working. One company's project management office planned, designed, tested, and launched US$4 million of advanced technology to automate a business process and reduce staff. Yet, the intended end users continued to work using the old processes. They organized and used their own processes, while devising an elaborate scheme to report to executives that they were implementing the new process. Why don't employees adopt project deliverables? The possible reasons are many, including the following:

- The project team did not understand the real business problem.
- Little attention was paid to the definition of the current and desired future state of the business process.

- The team had no defined approach to identify barriers and enablers for the change.
- Proper stakeholders (i.e., users, managers) were not engaged early in the project life cycle.
- The project team made a minimal effort to communicate "what's in it for them" to the users.
- No one listened to or validated user concerns.
- The team allowed a void in project communications, and voids tend to fill with negative innuendos and half-truths.
- Management systems were not modified to properly track and measure the change.

All of these items contribute to resistance for the change and increase the probability of benefit erosion. Blame does not necessary lie with a presumed lack of sponsorship. Sponsors are busy and attend to many duties. Savvy project managers understand how to keep sponsors actively involved without placing undue burdens on them that they cannot fulfill. The project manager is acting on behalf of the sponsor(s) and must be well versed in change management techniques, which involve stakeholders in the conception, planning, and execution of the change. People tend to react to change better with such involvement than they do with executive edicts to follow orders.

To be consistently successful in leading projects, leaders and teams should measure the organization's ability to adapt to the change, then continually target project work by increasing the organization's ability to assimilate the project deliverables and reduce resistance.

Key Measures

The first step for successful change management is assessing and benchmarking the current state of an organization, considering both its ability to change and its willingness to change. The ability to change is a function of the urgency to change and the organization's capabilities. The willingness to change is a function of the organization's collective attitudes.

Three key measures for second- and third-degree change initiatives are:

- Urgency associated with the change;
- Attitudes from executives to rank-and-file staff; and
- Capabilities of the organization, people, processes, and systems to change (Mourier & Smith, 2001).

The first factor to assess is urgency. Urgency drives action. When management, users, and employees who are impacted by the change do not feel urgency, they are less likely to engage and participate in the project and its outcomes. Therefore, measuring how the stakeholders view the coming organizational change is critical. The inclusion of representatives from the range of stakeholders (e.g., executives, managers, and end users) can jump-start discussion as to how best to proceed. Have these stakeholders weigh in on 10 potential business outcomes (e.g., sales revenue, customer satisfaction, and employee morale) and the impact that the change will have on them. Stakeholders' recognition of a strong impact on key business outcomes indicates an urgency to move forward with the project. When the feedback from the stakeholders does not indicate urgency to change, the focus of the plan should begin with creating and instilling urgency.

Even when urgency does exist, employees still may not embrace change; therefore, the project teams need to assess the attitudes of those involved. Are employees positive about this change? Are end users and managers passive? Is the sponsor ambivalent? The attitudes of stakeholders will also have a powerful impact on whether organizational change succeeds or fails.

The third key area of assessment is capabilities: What are the current capability levels of end users and workers involved in the change? What is management's ability to implement and support the change? In the organization itself, has a change such as this been made before, and, if so, how successful was it?

Evaluating urgency, attitudes, and capabilities requires measuring positive and negative factors, again seeking input from stakeholders at various levels in the organization. Among the possible positive factors are employees' understanding of their role in the change, visible sponsor support for the change, reward for change and innovation in the organization, and a dedicated and capable project team. Factors measured on the negative side may include an uninvolved or ambivalent sponsor, goals that seem vague, a clash between the change and the way things are done in the organization, and a lack of attempts to keep people informed (Mourier & Smith, 2001).

For organizational change related to a specific project, finding the average score for each factor identifies which of the positive and negative factors are significant to the project's success. Then, calculating the difference between the number of positive and negative factors indicates the likelihood of the project's success (Mourier & Smith, 2001). If the project's significant negative factors heavily outnumber the positive factors, then the project will likely struggle to succeed. However, identifying the factors that will present the greatest obstacles allows the project team to determine whether these factors can be overcome, and if so, what actions are required. This creates the opportunity to plan how to address the negative factors and enhance the positive factors.

Once the influential factors specific to the planned organizational change are identified, the project team selects specific tactics to strengthen or neutralize these factors, as appropriate, to increase the chances of a successful project outcome. Change tactics to consider include the following:

1. Define change as a compelling element of the organization's strategy.
2. Establish an infrastructure for the change.
3. Create and use a project plan.

4. Invest in the change and commit to the long haul.
5. Break the change effort into small, manageable parts.
6. Translate the change into job-level details.
7. Provide recognition for meeting expectations and consequences for failing to do so.
8. Incorporate the change into the management systems.
9. Follow up relentlessly (Mourier & Smith, 2001).

Regardless of the type of organizational change sought through the project, the potential positive and negative factors will be similar, and the tactics above will be applicable.

Change Management Effectiveness: Measuring During Project Execution

With understanding of the organization's urgency, capabilities, and attitudes toward the change initiative, the project team can tailor the project plan to address specific deficiencies and capitalize on the strengths of the organization to increase momentum. When urgency is lacking, the project team can plan events or create artifacts during the initiation and planning of the project to increase urgency, such as updating the need statements, conducting town hall meetings with sponsors, and enlisting integrators to address their employees. If capabilities are lacking as a result of employee skills or system limitations, the project plan may need to be expanded to include training programs or to acquire specific system engineering capabilities.

Other deliverables to enhance change are:

- A vision statement;
- Communication processes;
- Surveys;
- Current and desired future states;
- Gap analysis of processes and systems;
- Management system reporting analysis;
- Targeted communications;
- Educational deliverables;
- Demonstrations;
- Workshops;
- Prototypes;
- Simulations;
- Application training;
- Process training; and
- Other engagement activities.

These deliverables help internal and external parties comprehend the change itself, what the change implies for them, and how they need to adjust their behaviors and work processes. One key to communicating effectively is to identify targeted audience groups and to select which groups are appropriate for each communication. Not every stakeholder needs to know the same information, and overloading recipients with irrelevant communications often negates the important messages.

Measurement of the effectiveness of change management deliverables ensures that they fulfill their intended purpose. To measure readership and engagement, the project plan could include open and click rates of critical communications and participation rates in surveys. Participation, comments, and feedback are essential for engaging people in the change initiative. The next crucial area is comprehension: Do customers really understand what is changing? Tools to answer this question include simple assessments and test questions about the material provided, skills assessments, and engaging people in two-way dialogue.

Even when stakeholders understand the change, the project team should be sure that the stakeholders at all levels are ready to deal with the change. In this readiness category are measurements of the organization's ability to execute the change if it were to happen immediately, including tasks such as updating policies and addressing possible anomalies. On an individual level, end users' skills should be ready for new processes. These needed skills may comprise using new software, new hardware, or electronic methods for processes that were previously paper based. New requirements may include changed ergonomics, such as long periods of sitting in front of a screen rather than walking through an office complex or standing at a copier.

Communication Best Practice

Following a communication best practice for the initiative helps ensure the development of the proper awareness and educational content regarding the change—for example, why it must happen, its impacts to specific stakeholders, and the path to successful change. Communications must target specific stakeholder audiences and the methodology must include the measurement of both content comprehension and desired behavior changes (or lack thereof) and the application of corrective measures where needed. The model shown in Figure 9-8 is appropriate for second- and third-order changes.

It is critical to the communication mode to have specific content that explains why the change is occurring, perhaps in the form of a call to action that captures readers' attention, combined with job-relevant material to assist employees and business partners in understanding the change and how to apply the new processes and skills in their jobs. The content needs to be compelling and specific to the recipients. Targeting content to the individuals impacted is important; contacting people who are not affected will dilute recipients' attention. Eventually, they will ignore the material. Using the appropriate medium to deliver the content is also important, such as the use of a learning management system or interactive material. Overuse of blast emails is ineffective. Measuring readership and comprehension through

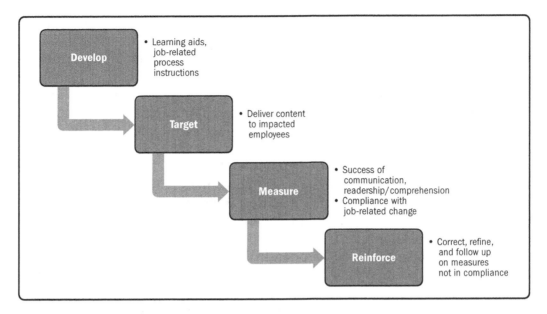

Figure 9-8. Change management communication model.

simple quizzes and interactive components helps ensure that the message is understood. Ultimately, the team should measure the key business metrics that should have been established early in the project to evaluate adoption of the change. Timely reporting of both comprehension and compliance measures is critical to drive mass change among large groups that are impacted by the change. Based on the measurements of readership and comprehension, change needs to be continually reinforced by project activities. Measuring once is not enough; timely feedback on key measurements allows for realistic appraisals of barriers that people face as well as the proper level of urgency, sense-making activities, and empathy.

Change Acceptance: Post-Deployment Measures

For projects requiring significant change, the achievement of specific change management measures provides an indication of readiness and a gating milestone to begin deployment activities. Too often, project teams focus on whether their deliverables are ready, but what is more important is whether the customer will be ready to use the deliverables and assimilate or master the change in a manner consistent with expected benefits realization. Knowing customer readiness requires assessment.

Even when users have read the provided material and indicated that they are ready for a change, the question remains as to whether they will actually accept it. Users often revert back to the familiar, comfortable processes that a project was designed to eliminate.

Measuring the outcomes and success of change management deliverables ensures that a change is on track to achieve lasting benefits. Measurements begin with the preplanning assessment of an organization's readiness and capability. During the course of the project, measurement continues with the evaluations of organizational readiness and effectiveness of communications that help stakeholders comprehend the change, understand what the implications are, and prepare for changed behaviors and processes. Finally, post-deployment measures ensure lasting, successful adoption of the change. To make certain that these measurements take place and realize their full impact, change management deliverables should have a level of visibility in the project documents that requires measurement and produces accountability.

The other essential measurement component is the metrics that are built in to an organization's systems. Embedding change into management systems is critical for the change to last. Far too often, organizations do not update their management systems to correspond with the implementation of an organizational change. Those legacy systems in general—and HR systems in particular—will present obstacles to lasting change. For example, an HR system may evaluate employees based on previous objectives rather than on the values of the new vision. Compensation may be tied to avoiding mistakes rather than moving change forward. Also, recruiting, hiring, and promotions may be highly subjective and reflect little that relates to the organization's transformation (Kotter, 1996). Aligning personnel and information systems with the vision of the change is essential, as is building metrics into the process to ensure that the changes are ingrained into organizational reports and scorecards. Without establishing new measurements, managers will continue to use existing measures to drive their behavior.

Once deployment begins, project teams should pay attention to the process measurements that point to a shift in desired behavior. They also need to look back to the benefits and objectives that are defined in the project mission statement. If the implementation is proceeding as planned, are users able to complete their work in a manner that achieves the project objectives? This includes quality, cycle times, cost measures, and customer satisfaction.

When the change requires large cutovers (switching from one system or process to a new one within a short time frame), establishing day one or week one teams to facilitate the initial rollout of the new system or process will help make users more comfortable. During one organization's large cutover, three individuals were designated as "change facilitators" and wore yellow project polo shirts. This provided users and managers with opportunities for direct, face-to-face discussion during the critical early implementation days when first impressions are drawn. People could ask for help, report an issue, or simply express frustration. The facilitators were trained and empowered to act on the spot, resolving most inquiries quickly. Other inquiries were directed to a centralized project support team for quick troubleshooting of the issues. Each issue was accompanied by survey and feedback data to assess how the implementation was truly proceeding. The data do not lie!

Summary

Change management processes are linking pins between strategy and execution teams. These processes connect strategy to portfolio management, to program management, and to project execution.

The role of change management is to consistently transition changes in strategy to portfolio managers, project management offices, and project teams to allow them to make sense of the changes, buy in to them, and empower them to act.

Changing portfolio components is difficult. In order to transfer the changes in strategy reflected in portfolio changes to program and project resources or project management offices, portfolio managers must execute change management activities in the definition, alignment, and authorization of these changes. These activities should be aimed at the goal of gaining consensus through the stakeholder community and achieving a sequenced, prioritized portfolio component list.

Portfolio changes flow down to the project management offices and execution teams that now need to adjust their cadence to shifting priorities. Delivery managers should have made sense of the change, and now need to be empowered to execute the change. To avoid the devastating impacts that multitasking has on productivity, workers must be able to prioritize tasks to increase throughput given their fixed capacity.

When it's time for a project to bring about change throughout an organization, the structure of the initiative is critical. The structure begins with the organization's resources rallying around a need to change and a well-crafted response to the need—the initiative's vision. Together, this need and vision are critical to properly aligning the project organization with the change. From the vision, the project or program organization structure arises. The proper structure of program and project research allows for the project mission to be achieved.

Any project that drives recognizable change requires change management to be ingrained in all aspects of the project and properly measured. Developing a communication best practice allows the effectiveness of change activities to be measured during pre- and post- deployment project phases.

References

Bourne, L. (2012, April). *What does a project sponsor really do?* [Web log post] Retrieved from http://blogs.pmi.org/blog/voices_on_project_management/2012/04/what-does-a-project-sponsor-re.html

Ferraro, J. (2012). *Project management for non-project managers*. New York, NY: AMACOM.

Fritz, R. (1999). *The path of least resistance for managers: Designing organizations to succeed*. San Francisco, CA: Berrett-Koehler.

Kotter, J. P. (1996). *Leading change*. Boston, MA: Harvard Business School Press.

Mourier, P., & Smith, M. (2001). *Conquering organizational change: How to succeed where most companies fail*. Atlanta, GA: CEP Press.

Project Management Institute (PMI). (2012). *The standard for portfolio management* – Third edition. Newtown Square, PA: Author.

Project Management Institute (PMI). (2013). *Managing change in organizations: A practice guide*. Newtown Square, PA: Author.

Tan, A., & Kaufmann, U. H. (n.d.). *What makes a good leader of change?* Retrieved from http://www.iqpc.com/redcontent.aspx?id=65804

Review Questions

1. What type of change activities link organizational strategy to portfolio management activities?
2. How does a prioritized list of portfolio components improve program and project resource productivity?
3. What is the importance of a developing a "real need" statement? Practice developing a needs statement with the key stakeholders for a current project.
4. Discuss the communications best practice discussed in this chapter and make some notes on how it can be adopted and incorporated into your organization's change initiatives.

CHAPTER 10

How Successful Project Organizations Deliver Change

By Gary Sikma, MBA, MSM, CSM, SAFe 4.0 (SA),
PMI-ACP, PMP

Abstract

When reframing the results of projects over an eight-year period at a national not-for-profit organization and reflecting on the criteria and promises made in order to gain approval, the chief operating officer reflected that if we had all the increased revenue, reduced expenses, and increased efficiencies, we would be able to do ten times as much with a fraction of the staff and have revenue that would astound anyone. But it does not take deep analysis to realize that none of those things happened. This organization came to a realization that was hardly an epiphany: That which is measured is improved. Unfortunately, there is a lack of detailed evidence revealed in postmortem analysis and the parade of project requests continues to proceed.

A chief financial officer at another not-for-profit organization echoed a refrain to that of other CFOs in other organizations—for-profit as well as not-for-profit organizations—that there is a need for measurements before and after projects. In an insurance firm in the Midwest, the CFO voiced demands on others in the executive suite to provide the essential details. This process proved effective, but it took time. Immediate results were not impressive, but eventually, there were improvements in the outcomes. Though initial studies were focused on projects that levered the waterfall methodology, it is being expanded to some of their more agile approaches as well.

This chapter will discuss some of the processes through which improvements can be made and the benefits understood. It will also outline a method of benefits planning to help track and realize results that reflect the desired return on investment (ROI). Through practical, low-impact methods, sponsors and key stakeholders can begin to make better estimates for success and begin to tout the success with credible evidence.

Why Change?

Organizations plan and implement change for a specific purpose. There is always some level of understanding as to what the benefits of the change will be. How well we understand those outcomes or how effective our plans are in getting the organization to the desired outcome is often overlooked. High-performing organizations are not only very deliberate in planning their changes, but these organizations also understand what key performance indicators (KPIs) will be achieved once the change has been put in place.

The more effective changes are those for which the change leadership has provided a compelling reason for the change. In many cases, there is typically an element to satisfy the WIIFM (what's in it for me) perspective. This is an important part of motivating others to facilitate the change. Another very important aspect of the change is getting approval. Typically, there needs to be a compelling reason for the change in order to "sell" the change to those who will authorize it.

These benefits are outlined as the business case for the change. This is articulated through the description of either a problem that the organization is trying to resolve or an opportunity that the organization is trying to capitalize on. In some cases, the problem may not have occurred yet, but the organization may feel that the problem is imminent. In this case, change is part of a risk mitigation strategy.

Project Success: Historical

Project success has traditionally been measured in terms of the project being on time, within budget, and within the scope or quality expectations. A plethora of studies show a range of success/failure rates, but it is clear that not all projects are successful based on these criteria. Though these are measured and typically valid, the measures are more associated with the quality of the project and not the outcome of the project. So, even under the traditional triple constraint values and measures of success, projects may lack the successes that were originally touted as the reason to move ahead.

Another method of evaluating success is the perceived value to the customer. How delighted is the customer with the implementation of the change initiative? The perceived value for the customer is becoming a common method for evaluating success, particularly when the project is not strictly an information technology change. These are typically anecdotal results and not empirical. The results are gathered in some form of a survey that typically attempts to assess the effectiveness of the project. Ultimately, the results are a perceived value and speak primarily to the effectiveness of the implementation team rather than a product of implementation.

The benefits of implementing any change amount to the value that is agreed upon by the key stakeholders. How well does the change impact the business problem or opportunity that motivated the change in the first place?

In order for a process to have value, there must be an agreed-upon perception of that value. If stasis is valued by a majority of an organization, then motivating to change will be a significant challenge. Not until there is an agreed-upon value and benefit will there be the motivation necessary to achieve the desired change.

Although the ability to change is one aspect that must be present, the willingness of the participants to change becomes an even greater hurdle. Training and coaching help with abilities in most instances; however, the willingness to change must come from within each of the stakeholders.

Figure 10-1 represents the scales of judgment for approving projects. On the left, we reflect the hard costs, which are the costs and investments necessary to complete the project. These may be in the form of costs for software, hardware, construction materials, and so on. These costs may also encompass the cost of labor. On the right of the figure are the proposed benefits that would result from the project. These benefits are broadly outlined in the business case and are intended as the return on investment for the expense.

All changes come at a cost. These costs can come in the form of soft provisions and may not be tied strictly to an organization's financial perspective. But in the end, all change requires a certain degree of hard costs. These hard costs come in terms of straight financial costs that are directly in the form of currency. Others may be in the less direct but still financial-oriented costs, such as those for human resources.

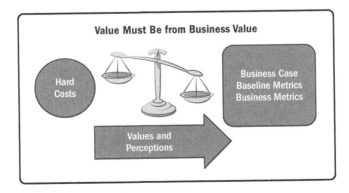

Figure 10-1.   Balancing costs with business value.

Irrespective of the type and source, in nearly all cases, there are hard costs associated with change. How the organization classifies these costs as well as the anticipated outcomes is a matter of what the perceived values are.

In some organizations, the value of customer satisfaction could be the preeminent driving force and the ruler against which all other costs and values are measured. In this type of organization, the outcomes for any change are measured in customer surveys, returning customers, and loyalty that typically will weather most mild storms in competition.

Others may take the perspective of valuing the shareholders' perspective. Even in the case of private or not-for-profit organizations, it is important to realize the value of making a profit for the organization.

Lastly, there are organizations that put the primary focus on the employees of the organization. Organizations strive to achieve high ratings for employee engagement and satisfaction. True artisans of this type do not take employee engagement surveys for the sake of superficial facades to placate the workforce. Rather, these organizations want to know what is valued by those who make up the workforce. They hire leadership that will value the engagement of employees.

Managers within any of these types of organizations are likely to understand the decision-making paradigm that exists. They are not quick to make decisions that will have a poor effect on the core of their corporate values.

Most successful organizations, however, take a more holistic perspective and balance the three dimensions. This balance helps achieve a consistent, long-term perspective. Though individual changes may more greatly impact or favor one area over another, the portfolio is typically balanced in such a way that the three are balanced in the long run.

A fourth aspect is sometimes included in the mix of values. Mission is a value that is a touted by many as a means of achieving success. Not many for-profit, and particularly publicly traded, companies can afford to have this perspective as a cornerstone of their value system. It is far more typical in a nonprofit company. Government, especially military organizations, may have this perspective. Mission success is the imperative.

Though there may be a significant number of organizations that tout any one perspective in change valuation, in the end, it is soon clear when it is only lip service rather than a true value.

Strategic Alignment

Another aspect of the change management process that was previously discussed is the aspect or purpose for change. In a deeper sense, this aspect refers to the need for all change to be in alignment with the corporate or business unit strategy. In the strategic planning process, it is typical to begin with a look at the organization and an external look at other businesses with like or similar business goals. Performing a SWOT (strengths, weaknesses, opportunities, and threats) analysis to assess the strengths, weaknesses, opportunities, and threats gives the leadership of the organization the opportunity to baseline their goals for the organization to achieve. In this way, the rest of the organization can begin to make initial proposals for how their segment of the business can help the overall organization achieve its goals.

Later in this chapter, we will discuss a method of creating healthy goals for each benefit to be realized. Here, let's a broader look at what the benefits should be at the tactical level in order to help the organization achieve the strategic goals it has set out after performing an analysis of the organization, along with the internal and external influences and aspects that affect the organization.

With a strategy created, the business units can assess their own outcomes that are critical to their success and to what degree they are contributing to the overall goals of the organization. These proposed changes come forward in a business case that is articulated to present either a problem statement that must be addressed or an opportunity statement that articulates an opening on which the organization may capitalize.

In the case of a problem statement, there are a number of challenges that a business unit may face, and these need to be dealt with. The changes that are proposed would generate the needed outcome or benefit to be realized. The strategic planning process is typically a top-down method of determining the overall benefits that need to be achieved and realized from the highest levels within the organization down to the tactical implementation of the strategic direction. These project proposals and change recommendations are the foundation for what the next layer of benefits should be.

The next phase of the strategic planning process is to determine the investments to be made. This is also an ideal place to make the change or project selections that will best achieve the outcomes needed. In many organizations, an investment level is determined based on the expected or anticipated outcomes. Careful calculations of the anticipated costs must be done in order to calculate the needed investment.

The most thorough portion of this phase is the total cost of ownership, or TCO. The TCO is an assessment of all costs, both hard and soft. Determining the costs that must be expended on the change initiative is considered a hard cost. This includes all capital and operational expenses that are new to the organization. In other words, these expenses are not built into the ongoing typical expenses that the organization would incur. Another hard cost is the cost of new full-time equivalents, or FTEs, that are needed to facilitate the change initiative. The soft costs for the change initiative are the salaries for the existing staff that would also be needed to perform the work of the change project. Although these costs are not new to the organization, they are part of the TCO for the change.

Understanding the total cost of ownership is necessary to help balance this investment against the anticipated reward that would have been portrayed in the business case. Knowing what the costs would be against the ROI helps ascertain the value. This is encompassed in the KPIs of the change. Ultimately, these are the expected benefits to be realized.

Once it is approved and scheduled, the change initiative can begin. Leveraging the science and art of implementation, project management, and the entire change management process, the change is put into place or implemented.

Though the benefits realization process starts long before this step, it is sometime during or immediately after the implementation that benefits begin to be realized. It is important to measure to determine how many benefits have been realized. What is measured, how it is measured, and who performs the measurements are all aspects that need to be planned in advance, but it is at this stage that the measurements begin. Has the anticipated value been achieved? Has the change initiative lived up to the promise of benefit? Unchecked, it is not uncommon for businesses to predict the same kind of benefits that a shiny infomercial might suggest. By planning and executing the measurement phase, stakeholders make a consistent and thorough estimate of the potential benefits.

Once measured, the values are reported to the group or individual responsible for oversight. If the predicted benefits have been achieved, the next step is to determine how long the process of measurements needs to continue.

But there are often times when the benefit is not realized. The next step at that point is to begin to analyze the reasons for not achieving the goal. If the cause can be determined, remediation can begin to take place.

This process is necessary, whether the change implementation is leveraging a waterfall or an agile approach. The agile approach can afford a quicker solution to the remediation process because it is built into the methodology. However, using traditional waterfall project management methodology is not an excuse for not performing remediation.

Remediation, in some cases, is a matter of adjusting the process slightly in order to achieve the goal. In others, a change scope order may be necessary in order to bring about a great change to enable the benefit to be realized. Of course, the change in scope will likely incur additional costs that were not originally anticipated during the planning process. In this case, it becomes imperative to perform thorough due diligence to determine if the anticipated costs are still required in order to achieve the benefit.

It is important to note that sunk costs should never be used to calculate the value of a troubled project. In the same context, it is important to realize that when the estimate to complete the change costs more than the anticipated benefit, serious contemplation should be given to canceling the project. It is not unusual for projects to be shut down in order for businesses to cut their losses rather than continuing to throw good money after bad. This, in essence, becomes the money pit of projects.

Science Versus Art of Benefits and Change

Change management, like many other things, consists of both science and art. The science and mechanics of change management are foundational and fundamental to effective change within organizations and the realization of the benefits from those changes. As the complexity of the change progresses, so does the need for a greater deal of the art of change management to be employed. The same is true with benefits realization.

Benefits realization can only be partially explained through the development and evolution of the science. Much of the science is articulated throughout this chapter. The art of benefits realization includes the wise use of tools and science in order to capture and measure the benefits of change, but also to use those data to continuously improve the processes and technologies.

The complexity of change and benefits realization can be measured through a straightforward assessment to determine in which order of magnitude the change can be categorized.

The first order of magnitude for change revolves around tasks. These include those changes that involve relatively simple changes in tasks and technology. This level or order of magnitude requires little art.

The second order of magnitude for changes is about changing people. This adds the dimension of people to the mix of tasks and technology. This requires a somewhat higher, yet still low, level of art to the change management and benefits realization process.

The third order of magnitude is when structure and culture are affected. At this point, science is only secondary to the need for the art of change management and benefits realization.

Lastly, the fourth order of magnitude consists of all the previous areas affected as well as the addition of external parties being affected.

Another aspect to this process is the dimension of a willingness to change along with the ability to change. With the lower order of magnitude changes, the primary inhibitor of effective change and benefits realization is the ability to change. In other words, getting players to engage is often merely a matter of ensuring that the right and adquate training is afforded to the staff.

As the order of magnitude increases, the ability to change is overshadowed by the willingness to change. This makes it far more difficult to achieve the benefits that were touted in the business case when the project or change for approval was first presented. As with anything, the greater the risk, the greater the reward. But also added into the equation is the added complexity with the risk. In fact, the added complexity compounds the risk asssociated with the change management process. Changing tasks is one thing, but as people, processes, and structure become a part of the mix, the complexity becomes far more challenging.

At this point, buy-in may be needed from those who are affected and those who must effect the changes in the organization; all must not only be able but, also willing to change.

Without this willingness, there can be no effective change. Without effective change, benefits will not be achieved or realized. This is why the art of change management is so vital to the process in inspiring, motivating, and managing the expectations of all the involved stakeholders throughout the change initiative.

A common mistake is to misinterpret the art of change management and view it as the manipulation of the people affected. Although manipulation may have some short-term, short-sighted benefits, the results will be short-lived and will not be sustainable over the long haul. Only through solid and effective change management and artful change management can long-term benefits be realized.

Whose Value?

As discussed earlier in regard to balancing costs, balance is the process of assessing value to both the cost and the business case. The values, however, are different based on the perceived value of the evaluator. The perspective of the evaluator is a significant contributor to what is held in higher regard. Figure 10-2 represents three of the primary viewpoints or perspectives that can be taken when making an evaluation of value. A Fortune 500 company in the United States made this a part of the decision-making paradim for their empowered managers.

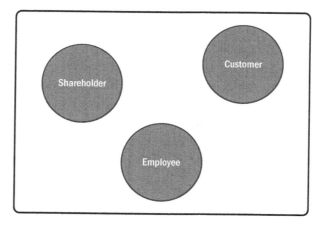

Figure 10-2. Values.

Key Performance Indicators

The value for the change can come in a number of forms. Earlier, it was pointed out that value can come from three viewpoints. From those perspectives, there are four areas in which value can be placed at the macro level. Financial benefits typically top the list of categories. Others include customer satisfaction, employee engagement and shareholder value. Moving into a more micro perspective of benefits realization requires companies to identify the specific key performance indicators (KPIs) that are going to be achieved or that the organization hopes will be achieved.

The KPIs selected are those goals that can give a measure of success to one of the four areas of value in the organization or ROI. Though we often look at a financial value as a return, there may be other perspectives, such as earlier, where we highlighted the idea of mission as a focus for some organizations.

How to Build KPIs

There are three primary aspects to building the KPIs that will mark success in change. First is understanding the value proposition for the organization—for example, shareholder, employee, customer, or mission. Second is to name the KPIs in a SMART goal which will be explained later. Finally, it is important to know who will be responsible for measuring.

The formula for value outcomes often seems like an overwhelming and complicated process. The perception of complication often keeps organizations from establishing this foundation of measures. Ultimately, several changes go without any real measured outcomes, and only anecdotal perspectives are garnered.

But how can we achieve empirical data based on the values of the organization and understand when a change has been successful or not? This process, as with others, is simpler when it is broken down into smaller, more manageable steps. Although there are any number of ways to do this, a common method is to use SMART goals (Doran, 1981)—an acronym that aids in the process as follows:

- S = specific
- M = measurable
- A = achievable
- R = relevant
- T = timebound

Specific

Though we can categorize goals in terms previously mentioned (customer-centric, employee-centric, mission-centric, or shareholder-centric), we need to peel back the layers of the problem that we are addressing or the business opportunity that we are using as a motive for our change. We have to be specific.

One of the more poignant lessons in specificity for me was one that I often used in my graduate classes in contracting. In this exercise, I provided the background of several cases and then I encouraged the class to debate how the judge would have decided. The examples that I used came from different states, so although there were some differences in the laws, the general terms of specificity were the same from state to state. One of the cases involved a contract to care for an elderly gentleman. The caretaker was to receive 10 acres of the gentleman's land upon his demise. After the man passed away, the family would not honor the agreement. Typically, the class would argue that the decision was in favor of the family and not the caretaker, citing a lack of a signed agreement or other formal codicil. Though they were right about the judgment, they were wrong in their reasoning. The reason for the decision was the lack of specificity. Had the agreement been for a *specific* 10 acres, the judge would have sided with the plaintiff.

Several other cases with very similar outcomes were the result of a lack of specificity. The same is true in reaching goals, outcomes, and, in particular, KPIs. Without the specific goal outlined in the agreements, success or failure is once again relegated to anecdotal data and a subjective perspective. Specifics are tantamount to realizing benefits.

Specificity requires us to name items that are less likely to be misconstrued than the broader description. For example, a change might be initiated to reduce turnover in an organization. Being more specific, in this case, is similar to moving from the strategic perspective to the tactical. So, a manufacturing organization might develop a plan to change a process that ultimately has the benefit or KPI of improving the employee satisfaction for a specific grievance that may have led many production employees to walk off the job and seek employment elsewhere. In this case, it would be a specific employee type that might be articulated for a specific goal.

Another is the general KPI of improved revenue to satisfy a shareholder-centric perspective. In order to be able to sell the change as well as to understand whether the change was actually the cause of the desired benefit being achieved, it must be associated with a more specific area. So, in one example, we could say that the increased revenue was from a particular service line, product, or other value stream that was generated by the company. In being more specific, we can see that there is a more direct connection to change.

Left to a broader or less-specified description, the overall income for a company may have dropped in the time period in question. But when you look further, you may discover that the reduction in revenue was the result of another change in the organization that happened simultaneously. Specifics help the organization understand this perspective more clearly.

Another solution is to limit the number of changes that are scheduled to occur simultaneously, but this will be addressed later.

Measurable

The second perspective to having and achieving effective goals is to ensure that they are measurable. Quantifiable outcomes take the specificity that we discussed earlier to a greater degree. In establishing goals, we want to avoid the generic adjectives that are typical in the mainstream public marketing of products.

Some good examples of measurable goals include a specific head count, as in the case of 85 employees who successfully completed a class. Another example is a percentage of an overall measurement, but this can be challenging, as in a case where the denominator of the equation is less static than what would be necessary to maintain that degree of certainty. Other examples of an outcome being measurable include temperature, weight, height, width, speed, currency, production rates, or units of time. In short, things that one can count may qualify as measurable components.

In terms of employment, what if you were asked to change jobs and, in return for your agreement to change jobs, your perspective employer offered you a "huge" salary increase? Most people would want to know what "huge" means before agreeing to such a deal. Having a goal be measurable removes ambiguity and limits the individual perspective or probability of a false inference.

Achievable

The third perspective in having solid goals for change outcomes is to ensure that the goal is something that can be achieved. Although having lofty, reach-for-the-sky goals may be fine for corporate vision statements (e.g., The airline of choice for all domestic travel), an outcome goal needs to be more realistic. A specific, measurable goal that is beyond the reach of the organization under present conditions discourages people from even trying to achieve the goal. What is the point? We cannot get there anyway, so missing the target by a little or a lot becomes moot.

Having stretch goals is a different perspective. Stretch is not the same thing as lofty, even though both goals are clearly higher-level, more challenging goals. Stretch goals provide the organization going through the change with the hope for success. Having hope, seeing light at the end of the tunnel, and knowing that there is a possibility of being successful is much more encouraging than the alternative.

By the same token, having goals that are not very challenging to achieve makes one wonder why the change is necessary in the first place. Finding the right mix of challenge versus achievability is a significant aspect in creating a solid, game-winning business goal.

Relevant

The relevancy of a KPI or its connection to the overarching strategic goals is an important aspect for any change. Without a relevant tie to the organizational goals, there is a dilution of purpose. Or, there is a tendency to create too many goals and the organizational focus is spread too thin.

Time Bound

Finally, appropriately established goals need to be time bound. The lack of a target date may precipitate an ongoing attempt to achieve the benefit regardless of the length of time and resources already expended.

Agreed upon

A bonus aspect of SMART goals is one more perspective on the benefits realization process where all the key performance indicators must be agreed upon by all stakeholders. Primarily, the sponsor, business owner, and the project manager should be in clear agreement as to which aspects or goals are worth the effort of going through the change management process.

Without a collaborative approach to this process, goals are only partially meaningful. This is a clear case where goal setting needs to be a dialogue and not simply a monologue. As was discussed in other chapters of this book, those having a change thrust upon them need to see a compelling reason for it. In particular, it is important and vital that all goals be agreed upon.

Baselines

Knowing the target you are aiming for in the benefits realization phase of the change management process will only have real value if the organization knows where it stands before the change begins. This is when a baseline of the current state becomes important to capture. Far too often, an anticipated benefit is never measured in the end simply because there was no beginning measurement. The sponsor or the business owners are so intent on getting started that some of the more vital aspects of planning and preparation are skipped, including the baseline measurement process.

In the parlance of the Old West, this is what is known as the ready, fire, aim methodology of change management. Though the team's enthusiasm is laudable, the outcome is often less than desirable. Measure twice and cut once, as the adage states. Keeping the sequence and timing of all aspects of the change management process in perspective is very helpful.

Determine everything that will be measured as a benefit. If you do not have a baseline measurement for that benefit, it can no longer considered a benefit.

Who Is Responsible for Benefits Realization?

When an organization is interested in capturing and reporting data regarding change management, benefits realization is not a task that is typically sought after. It is often considered one of the least-favored tasks of the change management process. If fingers are to be pointed at others for anything, this will often be the place they're pointing. In many sports, such as golf, tennis, and baseball, follow-through is important. Stopping the swing of the bat at the time of contact with the ball will certainly weaken the impact and ultimately shorten the distance and reduce the speed of the ball. Similarly, in golf and tennis, the follow-through of the swing is something that professionals are continuously coaching players on.

In change management, failure to take responsibility for benefits realization is the same as not following through on a swing. Ultimately, the impact of the change is either never realized or the benefits remain anecdotal and eventually lose their punch and effectiveness.

Historically, several scenarios and models have been tested along the way. Although there is no hard and fast rule for benefits realization ownership, there are a few principles that apply in most cases. Ultimately, the business owner is responsible for managing the outcome of the change; therefore, benefits realization is the business owner's responsibility. However, the entire process can be shared.

In cases where there is a center of excellence (COE) or a project management office (PMO) at the enterprise level, the responsibility for reporting belongs there. It is important to note that this is not the responsibility for benefits realization, but only the reporting of progress. The actual measurement itself is performed by a person or organization with the capability to gather the appropriate information. This could be a reporting group from the business unit or a person under the purview of the CIO.

Though a project team can implement a process, application, or any other change initiative, it takes the people in the affected business unit to make the sustained change and work toward realizing the benefit. These staff members are responsible to their managers who, in turn, have the overall responsibility for the benefits realization or lack thereof.

How Many Goals Are Appropriate?

The KPIs are established when working on the business case in the ideation phase of a change initiative. But how many goals are required? In some organizations, the list is limited to one to three benefits or KPIs that will be tracked. As organizations begin to assess and grow in their change management maturity, it may become grandly beneficial to limit the number of KPIs to one solid, SMART goal. In some cases, it may be helpful to increase this to two or three. More than that becomes extremely challenging to manage on the backside of the process.

When there is a need or organizational desire to have more than three goals, another step in the process becomes necessary. At the point when more than three KPIs are documented as benefits to the change management initiative, it is important to prioritize them. As in the case of requirements that need to be prioritized when one or more of the requirements can't be achieved because of crashing the schedule or de-scoping the project, it is not desirable to eliminate the deliverables that will help satisfy the higher-priority requirements.

Similarly, the benefits need to be prioritized when there are more than just a few. In the event that certain elements of the change need to be eliminated, revert to the original planning documents that established the requirement and the traceability for that requirement through the deliverable, test plan, and benefit that was expected to be realized.

Organizational Maturity

As mentioned earlier in this chapter, organizational maturity around the process of change management is important to understand. As in any organizational process, maturity can occur at different stages for different processes. Organizational project management maturity that is quite advanced does not inherently mean that change management maturity is just as advanced.

Likewise, having a very mature change management methodology and process in one part of the organization does not imply that the same maturity level exists throughout the organization. Understanding the maturity and change readiness posture of an affected portion of the business is important. In particular, it is vital to understand how this pertains to the benefits realization phase of the change management process.

Taking informal surveys of several organizations may provide limited and anecdotal data, but these surveys may indicate that benefits realization is not as prevalent as one would expect. Even in corporations with a very mature organizational project management methodology, the assumption cannot be made that the change management methodology is mature.

Benefits realization is lacking in many organizations. It is not fictional. It does exist. More and more organizations understand the need for it and are beginning to mature their processes. But typically, most organizations have a considerable way to go.

Benefits Plan

As with any aspect of project management or even management in general, it is important to start with a plan. This plan should guide the work through the project or program beyond the finished product and through the life cycle. The KPIs and quantitative measures must be defined and form the basis necessary to effectively monitor the delivery of program benefits management.

In order to realize benefits, it is important to have a plan that realistically understands the stakeholders' expectations of outcomes and benefits. This consists of the following key elements:

- Identifying planned benefits
- Analyzing and planning for delivery of benefits
- Delivering and monitoring benefits
- Transitioning benefits management to the organization and
- Sustaining benefits management.

The Benefits Register

The basic and simplest form of benefits planning is the benefits register. It is comprised of the following fields or aspects and can be used as a baseline as well as a summary report to the sponsors or key stakeholders:

- Program benefits;
- Stakeholders and their sphere of influence;
- Which benefit the stakeholder needs to know about;
- Which program component or deliverable delivers which benefit;
- The process for measuring benefits;
- KPIs for benefits;
- Thresholds for evaluating benefit achievements;
- Target dates and milestones for benefits achievement;
- Person, group, or organization responsible for benefits delivery; and
- Stakeholder preference for and frequency of communication.

Conclusions

The change management process is challenging. Understanding what the anticipated benefits are for any change is a vital part of justifying a change initiative. Benefits realization is one of the crowning jewels of the strategic planning process for an organization.

From strategy inception and creation to project ideation and approval, through the change management process and, ultimately, the benefits realization measurements, follow-through is paramount.

Change happens for a reason. Businesses are trying to solve a problem or capitalize on an opportunity. These changes have met with success and failure over the millennia, based on any number of success criteria.

Ultimately, there must be a reason; there must be value in the outcome of a change. The change must be aligned with the strategy. The change should be built on a solid method of planning and goal determination. Science will only get the organization partially there. Success is also a question of the art of change management. Goals must be agreed upon and SMART. As organizations mature, the need for understanding the impact of change and benefits realization will improve along the way.

References

Doran, G. T. (1981). There's a S.M.A.R.T. way to write management's goals and objectives. *Management Review, 70*(11), 35–36.

Review Questions

1. Why do organizations implement change?
2. Regardless of the perceived value of making a change, there is always some level of investment necessary to facilitate change in an organization. What are some of the hard costs associated with change?
3. When considering the value or benefit of change, nearly all organizations will consider the appropriate balance of the customer, employee, or owner. Some will also consider a fourth perspective. What is this fourth aspect and which types of organizations might want to view this perspective?
4. When creating key performance indicators (KPIs) in order to measure the efficacy and value of a change, what are five aspects that must be considered? How can we achieve empirical data based on the values of the organizations and understand when a change has been successful or not?
5. Who is responsible for benefits realization?

CHAPTER 11

Committing the Change Team

A Smooth Sea Never Made a Skillful Sailor

By Simona Bonghez, PhD, PMP

Abstract

In *Managing Change in Organizations: A Practice Guide* (Project Management Institute, 2013), change management is presented as an essential organizational capability that cascades across and throughout portfolio, program, and project management. The success of programs and projects is seen as being closely related to the successful implementation of the change it produces, and the contribution of the change team is essential. This chapter's effort is directed toward identifying the change team and the tools and techniques that can raise the commitment of its members. It addresses three major questions:

- Who is the change team and what are the roles and responsibilities within this team?
- What are the models that explain the dynamics of the change team?
- Which tools and techniques can we use to gain and increase the commitment of the change team?

Who is the Change Team?

The typical answer is that a change team is *a small group of employees appointed by the CEO (chief executive officer)*. This answer is incorrect on three levels, which will be explained throughout this section. The correct approach should:

1. Involve the people who are involved in the work;
2. Appoint some of the people in the task group, leaving them to appoint others who have the knowledge and competences; and
3. Select a team, not a group.

Many organizations' leadership approach for change was developed in the 1990s and as late as the early 2000s. Leadership sets up a task force that is required to develop a solution and an action plan for bringing to life the change envisioned by the CEO. The task force works as a closed group of people determining the right design and the way in which it could be implemented, reporting the solution to the CEO. While the change could be the right one for the company, the approach of not involving the impacted people, or even a limited number of people, is the certain formula for failure (Kotter, 1996, p. 7).

In 2005, a multinational Central European company acquired a well-established local (Eastern European) company with a long history of steady growth. Based on the condition of the acquired company, the new management decided that a restructuring was required and a consulting company was hired to support the restructuring. The consultants were asked to present the best structure within three months and access was given to all of the members of the new board of directors. The board of directors issued a formal announcement about the intention of restructuring, but this was the only piece of information the employees received. The reason was a very simple one: The board considered that there is nothing to be communicated before reaching an agreement within the board.

What happened next was that the employees began to gossip due to the lack of information. Everyone knew that something was happening, but no one knew exactly what it was. The employees started to build scenarios, discussing and debating all possible and impossible options. All of the breaks and most of the working time were devoted to these speculations. As time went on, the scenarios became darker as complete strangers (the consultants) were working to figure out the employees' future. Employees started to search for new jobs, some left the company, and rumors flooded the business market that the company was bankrupt.

Many examples exist of change initiatives ruined by poor communication. The need for communication is not a cliché, as it cannot be overused in this context. Everything that is done or is not done sends a message. It is human nature to take a poorly communicated message and interpret it in many different ways—often in a negative light. Humans can develop hundreds of perspectives to decodify the same message; therefore, communication must be in the forefront for clarification. Communication is expected by those who are affected by a change (Thill & Bovee, 2003, p. 12).

The second reason why the statement, *the change team is a small group of employees appointed by the CEO*, is wrong is the manner in which the change team should be selected. The CEO and senior management are not always clear about all the aspects of a change. The leadership can nominate some of the members of the core team and these team members should be responsible to recruit other members whose competences, knowledge, or relationship capital are required. While having the right functional experience in order to support a specific role is essential, the aspects related to having soft skills and a specific relationship capital are mostly underestimated, or not even considered. The term *relationship capital* defines the way we design our relationships in order to gain the esteem of those with whom we have direct engagement, socially or professionally (Carr Williams, 2013). The literature supports the importance of the leadership capabilities; Kotter insists on its importance in all of his works related to change. Cameron and Green even have a specific term for it: They call it "flexible leadership" (2009, p. 349). In a study conducted by Buss (2009), the impact of leadership and the relationship capital are examined on the acceptance of the change. His conclusions reveal that, although not visible most of the time, relationship capital alongside the leadership capabilities has a considerable effect in making the change actually happen.

Example

In early 2000, the accounting department of an East European, state-owned company was struggling with an old information system. Several years ago, a small IT company developed a simple reporting solution for the accounting department. This reporting solution was needed to meet state-mandated reporting requirements.

As time went by, new functionalities were added, and a simple reporting solution became a complex, unstructured IT system, taking care of all bookkeeping activities and the monthly mandatory financial reporting. As a result, more physical resources were required, more bugs were discovered, and the downtime required for fixing the system increased substantially. Based on the mounting users' complaints, the company decided to replace the existing system with a modern, flexible, reliable one.

Management carefully nominated a change team. Management considered all the required functional knowledge and experience. After two years of defining requirements, searching for the most appropriate solution provider, and customizing the solution according to the company's needs, they were totally surprised by the users' reaction—not only did the end users reject the new system, but suddenly the old system became the *best solution ever*.

Management focused on the technical part of the project, which was the part of the project where most of the team members felt comfortable. They neglected to build a relationship with the users by gaining their trust, making them feel that they were part of the team, involving them in the development and testing of functionalities, and communicating with them continuously. The result was discouraging—they had a great solution, but no one wanted to use it.

Assembling the Change Team

Crawford and Nahmias (2010) list the competences required to manage change based on their synthesis of findings from the literature and case studies. Among those competences are leadership, stakeholder management, communication, decision making, problem solving, and cultural awareness. We can conclude that when building a change team, organizations first need to consider the interpersonal abilities of the team member and, if they are in place, to then consider the required technical abilities that should be added. How we prepare our team for these roles is another tough question. Although there are many papers, articles, and books dedicated to change management, the competences of the change team and the role of the change manager are weakly supported in terms of the professional formation (Crawford & Nahmias, 2010).

Finally, the third reason why the statement, *the change team is a small group of employees appointed by the CEO*, is wrong is the term *group*. There is a marked difference between a group and a team. According to Kane (1998, p. 2) the difference between working groups and teams resides in the presence or absence of: (1) an incremental performance need or opportunity, (2) true interdependence, and (3) real shared accountability. Kane states that the first factor is the single best criterion for determining the appropriate type of organization for a given situation. Given the level of difficulty to implement a change and the fact that a change can be seen as an opportunity, it may be argued that there is a need for a *team* and not a group. Casey (1993) states that there is a clear link between the level of uncertainty of a task to be managed and the need for a team to handle it. This is another motivation for selecting a team when implementing a change.

Katzenbach and Smith also explored this difference and concluded, "A working group's performance is a function of what its members do as individuals. A team's performance includes both individual results and what we call 'collective work-products'" (1993, p. 112). It is clear that sometimes the working group can fulfill the needs of an organization; however, in the case of a change, a strong commitment toward a common purpose is required.

One of the best metaphors related to groups and teams is the one that compares a dog pack with a dog sled team. The members of the dog pack "work" together and they have—most of the time—an accepted leader. It might happen even that they share their prey but, at the end of the day, they "work" together only because it is easier to achieve their own individual goal: survival. In a dog sled team, things are different. When assembling the sled, the musher (driver of the dog sled) considers several specific roles as the leader dogs, point dogs, swing dogs, and wheel dogs. They strive for a well-balanced dog team in terms of size and speed in order to increase the overall team efficiency. The goal is that the team and the members of the dog sled work in perfect unison to achieve efficiency. According to Zenger (2012), "These dogs can pull a sled for 20 miles and they love every minute of their job."

More specifically, what do we mean by the term "change team"? There is no agreement in the existing literature regarding a specific composition of the change team, and this is most probably because of the diversity of changes implemented throughout various organizations. Nevertheless, if we draw an analogy between the project team and the change team, we can easily develop a definition of the change team. Project teams are teams that are formed for the specific purpose of completing a project; therefore, change teams are teams that are formed for the specific purpose of implementing a change. The change team will bring together individuals with different competencies, experience, knowledge, and relationship capital, fulfilling specific roles (as described in the following section), working transparently, and involving as many stakeholders as possible in their quest toward implementing the change.

Who Could Be Part of the Change Team?

When building a change team, several roles need to be considered. PMI's *Managing Change in Organizations: A Practice Guide* talks about developing "change-ready" employees within organizations (PMI, 2013, p. 10). These are the employees who are able to assume the roles required in a change team. In this guide, PMI lists six major roles and describes the major responsibilities of each (PMI, 2013, pp. 11–12):

- **Governance Board.** Ensures that the change process remains aligned with the organization's vision and direction;
- **Sponsor.** Has the ultimate responsibility for the program or project, and direct accountability for the change;
- **Leads.** Support the overall change management process and its implementation;
- **Integrators.** Carry the responsibility for the preparation and integration of the change into the business;
- **Agents.** Represent the resources for integrating the change in their respective environments; and
- **Recipients.** Consist of people directly and indirectly impacted by the change.

An excellent review of the existing literature regarding roles and responsibilities within the change team can be found in a paper by Michael Stummer

Table 11-1.   Comparison of change roles (adapted from Stummer & Zuchi, 2010).

Role	Lee and Krayer (2003)	Newton (2007)	Klewes and Langen (2008)	PMI (2013)	Murphy (2014)
Change owner	Upper management	Change sponsor and steering committee	Top management	Change sponsor and governance board	Sponsor/senior executive change leader
Change manager	Change manager	Change manager	Change project manager	Leads	Change manager/ consultant
Change agent	Employee representative and supervisors on steering committee	Change agent	Multiplier	Agent, integrator	Change leader (project manager/ division or unit head/middle management
Change Team	Change steering committee	Change team	Change project team	Change team (all of above)	Change team (all of above)
Other roles		Communication manager	Consultant, change controlling team	Recipient	Change champion

and Dagmar Zuchi where they compare the different change roles as described by (among others) Lee and Krayer in 2003, Newton in 2007, and Kewes and Langen in 2008. With the consent of the authors, we added to their work the roles listed by PMI (2013) and the ones identified by Murphy in her article "How to Build a Change Management Team" (2014).

What's the Relevance of Team Dynamics in the Context of Change

Teams are influenced by their members' behaviors, personality, and by the relationships within its members, just to name a few. Their results on the team's behavior and performance are what we call team dynamics. "They are like undercurrents in the sea, which can carry boats in a different direction to the one they intend to sail'" (Myers, 2013). Effects of team dynamics are considered by project and program teams as facilitators in order to increase the rate of success for their projects and programs. While implementation of change occurs through programs and projects, and sometimes with a high level of complexity, the topic is of utmost importance when talking about the change team. The over-discussed and debated aim of gaining the commitment of the team can be achieved when team dynamics are correctly understood and managed.

The effect of team dynamics can be beneficial because it can improve the overall team performance. However, team dynamics can also be destructive when not managed correctly, causing demotivating, conflictual situations. If the dynamics of a change team can be improved, so can its performance. The stronger the team is, the better the accomplishment of the expected change. This is why it is crucial to understand team dynamics. And this is why all change team leaders should continuously enable the evolution of the change teams.

One of the first researchers and thinkers concerned with group dynamics was Kurt Lewin. Some of his contributions discussed the main reasons why people form groups: interdependence of faith and interdependence of tasks. There is a psychological sense of being part of a group, "not because their members necessarily are similar to one another (although they may be); rather, a group exists when people in it realize their fate depends on the fate of the group as a whole" (Lewin, cited by Brown, 1988, p. 28). However, an ever more powerful dynamic is created when individuals within a group depend on each other for achieving a certain goal (Lewin, cited by Brown, 1988, p. 30).

> *Relevance for the Change Team:* All the members of the team should be aware of the fact that—in order to achieve success— they need each and everyone's abilities and cooperation. This interdependence will be reinforced during the project.

Another theory relating to group dynamics is the FIRO (Fundamental Interpersonal Relations Orientation) theory developed by Will Schutz (1958). It states that there are three basic needs that all human beings share—the need to feel significant, competent, and likable—which express themselves across three levels of human interaction: behavior, feelings, and self-concept. Within each level there are three main areas of human concern: inclusion, control, and openness. People need these elements in just the right amount in order to feel good about themselves. The better people feel about themselves, the higher the possibility of experiencing generosity and flexibility toward others, thus increasing the satisfaction at the work place (Schutz, 1958).

> *Relevance for the Change Team:* During the project, the level of satisfaction of each team member needs to be assessed. An atmosphere of trust is required, and this can be achieved when the change team members are constantly encouraged to share their needs, frustrations, and concerns. Solutions to the raised issues are discussed, agreed, and implemented; ideas, innovations, intermediate results, and success are celebrated.

Probably one of the most spread theories about group dynamics is Bruce Tuckman's Stages of Small-Group Development Theory. First developed in 1965, the theory explains that there are four inevitable phases for a group to experience in order to grow and deliver results: forming, storming, norming, and performing. In the forming stage, people get to know each other and tend to work independently. Once they start collaborating, differences of opinions arise and each member starts to impose his point of view, thus entering in to the storming phase. In the norming stage, a set of rules are established in order for the group to work and, once the rules are accepted and followed by all members, the group reaches the performing stage. This means that the group is now motivated and autonomous and can make decisions on its own. Considering the temporary nature of teams, in the later revision of the theory, Tuckman and Jensen (1977) have added a fifth stage—adjourning—in which the team completes the final tasks and then dissolves.

> *Relevance for the Change Team:* During a change program or project, special attention has to be paid to the change team development stages. The storming and norming phases could be used in order to release the possible tensions within the team. The change manager will build the framework that allows team members to share and discuss the blocking situations or the frustrating obstacles (whether these are feelings, attitudes, or behaviors) and to agree on the ground rules governing their collaboration.

Thinking about the roles that individuals play within a team, Meredith Belbin has discovered that there are nine roles that people feel comfortable to play within a team: plant, monitor evaluator, coordinator, resource investigator, implementer, completer, finisher, team worker, shaper, and specialist (www.belbin.com). Each role has certain strengths and weaknesses that should be taken into consideration when forming a team in order to be productive.

> *Relevance for the Change Team:* We often concentrate our efforts on the specific weaknesses that we identify in our team members, spending valuable time and effort on minimizing them. A more efficient approach—as proved by Gallup's research—is to focus on people's strengths. It is easier, more productive (as people do something they feel comfortable with) and what is more, it is a crucial way to show team members that they matter and that they can contribute based on the talents that make them unique. Belbin's theory states that each role people prefer to play indicates both some strengths and weaknesses. If preferences are known, one also knows the strengths and can combine the roles so the team has the desired mix of team members (and the weakness of one member is always covered by the strength of another).

Interactions within a certain group should be considered as well as the group dynamics that are influenced by the interactions with other groups.

This is referred to as the in/out group effect whereas people within a group work well but encounter difficulties in their relationships with other groups. This effect is created by boundaries (e.g., geographical location, separate offices, walls of cupboards dividing a room into two, opposite sides of a meeting table) and markers (e.g., clothing, title, accent/language, pay band). Group dynamics can also be explained through personality type theories. Interactions within a group are better once members understand that each one of them has different preferences (i.e., Myers-Briggs Type Indicator® personality inventory (see www.myersbriggs.org), behaviors (DISC Model at www.discprofile.com), or thinking habits (The Whole Brain® Thinking approach at www.hbdi.com).

> *Relevance for the Change Team:* Each of these influencers can be used by the change manager to allow the team members to better understand each other, to improve interactions, and to build better communication bridges.

What Tools Could We Use to Raise the Commitment of the Change Team

Now that we discussed team dynamics and we know that this is a result of the interaction of multiple components, such as personalities, roles, structure, culture, and so forth, it is clear that if we want to improve the team dynamics, we need to consider all of these factors. But knowledge is not equal understanding, and understanding is not enough to produce results. Knowing about all of these theories is interesting but ineffectual if we do not understand the specific context of the change and we do not apply the tools and techniques that are appropriate for the specific situation.

In order to raise the commitment of the team through improving team dynamics, we apply the concept of team dynamics. There are several steps to follow (very similar to the steps we follow in most of our continuous improvement initiatives) (see also Figure 11-1):

- **Step 1: Understanding.** We start with the diagnosis of the team:
  - Identify what is the best type of interaction to be applied (the intervention methods)—the most appropriate in the specific context or the one that could bring value for the particular case.
  - Investigate the primary factors that could cause problems or decrease team performance (e.g., using a team health check, interview, or questionnaire).

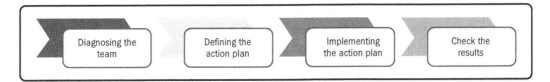

Figure 11-1. Process of improving team dynamics.

- **Step 2: Defining the action plan.** We continue with developing an action plan (with the identified intervention methods). Some of the possible strategies are:
    - Introduce new processes, tools, or technologies (e.g., the Belbin questionnaires in order to understand the preferred roles of each change team member, new technologies for facilitating communication, etc.).
    - Organize specific workshops for the change team members to:
        - Raise awareness of interpersonal dynamics, motivational value systems, and conflict management;
        - Improve individual, collective, and organizational learning (apply intervention methods such as feedback and reflection); and
        - Explain reactions to change, with the objective of minimizing the fear and resistance to change.
    - Organize cultural change programs to introduce new attitudes and behaviors.
    - Organize specific workshops with stakeholders with the objective of better understanding the different perspectives (e.g., discuss the change project scorecard).
    - Adapt the organizational structure, change the existing infrastructure, and change reporting structures within organizations.
- **Step 3: Implementing the action plan.** Implement the plan.
- **Step 4. Check the results.** Continuously check the results, understand the causes, and adapt the action plan accordingly.

The Team Health Assessment

People involved in projects are aware of the project health check questionnaires or surveys that are often used during a project to assess whether the project is moving in the right direction. Through answering a series of questions (for which the answers are scored), the project manager and the project team members obtain greater clarity regarding their project and the aspects that need to be improved. The application of the team health assessment is very similar although its purpose is different. Instead of focusing on specific project task, actions, plans, or results, the questionnaire aims to analyze team behavior, team cooperation, and the level of satisfaction the team has working together. By using a short questionnaire, the change team can easily achieve helpful outcomes about the team performance and energy, in a very short time, and it is a great beginning for open discussions regarding the team's success and what gets in a way.

A great example of a team health assessment is provided by Patrick Lencioni in his book, *The Five Dysfunctions of a Team*. The questionnaire proposed by Lencioni helps to evaluate a team's susceptibility to the five dysfunctions described in the book: absence of trust, fear of conflict, lack of commitment, avoidance of accountability, and inattention to results. The book also provides a simple explanation on how to tabulate the results and interpret the possible conclusions (Lencioni, 2002, pp. 191–194). The value of the book—and of the assessment itself—consists not only in identifying the specific issues a team might face, but describes how to interpret these "dysfunctions." Rather than didactically plead for sophisticated theories, Lencioni shows, in a very practical manner, how teams can succeed through embracing common sense with uncommon levels of discipline and persistence" (Lencioni, 2002, p. 220).

Case Study

This is a situation where Lencioni's proposed questionnaire was successfully applied. The board of a local professional association—where all the activities were performed based on volunteering, including the activities of the board—was struggling in further developing the association, namely in putting the ideas in practice. All of the board members were professionals with great experience and most of them held high positions in their companies. As experts in their field, all of them were used to having a strong voice and their decisions or opinions were followed without being questioned. Although each of the board members had the good of the association in mind, the perspectives and the ways of achieving the main goal were different. With so many strong personalities (all of them having the same authority level in the board), it was difficult to reach a consensus, and the meetings became unproductive with frustrating quarrels. Teamwork deteriorated and they realized soon that the situation needed to be urgently redressed. On the edge of a crisis situation, they applied Lencioni's team assessment questionnaire which proved to be a straightforward diagnostic tool for their dysfunctions. They reviewed the individual results, discussed the discrepancies in their responses (which was surprising to many of them), and identified the implications for them as a team. Far from being a magic wand, the tool initiated great discussions and concluded with concrete measures to improve the situation.[1]

---

[1] Good examples of team health check can also be found at www.stellarleadership .com or www.theteamhealthcheck.com. These examples can be applied for the teams involved in organizational changes.

Intervention Methods: Feedback and Reflection

One of the paradoxes of change is that trust is difficult to establish when you need it the most, according to Jeanie Daniel Duck, author of the book *Change Monster: The Human Forces that Fuel or Foil Corporate Transformation and Change*. Feedback and reflection are powerful tools, but they can be used only when the premises of a trustful environment are in place. Both tools can be used for learning, for reviewing team strengths and development needs, and for setting up ground rules for working in a team environment. The difference between the two resides in the perspective of the speaker: Feedback is directed toward a person or a team and provides an outside point of view (the one of the speaker); while in the case of reflection, the objective is to develop a common view of the current status of the team and to "equip the team members with the potential to address the problems of tomorrow" (Simmons, 2010).

Reflection, through its specific characteristic of positioning everyone on the same level, smooths the acceptance of the different perspectives. Unlike feedback, which can be perceived as finger pointing, reflection places the speaker in the same context as the rest of the team, considering the speaker as part of the situation being assessed or for solutions being investigated. The change team reflects on their potential or actual performance, identifying rules for enhancing the team work, actions for improving their performance, and new and better ways to gain buy-in from the rest of the organization. In order to be able to reflect and to bring out the best of the team during this process, there is a prerequisite: a safe and trustful atmosphere within the team. If team members fear of being seen as incompetent or think their relationship could be jeopardized, the entire reflection process become a simple exercise of saying nice things to each other and ends by falling into derision. The interdependence between reflection and trust could be perceived as paradoxical, yet the two synergistically develop each other. The more that reflection sessions are performed, the more assertive team members become. They prepare themselves, by sharing what they honestly think and feel, to be ready and able to hear, understand, and accept what their colleagues think and feel.

Reflection methods in projects are briefly described by Gareis who calls the reflection methods flash light, mood picture, or mood barometer (Gareis, 2005, pp. 123–124). In projects, the methods are usually applied during retrospective or lessons learned meetings, where teams reflect upon their previous accomplishments and prepare for future projects.

Figure 11-2 shows how we can position the results of the team reflection session. The members answer the question "How happy am I today [date] about the change project?" Each team member evaluates the satisfaction level considering the results achieved to date and the level of collaboration with the rest of the team. The discussions are focused on team members' impressions about what they experienced, what issues they faced, and how

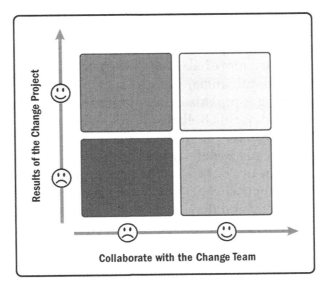

Figure 11-2. Example of reflection mood picture.

it affected them. By sharing their points of view, team members better understand each other's attitudes and behaviors and can determine a specific framework or set of rules which, if accepted by all of them, will allow them to perform better (the performing stage in Tuckman's stages of team development). These result mostly from the interpretation of the satisfaction level regarding the collaboration within the team. What could we change or what would we need to do in order to improve the collaboration are great questions for the team. It offers them the possibility to identify those ground rules that would allow them to reach a new and improved level of cooperation.

Figure 11-3 shows a frame that can be used for a reflection session held with the purpose of gathering lessons learned. Using Pendleton's rules of feedback (what went well, what went wrong, and what could be improved in the next project), we can gather ideas that will allow us to perform better in our future projects.

Figure 11-3. Example for frame used for reflection session for lessons learned.

The Change Project Scorecard

In early 1990, Drs. Robert Kaplan (Harvard Business School) and David Norton were researching for a more balanced view of organizational performance. They added strategic nonfinancial performance measures to the traditional financial metrics, asking companies to recognize the importance of the intangible assets as well. Today, this holistic approach is considered as being successful in project management as well. Change projects—due their increased complexity—would greatly benefit from such a tool. The idea is to measure the project performance not only from the triple constraint point of view, but to introduce other aspects such as customer satisfaction, team motivation, the relationship with stakeholders, and so on. This tool has the advantages of the known balanced scorecard (e.g., increased focus on results, focus on drivers of future performance) and it significantly improves the communication among team members and stakeholders. Developing such a scorecard with the contribution of the entire team, plus invited stakeholders, during a meeting helps significantly in gaining the buy-in of the stakeholders, aligning expectations, and keeping the team engaged (Bonghez, 2015, p. 15).

Case Study

A medium-sized Eastern European organization launched its first €5.5 million change project. This was the first complex project for the organization, and the employees had limited project management knowledge and experience. The team members were not aware of the effort required by such an endeavor. One of the decisions made by the sponsor during the early stages of the project was to work as closely as possible with the project team, involve them in all main project decisions, and keep them permanently connected with the project. The most successful tool used in that sense was the project scorecard.

Although it took more than two hours to go through the indicators each time the team met (the frequency was once every six weeks), the results were encouraging. The team took the project evaluation meeting very seriously and thoroughly discussed the indicators each time. Debates started for the score of almost every indicator and if its value was higher than two, the entire team was involved in searching for ways to improve it. Figure 11-4 shows the project scorecard at the end of the project after six iterations. Increased self-confidence, better understanding of the big picture (before and after the project), awareness about project risks and ways to mitigate them, and greater buy-in were only a few of the outcomes from the consistent use of the tool during the project.

Conclusion

A change team and a project team have a very similar purpose: They both need to migrate smoothly to a new, and in most cases, unknown situation.

Project Scorecard						

Legend		**009.12 Inv P10' Project - overview**					
		10.07.13	22.08.13	31.10.13	04.12.13	05.02.14	19.03.14
very bad	5						
bad	4						
ok	3	3	3	3	3	2	3
good	2						
very good	1						

Project objectives and context	10.07.13	22.08.13	31.10.13	04.12.13	05.02.14	19.03.14
Project objectives	1	1	1	1	2	2
Major deliverables	1	1	2	2	1	2
Business objectives	2	3	1	1	1	1

Project organization	10.07.13	22.08.13	31.10.13	04.12.13	05.02.14	19.03.14
Team work	3	3	2	2	2	2
Project communications	3	3	2	1	1	2
Project culture development	5	5	3	3	2	2
Task achievement	4	4	3	3	2	4

Planning, control	10.07.13	22.08.13	31.10.13	04.12.13	05.02.14	19.03.14
Schedule status	5	4	4	3	3	5
Costs status	4	4	3	3	3	5
Project resources	2	2	2	3	2	2
Project risks	4	3	4	3	3	3

Relationship with stakeholders	10.07.13	22.08.13	31.10.13	04.12.13	05.02.14	19.03.14
Stakeholder 1 BOD	4	3	3	3	3	3
Stakeholder 2 BOD	2	1	3	3	1	1
Stakeholder 3 (technical)	3	2	1	2	2	1
Stakeholder 4 (commercial)	3	5	4	4	2	1
Stakeholder 5	1	1	4	4	3	4
Stakeholder 6	4	3	2	1	1	1
Stakeholder 7	3	3	2	2	2	2
Stakeholder 8	5	4	3	2	2	2
Stakeholder 9 (authorizations)	2	3	3	3	2	1
Stakeholder 10	2	3	3	3	3	3

Figure 11-4. Sample project scorecard.

The journey is not a common one, the obstacles are diverse, and the result is unique each time. However, there is a difference in performing this very exciting job. The change team has an additional challenge. The members of the change team need to convince the rest of the organization that their endeavor is the right one and that the result of their struggle is the best solution.

The change team has to sell the change to be implemented and needs to gain stakeholders' trust and collaboration throughout the journey. In order to do so, the change team's motivation needs to be strong, and its level of engagement and commitment needs to be extremely high.

This chapter provides examples of how several group dynamics theories could contribute to raise the commitment of a change team and demonstrate how tangible results can be obtained by applying accessible tools. The catch is that as simple as these tools may look, their application requires time, patience, and willingness to hear and understand each team member's perspective—a time-consuming process, but one that pays back.

References

Belbin®. (2017). Retrieved from http://www.belbin.com/rte.asp?id=8

http://www.teamtechnology.co.uk/soft-skills/project-management-training
-part13.html

Bonghez, S. (2015). *Building positive project culture for navigating complexity: A case study.* Retrieved from http://www.pmi.org/~/media/PDF/learning/ project-complexity/building-project-culture.ashx

Brown, R. (1988). *Group processes: Dynamics within and between groups.* Oxford, England: Blackwell.

Buss, R. J. (2009). *Relationship capital and the dark side of change management,* PhD thesis, Southern Cross University, Lismore, NSW.

Cameron, E. & Green, M. (2009). *Making sense of change management: A complete guide to the models, tools & techniques of organizational change* (2nd ed.). London, England: Kogan Page.

Carr Williams, T. (2013). *What is the difference between relationship capital and social capital?* Retrieved from http://www.relationshipmanagement institute.com/2009/01/what-is-the-difference-between-relationship -capital-and-social-capital/

Casey, D. (1993). *Managing learning in organizations.* Buckingham, England: Open University Press.

Crawford, L. & Nahmias, A. H. (2010). Competencies for managing change. *International Journal of Project Management, 28*(4), 405–412.

Disc Profile. (n.d.). Retrieved from https://www.discprofile.com/what-is -disc/overview/

Gareis, R. (2005). *Happy projects!* Vienna, Austria: Manz.

Hermann International. (2017). Retrieved from http://www.hbdi.com/ WholeBrainProductsAndServices/programs/thehbdi.php

Kane, M. J. (1998). How to distinguish the important differences between teams and work groups. Retrieved from http://www.executiveevolution .com/docs/Work_Groups.pdf

Katzenbach, J. R., & Smith, D. K. (1993, March–April). The discipline of teams. *Harvard Business Review*.

Kotter, J. P. (1996). *Leading change*. Boston, MA: Harvard Business School Press.

Murphy, E. (2014). *How to build a change management team*. Retrieved from https://www.thechangesource.com/how-to-build-a-change-management -team/

Myers, S. P. (2013). *Definition of team dynamics*. Retrieved from http://www .teamtechnology.co.uk/team/dynamics/definition/

Project Management Institute. (2013). *Managing change in organizations: A practice guide*. Newtown Square, PA: Author.

Schein, E. & Bennis, W. (1965). *Personal and organizational change through group methods*. New York, NY: Wiley.

Schutz, W. C. (1958). *FIRO: A three-dimensional theory of interpersonal behavior*. Oxford, England: Rinehart.

Simmons, B. L. (2010). *Trust and team performance: Does reflection matter?* Retrieved from http://www.bretlsimmons.com/2010-10/trust-and-team -performance-does-reflection-matter/

Stummer, M. & Zuchi, D. (2010). Developing roles in change processes—A case study from a public-sector organization. *International Journal of Project Management, 28*(4), 384–394.

Team Technology. (2017). Retrieved from http://www.myersbriggs.org/ my-mbti-personality-type/mbti-basics/

Thill, J. V., & Bovee, C. L. (2005). *Business communication*. Upper Saddle River, N.J.: Pearson Education, Inc.

Tuckman, B. W., & Jensen, M. A. C. (1977). Stages of small-group revisited. *Group and Organization Studies, 2*(4), 419–427.

Zenger, J. (2012, December 26). The power of teams: A lesson in leadership from a Siberian husky. *Forbes*. Retrieved from http://www .forbes.com/sites/jackzenger/2012/12/26/the-power-of-teams-a-lesson -in-leadership-from-a-siberian-huskie/

Review Questions

1. What is the main reason why many change initiatives fail?
2. What is the second factor listed by Buss along with the leadership capabilities as having considerable impact in ensuring that a change happens?
3. What are the main competences required for the change team members, according to Crawford and Nahmias (2010)?
4. According to the Project Management Institute, what are the roles within a change team and their associated responsibilities?

5. What are the four steps proposed for the process of improving the change team's dynamics?
6. What is the difference between feedback and reflection, and when can these methods be used during the change project?
7. What are the main benefits of developing a project scorecard with the contribution of the whole change team and relevant stakeholders?

CHAPTER 12

"People don't resist change, they resist being changed."
—Peter Senge

Leadership Factors in Successful Organizational Change

By Frank P. Saladis, PMP, PMI Fellow

Abstract

Organizational change has become a common experience across all industries and requires strong leadership, specific goals, a vision the entire organization can buy into, and an understanding that change, though necessary and inevitable, will cause some disruption, will meet with some resistance, and will require empathy and a commitment to see it through. In many ways, it is the ultimate leadership challenge.

To lead (not just manage) change, organizational leaders must be prepared to deal with some significant, and often overwhelming, challenges. Organizational change, for the most part, is intended to drive improvement and strengthen sustainability. It may actually include some potentially destructive activities, and the executive management and those responsible for the initiation of the change can expect doubt, suspicion, criticism, and distrust from those who will bear the greatest impact of the change. Through effective and relentless (with emphasis on relentless) communication, a willingness to listen to those affected, and a defined and documented strategic view of the change initiative, the experience may become less painful for everyone involved. Using this approach, the leadership team will be more successful at influencing the organization's employees and smoothing some of the "rough waters" that may be experienced as change is implemented.

The main factor, or requirement, for successful change is the ability of senior management to create the appropriate environment and become "transformational leaders." This environment actually becomes a culture where change is not only expected, but embraced and initiated with passion.

Transformational leaders understand the complexity of change, prepare themselves by identifying the many components of change, and initiate the actions that will create a change-ready environment. The key topics and areas of knowledge the transformational leader must address to be successful in managing change are:

- Top drivers of change
- Systems thinking
- Stages of reaction to change
- Dealing with change—The leadership challenge
- Lessons learned about change
- Transformational leadership—The essential element of change
- Positivity—Toning down the doom and gloom and focusing on possibility
- Key points about leading organizational change

Top Drivers of Change

The subject of organizational change is not new, and it is difficult to develop fresh and creative ways in which to explain it, manage its impact, and provide suggestions about how those in leadership positions could improve on its implementation. Much of what is written today about change management addresses the same basic information: people resist change; change is uncomfortable but necessary; if you don't change, your organization won't survive; and so on. W. Edwards Deming summarized the essence of change when he said: "It is not necessary to change. Survival is not mandatory!" The subject, however, continues to draw attention and there are usually some nuggets of useful information embedded in many of the resources that are available. This chapter is intended to provide a few of those nuggets.

Every organization is different in terms of culture, leadership styles, the way information is communicated, and what the specific strategy for the future may be. There are, however, a number of elements in the management of change that apply to all organizations. One element is to identify the drivers of change that will affect an organization. Part of the strategic planning process requires the leadership team to develop a "view," not a prediction, of the future and to assess where the organization needs to change or adapt to meet the very fluid demands of the worldwide business environment. In the book *The Art of the Long View*, author Peter Schwartz (1996) refers to the "the gentle art of re-perceiving" rather than "how" to predict the future. This re-perceiving technique suggests that we should question our assumptions about how the world works. Another way to describe this would be to ensure that an organization is ready to re-tune its strategic view. Assessing the drivers of change will help managers see the world more clearly and continually fine-tune future plans. Developing scenarios about possible futures, based on a current awareness of the drivers of change, allows organizational leaders and decision makers to update their view of what they believe the future has in store for both them and their employees. It also helps them develop plans that are realistic and attainable and to formulate decisions that are more likely to create the value desired. A practice of preparing and then continually adjusting and refining a strategic plan will prepare the organization to more effectively prepare for and adapt to change.

The Drivers of Change

Research about change has provided us with a number of factors that will have a direct impact on organizational strategy. These factors are sometimes subtle and evolve slowly, but most are clearly visible and require immediate attention and action. The most common drivers of change include the following:

1. **Consumer preferences.** These may include anything from a new product, including the packaging of a product, sizes and shapes, convenience, operability, or how to actually purchase an item (online or in-person shopping).
2. **Energy costs.** These include the swing of oil prices, alternative sources, the increasing focus on green energy, and the impact of energy costs on the world economy.
3. **Tax policies.** Tax policies include changes to existing laws, new laws every year, and political activities to entice new business or change existing tax structures.
4. **Reverse innovation.** This refers to the examination of flagship products from a critical viewpoint to determine where improvements can be made. Basically, this is a practice of finding fault in the best products provided by a supplier and using the results to either improve a product or create potential new products.
5. **Nontraditional competitors.** These are competitors who will not play by the rules of the past and who will use very creative and innovative techniques to attract your customers and increase their market share.
6. **Extended enterprise risks.** These risks may include hackers, financial fraud, emerging markets, political unrest, disgruntled employees, global changes in the economy, and threats of terrorism.
7. **Exponential growth in information flow.** Today, information is produced 24 hours a day, seven days a week, in global communities—with projects creating 24-hour work days.

8. **Long-term growth strategy.** Changing economic conditions and consumer preferences, along with each factor listed here, will impact organizational strategy.

9. **Succession planning.** This refers to the exit of Baby Boomers from the workforce and the need to fill an increasing talent gap.

10. **Generation values.** Baby Boomer, Generation X, Generation Y, and Millennials—there are differences in how each generation communicates, sees the world, defines leadership, and interacts with others.

11. **Technology.** This involves continuous and unrelenting change in every aspect of technology in the business and social environment.

12. **Ethics and social behaviors.** Society continues to evolve and personal, family, community, and business place values drive the way people establish their relationships and how they live or work together.

13. **Agile approaches to project management.** These refer to the increasing popularity of agile methods within the software and IT industry and the slow progression of these techniques into the traditional and waterfall planning environment.

Other drivers of change may not be associated with improving the business environment, but may be more focused on individual gain. These include leadership ego, political ambition, greed, and the desire to make an impression even when major change is not actually necessary, and they are intended to create personal advantage and positioning. These "personal advantage projects" were commonly referred to as "pet projects." The change initiatives established under these conditions and personal objectives are likely to result in an exodus of highly skilled and valuable employees or a sharp drop in performance.

A simple message to leaders about change—as Tom Peters quotes in his book *The Little Big Things*—is: "To lead is to serve. Period." If you are going to introduce change, the reasons should be clear and, if at all possible, the benefits must be apparent to all, especially to those who will experience the greatest impact of the change.

It's All About Process

Any organization that is serious about its future will have processes in place for every element of its business. Clearly defined processes minimize conflict, reduce risk, create some degree of predictability, allow for smoother transitions, and accelerate problem solving.

In the project, program, and portfolio environment, processes will minimize the possibility of approving projects that will not connect with strategic objectives, that will fail to produce the level of value desired, or that will not improve the organization's position in the marketplace. Portfolio management, project management offices (PMOs), and project management centers of excellence (PMCoE) are maturing and, with that maturity, they are providing more effective and efficient governance to ensure that projects are appropriately selected and managed through their life cycles.

Indicators of Change

Another way to address change proactively is to look for *indicators* that change is about to engulf an organization. Many organizations analyze information about past performance. These findings are actually considered "lagging" indicators because they will tell you about what has already occurred. These indicators include factors such as past financial performance, a comparison of planned operating budget with actual expenditure, a comparison of project baselines to actual performance using earned value management techniques, and, basically, a comparison between what was expected to occur and what actually occurred. This type of analysis has value and many lessons learned can be derived from its use. There are, however, other factors to consider. Organizational leaders should also consider another type of indicator when managing organizational change. This relatively unused factor is referred to as the *leading indicator*. I first discovered this term while reading the book *How to Save a Failing Project* by Ralph R. Young, Steven M. Brady, and Dennis C. Nagle (2009). The authors' reference to *leading indicators* captured my attention and I wanted to find out more about this term and its value, not only regarding its relevance to organizational change, but its connection to managing projects more effectively. Leading indicators are actually very much related to the practice of risk management. The concept is to look more closely at what could happen or what is developing rather than to focus attention and energy on those events and situations that have already occurred. There is certainly value in the assessment and analysis of past performance, but there should be much more emphasis on preparing for what "could" occur and how to influence those potential changes before they become lagging indicators. Leading indicators are actually signals, signs, or, to use risk management terminology, *triggers* that require attention and might, if acted upon appropriately, make a huge difference in the outcome of a planned endeavor. Leading indicators require a much more proactive approach and need conditioning of team members and team leaders so these people will truly be in "scanning mode," continuously looking for potential red flags to begin emerging as well as opportunities that may develop. These items may appear very small and insignificant at first, but astute leaders will recognize potentials for disaster or great opportunities early enough to make appropriate decisions and initiate positive actions.

Examples of leading indicators from a change management viewpoint include:

- Mergers, acquisitions, and divestiture;
- Hostile takeover;
- New product or service;
- New leader or manager;
- New infrastructure;
- New major project;
- New business objective or requirement;
- New customer;
- New market;
- Sell-off of a business component;
- Shrinking market share;
- Niche or specialty area developing;
- Employee morale;
- Changes in the tone of internal communications;
- Complacency;
- Minimal to no conflict;
- Reduction in sales; and
- Loss of a key client.

These indicators, and many others, would drive an organization to focus more on the need for a comprehensive risk management strategy. The emphasis on planning for these types of changes would generate a highly active dialogue of "what-if" questions and a deeper dive into understanding the potential effects of the change. The outcome of these discussions would provide the basis for more informed decision making and would also encourage the development of more creative solutions. The SWOT analysis (strengths, weaknesses, opportunities, and threats) is an excellent tool for identifying and addressing leading indicators. A SWOT analysis allows an organization to clearly identify its current state of performance and efficiency and the areas where change will be necessary to remain competitive. It also identifies areas where the "human factors" of organizational management require attention.

SWOT Analysis Example:

- *Strengths:* This component of the analysis focuses on the experience, knowledge, financial reserves, location, price, quality, accreditations, and other attributes of the organization.
- *Weaknesses:* This component of the analysis addresses morale, competitive capability, cash flow, and other areas where improvement is necessary.

- *Opportunities:* This component is intended to identify areas based on organizational strengths that may create niche markets or increase global influence.
- *Threats:* This component of the analysis drives the participants to identify potential problem areas and risks that may negatively impact the organization. These may include loss of key staff, political turmoil, and major changes in a competitor's positioning.

A SWOT analysis can provide a basis for developing the change initiatives needed to boost organizational performance, prioritize the most important projects and operational issues, and gain the buy-in of the key stakeholders who must engage in implementing change.

Managing Change—A Place to Start

Organizational structure has changed significantly over the past few decades. The trends have led to leaner, flatter structures and greater emphasis on cross-organizational collaboration. Unfortunately, even with this emphasis on the need for internal cooperation, many organizations are dealing with silos and communications issues between business units, departments, and even small groups within a department. Rather than address how to work more efficiently across internal functional groups, managers and their employees argue about process, specific group requirements, and specific group performance measures. Rather than deal with internal conflict, the emphasis should be directed toward breaking down barriers between functional groups, simplification of processes, cooperation, and contributing visible value to the enterprise.

A good place to start addressing organizational change is to identify the silos that exist, why they exist, and what can be done to break down the walls that separate each functional group. The executive message to all internal groups should be: "Organizational success through value generation, cooperation, and resource efficiency."

Addressing organizational change by looking more closely at the factors that drive change, the leading indicators that signal a change is coming, and the silos and inefficiencies that exist will assist organizational leaders in developing a well-framed and grounded change strategy. This, in turn, will enable the organization to become more proficient at systems thinking.

Systems Thinking

Systems thinking has been defined as an approach to problem solving that views problems and issues existing within the system from a perspective that addresses the impact of the problem on the whole or "enterprise" level rather than addressing and reacting to distress signals and the operational dysfunctions of a specific part. This approach assists in developing solutions, the outcomes of which will contribute to overall efficiency and not potentially result in unintended consequences caused by addressing only a small element of the system. This type of thinking addresses the concept that component parts can best be understood in the context of relationships with one another and within the greater system rather than isolated attempts at resolving an issue. This is similar to the process of project integration management and integrated change control. The concept here is that a change to one specific area must be examined in a larger context to determine the impact of that change across the entire project, program, or system. In short, it is actually a form of impact analysis. The system-wide assessment of change is a core element of organizational change management, systems thinking, and any change process.

Systems thinking enables leaders and their teams to view an organization from a wider and more global perspective. The organization is a system. Each part should be clearly defined as essential and purposefully contribute to the whole organization's efficient and sustained operation. Leaders who are developing plans for a major change may want to consider creating a culture of systems thinkers, which means that everyone in the organization understands how the system works and why each functional part is important.

A system is a group of interacting, interrelated, and interdependent components that form a complex and unified whole. Any organization, large or small, generally operates as a system.

Relating organizational change to systems thinking, there are several factors to consider, including the following:

- All of a system's parts must be present and operating in order to carry out the intended purpose of the system. Knowledge of each part and its function is essential, including the rationale behind why that function is necessary.
- Each part is designed and arranged in a specific way to support the higher-level purpose of the system as a whole.
- Systems change in response to feedback and stimulus. The changing global business environment would be considered a stimulus of an organizational system change.
- Systems may be sustained or changed by making adjustments to feedback and stimulus.

As the environment changes, organizational leaders must analyze feedback and determine the appropriate change strategies. Is the current system flexible enough to sustain a major change, or is an entirely new system required to remain competitive?

As stated previously, systems thinking is a way of understanding reality that emphasizes the relationships among a system's parts, rather than the parts themselves. This type of thinking directly relates to managing organizational change. The organization is a system of multiple parts, each with its specific function. To understand the impact of change on an organization more completely, leaders must view how a change in each functional unit will affect the greater system. If a change is being considered at the higher systems level, it is important to assess how that change will affect each subsystem and component to determine the true impact of the change.

Systems thinking has a number of benefits and can have a highly positive impact when planning for and executing change.

Benefits of Systems Thinking

Applying the techniques of systems thinking results in a number of organizational benefits and should provide a more effective foundation when planning for a major organizational change. The process of systems thinking requires those engaged in managing organizational change to identify the linkages and interactions within the organization. This will help to fully understand the impact of the change and to plan for a more effective and efficient outcome. Utilizing a systems-thinking approach will assist the change leader in many ways.

- It can help you design smart, longer-view, sustainable solutions to identified problems and organizational challenges.
- It gives you a more reliable picture of business reality from both an internal and external perspective.
- You can work with a system's natural capabilities (communications, leadership effectiveness, employee competence, employee attitude, organizational culture, global presence, and customer relationships) in order to achieve the results you desire.
- It encourages you to think about problems and solutions with a focus on the "big picture" and long view. It creates the need to focus on risk management, for example:
  - Assessing how a particular solution or decision you are considering will play out over a long period of time (not just to solve the immediate problem); and
  - Identifying the unintended consequences that a decision might have, which emphasizes the need to address secondary risks and residual risks.
- It emphasizes the whole rather than the parts (i.e., breaks down silos).
- It drives a focus on interconnections and developing efficient internal relationships.
- It emphasizes continuous circular feedback, which will help identify potential new risk situations.

- It drives the development of reinforcing processes—processes that improve performance and create growth.
- It drives the development of balancing processes—processes that connect functional groups and create greater efficiencies between groups. These processes establish a certain element of stability that is necessary in any organization. We know that change is constant, but we also know that people need to feel that there is a degree of control even when dealing with a turbulent environment. Consider a ship's captain in a storm. The sea is changing by the second and the captain is at the helm directing, leading, and displaying a high degree of confidence and control of the situation.

Stages of Reaction to Change

It can be safely stated that everyone reacts to change differently. On the positive side, change is viewed by many as an opportunity to improve a product or a process or rejuvenate or revitalize an organization, which is necessary for progress and sparks innovation and growth. But just as legitimately, change can also be seen as a threat to stability, an upheaval of accepted or "normal" processes, a path toward unpredictability, a threat to one's job or position, disorientation, and confusion.

As we all know, change can be traumatic, and for those who will be affected, change really isn't very welcome. Most people, when you ask them about change, respond with similar views: change is uncomfortable; it's disruptive; if it isn't broken, don't fix it; things are fine just the way they are. Deep down inside, people all know that change will occur and, despite their opposition, they know they will eventually have to deal with it. Organization leaders are generally familiar with the impact of change and should be prepared to address the following responses and behavior:

- **Surprise and shock.** Why is this necessary? Who decided this was a good idea? Don't they know what this will do to my area of responsibility? Why didn't they ask me first?
- **Defensive retreat.** They can't do this! I won't cooperate. I will find a way to protect myself and my team. I will show them the errors in their thinking process.
- **Acknowledgment.** I realize that resistance is futile. I will have to make this work even if I don't like it. There must be a very good reason why this is occurring.
- **Acceptance and adaptation.** Okay, I see why the change was decided upon. I will make adjustments to my specific area and will inform my team. I will obtain the necessary information, communicate that information, and work with my team and employees to adapt to the change.

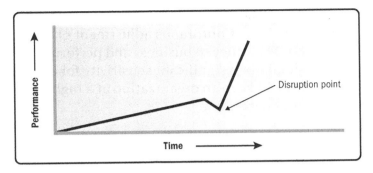

Figure 12-1.   The change disruption point.

The change leader, the originator of the change, must develop a strategy to minimize the time it takes for people to progress through these stages in order to establish an organization that has become conditioned to be "change-ready." This requires strong leadership and a well-thought-out plan.

An organizational change—despite the level of planning, the attention to detail, and the effectiveness of communications—will create a period of adjustment, or a "disruption point." This is the moment that the change is introduced. Orientation and training have been completed; processes are in place; equipment, tools, and other factors have all been distributed; and the workforce is deemed ready. The decision to "go live" is communicated and the change is implemented. At this point, some things don't quite work as planned: someone forgot a step in a process, people are not exactly sure who to contact about a problem, or a computer system or program seems to have a few "quirks"—there is some discomfort and a degree of stress. Doubt rises and hindsight runs rampant. The naysayers begin to materialize and, for a time, the change appears to be failing. Then, with some managerial effort and leadership, the change begins to take hold. Processes are smoothed out and people begin to adapt. Eventually, the change becomes normal operation. The leader's goal here is to minimize the duration of the disruption point, between when the change is introduced and when the change is fully accepted and becomes part of normal, day-to-day operations (see Figure 12-1).

Dealing with Change—The Leadership Challenge

Organizational change management is defined by the Project Management Institute (PMI, 2013) in *Managing Change in Organizations: A Practice Guide* as "a comprehensive, cyclic, and structured approach for transitioning individuals, groups, and organizations from a current state to a future state with intended business benefits" (p. 7). It provides the means for an organization to integrate and align people, processes, and culture with a strategy for moving forward. The key word here is *cyclic*. Strategic planning is an ongoing process that includes a long-term view of three to five years and a shorter-term view of one to three years. The further the organization looks into the future, the fuzzier the picture will be. Continuous adjustment of the plan as the organization proceeds on its journey to business and performance excellence is necessary, and there should be a significant sensitivity for detecting opportunity along the way. This will keep an organization at a high stage of readiness and equipped to adapt as necessary.

Getting Started

The first step in the process of dealing with change is to understand what it is. PMI's definition seems to provide a fairly universal view of change and actually suggests the very specific need for clear and intentional leadership. The leaders of organizations that have experienced continuous success understand that their organizations do not evolve randomly or through luck, but through purposeful and dynamic strategies that drive them to anticipate, influence, and respond appropriately to emerging and shifting global trends, financial and business patterns, and events that are both local and international in impact.

Effectively leading organizational change includes the encouragement of creative and innovative thinking, strong management influence on process improvement, relationship management among functional units, and an organization-wide understanding of stakeholder management and engagement. Leaders must also be aware that change places enormous stress on employees. When not managed properly, change may cause significant distrust of management and a perception that whatever change is initiated at the moment will soon be undone by another change that will be introduced before the previous change was fully accepted. Constant stress and a view that changes are not actually beneficial but more similar to busywork or to fulfill an individual objective rather than an organizational need can derail any attempt to create a change-ready organization. The ultimate goal for the leader is to convince everyone that becoming change-ready is a strategic necessity.

Leaders must clearly demonstrate that a proposed change will have defined and measurable objectives and obvious success points, but also ensure that there is awareness that there is no end to the business-change process. Change becomes part of the organizational culture. It should also be noted that the implementation of change will include some element of risk and uncertainty. This concern for uncertainty is captured in the statement:

> If people waited until changes could be performed perfectly, change would never occur. (*Harvard Business Review*, 1998)

Most people, especially experienced leaders will agree that there is basically no such thing as error-free change. What we can do is determine why a change is needed, communicate the need very clearly, anticipate the risks involved, encourage comprehensive planning, and be ready to adapt when necessary.

Leadership Actions to Prepare an Organization for Change

Leaders must develop a strategy for dealing with the results of change decisions. The strategy should be based on what is commonly known about change and its effect on people, plus an understanding of the unique aspects of the organization, its culture, and its position within the industry or marketplace. Regular, clear, and transparent communication is the key part of that strategy. In addition, the following items will drive the change strategy:

- People generally resist change. The leader should ensure that the reasons and the benefits of the change are clear, evident, and communicated effectively and often.
- Make sure the vision, the desired future state, has been carefully phrased.
- Provide an opportunity for those who will be involved and affected by change to provide input and suggestions.
- Establish trust by following through on commitments and displaying consistent leadership behavior.
- Match the stated vision with reality. People should believe that the vision is not only possible, but highly beneficial to achieve.
- Insist on an enterprise-wide focus on risk management.
- Adopt and implement standard processes and practices for managing projects and portfolios. This will provide some of the factual information necessary to communicate the need for a change.
- Package and communicate the change in such a way that employees and team members will embrace the solution being offered.

Organizational change is challenging, and there is no secret formula that will guarantee success. A common-sense approach that includes strong and sensible leadership, a well-thought-out communications process, and a continuous awareness of the risks associated with change should increase the probability of achieving a successful outcome. Caution should be taken to minimize the perception that the change initiative is unorganized and is only a spontaneous reaction to an internal or external factor. (There are times when spontaneity is actually appropriate. Use good judgment to avoid discouraging the development of new and creative ideas. In some cases, brilliant ideas emerge unexpectedly and require quick action to capitalize on an opportunity.)

One thing that most successful leaders know about change is to celebrate successes along the way. This approach actually increases momentum and creates a desire to reach the next milestone. Acknowledge progress all along the way. Make your acknowledgments sincere and show some enthusiasm, but don't overdo it. Use good judgment and avoid acknowledging the same person or small group repeatedly. Change is a large team effort and it is important to ensure that everyone feels a sense of belonging and importance.

Lessons Learned About Change

The list of lessons learned about organizational change could probably fill several volumes of a "best practices in change management" manual. However, there are some lessons learned that will naturally float to the top of the list. The Harvard Business Essentials (2003) publication *Managing Change and Transition* provides an excellent reference about managing change—specifically, managing change during turbulent times. Considering the past, the current state of world business, the social and political environment, and the seemingly endless predications about a not-so-pleasant future (mega-storms, climate change, political rivalry, tensions in the Middle East, pandemics, and more), it is difficult to imagine anything but turbulent times. There are, however, some key lessons learned that should be reviewed and used as a guide when planning a major organizational change, including the following:

- **There are numerous phases associated with change.** The organizational change process utilized by a company or enterprise can be directly associated with the change processes used in managing a project. The steps include: Determine the need for change—prepare a business case. Assess the benefits and costs—conduct a cost/benefit analysis. Assign a team and team leader to manage the change. Define the objectives and desired future state of the organization. Provide the appropriate resources and ensure highly visible executive support. Iterate the plan—apply the appropriate level of effort to revise, enhance, and improve. Approve and execute the plan. Effectively manage all changes to the change initiative. Review milestones, adjust as necessary, and celebrate successes. Communicate relentlessly—keep everyone informed. Evaluate progress and, when completed, review to ensure objectives were met and to capture new lessons learned.
- **Don't take shortcuts or skip steps.** Doing these things usually creates an illusion that things are moving fast. My project management mentor was fond of saying: "Go slow now so you can go faster later." Shortcuts usually mean leaving something out. In a major change initiative, this can lead to disaster. Take the time to create a workable plan and then work that plan.
- **Errors will be made.** Expect some mistakes at the executive level and throughout each level of authority and responsibility in an organization. No one is perfect, so don't try to create that illusion. Attempting to do so will undoubtedly lead to suspicion, uneasiness, and a lack of confidence. Own up to mistakes and learn from them. People trust others who are willing to admit their errors and their willingness to learn.

- **Make incremental changes—sometimes small steps lead to significant advances.** I recently added the term *inchstone* to my vocabulary. It may have been around for a while, but it was a new term for me. As simple as it may sound, it is incredibly smart. A milestone, by its very name, indicates a long journey. Sometimes the "distance" between milestones leaves the entire team feeling discouraged and too challenged to make it. The notion of an inchstone provides the team with a series of small successes and the motivation to get to the next. With this approach, the milestones seem less daunting.

- **Continue to assess your organization's competitive position.** Analyze products and services. Benchmark best-in-class products and compare with what your organization offers. If there is a gap, assess what is needed to change that scenario. The goal is to cause competitors to try to catch up to your organization. Provide your entire organization with information about your position in the marketplace. Everyone should be interested in the overall performance. Keep your people in the know. When they are provided with straightforward information, they will be more willing to work toward change that will be beneficial. In fact, they may actually become catalysts for the change.

Transformational Leadership—The Essential Element of Change

Transformational leadership is a style that enhances the performance of an organization through a combination of motivation, building morale, conditioning employees and teams to expect and deal with change, and demonstrating confidence in the capability of those involved in a major change to overcome the challenges and achieve the stated objectives. This type of leadership includes connecting with everyone in the organization and creating an individual sense of value and importance to the change initiative. This, in turn, contributes to a desire to work toward the collective needs of the organization. The leader becomes a role model and inspires employees to adapt, collaborate, and develop creative solutions to problems encountered during the change. Transformational leadership creates a sense of ownership, sustains the interest of everyone involved, and ensures that people are aligned with the tasks that they are most suited to perform.

According to the writings of James MacGregor Burns, referenced in an article about transformational leadership published by Langston.edu, transformational leadership is attained when the leaders and followers are working together and motivated to advance to a higher level of performance. Transformational leaders inspire their followers to adjust expectations, rethink perceptions, and work toward common organizational goals.

The transformational leader creates a vison and a specific map to guide the organization and achieve the vision that was created as part of the change initiative.

The transformational leader provides direction through a set of phases or a life cycle. The following is a 12-step process or set of phases that may produce the desired results for a change initiative:

1. **Determine the need for change.** Conduct a needs analysis. Understand where the organization is and where it should be going.
2. **Create a vision.** Create a vision that is clear, attainable, and sellable to those who will be affected.
3. **Define the scope of the change.** What is needed? Why? Who will manage the change? When is it needed?
4. **Conduct an impact analysis.** This is the fundamental element of change. Look at the entire picture—the systems view.
5. **Communicate the change initiative to everyone.** Explain the rationale. Transparency is critical.
6. **Plan the change.** Consider risks, cost, immediate and future benefits to be realized, consequences, and opportunities.
7. **Initiate the change.** Ensure highly visible enthusiasm and commitment.
8. **Monitor and control the change.** Maintain awareness of variances, obstacles, and levels of stakeholder engagement. Look for opportunities as well as threats.
9. **Celebrate completion of deliverables.** Incremental successes will drive more successes.
10. **Review lessons learned along the life cycle.** Emphasize continuous improvement.
11. **Watch for signs of stress and slowing momentum.** Take care of the people involved. Find time for some fun. It helps to rejuvenate and can help to generate creative ideas that may enhance the final outcome.
12. **Take time to thank your change team at completion.** A sincere thanks, some reflection on what has transpired, a recognition of the sacrifices that have been made, and some words of encouragement about the future as the change takes hold all go a long way. Remind everyone that the next change will come sooner than they may think. Keep them prepared and change-ready.

Transformational leadership creates a sense of urgency among those who will be affected by the change and those who will actually perform the change. This type of leadership creates a connection with employees and team members and establishes a high degree of trust. This does not mean that the tough decisions will be avoided. It means that a certain degree of empathy and compassion for the people directly affected by the change is present and the change initiators are prepared to deal effectively with the sometimes unpleasant elements of change.

Positivity—The Mind-Set of the Change Manager

Change certainly can bring about a negative atmosphere. Fear, anxiety, a sense of uncertainty, unwillingness to accept the change, a feeling of unfairness, and a "why do we have to do this" attitude are common obstacles and hurdles for the change manager. Finding ways to tone down the gloom and despair of change is important, but amplifying the positive aspects is the critical success factor in orchestrating successful organizational change. Every project is a challenge and a journey. Throughout organizational change, there will be difficult times and more than an occasional encounter with a "stakeholder in despair." Imagine the leader displaying an attitude of frustration, doubt, short temper, and impatience when communicating with people who are genuinely concerned about the end results of the change and its impact on their assignment or job security. The change leader who understands emotional intelligence and applies that knowledge while managing the change team will experience the effects of its application. Providing answers, keeping people informed, and accentuating the benefits of the change and the necessity for the change will create a more positive experience.

Though a positive attitude is critical during major organizational change, it is important for the change leader to remain fully connected with reality. Most changes are not easy to implement, and it should be understood that efforts to gain support for the change may not be as successful as desired. It will take continuous work and a clearly defined strategy to achieve the defined objectives.

The following is a list of possible approaches and techniques that could maintain a fairly high level of positivity:

1. **Remain approachable.** Bring a smile to the office each day. There will always be something to thank someone for, even during the most difficult times.
2. **Be visible.** Walk around and remain connected to your team. Make sure you also connect with your virtual and remote teams.
3. **Schedule frequent status sessions.** Brief updates keep the level of stress down.
4. **Remind people of the objective.** Reiterate why the change was necessary.
5. **Assign meaningful work.** Assign meaningful work to each team member and acknowledge accomplishments.
6. **Demonstrate that you are human.** Manage your behavior through emotional intelligence.

7. **Make sure you are fully committed to the change.** Maintain consistency when speaking to anyone about the change. Side conversations that indicate you are less than sincerely committed or critical of the change will eventually surface, and that could trigger some very uncomfortable situations.

Positivity should not be a façade and it should not be a "disconnect" from reality. It is simply a way to make reality more acceptable. The atmosphere of positivity will very likely lead to higher levels of quality, greater loyalty to the change project, and a deeper sense of respect for the leaders involved in the change.

Key Points About Leading Organizational Change and Summary

Managing organizational change is a challenging, often emotionally draining experience. It requires an understanding of the capabilities of the entire organization and a systems-thinking approach. It is not something that is led by one person; it is an enterprise-wide event that requires buy-in from each board member, business unit manager, supervisor, and employee. In most cases, it will not be easy and will be disruptive to some. There will be some loss of key employees and there may be a short period when operations and internal processes actually drop in performance. Effectively managed change will minimize the duration of the performance drop. It is important for the change leader to understand that it is not easy to drive people out of their comfort zones. There will be some resistance and a tendency to hang on to existing processes and tools. The effective leader will empathize with the workforce, listen to their concerns, communicate the specific reason for the change and "sell it," and be prepared for the naysayers who will attempt to block change.

The change leader describes the urgency behind a change, accepts responsibility for the decision to change, and attributes the successful change to the people who actually implemented it.

Leaders understand the potentially destructive nature of change and work to minimize the fears that are naturally associated with change. An informed employee base and a unified management team are the key elements in the planning and implementation of organizational change.

Change is part of organizational life and is essential for business survival. It requires the leadership to nurture a culture that encourages creativity and innovation. It is about the need to occasionally reinvent itself by taking a good look at performance, internal processes, and its overall efficiency and compare these with the competition.

Today, change is clearly a given. The entire organization must be conditioned to prepare for change, embrace change, and when necessary, cause change. This is the real leadership challenge.

An organization is change-ready when:

- Leaders at every level are respected and demonstrate fairness, competence, and respect for their employees;
- Leaders have successfully created an environment where people feel personally responsible and motivated to accept change or change behaviors that will enable organizational success;
- Leaders have created an organization that has matured to a state of collaborative work without silos;
- Leaders have provided their employees with a strong sense of purpose and meaningful work that enables them to realize personal-value growth while contributing to the organization; and
- Leaders show genuine appreciation for the contributions of employees.

Fire up your organization through a positive leadership approach, condition all employees to expect change, and encourage them to look for opportunities to make positive changes. Louis Pasteur provided us with a thought about change: "Chance favors the prepared mind!" (Lecture, University of Lille, 7 December 1854). This quote should be on or near the desk of every change manager and organizational leader. Prepare yourself and your organization. Luck has very little to do with anything. Your leadership will make positive and beneficial changes happen.

To prepare a plan of action to deal effectively with organizational change and to lead it with confidence, consider the following questions:

1. On a scale from 1 to 10, how would you rate the change-readiness of your organization, where 1 indicates that change is feared and the entire organization is stuck in its comfort zone and 10 indicates that change is the norm and everyone has a "let's get it done" attitude?
2. How well are you setting the stage for change? How frequently do you communicate the "state of the business" to your employees?
3. How well do your employees understand your market position and your rating against your competitors?
4. How are your flagship products performing against your competitors' products?
5. What are the greatest concerns identified by your employees?
6. How often do you offer town hall-type meetings to ensure that employees are kept in the know?
7. How does your management and leadership team nurture creativity and innovation?
8. How well do you listen to your clients, and more importantly, your employees?

9. What are your employees saying about the organization's leaders? What is the "unofficial buzz"?
10. How has the organization's leadership conditioned employees to respond positively to change?
11. When communicating about a change initiative to employees, how well do you describe what's in it for them?
12. How emotionally intelligent are you?
13. During a major organizational change, how well do you remain connected to organizational values?
14. How well can you change the perspective about change from "your vision" to "our vision"?

If we think about it, we realize that change occurs every minute of every day. It is something that we deal with, sometimes on a small scale and sometimes on a very large scale. Just like risk, the results of change can be either positive or negative. It is advantageous to every organization to practice effective leadership tactics. Along with those tactics, it is important to maintain a connection to emotional intelligence. Your consciousness of your own behaviors and your ability to be sensitive to the behaviors of the people who will be impacted by change are essential success factors.

Keep in mind that if your organization has been successful up to this point in time, it can be safely said that it is not an indication or guarantee that you will still enjoy success tomorrow. The organization that is "change-savvy" will have an edge over its competitors. This means that the culture of the organization revolves around change and, if change isn't occurring, a shift is necessary. New questions must be asked. Processes and rules must be challenged, and leaders must initiate actions that will be a catalyst for positive organizational change.

References

Creative Commons. (n. d.). Transformational leadership. *Langston.edu* Retrieved from http://www.langston.edu/sites/default/files/basic-content-files/TransformationalLeadership.pdf

Deming, W. E. (2017). *Management and leadership quotes.* Retrieved from http://managementquotes.net/authors/W._Edwards_Deming?page=2

Harvard Business Essentials. (2003). *Managing change and transition.* Boston, MA: Harvard Business School Publishing Corporation.

Harvard Business School Press. (1998). *Harvard Business Review on change management.* Boston, MA: Harvard Business School Publishing.

Peters, T. (2010). *The little big things: 163 ways to pursue excellence.* New York, NY: Harper Business.

Project Management Institute (PMI). (2013). *Managing change in organizations: A practice guide.* Newtown Square, PA: Author.

Schwartz, P. (1996). *The art of the long view.* New York, NY: Doubleday.

Young, R. R., Brady, S. M., & Nagle Jr., D. C. (2009). *How to save a failing project.* Vienna, VA: Management Concepts.

Review Questions

These questions will challenge your knowledge and assist in developing strategies for the advancement of your organization.

The answers to these questions depend on the situation and the organizational culture one has to work within. There are certainly multiple ways to answer them. The important element here is to take a very close and objective look at your organization and then determine the most effective and least disruptive way to execute and successfully complete organizational change.

1. Considering the need for periodic assessments of an organization's capabilities to ensure its sustainability and growth in the business environment, what actions may be taken to prepare the organization and its employees for business changes that are not clearly foreseeable?

2. Many organizations rely on a specific set of metrics to determine how the organization is performing. Most of these metrics are actually "lagging" indicators. How would you describe the difference between a lagging indicator and a leading indicator?

3. Systems thinking allows organizational leaders to fully conceptualize the current and short-term future of an organization. How would you describe the concept of systems thinking?

4. Organizational change can be hindered by a number of factors. What is generally considered the primary factor that must be addressed when developing plans for making a significant organizational change?

5. How would you explain "transformational leadership" to your peers and colleagues? Why is this concept key to achieving successful organizational change?

CHAPTER 13

The Importance of Sponsorship for Successful Change

By Alfonso Bucero, MSc, PMI-RMP, PMP, PMI Fellow

Abstract

This chapter describes a process of leading change from the sponsorship perspective in order to increase acceptance to change and to take advantage of favorable existing conditions. PMI's *Pulse of the Profession*® in-depth report *Enabling Organizational Change Through Strategic Initiatives* shows that change success "is likely fueled by the significantly greater support received from executive sponsors" (PMI, 2014, p. 13). The sponsor's role is crucial to manage the change successfully.

Introduction

Whatever the level or degree of organizational change, the people on the receiving end are human beings. Without looking at the implications of change on individuals, we can never really hope to manage large-scale change effectively. According to Blacker and Shimmin (1984), when considering human behavior, there is no objective reality. People behave in accordance with how they perceive the situation to be. Perceptions vary because individuals approach the same situation with different key meanings. Changes that appear reasonable and straightforward to some may, in altogether unforeseen ways, undermine certain key attachments felt by others. The executive who believes in the change buys into it. It is essential that the executive supports the change. The sponsor plays a key role in any organizational change.

The behavioral approach to change, as the name implies, focuses on how one individual can change another individual's behavior using reward and punishment to achieve the intended results.

When the sponsor spends some time with the project stakeholders in order to elicit the preferred behavior, the individual needs to be encouraged to behave in a specific way and discouraged from behaving in any other way. The sponsor is the one with enough power and authority to support and embrace the change. The sponsor is responsible for creating an environment that enables the selected change to be made on time and within budget.

According to Harrington and Nelson (2013), ideally, once the sponsor has legitimized the project, everything will run smoothly, and the project scope will remain constant. By providing the resources required to implement the project, the sponsor's involvement is negligible until the final results are available for evaluation. However, seldom do things run this smoothly in the real world.

The Economist Intelligence Unit (2013) found that approximately 50% of strategic initiatives do not receive appropriate executive-level attention, and 28% of organizations admit that individual projects to implement strategy do not typically obtain the necessary senior-level sponsorship. Better sponsor involvement in organizational change management can improve these numbers.

Managing Change in Organizations: A Practice Guide states:

> A sponsor provides resources required for change and has the ultimate responsibility for the program or project, building commitment for the change particularly at the senior management level across the organization. Direct responsibility and accountability for the change needs to be clearly defined and accepted at an appropriately high level within an organization. Consequently, the sponsor for a change effort should be someone who has sufficient authority, influence, power, enthusiasm, and time to ensure that any conflicts that could impede the change are resolved in a timely and appropriate fashion. (PMI, 2013)

The *Chaos Manifesto* states: "The single most important advancement to improve project success rates is the increase in competency of the executive sponsor" (Standish Group International, 2013, p. 8).

I will use a real case study from a financial institution to show how to get buy-in from both the sponsor and the stakeholders to make change happen. In the case profiled, the entire organization needed to change in order to accomplish the project's objectives, and the project sponsor was a key to the success.

Background

The organization was a financial institution and had traditionally been a very large user of UNISYS computer systems and solutions over a 10-year period, experiencing stability and good business results throughout that time. However, systems and methods that had remained static for many years and did not allow for rapid and substantial change were under tremendous competitive pressure.

The customer had a very clear idea that users were happy working with the old system. But a change was needed as quickly as possible in order to survive among all the banking competition. The proximity of Y2K was forcing all financial entities to be prepared, meaning they needed to update or create processes, train people, and upgrade or change their technology. The project in question started in September 1999.

It was an information systems strategic project. It consisted of functional and technological innovations that answered market and environment needs, implementing a hardware and software platform, developing a customized software package, and managing the change. Looking at all the changes required, my challenge was to start working with a new customer and to understand the project stakeholders and their behaviors.

The client's business objectives were:

- To achieve a performance improvement of 30%—some processes caused hours of delay while offices demanded more transactions;
- To increase the number of branches of the organization by 20% without any loss of performance; and
- To implement new technologies—the client needed more value-added competitive offerings—changing its platform and software to open systems was a necessity.

This financial institution needed to embrace and adopt change in its strategy to ensure long-term success for the organization.

A multinational firm and professional services provider was chosen as the main contractor. As the project manager, I took on the task with the team to make things happen using project management skills and processes. The entire organization needed to change to accomplish the project objectives. Success was possible because of the organization's willingness to learn, ability to motivate the project team, and the fact that it never gave up in the face of extremely difficult situations.

Challenges

One of the most complicated tasks was to convince the senior managers of the financial organization about the need for project planning. In the beginning, the customer was very involved. After the first month, the customer asked for tangible results. I explained that planning is absolutely necessary for project success. I borrowed equipment and dedicated one team member

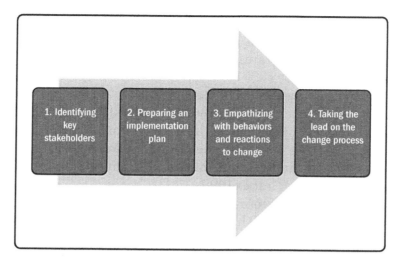

Figure 13-1. Change process steps.

to the startup of one machine in order to demonstrate to the customer how we, as project providers, were able to operate in this platform. That diminished customer pressure for a while.

Managing challenges throughout the project was part of managing the change and is considered a project manager responsibility. Clear communication and intimacy with financial institution managers were critical success factors. I was able to determine that this project was clearly linked to the financial institution strategy; that link proved very helpful for us throughout the project. At my prodding, senior management assigned the highest priority to this project.

The Process

The multinational project management initiative (a form of project management office [PMO]) had summarized a process for *take the lead on the change*. I applied the process in order to get support and minimize impact on the customer organization. The process steps are shown in Figure 13-1.

Identifying Key Stakeholders

It took more than two months to analyze all of the critical players in the customer organization. During the first month, I organized periodical meeting sessions in order to get people involved and informed about the project status. One of my daily tasks was to be available to everyone and to facilitate the information flow and communication among team members.

One critical success factor was getting sponsors on board who had the authority to commit resources and would support the project manager.

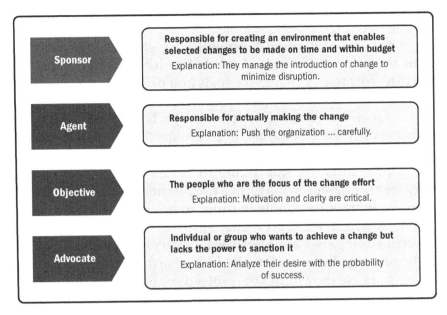

Figure 13-2.   Categories of key players.

The customer considered this project strategic and totally linked with its business objectives. The model used establishes four categories of key players: sponsors, agents, objectives (targets), and advocates (see Figure 13-2).

I was the agent for the change. Honestly, at the beginning, I felt more like an advocate. I had to be proactive, self-confident, and gain customer confidence to create an open line of communication.

Preparing an Implementation Plan

The first thing we did was identify events that would guarantee the change and help everyone understand its value. We involved all team leaders early in the planning phase, discussing different options to be implemented. This was not difficult because every team leader was responsible for a different functional area and knew the old system very well.

We analyzed the gap between the old system and its applications and the new system. Also, the plan needed to take changes into account regarding processes, systems, people, and the organization. We developed a plan for implementing the change, looking at the possible impacts and contingencies in terms of processes, people, and technology.

We needed to ask for support from the financial institution's senior management in order to facilitate the change. I persuaded them by sharing facts and a rationale to help them conclude that the change management plan was effective. When the plan was finished, we asked for approval for the implementation plan from the sponsor, and we received a consensus from the steering committee and from the other stakeholders in the organization.

Empathizing with Behaviors and Reactions to Change

As usual in this type of project, inhibitors to the change were detected throughout the project life cycle. I needed to have personal meetings with all branch directors to clarify project goals and objectives and convince them about the major benefits of the project for them and for their business.

The financial institution imposed the change, but the reasons and justifications for that change were explained to all groups. This resulted in diminished resistance because good mechanisms for communications were established.

The customer situation was stable in terms of processes, people, and technology, but the senior managers of the financial institution knew how to motivate and compensate people in order to ask for extra effort. They knew they could not ask for extra effort without providing compensation. Then they defined metrics and personal objectives for every team leader in the project.

In the beginning, there was a major lack of involvement from end users at the branches because they were not involved in the initial study. One success factor in this process was to recognize different behavioral patterns and to allow enough time to work with everyone in the organization.

Change Process

You need to go through the following steps:

- **Lead.** Eight functional groups were set up, defining different goals for individuals. Team leaders were empowered to participate in most decisions. I needed upper management and customer support for getting these things done most times, but I was able to have influence without a lot of power.
- **Test.** People were invited to express their reactions to the changes. This feedback was very valuable in order to learn from the errors and make improvements.
- **Recognition.** Metrics were established that allowed for improvement and recognized the efforts and achievement of the team and team leaders.
- **Follow.** Every project is alive and needs to be monitored. In this case, the follow-up consisted of weekly brief reviews with team leaders, analyzing the results and learning from our experiences.

Assessing the Change

Before making the decision to change, we needed to consider the three following aspects:

- Assess the readiness for the change.
- Assess the resistance to the change.
- Assess the risk for the change.

Figure 13-3. Assessing the readiness for change.

To consider these aspects, I used three assessment surveys. I had used all three for several change management projects previously, and they were quite useful for all project stakeholders (see Figure 13-1).

Assess the Readiness for the Change

The purpose of this tool is to increase the organizational awareness regarding the change. It provides a high-level risk analysis of the potential areas affected. This is a first-level assessment of the situation. The risk is assessed regarding the eight critical success factors of the foundation for the change.

This tool needs to be used with all stakeholder groups (Figure 13-3). It is useful at different levels and with several functional groups. This tool serves to contrast opinions and can be used as a test for the issues that might arise. The tool assesses:

- Motivation to change;
- Change commitment;
- Change shared vision;
- The culture fits the change;
- Organizational alignment;
- Communication;
- Transition planning; and
- Skills.

Change Assessment Tool

The purpose of this tool is to increase organizational awareness in an organization that wants to make a change. This tool provides a high-level analysis of potential risk areas for the planned change. This is a first-level evaluation used to get a sense of the situation. Risk is assessed regarding eight critical success factors, which became the foundation for the change.

Important: This tool may be used with all stakeholder groups. It is useful for different levels of several functional groups. This serves to compare opinions and can be used as a test for any issues that might arise.

Administration: This survey may be used directly with the target public, or an interviewer can ask questions and fill in the answers. People who administer the tool need to understand change management concepts.

Select a number from 1 to 5 and place it in the right column of Table 13-1 as a score for each sentence. The scoring shown is an example.

The meaning for each score is as follows:

1 = Totally agree
2 = Agree
3 = Neutral
4 = Disagree
5 = Totally disagree

Scoring instructions: First, add up the scoring from each section and then divide the score by the identified factor to create an adjusted scoring. The change-assessment tool in Table 13-1 and Figure 13-4 evaluates the readiness of the organization to move forward with the change.

Assess the Resistance for the Change

This tool helps manage the human aspects when adapting to any change. As a diagnostic tool, it can be used to determine global resistance for an organizational change and determine its contribution to the risk of failure when implementing the change.

This tool can be used during the initial planning phase, when an organizational change is being considered, before announcing the change, or at any moment after the change has been announced. It can also be used after the implementation has been finished.

The Reason to Use It

Based on practical experience, I found several reasons:

- As a warning for potential failure at implementation phase;
- To determine the disposition from the objective public facing the change;
- To analyze any resistance during the implementation process; and
- To identify the nature of resistance problems once implementation is complete.

Table 13-1.   Example of organizational awareness assessment.

1. Motivation to Change	
Statement	**Score**
1.1 There is a clear business need that forces a necessary change.	1
1.2 There are meaningful business risks if the change is not successful.	5
1.3 Lack of satisfaction level for the current situation is shared among the employees and management.	4
1.4 There is a common feeling of urgency for the change.	5
1.5 The impact for those affected by the change is minimal (habits, power, security).	3
Total	18
2. Change Commitment	
Statement	**Score**
2.1 Management is publicly committed to the change.	1
2.2 Resources, time, and money are committed to sustain the change.	5
2.3 The sponsor is at the right organizational level to have power for decision making.	4
2.4 Those who are implementing the change have enough credibility with the people affected by the change.	3
2.5 The sponsor understands his/her responsibility, especially in the case of conflict.	5
2.6 Other leaders (coalition) support the sponsor who is conducting the change.	5
2.7 Senior managers support the change.	3
Total	26
3. Change Shared Vision	
Statement	**Score**
3.1 There is a close relationship between the change vision and the global organizational vision.	1
3.2 People can count on the change vision from a positive perspective.	1
3.3 There is an understandable and shared vision from the change.	3
3.4 There is strong leadership to sustain the change vision.	3
Total	8
4. The Culture Fits the Change	
Statement	**Score**
4.1 Change is aligned with the organizational culture.	2
4.2 The implementation approach is appropriate for the organizational culture.	2
4.3 Cultural strength may reinforce the change direction.	2
4.4 Previous changes have been managed well at this organization.	4
4.5 The organization makes and implements decisions on time.	4
4.6 Managers and employees tell the truth to one another regarding the areas affected by the change.	5
Total	19

(continued)

Table 13-1. Example of organizational awareness assessment. *(continued)*

5. Organizational Alignment	
Statement	**Score**
5.1 The planning cycles support change resource requirements.	2
5.2 Award structures encourage change adoption by all people affected.	4
5.3 Processes support change sustainability.	4
5.4 All consequences are articulated and there is follow-up on them.	5
5.5 Management practices and behavior support the change.	3
5.6 There is a low level of stress in the organization.	2
Total	20
6. Communications	
Statement	**Score**
6.1 The organization uses three communication channels: across, up, and down.	3
6.2 Communication usually arrives and is understood at all levels.	5
6.3 The communication plan is complete and is completed on time.	5
6.4 There are different communications means within the organization.	4
6.5 The change magnitude is small, both vertically and horizontally.	4
Total	**21**
7. Transition Planning	
Statement	**Score**
7.1 There is an ongoing transition plan that allows adequate time for the change.	1
7.2 The transition plan is complete, covering human dimensions about processes and techniques.	2
7.3 Transition measures are incorporated in the plan.	3
7.4 Risks and potential problems have been identified with plans to solve them quickly.	4
7.5 The implementation approach is aligned to the scope of change (time, methods, involvement, and leadership style).	5
Total	15
8. Skills	
Statement	**Score**
8.1 Change agents have the skills to implement the change.	1
8.2 Those affected by the change have the necessary technical skills to perform the new activities.	3
8.3 People understand their personal transition process.	5
8.4 There are mentors available to help people through the change.	5
8.5 Employees feel they have the appropriate power for the change.	5
8.6 Organizational teamwork is developed by the organization.	4
Total	**23**

SECTION	SCORING	DIVISOR	ADJUSTED SCORING	
1	MOTIVATION	18	5	4
2	COMMITMENT	26	7	4
3	SHARED VISION	8	4	2
4	CULTURE	19	6	3
5	ALIGNMENT	20	6	3
6	COMMUNICATION	21	5	4
7	PLANNING	15	5	3
8	SKILLS	23	6	4

Step 1: Add up the adjusted scores.

Step 2: Multiply total adjusted score by 2.5 to create the risk evaluation score.

Step 3: Select the corresponding cell to show the risk evaluation.

Global Risk Evaluation	Precaution
	41–70
Motivation to change	18
Change commitment	26
Change shared vision	8
The culture fits the change	19
Organizational alignment	20
Communication	21
Transition planning	15
Skills	23

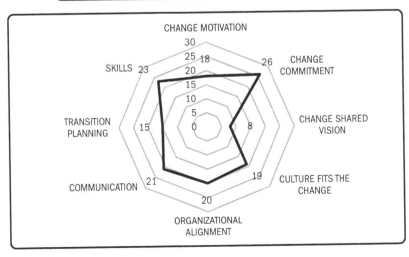

Figure 13-4.   Change evaluation tool.

Change Resistance Tool

This tool helps manage the human aspect of change adaptation. As a diagnostic tool, it is used to determine global resistance for an organizational change and its contribution to the risk of failure in the implementation.

Each of the 25 elements in Table 13-2 includes a scale from 1 to 10, where 1 indicates a low impact and 10 indicates a high impact. Choose the most adequate. Below it is an example.

Table 13-2. Sample change resistance tool.

Statement	Scoring
1. PURPOSE	
Do you understand the purpose of this change?	10
2. NEED	
Do you believe this change is necessary?	1
3. INVOLVEMENT	
Have you been involved in the planning of this change?	1
4. CLARITY	
Has communication been clear regarding this change?	2
5. COSTS	
How meaningful are these changes to you with regard to tangible, intellectual, or emotional costs?	2
6. REWARDS	
Do you believe that the appropriate awards have been established?	3
7. COMPATIBILITY	
How compatible is this change with the organizational values?	1
8. SUPPORT	
Do you believe that your boss or other politically important people are supporting this change?	1
9. EMOTIONS	
Do you believe that this change will impact your relationship with others in the organization who are important to you?	8
10. CONFIDENCE	
What is your confidence level that the necessary resources will be available for this change?	5
11. IMPACT	
What budgetary impact are you expecting to have at your operational area because of this change?	6
12. TIME	
Do you believe there was adequate time between the change announcement and the implementation starting date?	8

Statement	Scoring
13. DAILY WORK	
Do you believe work patterns were taken into account when the change was planned?	8
14. YOUR WORK	
Do you think this change will negatively impact any key aspect of your work?	10
15. SIGNIFICANCE	
Is this change meaningful to you?	7
16. PENALTY	
Do you think you will be punished in an inappropriate way if you make mistakes while you are learning what is needed for the change?	8
17. NEW WORK	
Do you feel secure about how you will perform your job after the change?	10
18. SKILLS AND KNOWLEDGE	
Do you think that you have the necessary skills and knowledge to implement this change?	10
19. SPONSOR	
Do you respect this change's sponsor?	9
20. CHANGE AGENTS	
Do you respect the change agents?	10
21. STRESS	
Are you currently stressed in your job?	9
22. THREATS	
Does this change represent any threat to your personal interests?	5
23. PERSONAL OBJECTIVES	
How compatible are these change objectives with regard to your personal career path objectives?	4
24. WITHDRAWAL	
If this change is given up or is not implemented completely, how difficult will it be to withdraw?	8
25. PERFORMANCE	
Do you feel this change will be reflected in your previous performance?	9

Scoring Instructions: In order to compute your problem evaluation during implementation, please follow these steps:

Step 1: Add up all the answers from all items (146).
Step 2: Divide total by 25 (5.8).
Step 3: Multiply the result by 10 to obtain its problem implementation factor (58.4).

Implementation Problem Factor = (TOTAL/25) × 10 = 58.4.

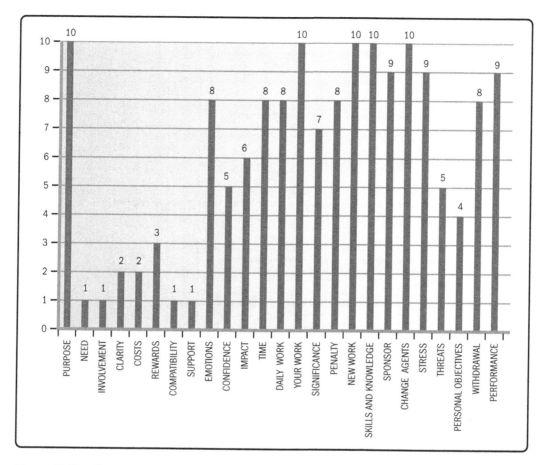

Figure 13.5. Change resistance tool scale.

Assess the Risk for Change

This tool provides a high-level analysis of the change effort. We examine risk in the following five dimensions:

- Motivation level for change
- Change sponsorship level
- Change organizational resistance level
- Transition planning and the process
- Appropriate change culture for the organization

The purpose of this tool is to elevate awareness of the critical success factors for change and to identify where an intervention to increase the probability of success is needed.

Important: The targeted tool users are consultants, project managers, or business developers. The tool is used to verify opinions and as a test for the issues that might arise.

Write a number from 1 to 5 as the most appropriate answer for the following questions:
Scoring:

1 = Totally agree
2 = Agree
3 = Neutral
4 = Disagree
5 = Totally disagree

All the data in Table 13-3 are an example.

The Sponsor Role

The project sponsor was the IT manager from a financial organization. He had enough authority in his organization because he had been assigned by the board of directors to sponsor the project. He was a respected professional who had joined the organization 20 years ago and had a good reputation. He believed in the change and required my time and support as a project manager.

The project sponsor provided the resources required for the change and had the ultimate responsibility for the project. He worked well at building senior management commitment across the organization. I spent many hours talking to him about how he would be directly responsible and accountable for the change, but explained that I would be helping and working with him so that the change would be successful. The sponsor had a lot of enthusiasm, power, and influence over the entire organization. His support was visible and was one of the key reasons for the change success.

In change projects, the normal hierarchy of management control is often broken as the project stretches across many parts of the organization. This hierarchy is replaced with sponsorship, where individual managers in the organization take on the temporary role of providing the formal authority by which changes are made. A change manager needs to have a good understanding of the nature of sponsorship and to carefully assist and manage the various sponsors of the project.

The Sponsor Evaluation

Table 13-4 reflects the key elements of sponsor commitment. Each element has a scale from 1 to 7, with a 7 indicating high sponsor commitment, and a 1 indicating low sponsor commitment. The scales are as follows: From 1 to 2 is considered low; medium, from 3 to 5; and high, from 6 to 7.

The sponsor factor, generated by the evaluation above, reflects the risk of implementation failure of a project. The lower the factor, the greater the risk of implementation failure. I used these questions with the project sponsor and it helped me obtain his commitment for the project.

Table 13-3. Risk assessment questionnaire for a change (example).

1. Change Motivation	Scoring
1.1 Is there a clear business need that demonstrates the need for the change?	1
1.2 Are the reasons for the change perceived by everyone in the business unit?	5
1.3 Is there a strong sense of urgency for the change from management?	4
1.4 Are there significant risks for the business if the change is not successful?	5
1.5 Is the lack of satisfaction level regarding the current situation mutually shared by employees and managers?	3
1.6 Is there a well-articulated vision about the organization's future, and is that vision understood?	5
1.7 Does the future vision for the organization motivate the employees?	4
Total	**27**
2. Sponsorship for the Change	**Scoring**
2.1 Is there a sponsor committed to initiating the change?	1
2.2 Is there a sponsor committed to sustaining the change (resources, money, and time are committed)?	5
2.3 Is the sponsor at a high-enough organizational level to have decision-making power?	4
2.4 Does the sponsor have credibility from the people affected by the change?	3
2.5 Does the sponsor understand his or her role as sponsor?	5
2.6 Did the sponsor set up some clear expectations with the other change leaders in the organization?	5
2.7 Does the sponsor have allies?	3
2.8 Does the sponsor understand how people will react to the proposed changes?	4
2.9 Does the sponsor consider and respond to people's feelings when the change is introduced?	5
Total	**35**
3. Change Shared Vision	**Scoring**
3.1 Is the effort of the change visibly linked to other main strategic efforts inside the organization?	1
3.2 Have the change priorities been communicated in a clear way?	1
3.3 Does the organization have the key abilities to maintain the "momentum" in the transformation process?	3
3.4 Do the key stakeholders incorporate the change process into their plans and actions?	3
3.5 Can management mobilize all relevant parts to take action?	5
3.6 Are changes perceived as a success by most people?	5
3.7 Does the organization respond to market needs?	5
3.8 Are incentives established and consequences monitored?	5
3.9 Does the organization remain focused on the change, even when there are "fires" to put out?	5
3.10 Are problems solved in a quick and effective way?	5
3.11 Are managers authentic and do they practice integrity?	5
3.12 Does the truth flow between employees and managers?	5
3.13 Has the organization been successful implementing other changes?	5
Total	**53**

4. Transition Management Plan Process	**Scoring**
4.1 Is there an ongoing transition plan?	2
4.2 Is the transition plan complete (technical, human, and processes)?	2
4.3 Is there a leader and a team identified for the transition?	2
4.4 Are the key stakeholders identified and involved in the change process?	4
4.5 Have the transition-monitoring mechanisms been incorporated into the plan?	4
4.6 Have potential problems or risks with the plans been identified for quick resolution?	4
4.7 Are there some plans regarding skill assessment and people transition?	4
4.8 Does the organization have several mechanisms for two-way communications?	4
4.9 Are communications understood at all levels?	4
4.10 Are the change details communicated as soon as possible?	4
4.11 Does management communicate in an open and honest way about all aspects of the change?	4
4.12 Are the key communicators able to influence opinions and behaviors?	4
Total	**43**

5. Appropriate Culture for Change	**Scoring**
5.1 Does the organization know its customers?	2
5.2 Are performance metrics aligned to economic ones?	4
5.3 Do performance metrics encourage the desired behavior?	4
5.4 Is the change aligned to organizational culture?	5
5.5 Is the implementation approach appropriate for the scope change?	3
5.6 Is the implementation process consistent with the organizational value?	2
5.7 Are the implementation periods consistent with the organizational rhythm?	4
Total	**20**

Scoring Instructions:

> Step 1: Add up the scores from each section.
> Step 2: Divide the scoring by the identified factor to create an adjusted score.

SECTION	SCORING	MULTIPLIER	ADJUSTED SCORE
2.1	Motivation	27	2.85	77
2.2	Sponsorship	35	2.00	18
2.3	Resistance	53	1.42	37
2.4	Transition	43	1.66	26
2.5	Appropriate culture	20	2.85	7

Step 3: Total = 165

Step 4: Multiply the total adjusted scoring by 0.40 to create the risk evaluation score = 66.

Step 5: Select the correspondent box to show the risk evaluation.

Risk Global Evaluation	Low risk 20–40	Precaution 41–70	High risk 71–100
MOTIVATION FOR THE CHANGE	27		
SPONSORSHIP FOR THE CHANGE	35		
CHANGE SHARED VISION	53		
TRANSITION MANAGEMENT PLAN AND PROCESS	43		
APPROPRIATE CULTURE FOR THE CHANGE	20		

Selecting the Right Sponsor for the Change

In managing change, one needs to understand and work with different types of sponsors, such as the following:

- **Initiating sponsor.** This is the person who starts the change project and may be the person with whom you first meet. This may be the key sponsor or someone lower down the order. He or she may be the one who asks you to manage or facilitate the change project.

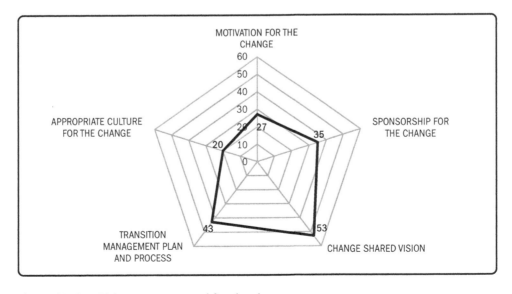

Figure 13-6. Risk assessment tool for the change.

Table 13-4. Sponsor evaluation survey.

Questions	LOW (1–2)	MEDIUM (3–5)	HIGH (6–7)
1. How dissatisfied is the sponsor with the way things are?			
2. Are the sponsor's goals for this project clear?			
3. Does the sponsor believe that there is a real need for the project?			
4. Does the sponsor understand the long-term impact the change will have on the organization?			
5. Does the sponsor understand what people are being asked to change about the way they operate?			
6. Does the sponsor understand how many people or groups will be affected by the project?			
7. Does the sponsor understand what resources are needed for the project to be successful?			
8. Is the sponsor willing to commit the resources needed for the project to succeed?			
9. Does the sponsor publicly convey the organization's strong commitment to change?			
10. Is the sponsor willing to meet privately with individuals or groups to convey strong personal support for the change?			
11. Will the sponsor use rewards and pressures to gain support for this project?			
12. Will the sponsor ensure that procedures to track progress and problems are established?			
13. Is the sponsor aware of the prices that must be paid for the project to succeed?			
14. Is the sponsor willing to make sacrifices to ensure the success of this project?			
15. Will the sponsor show consistent, sustained support for the project?			

- **Key sponsor.** This is the person (often the most-senior manager) who can resolve the stickiest of problems, such as differences between other primary sponsors, and is the one who provides the ultimate authority for the project and may have a hand in direction and approval. Spend quality time up front with the key sponsor to understand what his or her real needs are. Then meet regularly during the implementation of the change to ensure that the key sponsor is in the loop and remains committed. If the key sponsor drifts away and shows insufficient interest, you may need to consider closing down the project.

- **Primary sponsor.** This is a small group of managers whose support is critical and who have sufficient clout to unblock most problems, including problems with secondary sponsors. These people are sometimes also called "sustaining sponsors," and they often work together as a core team. To get the time and commitment you need from the primary sponsors, spend time with them, both individually and collectively, showing how close collaboration is very much in their interest (if it is not, then you need to connect with the key sponsor to resolve this). You will also need to put appropriate effort into building this group into a cohesive and effective team.

- **Secondary sponsor.** These are managers whose support is needed, albeit at a limited level. They are important because they have the ability to block change. However, if they were all members of the core team, then that team would become unwieldy and difficult to manage. Excluding them, however, may be a bad political move because they can take revenge by refusing to cooperate or otherwise blocking progress. Therefore, they require careful handling and usually need to be communicated with on a very regular basis. If you can't invite them to all meetings, at least keep them up to date with progress and demonstrate that you are listening to them and taking their concerns into account.

Other Potential Sponsor Roles

The sponsors of the project can play a number of roles in the change project. The only role that they must not be allowed to play is sitting back and letting you get on with it. If any of the roles are not undertaken, then it will be necessary to discuss how they will be effectively performed.

Table 13-5 is based on my experience regarding some potential roles a sponsor may play.

Table 13-5.   Potential roles for sponsors.

Role	Actions
Visionary	Presenting and selling his or her vision of the new future, motivating people to work toward this future
Milestones keeper	Reviewing progress at defined milestones, and only allowing continuation if milestone criteria are met
Budget owner	Holding the budget for changes and only paying for those projects and changes that meet the change criteria
Clearer	Acting to remove resistance and other organizational blocks that hinder the changes being implemented
Negotiator	Resolving disputes between people affected by the change
Planner	Active involvement in planning the change, then reviewing implementation of the change
Leader	Full involvement in all stages of the change

Sponsorship Traps

Mismanaging sponsorship is, perhaps, one of the main reasons why change projects fail. A common sponsorship trap occurs when sponsors see their role as an early agreement, but have no further engagement, taking an open option to back out at any time. Such weak commitment is highly hazardous and must be exposed and managed if the change is to succeed. Another trap occurs when the change manager does not engage with sponsors early on, either not realizing they exist or assuming they will be no problem. When the project gets under way and things start to change, these sponsors may feel left out and take revenge by obstructing the change. When things are going wrong and your sponsors are washing their hands of the project, you are doomed. When sponsors are managed well, however, they will find it impossible to wash their hands of the project because good management ensures they are well connected to the project, not only physically but also mentally and emotionally.

The Team

The project team in the case study consisted of functional team leaders who owned the entire project life cycle for every functional area in the financial institution. Every functional leader was responsible for talking and meeting with end users, leading his or her software development team, and managing all tests. Hewlett Packard consultants trained these leaders to be prepared for managing and motivating their teams, and the leaders were supported by a project manager.

Steering committee members also participated, not only in sponsorship tasks, but also in all communication and dissemination tasks that contributed to project success. They talked to and supported people, boosting morale and recognizing everyone's efforts in public ways.

The Tools Used

Several tools were key for the project success, including:

- Teamwork exercises, using real meetings to put ideas into practice;
- Roles and responsibilities definitions that were then published in planning documents;
- Change agent training;
- Daily communication among team members;
- Asking for feedback from every team leader; and
- Communication and respect among team members.

Projects frequently fail not for technical reasons, but because people in the organization refused the change. The critical success factor to implement systems is the way human and organizational factors are planned; technology is a secondary priority. This message was not understood by the entire management team at the beginning. It took six months of work to convince everyone.

The Results

Based on the organization case's study, we can measure results according to a number of parameters, but when we talk about the management of change, we are talking about process, people, and technology—the enablers of a change:

- **Process.** Because of the new application's implementation, customer processes needed to be defined, modified, and used by people. This was one of the most difficult parts of this project, but the people involved in that area were proud because they had the opportunity to contribute to the project's success and be members of a successful financial institution. By reviewing their old processes, they were able to define new ones that enabled them to introduce new products to the market. Process ownership was a key aspect.
- **People.** Another important result was the use of the system by end users. Step by step, all users adapted their behavior to the new system's functionality and to the new processes. Systems were tested, measured, and evaluated by the end users. In this particular case, the level of involvement by end users grew in a positive way over a period of months.
- **Technology.** All software modules in the new application were working, and the customer had a foundational platform for building future information systems. Technical results were improved over the old system. Performance became much better, and the system placed the customer in a technological, competent position within the financial market.

Summary

This project was almost two years long—its implementation was delayed, but it was finally successful. The key points to remember are the following:

- To be a leader in the market depends on the capacity to change behaviors, skills, and processes.
- The project manager created an effective communication strategy to deal with everyone in the organization.

- Managing difficulties was part of managing the change.
- All changes require initiatives from many people, and those people need time, patience, persistence, and management support.
- One of the critical success factors was recognizing the different behavioral patterns among the different stakeholders.

References

Harrington, H. J., & Nelson, D. (2013). *The sponsor as the face of organizational change.* Newtown Square, PA: Project Management Institute. Retrieved from http://www.pmi.org/~/media/PDF/Knowledge%20 Center/Change_Mgmt_whitepaper_v4.ashx

Project Management Institute (PMI). (2013). *Managing change in organizations: A practice guide.* Newtown Square, PA: Author.

Project Management Institute (PMI). (2014, March). *Pulse of the profession® in-depth report: Enabling organizational change through strategic initiatives.* Newtown Square, PA: Author.

Standish Group International. (2013). *Chaos manifesto 2013: Think big, act small.* Boston, MA: Author.

Review Questions

1. What process was used by the project manager to lead the change?
2. What aspects need to be considered before making a decision to change?
3. What did the project sponsor do during the project?
4. Who is the right sponsor for a change management project?
5. Which tools were used by the project manager to manage the change?

Appendix: Case Study

Keeping a company—in this case, a banking company—among the leaders in the market depends on the capacity to change behaviors, skills, structures, and processes. It becomes important for people to exchange information regarding the process of change and have that information accepted as valid.

This study describes a process of leading change that was necessary in Caja Granada, a Spanish banking company, in order to reduce resistance to change and to take advantage of existing favorable conditions. Every change is traumatic by itself; this project required effort from everybody in the organization. Some individuals responded well; many others resisted efforts to change their behavior.

Hewlett-Packard Consulting in Madrid, Spain was chosen as the main contractor. As the project manager, I (Bucero) took on the task with the team to make things happen through project management skills and processes. The entire organization needed to change to accomplish the project objectives. Success was possible because of the willingness to learn, ability to motivate the project team, and never giving up in the face of extremely difficult situations.

Project Background and Customer Objectives

The customer is a leading banking company in the south of Spain, and had traditionally been a very large user of UNISYS systems and solutions over a ten-year period, experiencing stability and good business results throughout that period. Systems and methods that remained static for many years and did not allow for rapid and substantial change came under tremendous competitive pressure.

The customer had a very clear idea that users were happy operating with the old system. But a change was needed as quickly as possible in order to survive among banking competition. The proximity of Y2K forced all financial entities to be prepared, meaning update or create processes, train people, and upgrade or change technology. The project started in September 1999.

Red Castle was an information systems strategic project. It consisted of functional and technological innovations that answered market and environment needs, implementing a hardware and software platform, developing a customized software package, and managing the change.

Looking at all the changes required, my challenge became to start work with a new customer and understand all project stakeholders and their behaviors.

The client's business objectives were:

- Performance improvement: Some processes caused hours of delay while offices demanded more transactions.
- Growth: They needed to increase the number of branches in their organization without any loss of performance.
- New technologies: They needed more value-added, competitive offerings; changing their platform and software was a must.

Challenges

One of the most complicated tasks was to convince upper managers of the bank about the necessity of project planning. At the beginning, the customer was very involved. After the first month, the customer asked for tangible results. I explained that planning is absolutely necessary for project success. I borrowed equipment and dedicated one team member to the startup of one machine in order to demonstrate to the customer how HP was able to operate in this platform. That diminished customer pressure for a while.

Managing challenges throughout the project was a part of managing the change and is a project manager's responsibility. Clear communication and intimacy with bank managers were critical success factors. I tested that the Red Castle project was clearly linked to the bank strategy—that link proved very helpful for us throughout the project. At my prodding, upper management assigned the highest priority to this project.

The Process

Hewlett-Packard's corporate Project Management Initiative (a form of project office) had summarized a process for *leading change*. I applied the process in order to get support and minimize impacts to the customer organization.

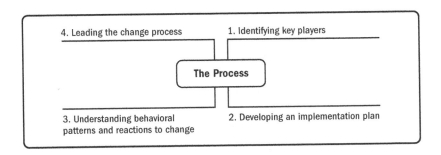

Project Key Players

It took more than two months to analyze all critical players in the customer organization. Starting the first month, I organized period meeting sessions in order to get people involved and informed about project status. One of my daily tasks was to be available for everybody in order to facilitate information flow and communication among team members.

One critical success factor was getting sponsors on board who had authority to commit resources and would support the project manager. The customer considered this project strategic and totally linked with business objectives. The model establishes four categories of key players: **advocates, sponsors, agents,** and **targets**. I was the **agent** of the change. Honestly, at the beginning I felt like an **advocate**. I had to be proactive, self-confident, and had to get customer confidence to create an open line of communication.

Implementation Plan Development

The first thing we did was identify events that would guarantee the change and help everyone understand the value of the change. We involved all team leaders early in the planning phase, discussing different options to be implemented. This was not difficult because every team leader was responsible for a different functional area and knew the old system very well.

We analyzed the gap between the old system and applications and the new one. Also, the plan needed to take changes into account about processes, systems, people, and the organization. Then, we developed a plan for implementing the change, taking into account the possible impacts and contingencies in terms of processes, people, and technology.

We needed to ask for support from the bank's upper management in order to facilitate the change. I persuaded them by sharing facts and rationale to help them conclude that the plan to change was effective. When the plan was finished, we asked for approval for the implementation plan from the sponsor and I got consensus from the steering committee and from the other stakeholders in the organization.

Understand Behavioral Patterns and Reactions to Change

As usual in this type of project, we detected inhibitors to the change throughout the project life cycle. I needed to have personal meetings with all branch directors to clarify project goals and objectives and convince them about the major benefits of the project for them and for their business.

The bank imposed the change, but we explained, group by group, all the reasons and justifications for that change. The result was that resistance diminished because we established good mechanisms for communications.

The customer situation was stable in terms of processes, people, and technology, but the upper managers of the bank knew how to motivate and compensate people in order to ask for extra effort. They knew they could not ask for extra effort without compensation. Then they defined metrics and personal objectives for every team leader in the project.

In the beginning, a major lack of involvement was from end users at the branches because they were not involved in the initial study.

One success factor in this process was to recognize different behavioral patterns and to allow enough time to work with everybody in the organization.

Lead the Change Process

Lead – We defined eight functional groups defining different goals for individuals. We empowered those team leaders to participate in most decisions. I needed upper management and customer support for getting these things done most times, but I could influence without a lot of power.

Test – We invited people to express their reactions to the changes. This feedback was very valuable in order to learn from the errors and make improvements.

Recognition – We established metrics that allowed room for improvement and recognized the efforts and achievement of the team and team leaders.

Follow – Every project is alive and needs to be monitored. In this case, the follow up consisted of weekly brief reviews with team leaders, analyzing the results, and learning from our experiences.

The Team

The team consisted of functional team leaders who owned the whole project life cycle for every functional area in the bank. Every functional leader was responsible for talking and meeting with end users, leading their software development team, and managing all tests. HP consultants trained these leaders to be prepared for managing and motivating their teams, and the leaders were supported by an HP project manager.

Steering committee members also participated—not only in sponsorship tasks, but in all communication and dissemination tasks that contributed to project success. They talked to and supported people, boosting morale and recognizing their efforts in public ways.

Tools Used

- Teamwork exercises, using real meetings to put ideas into practice
- Roles and responsibilities definitions that were then published in planning documents
- Change agent training
- Daily communication among team members
- Asking for feedback from every team leader
- Communication and respect among team members

Frequently projects fail, not for technical reasons, but because people in the organization refuse the change. The critical success factor for implementing systems is the way in which human and organizational factors are planned; technology is a second priority. This message was not understood by the whole management team at the beginning. It took six months of work to convince everybody.

Results

From the customer's perspective, we can measure results according to a number of parameters, but when we talk about the management of change, we talk about processes, people, and technology that are the enablers of a change.

Processes

Processes need to be defined, modified, and used by people. It was one of the most difficult parts of this project, but people involved in that area are proud because they had the opportunity to contribute to project success and then be members of a successful bank. By reviewing old processes, they defined new ones that enabled them to introduce new products to the market. Process ownership was key.

People

Another key result is the use of the system by end users. Step by step, each user adapted their behavior to the new system functionality and to the new processes. Any system is tested, measured, and evaluated by the end users. In this particular case, the level of involvement by end users grew in a positive way over a period of months.

Technology

All software modules in the new application are working, and the customer has a "foundation platform" for building future information systems for the new century. Technical results are improved over the old system. Performance is much better, and the system places the customer in a technologically competent position within the financial market.

Learning Perspective

Key factors for project success:

- Upper management sponsorship from the customer is mandatory.
- Linking the project to the bank's strategy was fundamental.
- Quality management was helpful.
- Communications planning and deployment was difficult, but was key for the change agent.
- Encouragement of the end user is mandatory.

I found that I had to work with everybody on the team with different degrees of involvement. The percentage of time spent working with everyone can be classified by project phase:

Initiation and Planning Phase

- 100% scope validation and planning (time spent with the customer's project manager, team leaders, and other stakeholders)

Execution and Controlling Phase

- 75% of my time spent in "communications management" (with the whole team)

- 40% of my time (weekly) spent in project meetings (team leaders, management, steering committee)
- The rest of my time involved planning, monitoring, and controlling

To create success in big organizations and complicated projects like Caja Granada, even with excellent leadership skills, all changes require initiative from many people. This requires time, patience, persistence, and, especially, upper management support. An explicit change management process is an indispensable tool in the project manager's tool kit.

CHAPTER 14

The Future and Organizational Change Management

By Emad E. Aziz, PRINCE2P, CSSGB, PMP, PgMP, PfMP and Wanda Curlee, PhD, PMI-RMP, PMP, PgMP, PfMP

Overview

Organizational change is required anytime changes are done to an organization's strategy, and occurs when a portfolio and its component programs and projects is/are implemented. Aspects pertaining to organizational change have been recently documented by the Project Management Institute (PMI). In 2013, PMI published *Managing Change in Organizations: A Practice Guide* (2013a). This practice guide helped define the areas associated with actual change in organizations and provided a framework for the implementation, deployment, and sustainment of portfolios, programs, and projects.

There have been numerous articles that discuss innovation and its importance to change. Whether the innovations are for megaprojects/programs (Biesek & Gil, 2014; Davies, MacAulay, DeBarro, & Thurston, 2015; Flyvbjerg, 2014) or innovations within a company or organization (Thomas, George, & Cicmil, 2013), each innovation will drive change. Each of the authors referenced in this paragraph would imply that innovation is change, and without a concerted effort to allow innovation or change to be deliberately introduced into organizations and megaprojects, projects and organizations will stagnate. Such stagnation may result from:

- Relying on historic success;
- Disregard of current and near-future changes in the market; and
- Disregard of technological advances.

Many household brands that were popular through the 1980s, 1990s, and even more recently have ceased to exist as a result of one or more of the above reasons. Examples include Polaroid, Kodak, and Nokia. Other companies significantly lost their market share and customer loyalty, such as Cadillac.

Organizational change for some companies is an afterthought. Astute executives as well as project management practitioners understand that effort is needed to help those who are affected by change. Changes may be small and affect only a few people, while other changes may affect everyone in the company. The approach used needs to be appropriate to the need.

With any organizational change, planning needs to occur as it does for all other parts of the portfolio, program, or project. The effort may be limited to training, or could involve layoffs, skill reassessments, or a complete reorganization of a business unit or company, including restructuring of its business processes, practices, and even reconsideration of its values. Each type of change is very important to the success of the organization and is brought about effectively through the use of portfolio, program, and project management. In turn, program management should be the focal point for the success of every type of change. Some organizations have gone as far as naming their enterprise portfolio management office (EPMO) the "Organizational Transformation Department," a trend that has been seen in global, multinational companies with high levels of maturity since the turn of the century.

The project management discipline is essential for successful organizational change. The change may be the result of a strategic goal that drives the portfolio and programs. The projects implemented would support the strategic initiatives of the portfolios and programs. The projects implement the tactical requirements of the change. These changes will drive the benefit realization and the road maps at the program and portfolio levels (PMI, 2013a, 2013b).

Organizational change may also be driven by a tactical or legal requirement. Projects drive organizational change because of a new software initiative, a new workflow, an updated process/procedure, or many other tactical requirements. When a company uses a specific software or operating system and the software company has a major update, there is a ripple effect to its customers. First, the customers need to decide whether to update. Second, when an update is implemented, an organizational change may occur. The change may be limited to a single organization or may affect the entire enterprise. The change may drive workflows and/or a need for training. Decisions will be made based on the maturity of the organization.

The organizational change drives how and with whom the project professional will plan and implement the change. Project professionals' own biases may also influence the management of change. Project professionals who are averse to change may be reluctant to plan, discuss, or even implement change. They may need to oversee the implementation, but have the fortitude to delegate the responsibility. Delegation in any scenario is scary because what the project professional has done successfully on his or her own is now the responsibility of someone else, even though the project professional is responsible (PMI, 2013a).

Delegation is beyond the scope of this chapter; however, delegation is a viable means for achieving organizational change. The Project Management Institute (PMI), other project organizations, and standards organizations, such as ISO, will continue to develop articles, standards, practice guides, blogs, and news articles that provide updates on organizational change. Organizational change management will mature through those who practice the various aspects of project management.

PMI (2013a) advocates three levels of change. The first level of change is described as nonthreatening to those who are affected by the change. Technology will drive dashboards to be seen at any time with the latest data on smartphones. Executives expect this change. Those involved in project management will need to understand the data presented and understand how those data may best be presented to leadership.

The second order of change may have a greater impact on employees. These changes are irreversible, as they are driven by the organization or the enterprise. In most situations, these changes are driven by strategic directives. Market forces, changes in regulatory requirements, competition, politico-economic factors, and the quest for cost efficiency will drive changes at this level as well, whether companies want them or not.

The third order is when the organization wants to change a fundamental aspect of the organization. Environmental forces will fundamentally change almost every industry. Project management will be changed significantly. Project managers will be working from their smartphones, laptops will be a thing of the past, dashboards for leadership will be on smartphones, and decision making will almost be instantaneous. Companies requiring employees to report to the office may have to rethink this requirement. Taken a step further, one might wonder if there will even be a need to have full-time employees. One may argue that in the near future project progress will be reported by machines, and so will estimates be derived: For example, the amount of work performed by an excavator to dig a ditch, the number of man-hours contributed by the driver, and the consumption of fuel, may be reported directly from the excavator in the near future, should creators of project management information systems allow such integration. Will there be a shift to a company that hires artisans who bring their own toolkits to provide the required service? Companies are already demonstrating a shift with contractors, as is the overall economy, which has come to be known as the Gig Economy, providing anyone with an internet connection with access to a vast array of qualified individuals at highly competitive costs who can be hired almost instantaneously to perform specific tasks for which they are licensed/

Table 14-1. The three levels of change.

Category of Change	Area of Application	Difficulty	Length of Initiative	Reversibility
First-order change	Procedures: Modifications in how work is done	Minor	Short	Easily reversed
Second-order change	Policies: Doing something significantly different	Moderate	Medium	Irreversible
Third-order change	Values: Rethinking the governing values	High	Long	Irreversible

certified at preannounced rates, without the need for a lengthy tendering process and the engagement of general contractors who, in turn, will hire the same tradesmen. Table 14-1 differentiates among the three levels of change.

Examples of Organizational Change and Its Drivers

There are many things that drive organizational change: a change in leadership, a change in strategic direction, a change in a new product or processes introduced, or a change in market forces and dynamics. However, one of the most tumultuous organizational changes in the 20th century was technology. Computer technology transitioned from mainframe to desktops and an entirely different way of crunching data or producing reports. Organizational change may be a factor of Moore's law, which states that technology hardware changes approximately every 18 months. Further, silicon chips double their capacity within the same time frame. With that change came more computing power. Whether change comes from technology or a new business initiative, it affects people. People are unpredictable, and that is why change is so difficult.

Companies and individuals continue to deal with many different versions of technology and operating systems that change almost yearly, and IT departments do not have the funds needed to keep up with the changes. The companies have to decide whether to keep a myriad of different technologies and create a spider web that can not be efficiently tested. These companies' IT departments hope that when a change is made, a catastrophe will not happen. With these technology spider webs, it is impossible to replicate or bring down the system to see if the change is working prior to going live.

There are companies that want to be on the cutting edge of technology and adopt new versions of an operating system or an application as soon as possible. These companies are in a steady state of flux because of the speed with which software is updated. However, software is not the only organizational change companies are facing.

Drones are vastly changing the expedited delivery of parts; for example, oil and gas parts for oil rigs or automotive industry parts from suppliers that are normally within a five-mile radius of the plant. Drones will reduce expenses and safety issues for oil rigs. Deliveries to an oil rig is currently done via helicopter or boat, both of which have inherent dangers for human life. Drones will reduce the need for spare parts being delivered by these two modes. Drones can be constructed in various sizes to deliver the largest spare part needed. Drones could even reduce the need for a supplier to be in near proximity to the plant.

Drones are changing organizations. Depending upon where a delivery is located, the item being delivered may never be touched by human hands until receipt. This may radically decrease the need for delivery trucks and drivers, will reduce the carbon footprint, and may ultimately increase satisfaction. Will delivery drivers now be trained as drone drivers? Will the behavior of the customers change?

3-D printers are also changing the landscape of retail and overnight delivery service. Instead of storing spare parts or pallets of goods to stock shelves, industrialized 3-D printers will be able to print the spare part or reproduce the item desired by a customer. Will retail in the future be a storefront with a vast amount of industrialized 3-D printers and customers queued at a kiosk to select what is wanted, similar to a self-checkout in stores today? The customer would be able to pay for the goods printed and pick them up in a matter of minutes. Is this retail's next radical shift? 3-D printers will also change the inherent mechanism of building cars. Will cars eventually be created using a 3-D printer?

All of the above are examples of questions strategists are trying to answer in organizations that want to remain viable in the future. Every positive answer to any of the above questions will inevitably result in the need for one or more change initiatives in any organization.

There are companies that charge ahead with change, and there are other companies that wait until the technology is proven or until the software company no longer provides version support. These companies do not change as often; however, when a new operating system or new application is adopted, the change can be traumatic for them. The company's employees have not been exposed to the incremental changes that others have been exposed to. Because of this, changes that were made slowly through version changes are now presented to the employee in one version. Most importantly, there are companies that deny or disregard the changes occurring around them and do not embrace such changes (or resist them altogether), and these companies are faced with the consequences of becoming irrelevant or obsolete.

The generation entering the workforce today has grown up with smartphones and new ways of dealing with technology. This generation enjoys the convenience of technology and wants technology to make their life and work easier. This means driving usage away from modern conventional methods and tools and doing work on hand held devices instead.

Given the rising awareness and evident impact of global warming and the damage the environment has sustained as a result of the Industrial Revolution, entire industries are now embracing change. Some—like the utilities industry—are turning to solutions that are less harmful for the environment. For instance, companies that generate electricity are turning to hydropower, wind power, and solar power. Could you imagine what the fate would be of companies that continue to generate power through burning fossil fuels in 10 years' time? A similar awareness has trickled into other industries as well. Hybrid vehicles form the vast majority of vehicles on the streets of New York today. Large automakers are finding ways of generating the same output (if not more) through smaller engines equipped with advanced turbo systems that use air to supplement gasoline. Equally, the construction industry is using lighter, more environmentally friendly materials.

The financial industry is one that has also seen drastic changes over the past years. In London, New York, and other cities, you can visit restaurants, museums, and other attractions in what once were banking halls. Technology is being harnessed by players in the financial industry to facilitate services to the extent that the concept of a physical banking branch is becoming obsolete in many areas. Today, there are some financial institutions—insurance companies, for example—that are based entirely online. In recent years, there has been a surge in the adoption of technology in the financial industry, the automotive industry, retail, and many others.

But technology is not the only way the financial industry is changing. Banking products, for example, used to focus on individuals with a certain income or net worth. More recently, banks and lenders have diverted their focus to individuals they would have not entertained 10, 15, or 20 years ago: Small-net-worth, low-income individuals, and small and medium businesses are now receiving micro loans and financing. On the other side of the spectrum, banks and financial solutions are also innovating to serve what have now emerged as ultra-high-net-worth individuals. Both customer groups are new to the industry, each has their unique set of requirements, and the most successful financial institution is the one that will be able to deliver products and services to those customer groups in the fastest, most efficient way, while catering to all the requirements of those groups. This can only be achieved through robust portfolio, program, and project management.

How Successful Organizations Implement Change

As is evident from the previous examples, the world around us is changing, and so are the organizations that deliver products and services. In today's world, the abundance of information, communication, and alternatives for every single product obligates organizations to change their strategy-formulation techniques. PMI's (2013a) *Managing Change in Organizations: A Practice Guide* states that strategic planning "can no longer be an annual, top-down process, [and that] organizations need to embrace and adopt change in their strategy to compete and to ensure long-term success" (p. 9). It further specifies, "Organizations need to react to change internally with the same intensity as they react to changes in their external environments" (p. 9). This presents organizations with significant levels of complexity.

In the past, organizations conducted their strategic planning once and then strove to deliver the constituents of that plan for the rest of the year while maintaining a focus on business as usual. The new (or current) approach to strategic planning requires organizations to be more flexible and agile in their formulation and delivery of strategy (see Figure 14-1). Influencers from outside or inside the organization may emerge at any time, requiring an attentive response and immediate action. The challenges associated with strategy formulation are not part of the scope of this chapter, but the challenges associated with the responsiveness to such changes and the ability to create, terminate, suspend, or change projects and programs are. We advocate that these are best addressed through a centralized, accountable, and authorized portfolio, program, and project management office (PMO).

Project managers drive the tactical aspects of organizational changes. However, program and portfolio managers drive the strategic changes. Should companies decide not to implement new strategies in years to come, their leadership may find that either the company is no longer a leader or that a former follower is now a leader. Companies that are powerful today may end up in bankruptcy, while small innovative companies may flourish.

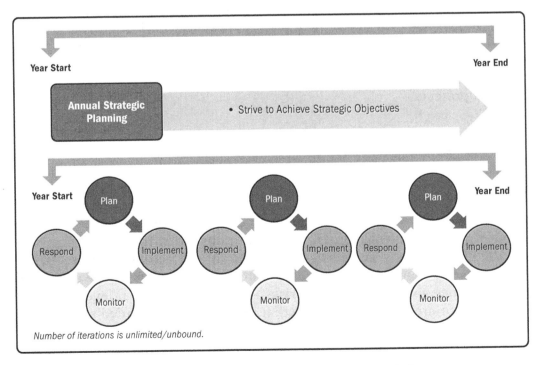

Figure 14-1.   Example of conventional versus modern strategy formulation.

Organizational Change and Portfolio Management

PMI (2013a) considers portfolio management the highest level of strategic management within the project management discipline. The portfolio manager should drive the executive suite's strategic view. The C-suite and the portfolio manager work together on strategy.

When the C-suite determines the strategic direction, the C-suite leadership then focuses on other issues. The portfolio manager is now responsible for implementing the organization's direction and ensuring that business units and middle management stay focused. All parties involved in the strategic direction have good intentions. However, strategic change is difficult. Without careful monitoring, people naturally revert to what is comfortable.

The portfolio manager does the implementation for the C-suite. The establishment, monitoring, and health of the portfolio is the responsibility of the portfolio manager. The portfolio manager reports back regularly to the C-suite regarding the health, benefits, and recommended changes. Organizational change needs to be within the scope of the portfolio manager. These organizational changes drive benefits. Organizational changes should be part of the road map to drive the portfolio and keep the organization focused.

In his paper, "The Case for the Chief Project Officer," Andy Jordan (2014) identifies the portfolio manager as "an executive responsible for project execution," which is a key part of the role in any organization, as well as participation in strategy formulation, implementation of organizational change, and responsibility to ensure that organizations attain and sustain the maturity levels that best serve their needs. Ed Kozak (2012), author of "The Chief Project Officer and How One Can Benefit your Organization," defines the portfolio manager as "a single individual at the senior management level who is responsible for providing governance over the organization's internal projects."

Why Do Organizations Need Portfolio Management to Oversee and Implement Change?

Governance

Governance can mean different things to different people. Despite the hype about it in government, corporations, and nonprofits, there is no one, single definition that is universally agreed upon and accepted. However, research reveals that two of the most common components of the definition of governance are "assurance that risks at the organizational level are managed appropriately" and "assurance that resources are expended and utilized responsibly" (Crawford, 2012).

Crawford (2012) demonstrates the link between having a portfolio manager and good governance in organizations. The McKinsey's Investors Opinion

Survey of June 2000 revealed, "Organizations that have good governance practices in place are able to realize a premium of more than 20 percent from their investors" (Crawford, 2012). Furthermore, Crawford (2012) argues, "To have effective governance in the enterprise, the lower layers need to apply the same principles as executive management—setting objectives, providing and getting direction, and providing and evaluating performance measures."

To achieve such synergies in an organization, it is important to differentiate between two verticals: (1) the organizational breakdown structure reporting to the chief operating officer (COO), whereby the COO is responsible for cascading governance into daily recurrent operations of the organization; and (2) the project management vertical. In many organizations, project management either occurs on an ad hoc basis or is the role of the PMO, with the PMO situated below the executive level. In these situations, the head of the PMO has little or no authority in enforcing organizational governance on the projects and programs run by the PMO in view of the matrix setup in which they are run and the shared authority with the line/functional heads that have different—if not conflicting—priorities. Despite such situations, the head of the PMO is still accountable for governance, and that leads to a situation of complete dependence on that individual's personal skills and influence. By having a portfolio manager at the executive level of the organization, not only is the importance of portfolio, program, and project management (PPPM) highlighted and clearly emphasized, but also the appropriate levels of authority and control are afforded to implement organizational governance.

Strategic Alignment

Kozak (2012) states that it is the portfolio manager's responsibility to "link all projects to strategic and operational business plans; make sure that every project supports the right business goals; require that every project have an effective manager or leader in charge; implement and maintain an appropriate PM methodology; rigorously and formally manage changes to project scope, budget, schedule, and requirements; group similar projects to them in a similar manner; and implement, lead, and coordinate project portfolio management."

One of the vehicles—for lack of a better term—that help organizations with the alignment of programs and projects guarantees consistency in their practices and helps maintain visibility, governance, and efficiencies is a PPPM methodology. Typically, such a methodology is developed, applied, governed, and continuously improved by the PMO (portfolio/program/project management office). The extent and magnitude to which such methodology is developed and applied is correlated to the type of PMO within the organization. As Aziz (2014) explains, a PMO would need to be a Tier-4 PMO—one that has control over portfolios with down-reach to the project level and is headed and directed at the executive level by a chief project officer—in order to effectively perform this role, having enough power and influence throughout the organization both vertically and horizontally.

The PMO and the Portfolio Manager Are Not Mutually Exclusive

But both Jordan (2014) and Kozak (2012) have adverse views on the PMO, its role in the organization, and its value. Research, however, has proven that the ideal situation would be to have a T-4 PMO headed by a portfolio manager. Jordan, Kozak, and a number of other authors tend to present a mutually exclusive proposition—that an organization should have either a portfolio manager or a PMO. As Jordan (2014) states:

> Ask a CEO today what benefits their PMO is delivering, and they'll struggle to answer; ask them who is ensuring that the portfolio delivers on its objectives, and they may well list everyone that they know of who is working on projects. Neither answer should be acceptable; there should be a clearly identified individual who is accountable for the portfolio and a single person who is ensuring that the PMO is delivering a return on the investment.

Kozak (2012) argues, "Many [organizations] have tried to achieve this governance by creating a project management office, or PMO, at their sites. Unfortunately for many organizations, this costly endeavor has not been successful, providing limited, or no, value." He further justifies this phenomenon by claiming, "A PMO is not for every organization." It is a fact that many organizations have tried to achieve governance through creating a PMO, but I disagree with Kozak that a PMO is not for every organization. In fact, research conducted by my own organization has revealed that the value delivered by the PMO in any organization is strongly correlated with the amount of authority and empowerment vested in it by the organization. If a PMO is tasked with the development of a methodology, but is incapable of ensuring the adoption of such methodology throughout the organization, little value can be expected from that PMO. Therefore, a PMO headed by an executive (i.e., the portfolio manager) would deliver value to the organization and achieve governance.

Arguments against a PMO that is not headed by a portfolio manager are plentiful, and all arguments are viable. A PMO is a costly endeavor that is expected to perform the work of an "engine" that delivers projects and changes the organization by implementing the strategy. What Jordan (2014) and Kozak (2012) did not consider in their work was whether or not such PMOs are endowed with adequate authority. If the PMO did not have enough authority, it would not be able to fulfill its responsibilities to the organization, and would not have enough influence over the matrix structures with which it operates. On the other hand, replacing the PMO with a portfolio manager can be equally damaging to the organization. A portfolio manager without the appropriate organizational structure for support would (1) be incapacitated to perform all the necessary duties; (2) leave the organizational vulnerable to the limitations of the capacity, knowledge, and skills of the person occupying the position of portfolio manager at any given time; and (3) leave the organization vulnerable to the availability of that person. Consider the consequences to the organization should that individual leave his or her job for any reason.

However, empowered with the right PMO, the portfolio manager would be the executive responsible for the development, adoption, deployment, and constant improvement of PPPM methodology as well as its penetration "into areas that have not historically been exposed to structured project and/or PMO structures, which will in turn help to further improve the overall quality of project execution" (Jordan, 2014). Furthermore, Jordan (2014) argues that the portfolio manager will receive enough empowerment and authority, as a result of his or her formal position, to instigate the practices of PPPM that fragmented PMOs otherwise would not, giving the example of "benefits realization." "From a portfolio management perspective, the benefits that a project is expected to deliver are much more important than the specific deliverables that are outputs of a project. This is because the goals and objectives of the organization are based on those business benefits, not on scope items" (Jordan, 2014). The specific scope items or deliverables of a project would be the focus of a departmental PMO, one that is focused on delivery of projects for a certain department—hence, increasing the probability that projects deliver their scope while that scope goes astray from the desired business benefit. In the context I propose, the specific deliverables of every project (the scope) would always be the focus of the PMO, and so would the benefits anticipated from the portfolio, creating a de facto mission of the PMO to align the two together, all in the best interest of the organization.

It can be derived that the portfolio manager is, in effect, an executive-level owner of project execution who provides clear accountability for project success as well as clear accountability that the organization will conduct the right projects to achieve strategic outcomes, aided and supported by a viable and capable PMO.

Organizational Maturity

Another element of the role of the portfolio manager is to act as "the sponsor of project management." Our research has revealed that in various large organizations, fragmented PMOs lead to fragmented practices and methodologies, and consequently, conflict among them. Each PMO or departmental project team should typically adopt the program and/or project management practices that best suits it, creating an unintentional "comfort zone," and leaving out tools and techniques or methods that the PMO or project team finds challenging or unfamiliar, despite their vitality to the success of programs and projects and their alignment to strategy. Such disparity in practices across the organization consequentially leads to the rise of conflict among different PMOs, each claiming that "it knows better" or is the one whose methodologies and practices should prevail. Such conflict eventually leads to a decline in the level of maturity with which the organization manages its programs and projects. The portfolio manager, in a formal capacity, would avoid such adversity for the organization, acting as the "sponsor" for all program and project management practices and ensuring that the organization adopts only a unified methodology, tools and techniques, governance, and processes that best fit its strategic objectives, while continuously overseeing their improvement and customization to serve the implementation of that strategy.

Why Can't Another CxO Perform This Role?

Research has also revealed that many organizations make the fundamental mistake of assigning the role of the PMO to another executive, most commonly either the chief information officer (CIO), chief financial officer (CFO), or the chief operating officer (COO). The reasons why this mistake can have detrimental consequences to the organization are obvious.

Conflicting Priorities

Regardless of his or her original role, the CxO, who has been tasked with overseeing the PMO and the practice of project management within the organization, would always have conflicting priorities. For instance, the CFO prioritizes the bottom line and treasury, the CIO prioritizes IT strategy, and the COO prioritizes the day-to-day recurrent business over implementation of strategic change and projects that lead to it. The conflicting priorities are not only for focus, time, and dedication, but also for resources and decisions.

If the CxO needs to choose what to allocate more time to, he or she would obviously opt for his or her "native" function, because this is what his or her appraisal and performance measurement are based on, and is more definitive of the CxO's career objectives. The same applies to resources. Would it be more viable to maintain the current operation or IT infrastructure or reallocate scarce resources to new projects? It doesn't really matter how strategic they are.

The presence of a COO in any organization tips the scales in favor of operational efficiency as opposed to strategic change. Marshall (n.d.) says, "A portfolio manager will provide a good balance to the COO." The ultimate conflict between the CxO and his or her acting role as portfolio manager happens in decision making. Any CxO, by virtue of the position, is expected to make decisions at the executive level. Those decisions can often conflict with strategic change. For example, if a CIO expended time on building and implementing specific enterprise resource planning (ERP) systems and the company strategy requires more agile and dynamic solutions based on software as a service (SaaS) platforms, the CIO may influence the decision-making process against the latter, undermining the strategic direction. Such influence or decisions may or may not be intentional.

Lack of Know-How

Another reason why another executive within the organization cannot perform the role of CxO is the need for a person to possess specific knowledge and skills related to the role of the CxO. Such knowledge is demonstrated in the growing number of standards, practice guides, and white papers published by organizations such as PMI. These include, but are not limited to, *The Standard for Portfolio Management*, *The Standard for Program Management*, *A Guide to the Project Management Body of Knowledge (PMBOK® Guide)*, *Managing Change in Organizations: A Practice Guide*, *Navigating Complexity: A Practice Guide*, and many more. Because the body of knowledge is constantly evolving, in order for portfolio managers to be successful, they would need to (1) acquire respective certifications and (2) keep themselves abreast and updated with all such knowledge. Neither can be considered an easy or brisk task, and it would be daunting to other CxOs who need to enrich themselves with the knowledge and best practices in their organizations. Therefore, the CxO acting on behalf of the portfolio manager will never provide the organization with sufficient know-how.

Lack of Experience

The lack of experience is very similar to the lack of know-how. A CxO who has not been managing multiple projects and programs would find it difficult to understand the special circumstances related to the planning, monitoring and controlling, and executing of such projects and programs. The portfolio manager needs to have a clear vision of what it takes to manage and successfully deliver programs and projects—the body of knowledge for such undertakings being dense and diverse, as well as fundamentally different from ongoing operations or discipline-specific tasks that other functional heads are tasked with in their native roles. The portfolio manager would need to have extensive practical experience with tools and techniques, methods, and implementation of matters specific to this practice, including, but not limited, to planning, execution, change control, benefits realization, benefits tracking, and so forth. Therefore, should a CxO be tasked with performing the role of the portfolio manager that CxO would struggle to speak the same language as those managing the projects and programs and to understand and cater to their specific needs and requirements. Ultimately, this would shift the balance of the matrix organization toward the functional heads, which very well may not be in the best interest of delivering strategy.

Multimodality

Strategy in any organization rarely involves one specific discipline; therefore, the programs and projects that are necessary to deliver strategic outcomes are multidisciplinary. Let's consider the example of an oil and gas company that decides to revamp its downstream operations by refurbishing and enhancing its gas stations; giving customers a better, more pleasant experience; and attracting more customers to stations, thus increasing revenue. Such a program would be split into multiple projects, all of which contain IT, construction, marketing, customer service, civil, electromechanical, business process reengineering, and human resources work streams. Should the leader of that program or the portfolio manager come from one specific background—for instance, civil engineering—the likelihood of the successful realization of strategic benefits diminishes, because that person would primarily focus on delivering an outstanding product based on civil engineering, giving less emphasis to the other work streams and providing little to no alignment with the strategic purpose of the program.

One very important argument that Jordan (2014) makes is that by embedding portfolio management into a departmental PMO,

> At best, the PMO (and by extension, PPM) is a subset of the accountabilities of a CIO or COO—and the focus and objectives of those functions reflects that. Sooner or later (probably sooner), that is going to send the message that portfolio management is not a top organizational priority—which will in turn result in a loss of focus and a degradation of performance. To address that, there needs to be a meaningful strategic accountability.

Thus, the person best suited to undertake the role of portfolio manager is someone who has extensive experience in managing projects, programs, and portfolios and is not tied to any one discipline or industry—someone who understands strategic vision, is capable of accessing the expertise necessary to do the work, and is primarily focused on delivery of strategy.

Why Do Organizations Need a Portfolio Manager to Implement Change?

According to Jordan (2014), by having a portfolio manager in an organization,

> From a perception standpoint, project execution and project management will be elevated to a level of importance where they can no longer be viewed as 'optional' by areas of the business that have historically created their own approach to getting work done. This will make it easier to manage those initiatives, will reduce the organization's risk exposure, and drive lower costs, better results, and a more engaged employee base.

Paul Marshall (n.d.) claims that a portfolio manager role "will help demonstrate just how important projects are in the continual development and maturity of an organization. Effective project delivery will be viewed as a 'must-do' rather than resourcing projects with existing staff using a 'best-endeavors' approach. The future of an organization might be dependent on benefits being realized through the delivery of a successful project." He continues to explain the vitality of the portfolio manager role in resourcing projects adequately. He says, "Historically, there has been a tendency for the functional areas to put their departmental needs and priorities above the needs of projects, even if those projects are aligned to strategic objectives of the organization." By having a portfolio manager, such imbalance would be avoided in the best interest of program and project delivery.

Jordan (2014) states, "An executive project execution function would also assume responsibility for any PMOs that exist within the organization, and can begin to drive an EPMO whose mandate aligns with portfolio management." Although this is true, we strongly advise against an organizational structure where multiple PMOs exist, because this may lead to continued disparity in program and project management practices, as well as possible rivalry and conflict, ultimately resulting in misalignment of projects and programs to organizational strategy. The centralized PMO, reporting to the portfolio manager directly and utilizing resources across the organization by means of a strong matrix organization, is what we advocate. This would create accountability and ownership of successful strategic execution across the organization as well as vertically, from the strategic level down to the lowest project scope element. Jordan (2014) supports this by saying, "It may be easier because departmental politics from member PMOs are removed."

Another argument that Jordan (2014) makes is that organizations often embed the portfolio management function into the PMO, and such an undertaking can be beneficial for the purpose of strategic alignment and implementation. In that instance, the head of the PMO would evolve into the portfolio manager role. However, Jordan makes a very important observation: that many PMOs are incapable of delivering strategies as they are set up departmentally (Jordan mentions the IT PMO as an example). Therefore, they are not empowered at the strategic level as in a Tier-4 PMO (Aziz, 2014). Jordan (2014) argues that creating a portfolio manager role indicates that organizations are committed to aligning their projects and programs to their organizational strategies, as well as delivering them effectively and efficiently.

This idea is further enforced through Kozak's (2012) observation, "Only someone at the senior level has the authority and wherewithal to link projects with strategic goals and to reach horizontally across departments to review expenditures and schedules, to regulate resource utilization, and to cancel projects that no longer are in alignment with strategic objectives."

Organizational Change and Program Management

The program manager overlooks the strategic initiative of a part of the portfolio. In some cases, the program may be stand-alone. The program manager watches the governance, monitors the landscape within the company for competing projects and programs, and keeps project managers focused on the goal. Major organizational changes should be overseen as a program. There are many different parts to an organizational change. To ensure that change meets the leadership's strategy, it needs the expertise of a program manager.

The program manager is responsible for ensuring that the program meets the strategic goals. The strategy may be at the enterprise or organizational level. Major initiatives will result in organizational change. The change may be a complete transition of people skills, processes and procedures, tool sets, and systems. All this may need specialized user acceptance testing, along with training and a restructuring of personnel duties.

Each of the previously mentioned initiatives may be accomplished by consultants with specialized skills who work with the appropriate part of the enterprise. For example, if job skills and duties need to be redone, then the company's human resources department must be involved and the program manager will coordinate necessary resources from the company. The program manager is the one point of contact.

Organizational change management is complex. Many organizations have attempted to implement a radical change via a project, not realizing that there are many interdependencies with other projects; a need to coordinate resources within the company and most likely with outside sources; and, more importantly, a need to understand how to keep the various aspects focused on the final strategic objective.

In fact, when senior leadership buys a company or there is a merger with another company, the people aspect is often an afterthought. This can, and often does, result in a less than adequate partnership between the two organizations. Without proper organizational change, a finger-pointing game may result. Those from the acquired company point to the buying company personnel for any failures (e.g., not making financial progress). Those from the buying company point to the acquired company and state that the new employees just don't know how things are done here. Both sides are right and both are wrong. An astute program manager would have realized that organizational change management was needed. The program manager would have worked with communications, human resources, training, process re-engineering personnel, IT, and others, as needed, to harmonize the two organizations into one. This is hard work.

Conclusion

Organizational change occurs at various levels and is a constant in all companies. To survive, companies have to continuously evolve. This can be the result of an acquisition or merger with another company, implementation of a new system or systems, or changes made to meet the needs of the industry, meet a niche need in an industry, or deal with evolutions within technology.

Drones, 3-D printers, and other factors including, but not limited to, market forces, changes in regulatory requirements, competition, politico-economic factors, and the quest for cost efficiency are driving organizations to change. Portfolio managers drive the strategy of the company or organization by selecting the correct programs and projects to meet the need. Program managers are the instruments that will drive major organizational shifts within a company or organization. This will be done via projects and their interdependencies. Project managers drive the implementation of the need. As stated previously, portfolio managers do the right work and program and project managers do the work right. It's a symbiotic relationship where all aspects must be working correctly in order to be successful.

IT, the energy industries, the financial industry, and automotive industries will all see radical changes in the years to come. These changes will drive organizational change at all levels and within every organization. Skills will have to change, visionaries will have to see the future differently, middle management will have to respond to a different mode of working, and those on the front line will also have to be redirected in their efforts.

What better way to implement the future than through the project management discipline? Through project management, organizational change will still be painful and hard, but will be in good hands during all phases of the implementation.

Organizations are forced not only to change their strategies, but also to implement those changes in an increasingly rapid and cost-effective manner, and in frequent iterations. Therefore, organizational change will become more commonplace, more frequent, and a part of daily life. Instead of only a few individuals within an organization having a direct effect on the implementation of change, tomorrow's organizations will become abundant. Change program managers will help transform such organizations, rendering them agile organizations, because only the most agile of organizations will be able to stay ahead.

References

Aziz, E. (2014a). *The PMO: Your key to strategy execution and results delivery*. Proceedings of the PMI® Global Congress —EMEA 2014, Dubai, UAE.

Aziz. E. (2014b). *The chief project office (CPO) position is vacant*. Proceedings of the PMI® Global Congress—North America 2014, Phoenix, Arizona, USA. Retrieved from https://www.pmi.org/learning/library/importance-role-chief-projects-officer-9308

Biesek, G., & Gil, N. (2014). *Building options at project front-end strategizing: The power of capital design for evolvability*. Newtown Square, PA: Project Management Institute.

Crawford, D. B. (2012). *Governance and the chief project officer.* Glen Mills, PA: PM Solutions. Retrieved from http://www.pmsolutions.com/resources/view/governance-and-the-chief-project-officer/

Davies, A., MacAulay, S., DeBarro, T., & Thurston, M. (2015, December–January). Making innovation happen in a megaproject: London's Crossrail suburban railway system. *Project Management Journal, 45*(6).

Flyvbjerg, B. (2014, April–May). What you should know about megaprojects and why: An overview. *Project Management Journal, 45*(2).

Jordan, A. (2014). The case for the chief project officer. *ProjectManagement.com* Retrieved from https://www.projectmanagement.com/articles/284159/The-Case-for-the-Chief-Project-Officer

Kozak, E. (2012). *The chief project officer and how one can benefit your organization.* LaGrange, IL: Successful Projects for Leaders. Retrieved from http://www.slideshare.net/Edmkozakjr/the-chief-projectofficerand howonecanbenefityourorganization

Project Management Institute (PMI). (2013a). *Managing change in organizations: A practice guide.* Newtown Square, PA: Author.

Project Management Institute (PMI). (2013b). *The standard for program management* – Third edition. Newtown Square, PA: Author.

Thomas, J., George, S., & Cicmil, S. (2013). *Project management implementation as management innovation: A closer look.* Newtown Square, PA: Project Management Institute.

Review Questions

1. Who should normally implement an organizational change? Why?
2. Which PMI publication describes the three levels of organizational change? Provide an example of each and explain why it meets the criteria for that level of organizational change.
3. Describe what the portfolio, program, and project managers do for organizational change management.
4. How will the project management discipline look in the future as it relates to organizational change management?

Answers to Chapter-End Questions

Chapter 2: Complexity and Turbulence as Triggers for Change

1. *How do I recognize complexity?*

   Answer: Complexity is a matter of perspective: What is complex for one person may not be complex for someone else. To better understand what is complex for you, undertake a complexity assessment. There is an assessment in PMI's *Navigating Complexity: A Practice Guide.*

2. *How is complexity different in change projects from other projects?*

   Answer: Many, if not most, change initiatives are reliant upon individuals changing their behavior and ways of doing things. Often, these individuals do not see how these changes will benefit them and generally are negative toward the change.

3. *How will I know if the actions I take are the right ones?*

   Answer: There are no right or wrong answers. Remember that not all complexity can be resolved or even reduced. It is often a case of trial and error, based on your own experience and the experience of others. To understand if the changes have a positive effect, it is recommended that you undertake another complexity assessment, which can be found in PMI's *Navigating Complexity: A Practice Guide.*

4. *How does knowing the causes of complexity help?*

   Answer: It is very hard to know how to address the root causes of any elements of complexity until the causes are recognized, even if they are not fully understood.

5. *What is the difference between stakeholder communication and stakeholder engagement?*

   Answer: All too often, all stakeholders are communicated to in the same way, with the same information. In reality, their needs are likely to be different, and these needs should be recognized, understood, and taken on board. Without engagement, stakeholders will not be on board, and if they are not on board, they are likely to introduce or contribute to complexity.

6. *How does reflective thinking help manage complexity?*

   Answer: Project managers have a natural tendency to look to and plan for the future and the actions and tasks that are next in the project. Reflective thinking is about looking at what has been done and how effective it was. Consider how things could be done better and review what worked and how these lessons may be used for future project tasks.

7. *Why is influencing important?*

   Answer: In many cases, managing internal-change initiatives involves working with stakeholders and getting their buy-in, with little or no power, control, or organizational influence over them. Therefore, the skill of influencing is essential if these stakeholders are to be brought on board.

8. *What else do I need to know or do?*

   Answer: Do not stop. Carry on learning and be vigilant. Even if some complexities are reduced or removed, in many cases new ones will emerge and others may return.

Chapter 3: Organizational Agility: A Catalyst for Organizational Change

1. *What indicates that the economic environment today is more turbulent than it used to be?*

   Answer: Turbulence can be assessed by measuring and comparing today's market with the market in the past. The number or the percentage of products with new features on a given market is a good indicator. The number or the percentage of new firms in the market is also a good indicator. Another indicator is the market-size variation (measured by the amount of sales) between two periods.

2. *Why is organizational agility a good strategy in a turbulent economic environment?*

Answer: The challenge of turbulent economic environments is that nobody knows for sure what the market demand will look like in the future. Companies need to be agile to adapt to possible changes. Other strategies rely on anticipation of the future: They assume that the future will remain unchanged.

3. *What is the risk for an organization to avoid change in the long term?*

   Answer: Avoiding change includes offering the same products and services to consumers and forgetting about innovation. This is typically what Michael E. Porter calls *cost leadership strategy*—it works only for large companies that benefit from large production volumes and large market shares when customer demand is stable. It no longer works when customer demand changes. For example, one can provide electricity at low cost on a long period from a nuclear power station. There will be no change for 30 or 40 years. Should customers require non-nuclear power for any reason, however, it would put the entire nuclear power station business at risk.

4. *Is organizational agility the same as agile project management?*

   Answer: Agile project management is an iterative and incremental manner of managing a project. It is highly flexible and open to stakeholder requirement changes. It can be used to make an organization more agile. However, organizational agility is more than using agile approaches in project management. Organizational agility includes strategic agility (staying in the market until an opportunity arises), portfolio agility (shifting resources from low-potential businesses to high-potential ones), and operation agility (seizing revenue-enhancing and cost-cutting opportunities faster and more effectively than competitors do).

5. *What are the risks of centralized decision making for an organization that needs agility?*

   Answer: Centralized decision making requires time to collect and analyze information. Being agile requires the ability to react quickly.

   Centralized decision making separates those who know (the ones who make decisions and control execution) from those who execute. Can doers be responsible for what they do when they are told what to do? When decisions are centralized, people are less engaged at work and their responsibilities are difficult to identify.

6. *What is the purpose of team building for agile organizations?*

   Answer: Agile organizations achieve higher collective results. The purpose of team building is results. It starts with creating trust among team members. When people trust one another, they create healthy ideological conflicts in order to make better collective decisions. Then, team members are accountable for what they do. Finally, organizations must consider collective results as the ultimate performance indicators and forget about measuring individual performance.

7. *What are the specific skills required to lead an agile organization?*

   Answer: Agile organization leaders develop the following skills: (1) They are tolerant to turbulence; (2) they are able to create trust among team members; (3) they are willing not to control everything and they learn to let go and trust their team; (4) they are supportive servant leaders; and (5) they are able to envision a clear goal and communicate it clearly to the organization.

8. *How can employees be engaged and help make the organization more agile?*

   Answer: Employees are more engaged when they are given a clear objective. They can even contribute to defining their objectives. In highly agile organizations, employees define their own objectives; they are free to take initiatives that they think will help the organization achieve its goal. Employees are more engaged when they are given freedom to do their job their own way. At the same time, they are responsible for achieving their objective. Freedom without responsibility would be anarchy. And responsibility without freedom would be a kind of mental harassment.

Chapter 4: The Role of Portfolio, Program, and Project Management in Organizational Change

1. *Of the three disciplines, which is the most similar to the practice of organizational change management, and why?*

Answer: Of the three disciplines, program management is arguably the closest to the practice of organizational change management. Both programs and organizational change initiatives are defined by their strategic direction, subject to change as they evolve, require a high degree of stakeholder engagement, contain a number of components that are all different and yet related, and complete their work by transitioning the results to the operational areas and ensuring that these results are sustained. In both cases, the key to success is to integrate and align people, processes, structures, culture, and strategy. In addition, the phases of the program life cycle are easily mapped to the phases of the change life cycle (see Table 4-3).

2. *Of the three disciplines, which is the most different from the practice of organizational change management, and why?*

Answer: Project management is the discipline that is most different from the practice of organizational change management. As noted in the text, there is a fundamental dissonance between the disciplines of project management and organizational change. Projects, by definition, are subject to the well-known triple constraint (schedule, scope, and cost). Projects are, literally by definition, limited in time and in scope. Change management, on the other hand, is subject to continuous change. As circumstances evolve, the change initiative will be modified iteratively, as will the underlying components that are charged with delivering the change. Thus, there is a basic conflict when a project manager manages projects that are part of a change initiative. On the one hand, project management discipline requires the project manager to define the expected scope, schedule, and cost of the effort, and manage the team to execute the resulting plan. On the other hand, the needs of organizational change management require the project manager to be ready to upend that plan if the changing needs of the initiative require it.

3. *With respect to the roles of the portfolio, program, and project managers, what are the key differences between initiatives that are part of an organizational change and those that are not?*

Answer: Although stakeholder interaction is very important in the management of any portfolio, program, or project, this importance is significantly higher in the context of organizational change management. There is much greater than usual sensitivity among stakeholders, and there is likely to be greater polarization of their positions relative to the initiative. Second, organizational change initiatives require a greater degree of flexibility and willingness to change direction than other types of initiatives. Finally, organizational changes typically have a higher degree of risk associated with them (both positive and negative), and so even greater attention must be paid to risk management in such an initiative.

4. *What is the most important consideration for a portfolio manager to keep in mind when setting up and running an organizational change portfolio?*

   Answer: At the portfolio level, the most important consideration is the assessment of the organization's readiness for change. If the organization is not ready for the required strategic change, but that is nonetheless the announced strategy of the organization, then the first task of the portfolio must be to alter that position.

5. *What is the most important consideration for a program manager to keep in mind when planning and executing an organizational change program?*

   Answer: At the program level, as at all levels, it is critically important to work closely with the stakeholders to ensure that they remain supportive (or can be convinced to become supportive) of the change initiative. Specifically, in the context of program management, the most important consideration specific to organizational change management is the careful planning of the transition of the organizational benefits (i.e., the change) into the operational areas. The program manager must ensure that the operational area has been prepared to receive the change and that the processes are in place to measure and sustain that acceptance after the transition is complete.

6. *What are the most important considerations for a project manager to keep in mind when running an organizational change project?*

   Answer: At the project level, the most important consideration is, of course, to produce the project deliverables. However, having done that, the second most important consideration—and the one that is perhaps more important in the context of organizational change than in other contexts—is the need for an increased focus on stakeholder engagement, communication management, and on managing risks related to possible stakeholder resistance to change. The connection between the stakeholders and the change initiative is direct and personal at the project level, and this is where the project manager must pay very careful attention.

7. *In which of the five phases of the change life cycle does the portfolio manager make the greatest contribution? The least contribution? Please explain.*

   Answer: The portfolio manager makes the greatest contribution to the organizational change in formulating change, defining the overall strategy, and starting to set up the components that will then implement the strategy of change at the program and project level. At the portfolio level, the team is much less involved in managing the change transition or sustaining the change.

8. *In which of the five phases of the change life cycle does the program manager make the greatest contribution? The least contribution? Please explain.*

   Answer: The program manager's greatest contribution is to the plan change phase of the change life cycle. The program manager receives the desired organizational benefits from the portfolio and then determines the most effective and efficient way to deliver those benefits by establishing, approving the initiation of, and overseeing the successful execution of the program components. The program manager could be said to have the smallest contribution to formulating change, focusing instead on the implementation of the organizational changes that were already formulated when the program manager was assigned to the program.

9. *In which of the five phases of the change life cycle does the project manager make the greatest contribution? The least contribution? Please explain.*

   Answer: The project manager is most involved in the phase of implementing the change. Project managers are all about execution—it is their job to get things done, and this is the focus of the implementing change phase. Note that this also involves managing the transition and ensuring that the change can and will be sustained, but those are not useful if the deliverables are not there in the first place, so that is the project manager's greatest contribution. The project manager is least involved in formulating change. By the time the change initiative is under way at the project level, the changes have already been defined.

Chapter 5: The Change Process in Practice

1. *What is a change trigger? Identify a trigger for organizational change and describe a best practice for responding to the trigger.*

    Answer: Change in organizations is often a response to a trigger. Events may trigger change and such triggers may arise both internally as well as external to the company. Although change is said to be triggered, how a company responds to triggers may or may not follow theorized change processes. For example, the decline of IBM triggered the action of the board of directors to bring in an outsider, Lou Gerstner, in 1993. In this example, action immediately followed a trigger that, in turn, was followed by change led from the vision of the executive (DiCarlo, 2002). On the other hand, some companies face change triggers but do not recognize them as such. For example, the introduction and success of the first touchscreen phone offered by Apple would appear to be an obvious trigger for legacy companies offering smartphones that their product lines would be in dire need of change in order to react to this new type of product. As is often the case, the trigger was apparently dismissed by most legacy companies and not acted upon until too late. The literature of change management focuses on the leadership and implementation of change, but does not apparently emphasize the importance of management sensitivity to change triggers or how to recognize such triggers (Manuele, 2012).

2. *Describe the importance of framing the problem as it relates to organizational diagnosis and data collection.*

    Answer: The data collection process in OD (organizational development) terms is referred to as diagnosis. In practical terms, it involves acquiring an in-depth understanding of the problem developed by the collection of supporting evidence. Unfortunately, change managers receive mixed signals from data that may at times be contradictory. This is because the problems that OCM (organizational change management) attempts to address are not well-structured problems. They are, at times, ambiguous and they resist facile troubleshooting by change practitioners (Connor, 2011). Because of this, the change management professional will likely structure or frame the problem in a way that makes most sense based on the experience and know-how of the practitioner. Unfortunately, this manner of viewing the problem, although convenient, may miss key elements of the reality of the underlying problem or situation. If this is the case, the proposed change solution that results may not solve the intended problem. In fact, in the worst case, it may increase the problems faced by the organization, and in the best case, it may cause unintended consequences. Change managers often experience changed processes or methodologies going unused because the proposed solution either does not solve the problem, is inconvenient for those expected to use it, or causes other problems that make the solution not worth the cost of acceptance and implementation. The fields of problem solving and decision making both begin, therefore, with the identification or framing of the problem (Jansson, 2013).

3. *Define "triangulation" as it applies to root cause analysis in change management. Explain how it relates to the concept of "the wisdom of crowds."*

   Answer: How do practitioners "get to the bottom of things" and make sure they are solving the right problem? The first step in accomplishing data analysis is the recognition that all data sources within the organization are imperfect measures. Different employees may see the same thing, but report different phenomena. The true picture may emerge only if everyone who sees the phenomena are queried. This suggests that managers of change talk to employees—many employees at all levels and functions. On the other hand, although the opinion input of large numbers of employees may well lead to the uncovering of the "wisdom of crowds," the collection of opinion may not capture the entire story. Research suggests that human memory is imperfect, so qualitative interview data of employee opinion are best validated by comparison with hard data from sources such as budgets, business metrics, meeting minutes, documented plans, and company presentations. The resulting comparison and conclusions may then be validated in a facilitated group meeting of key employees selected from multiple functions and levels. Such ongoing comparison and validation of data using multiple imperfect sources is referred to as "triangulation" (Miles & Huberman, 1994). Because the term *triangulation* is used in path-finding and distance estimation, it appears to be particularly appropriate in change management settings. The saying, "If you don't know where you are going, you may end up somewhere else," would appear to apply in this context. Above all, successful practitioners who are embarking upon a journey of change first determine clearly what the issue is prior to setting the direction for change.

4. *Compare and contrast the concept of "context" in change management versus "initial conditions" in chaos theory. Discuss the validity of this analogy.*

Chaos theory informs us that the beating of the wings of a butterfly in one part of the world may lead to storms in another part of the world. This view into chaotic systems speaks to the importance of initial conditions. It could be argued that organizations have elements of chaos in that events faced by managers on a day-to-day basis tend to be unpredictable. Further, some have proposed that results obtained by a business are not related to the skill of any particular manager at all, but instead are the result of random and fundamentally indeterminate events (Singh & Singh, 2002). Imagine the difficulty of change managers who seek to diagnose the issues that have led to the need for change and seek to embark on change initiatives that will eventually produce improved results. This cannot be done without a deep understanding of the context in which the change is being initiated. To continue with the analogy with chaotic systems, the initial conditions in a system are key; likewise, the context in which change is proposed informs the means by which change is undertaken. This intuitive view of change at the level of practice would appear to argue against prescriptive methodologies for initiating and managing change. For this reason, change practice would suggest that an understanding of the context of the organization is an important predecessor for understanding the underlying cause of the problem.

5. *Identify reasons (if any) why companies might seek to initiate change in the absence of obvious triggers.*

Change within a successful company may be viewed as change that is initiated in order to solve a problem that has not yet materialized. This situation may naturally lead to resistance to change—but unlike in traditional prescriptive change management models, such resistance is not merely a reluctance to adopt something new or to do something different. Rather, this form of resistance in practice is linked to legitimate concerns regarding the productivity and profitability of the overall business (Clarke & Garside, 1997).

Although the prospect of reduced earnings often leads to resistance, change becomes progressively difficult when companies fail to recognize key opportunities to change and begin to decline. Funding required for initiating change projects or new product feasibility efforts is less available than what existed during years of high profit. Further, the fundamental management bandwidth and overall energy of the company is often preoccupied with resisting the decline in revenues. By the time the need for change is recognized, it may be too late to initiate change and later still to implement it.

Chapter 6: Applying Agile Techniques to Change Management Projects

1. *Why can agile be more accommodating of changes in a project than more traditional approaches?*

    Agile takes full advantage of the concept of rolling-wave planning; therefore, detailed plans are not made at the beginning of the project. Because the detailed planning is deferred, making changes to a high-level plan does not require the same level of effort that changes to a detailed plan would require.

2. *How does the product owner manage changes to the project?*

    The project work is organized in the backlog—a high-level description of the work to be completed on the project—that is, the scope. The product owner is responsible for maintaining the backlog. If a new scope is required, the product owner can place it in the backlog and let it replace some scope that is now less important, thus keeping the overall scope constant.

3. *How can agile be used in an organizational change project?*

    An organizational change project can be organized just like any other agile project. A backlog of the scope is created. This backlog is prioritized, and the team organizes around the work to be completed. The project can follow an iterative approach, with reviews of completed work at the end of each iteration, or it can use a Kanban approach, where the team continues to pull new work to do as it completes the task it is working on.

4. *Does agile work at the program and portfolio levels?*

   Yes. There are a number of approaches that have been successfully implemented to scale agile projects. A common approach is the Scaled Agile Framework (SAFe®) developed by Dean Leffingwell. This framework addresses how work can be organized first at the portfolio level and then flow to the program and project levels.

5. *Can agile and traditional approaches be combined on a program?*

   Yes. A program may be composed of some project teams using agile techniques while other project teams follow a more traditional approach. An important activity will be monitoring dependencies between the teams to ensure that they are aligned so one team isn't waiting on another team to complete its work.

Chapter 7: The Role of Organizational Culture in Successful Change

1. *What is the model that will support organizational change by leveraging culture?*

   The model is:

   - Understand–Build–Launch,
   - Understand the culture;
   - Build the foundation for organizational change; and
   - Launch the change with organizational culture.

2. *Why is monitoring and measuring the change so important?*

   It is important because it is the only way to ensure that the change has been implemented. It also provides the organization with a true measurement of empirical success. Without a measurement, success is being measured subjectively, rather than objectively.

3. *Explain the Hawthorne effect.*

People behave differently when they know that they are being monitored, and so monitoring a change will give people within the organization the incentive to maintain the new process rather than going back to their old ways.

4. *How is implementing change like a blooming flower?*

If one thinks of change as a blooming flower, it will help in understanding that there are different elements that need to be successful for the bloom to appear. Just having a petal or two does not make a flower, and the most successful flowers are those that have multiple petals formed together in a tight grouping. Just like change, different elements need to work together to be successful.

Chapter 8: The Importance of Stakeholder Engagement

1. *Why is change good for organizations?*

Everything about our world is in a constant state of change: the way we work, the way we play, the way we communicate with others, the natural world around us—in short, nearly every aspect of our lives. At the extreme, consider the lives of early humans and how little they resemble our lives today. It's easy to imagine that there were some early humans who resisted the change around them at various points in history. There were those who lived off the land who couldn't adapt when there was a natural disaster or climate shift that made their food sources disappear. There were those who hunted animals who couldn't adapt when disease wiped out the animal population in their area. The world around us continues to change. Think for a moment how different life was before the proliferation of technology and the internet in our daily lives. Cell phones allow us to distribute messages quickly and widely with little effort—either by phone call, text, email, tweet, or other social media posts. There are good and bad things about this change, but there is change, and those who adapt better navigate that change. Companies that recognize that change is coming, which will affect how they do business or how their customers view their products, are better able to navigate that change to seize opportunities, minimize negative impacts, and, when necessary, reinvent themselves completely.

2. *Can I hire people to help me identify and make changes necessary for my business to succeed?*

Yes, you can. However, for the right changes to be made, and for those changes to be sustainable in the long run, you need to engage people at all levels of your organization in the change process, elicit their comments and feedback, and make changes that are tailored to your particular organization rather than outlined rigidly in a book or guide about change.

3. *Who are my stakeholders?*

The easy way to identify a stakeholder is to think about anyone who may have something to say, positive or negative, about the change you're making. Employees, shareholders, vendors, suppliers, customers, local government, and concerned citizens are good examples.

4. *I'm the boss—why should I care about how my employees "feel" about the proposed changes?*

This question has two answers. First, your front-line workers—those working with your customers and/or products—are more likely to spot flaws or improvement opportunities with a proposed change plan than high-level executives. These employees work directly with the heart of the operations—they know what works and what doesn't, what's easier, and what's harder. If management leverages this information while planning a change, it is often better than if worker feedback is not considered. Second, most workers either have a need to be heard or feel the need to resist what they consider to be a poor decision by management (or both!). Those who want to be heard, but don't feel that anyone is listening, can become disloyal. Those who resist changes they don't agree with can spread discontent among their fellow workers, which lowers both morale and productivity. Good leaders consider all feedback, incorporate the valuable feedback into their change plan, and plan communication strategies to help explain why decisions are being made. The workers proposing the rejected changes may not agree with the decision, but they'll at least know that they were heard.

5. *What is "legacy thinking" and why is it dangerous to an organization?*

Legacy thinking is when people are rooted in doing things "the way we've always done them." They resist change. One reason for this could be job security (believing their job is safe if they are the only one who knows how to do a specific task). It could also be because of a lack of skills or training—they don't have the ability to adapt to the change. Another reason could be that the employees want things to stay the same so they don't have to learn something new out of fear of the unknown or fear of their work becoming more difficult. Those who "legacy think" out of fear may be able to be coached or provided with training so they become comfortable with change. Those who resist change and do not embrace coaching or training are dangerous to the organization. They hold back, and worse yet, because they have been around long enough, they are often looked up to by others, and those others may follow suit and also resist change.

6. *What is "change collateral"?*

After an organization has successfully demonstrated its ability to perform change well, it earns this "change collateral": Those inside the organization begin to trust that the future change requests that the leadership proposes are based on good reasons.

Chapter 9: How to Structure, Plan, and Measure Organizational Change Management

1. *What type of change activities link organizational strategy to portfolio management activities?*

Effective communications, sense-making activities, and personal and organizational impact assessments are some areas in which change activities should be targeted. When defining new portfolio components, portfolio managers should ensure that certain change management activities (such as assessments of readiness, crafting of need and vision statements, and definition of done) are conducted to allow executives to properly assimilate and validate the new components, to allow program resources to conduct high-level planning activities, and to allow other impacted stakeholders to assess feasibility and readiness. This will provide portfolio managers with the ability to act decisively regarding portfolio management activities. The quality of portfolio change activities determines the level of change activities that the execution teams will need to apply to achieve buy-in and support from stakeholders who are not involved in the portfolio management activities.

2. *How does a prioritized list of portfolio components improve program and project resource productivity?*

To avoid the devastating impact that multitasking has on productivity, workers should be able to prioritize tasks to increase throughput given their fixed capacity. The focus of previous change activities should have been to gain stakeholder consensus, leading to a sequenced, prioritized portfolio component list. If the portfolio manager cannot provide such a definitive list, the PMO will not be able to optimize resources using critical chain or agile methodologies. To optimize portfolio performance measured as throughput, portfolio managers should provide the PMO with a clear prioritization of all components so that component task-level resource conflicts can be resolved against the prioritized list.

3. *What is the importance of a developing a "real need" statement? Practice developing a needs statement with the key stakeholders for a current project.*

Change starts with the organization being truthful with itself about what its real needs are. Without executives, managers, and line workers facing the truth about the current state, meaningful change will be impossible. The challenge of pursuing the real needs often implies a level of "indictment" of the current leadership. Getting to the truth requires the competencies of a service-based project leader. Basic questions should revolve around the following:

- What changes are required and why?
- Which people, systems, and processes are needed to make this change? Change begins with the collective organizational resources' willingness to adopt new attitudes and behaviors. Understanding the real need of the change effort and its stakeholders is a discovery process that involves continual dialogue and collaboration.
- What are the three key measures that should be measured in second- and third-degree change initiatives? Three key measures for second- and third-degree change initiatives are:
  - The level of *urgency* associated with the change;
  - The *attitudes* from executives to rank and file staff. Attitudes drive behaviors, and the correct attitudes must be formed with key stakeholders to drive changes in behavior; and
  - The *capabilities* of the organization, people, processes, and systems should be measured before significant monies are

spent to attempt to implement second- and third-degree changes within organizations.

4. *Discuss the communications best practice discussed in this chapter and make some notes on how it can be adopted and incorporated into your organization's change initiatives.*

The ability to develop content for change initiative communications to target specific stakeholder audiences is an art form. Seek out the creative types and secure executive support for the approach. Use the correct mix of facts or truth about the current state, the vision, and optimism; and utilize humor, as appropriate.

Targeting content to the individuals who are impacted is important; contacting people who are not affected will dilute the recipients' attention and, eventually, they will ignore the material.

Measuring readership and comprehension through simple quizzes and interactive components will help ensure that the message is understood. Ultimately, the team should measure the key business metrics that should have been established early in the project to evaluate adoption of the change.

Based on the measurements, change must be continually reinforced by project activities. Measuring once is not enough; this is a continual process throughout the course of the change initiative. Reinforcement through timely feedback to stakeholders on key measures should recognize the reality of the barriers that people face as well as the proper level of urgency, sense-making activities, and empathy.

Chapter 10: How Successful Project Organizations Deliver Change

1. *Why do organizations implement change?*

The reasons are varied and vast, but there is typically a benefit that the organization is attempting to achieve. In some cases, the benefit is to achieve or stay within compliance. There is typically an alignment with a strategic goal, and that strategy will be tied to some benefit. Subsequently, the reward for the investment of change typically will be for the customer, the employee, or the owner (shareholder, board of directors, etc.).

2. *Regardless of the perceived value of making a change, there is always some level of investment necessary to facilitate change in an organization. What are some of the hard costs associated with change?*

Hard costs are the costs and investments that are necessary to complete the project. These may be in the form of costs for software, hardware, construction materials, and so forth. These costs may also encompass the cost of labor.

3. *When considering the value or benefit of change, nearly all organizations will consider the appropriate balance of the customer, employee, or owner. Some will also consider a fourth perspective. What is this fourth aspect and which types of organizations might want to view this perspective?*

A fourth aspect is sometimes put into the mix of values: Mission is a value that is touted by many as a means of achieving success. Not many for-profit, particularly publicly traded companies, can afford to have this perspective as a cornerstone of their value system. It is far more typical in a nonprofit or not-for-profit company. Government, especially military organizations, may have this perspective. Mission success is their imperative.

4. *When creating key performance indicators (KPIs) in order to measure the efficacy and value of a change, what are five aspects that must be considered? How can we achieve empirical data based on the values of the organizations and understand when a change has been successful or not?*

In order to achieve empirical data based on the values of the organizations and understand when a change has been successful or not, a common method is to use SMART goals—an acronym that stands for specific, measurable, achievable, relevant, and timebound.

5. *Who is responsible for benefits realization?*

Though a project team can implement a process, application, or any other change initiative, it takes the people in the affected business unit to make the sustained change and work toward realizing the benefit. These staff members are responsible to their managers who, in turn, have the overall responsibility for the benefits realization or lack thereof.

Chapter 11: Committing the Change Team
A Smooth Sea Never Made a Skillful Sailor

1. *What is the main reason why many change initiatives fail?*

    Poor communication is the main reason for the failure of change initiatives. The need for communication is not a cliché; communication cannot be overused in the context of the change.

2. *What is the second factor listed by Buss, along with the leadership capabilities, that has a considerable impact on ensuring that a change happens?*

    A study conducted by Buss revealed that, although not visible most of the time, relationship capital—alongside leadership capabilities—has a considerable effect in making a change actually happen.

3. *What are the main competences required for change-team members, according to Crawford and Nahmias (2010)?*

    Crawford and Nahmias list the competences required to manage change based on a synthesis of findings from the literature and case studies. Among those are leadership, stakeholder management, communication, decision making, problem solving, and cultural awareness.

4. *According to the Project Management Institute, what are the roles within a change team and their associated responsibilities?*

    PMI lists six major roles in *Managing Change in Organizations: A Practice Guide*, describing the major responsibilities of each:
    - *Governance board*, ensuring that the change process remains aligned with the organization's vision and direction;
    - *Sponsor*, having the ultimate responsibility for the program or project and direct accountability for the change;
    - *Leads*, supporting the overall change management process and its implementation;
    - *Integrators*, carrying the responsibility for the preparation and integration of the change into the business;
    - *Agents*, representing the resources for integrating the change in their respective environments; and
    - *Recipients*, or the people directly and indirectly impacted by change.

5. *What are the four steps proposed for the process of improving the change team dynamics?*

The four steps are: understanding the team, defining the action plan, implementing the action plan, and checking the results.

6. *What is the difference between feedback and reflection, and when can these methods be used during the change project?*

The difference between feedback and reflection resides in the perspective of the speaker: Feedback is directed toward a person or a team and provides an outside point of view (the one of the speaker), while reflection is used to develop a common view of the current status of the team and to equip the team members with the potential to address the problems of tomorrow. The methods are usually applied during retrospective or lessons learned meetings, where the team reflects upon previous accomplishments and prepares for future phases or projects.

7. *What are the main benefits of developing a project scorecard with the contribution of the whole change team and relevant stakeholders?*

Developing such a project scorecard with the contribution of the entire team plus invited stakeholders significantly helps gain buy-in from the stakeholders, align expectations, and keep the team engaged.

Chapter 12: Leadership Factors in Successful Organizational Change

1. *Considering the need for periodic assessments of an organization's capabilities to ensure its sustainability and growth in the business environment, what actions may be taken to prepare the organization and its employees for business changes that are not clearly foreseeable?*

Establish an ongoing process of "retuning" the organization's strategic plan. Assessing the drivers of organizational and business change will help managers see the world more clearly and continually adjust to the environment. Developing scenarios about possible futures, based on a current awareness of drivers of change, allows organizational leaders and decision makers to update their view of what they believe the future has in store for them and their employees. It also helps them develop plans that are realistic and attainable and formulate decisions that are more likely to create the value desired.

2. *Many organizations rely on a specific set of metrics to determine how the organization is performing. Most of these metrics are actually "lagging" indicators. How would you describe the difference between a lagging indicator and a leading indicator?*

   Lagging indicators are references to activities and events that have already occurred. Examples would be cost variance, schedule variance, cost performance indicator (CPI), and schedule performance indicator (SPI). Leading indicators are trends and signs that something might occur that has the potential to be mitigated. Leading indicators are associated with warning signs, changes in trends, and an assessment of potential risks that could impact the desired outcome of a project.

3. *Systems thinking allows organizational leaders to fully conceptualize the current and short-term future of an organization. How would you describe the concept of systems thinking?*

   Systems thinking has been defined as an approach to problem solving that views problems and issues existing within the system from a perspective that addresses the impact of the problem on the whole or "enterprise" level rather than addressing and reacting to distress signals and operational dysfunctions of a specific part. Fixing a specific part may return a system to its original functional intent, but systems thinking is about enhancing the higher-level value of the system and improving the actual purpose of why it was conceived.

4. *Organizational change can be hindered by a number of factors. What is generally considered the primary factor that must be addressed when developing plans for making a significant organizational change?*

   A good place to start in addressing organizational change is to identify the silos that exist, why they exist, and what can be done to break down the walls that separate each functional group.

   The natural response of resistance to change must be anticipated. The leader should develop strategies that will reduce resistance to change by focusing on the actual benefits of the change and looking for ways to show why support for the change is beneficial to the individual, the organization, and customers who, all things being considered, are actually the ultimate stakeholders.

5. *How would you explain "transformational leadership" to your peers and colleagues? Why is this concept key to achieving successful organizational change?*

Transformational leadership is a style that enhances the performance of an organization through a combination of motivation, building morale, conditioning employees and teams to expect and deal with change, and demonstrating confidence in the capability of those involved in a major change to overcome the challenges and achieve the stated objectives. This type of leadership includes connecting with everyone in the organization and creating an individual sense of value and importance to the change initiative.

Transformational leadership is at the core of successful organizational change. If an organization is expected to survive in the business world, the leadership must be aware and must continually communicate that change will occur regardless of the desire to maintain the status quo. The message to deliver is that being comfortable is an indication that an organization has become complacent and may not actually step up to the signs of competitive advancement. The truly effective leader will communicate that attaining a comfort level is highly dangerous and full of risk. Challenging what is comfortable is the major factor for the advancement of an organization.

Effective leadership, transparency, engagement of the stakeholders, and a sincere and clearly visible commitment to change from the organization's leaders is the main factor in gaining buy-in, enlisting the support of the organization's employees, and achieving the objectives of a major organizational change.

Chapter 13: The Importance of Sponsorship for Successful Change

1. *What process was used by the project manager to lead the change?*

In order to lead the change, the project manager needs to:

- Identify key stakeholders.
- Prepare an implementation plan.
- Empathize with behaviors and reactions to change.
- Take the lead on the change process.

2. *What aspects need to be considered before making a decision to change?*

   - Assess the readiness for the change.
   - Assess the resistance for the change.
   - Assess the risk for the change.

3. *What did the project sponsor do during the project?*

   The project sponsor provided resources required for the change and had the ultimate responsibility for the project. The project sponsor worked well building senior management commitment across the organization. The sponsor had a lot of enthusiasm, power, and influence over the entire organization. The project sponsor's support was visible and was one of the keys for the change success.

4. *Who is the right sponsor for a change management project?*

   In managing change, you may need to understand and work with different types of sponsors, for example:

   - Initiating sponsor;
   - Key sponsor;
   - Primary sponsor; and
   - Secondary sponsor.

5. *Which tools were used by the project manager to manage the change?*

   - Teamwork exercises, using real meetings to put ideas into practice;
   - Descriptions of roles and responsibilities that were published in planning documents;
   - Change agent training;
   - Daily communication among team members;
   - Asking for feedback from every team leader; and
   - Communication and respect among team members.

Chapter 14: The Future and Organizational Change Management

1. *Who should normally implement an organizational change? Why?*

   A project or program manager should implement organizational change. The project and program manager will work with the stakeholders to coordinate all activities.

2. *Which PMI publication describes the three levels of organizational change? Provide an example of each and explain why it meets the criteria for that level of organizational change.*

Managing Change in Organizations: A Practice Guide describes the three levels of organizational change. The first order is when a process is updated, such as the project management methodology. The second order is transformational; this might be the implementation of an ERP system or other type of enterprise tool. The third order is a cultural change to the organization. This might be the result of hiring a new business unit president who may implement a new quality control system.

3. *Describe what the portfolio, program, and project managers do for organizational change management.*

The portfolio manager will determine which projects and programs are performed with respect to all projects/programs affecting the organization. These will drive the strategy for the entire organization. The program manager ensures that projects under the program drive to the correct strategy being implemented. The project manager is the tactical implementer of the change.

4. *How will the project management discipline look in the future as it relates to organizational change management?*

Organizational change is difficult because people are resistant to change. Leadership needs to realize that organizational change is not an HR issue; it needs the skills of a project management practitioner. The project management practitioner can bring a consistent approach to organizational change.